Industrial Evolution
in Developing Countries

Industrial Evolution
in Developing Countries

Micro Patterns of Turnover, Productivity, and Market Structure

Edited by
Mark J. Roberts and James R. Tybout

PUBLISHED FOR THE WORLD BANK
OXFORD UNIVERSITY PRESS

Oxford University Press

OXFORD NEW YORK TORONTO
DELHI BOMBAY CALCUTTA MADRAS KARACHI
KUALA LUMPUR SINGAPORE HONG KONG TOKYO
NAIROBI DAR ES SALAAM CAPE TOWN
MELBOURNE AUCKLAND

and associated companies in

BERLIN IBADAN

© 1996 The International Bank for Reconstruction
and Development / THE WORLD BANK
1818 H Street, N.W.
Washington, D.C. 20433, U.S.A.

Published by Oxford University Press, Inc.
200 Madison Avenue, New York, N.Y. 10016

Oxford is a registered trademark of Oxford University Press.

Manufactured in the United States of America
First printing December 1996

The findings, interpretations, and conclusions expressed in this study are entirely those of the authors and should not be attributed in any manner to the World Bank, to its affiliated organizations, or to members of its Board of Executive Directors or the countries they represent.

Library of Congress Cataloging-in-Publication Data

Industrial evolution in developing countries : micro patterns of turnover,
   productivity, and market structure / edited by Mark J. Roberts and
James R. Tybout.
      p.   cm.
   Includes bibliographical references and index.
   ISBN 0-19-521110-3 (casebound)
   1. Industrialization—Developing countries—Case studies.
   2. Industrial productivity—Developing countries—Case studies.
   3. Labor turnover—Developing countries—Case studies.
   4. Developing countries—Manufactures—Case studies.   5. Developing
countries—Commerce—Case studies.   I. Roberts, Mark J.
   II. Tybout, James R., 1953–
HC59.7.I4763   1996
338.09172′4—dc20   96-14987
                                                                  CIP

Contents

      Investment in Côte d'Ivoire, Morocco, and Venezuela** 163
      Ann Harrison

      Characteristics of Foreign Direct Investment in
          Côte d'Ivoire, Morocco, and Venezuela 164
      Description of Domestic and Foreign Firms 167
      Testing for Spillovers of Technology from Foreign
          Investment 173
      Trade Reform, Productivity, and Ownership in
          Côte d'Ivoire 182
      Conclusions 183
      Notes 185
      References 186

**Part II   Markups and Producer Turnover: Case Studies of
             Five Countries** 187

8   **A Preview of the Country Studies** 188
      Mark J. Roberts and James R. Tybout

      Descriptive Overview 189
      Entry and Exit Analysis 189
      Price-Cost Margins 193
      Conclusions 196
      Notes 197
      References 198

9   **Chile, 1979–86: Trade Liberalization and Its Aftermath** . . . 200
      James R. Tybout

      Chile's Radical Reforms of the 1970s 200
      Patterns of Entry and Exit 202
      Competition 211
      Conclusions 217
      Appendix: Data Preparation 218
      Notes 224
      References 225

10   **Colombia, 1977–85: Producer Turnover, Margins,
      and Trade Exposure** 227
      Mark J. Roberts

      Trade Policy in Colombia 227
      Characteristics of Manufacturing Plants 229
      Patterns of Entry and Exit 230

Preface

The research effort that has resulted in this volume began nearly a decade ago, when the "new" trade theory could more rightfully be called new, and development economists were asking how relevant it was for the semi-industrialized countries. How did commercial policy affect market structure in these countries? Were the models that justified strategic intervention empirically relevant? Did trade policy lead to significant changes in the exploitation of scale economies?

To address these questions, in 1987 we initiated the World Bank–funded project "Industrial Competition, Productivity, and Their Relation to Trade Regimes." Unlike earlier work in the area, this project was designed to link changes in trade policy with patterns of producer entry, exit, and adjustment, thereby revealing micro aspects of the relation between commercial policy and industrial sector performance. This required us to compile panel data sets on the population of producers in a number of semi-industrialized countries.

We ultimately chose Chile, Colombia, Morocco, and Turkey for analysis. These countries had collected the necessary micro-level data (specifically, they had annually surveyed the population of manufacturers with at least ten employees), they were willing to share these data, and they had undergone significant commercial policy reforms during the sample years. Several had also undergone major macroeconomic shocks. After a lengthy period of data acquisition and cleaning, the project produced a set of descriptive country studies, followed by papers on market structure, productivity, and their relation to trade policy.

As we worked with the micro panels, we became increasingly aware that commercial policy was only one of the many forces acting on the industrial sectors of our sample countries. In particular, the descriptive analysis and the studies of productivity growth revealed that micro patterns of entry, learning, growth, and exit in each industry were fundamental in shaping sectorwide performance. However, these evolutionary forces were only weakly associated with trade policy.

We thus became interested in the broader question of how the industrial sectors in the developing countries evolve. Researchers had begun to document and interpret these phenomena in the industrialized countries by the late 1980s, but very little was known about them in the developing world. On the one hand, developing countries are often characterized as stagnant, noncompetitive environments dominated by a few producers. On the other hand, they are also frequently described as undergoing rapid structural transformation and subject to relatively large macroeconomic shocks. Given our data sets, we were in a unique position to shed light on the relative merits of these different views and to generate a new set of stylized facts for developing countries on the patterns and consequences of producer entry, growth, and exit.

Motivated by these objectives, we began working with our collaborators on the present volume. First, we refocused and shortened our country studies to highlight the patterns of entry, exit, and change in market share observed under the various macroeconomic, trade, and regulatory regimes. We also analyzed the industrial sector of a fifth country, Mexico, using data obtained by James Tybout and M. D. Westbrook from the Mexican government in connection with another project. The country studies are collected in part II, with an overview provided in chapter 8.

Our next step was to prepare a set of papers that draw together evidence on a single issue from a number of the countries. These are collected in part I. One chapter focuses on the employment shifts that result from the entry, growth, and exit of manufacturing plants. Two chapters address the cross-firm differences in productivity at the micro level and quantify how the turnover process sorts out efficient and inefficient producers. Other chapters address the sources of heterogeneity across producers, with emphasis on the role of economies of scale and foreign direct investment. Chapter 1 summarizes the main lessons.

Although this book presents a new body of evidence and some clear messages, we view it as a beginning. The analytical literature on industrial evolution is still quite abstract, so we have not yet estimated structural models of the turnover processes we document. Without these models, it is difficult to arrive at policy conclusions. Nonetheless, we hope that our findings shed new light on the basic patterns, attract attention to the phenomena, and provide a first step toward formal empirical representations. We hope that as second-generation studies emerge, they will provide new insights as to how severance laws, credit markets, antitrust policy, bankruptcy law, and macroeconomic shocks affect industrial performance.

In addition to the individuals who contributed papers to the original project or to this volume, we owe thanks to many others. Our greatest debt is to the World Bank for its ongoing financial support, through both the Research Administration Department and the Country Economics

Department. Further, the data would not have been available without considerable assistance from World Bank staff and government representatives in each country we have studied. For help with data acquisition we are extremely grateful to Kristin Hallberg, Richard Newfarmer, Brendan Horton, Hamid Alavi, and Carlos Basterra (World Bank), Gerardo García (Chile, National Institute of Statistics), Suleyman Ozmucer (Turkey, Bogazigi University), Mohamed Alami (Morocco, Ministry of Commerce and Industry), Fernando Clavijo (Mexico, Economic Advisor to the President), and Adriaan Ten Kate (Mexico, SECOFI). John Newman (World Bank) and Victor Levy (Hebrew University) initiated a study of Côte d'Ivoire for the project as well. Unfortunately, problems with erratic survey coverage and the unavailability of good price deflators prevented inferences concerning entry, exit, and growth patterns, so their effort was ultimately abandoned.

Cleaning the data and constructing descriptive statistics were major endeavors. Under our supervision the unglamorous task of data preparation was performed mainly by Lili Liu (Chilean and Turkish data sets), Shoichi Katayama and Jinsung Park (Chilean data set), Constantina Backinezos (Colombian data set), Mona Haddad (Moroccan data set), and Jean-Marie Grether and Hans-Martin Boehmer (Mexican data set).

Finally, we received a great deal of help preparing the manuscript. Meta de Coquereaumont did a superb job of editing the initial draft, and Kathryn Kline Dahl ably oversaw the final round of editing and the production work. Ghislaine Bayard typed the first drafts of most of the chapters with great care, and Jennifer Ngaine prepared the revisions. Sherman Robinson, Elio Landero, Howard Pack, and two anonymous reviewers provided many helpful suggestions, as did seminar participants at the World Bank, the U.S. Bureau of the Census, and the 1994 Latin American meetings of the Econometric Society.

Contributors

Chapter authors and their affiliations as of late 1996:

Jaime de Melo	Professor of Economics, University of Geneva; Visiting Professor, Université d'Auvergne; Research Fellow, International Trade Programme, Center for Economic Policy Research
Mark A. Dutz	Senior Industrial Economist, The World Bank
Faezeh Foroutan	Economist, The World Bank
Jean-Marie Grether	Lecturer, Université de Neuchâtel; Researcher, University of Geneva
Mona Haddad	Economist, The World Bank
Ann Harrison	Assistant Professor of Economics and Finance, Columbia Business School, Columbia University; Associate, National Bureau of Economic Research
Brendan Horton	Senior Trade Economist, The World Bank
Lili Liu	Economist, The World Bank
Mark J. Roberts	Professor of Economics, Pennsylvania State University; Associate, National Bureau of Economic Research
James R. Tybout	Professor of Economics, Georgetown University
M. Daniel Westbrook	Assistant Professor of Economics, Georgetown University

1

Industrial Evolution in Developing Countries: A Preview

Mark J. Roberts and James R. Tybout

A s a country's demand conditions, technological opportunities, and policy regimes evolve, the micro characteristics of its industrial sector respond. New, inexperienced producers enter the market and begin to learn and grow, while other producers exit. Simultaneously, market shares shift among existing producers who differ in their technology, managerial expertise, and profitability. The premise of this book is that much can be learned about sectorwide performance by studying these plant-level dynamics.

Although the dynamics of industrial evolution have recently been studied in North America and Europe, these micro processes have attracted much less attention in the semi-industrialized countries, where they may be especially significant. Many of these countries are undergoing a rapid structural transformation from agrarian to industrial production and from cottage to factory production. They are often struggling to catch up technologically, and their labor markets have the formidable task of moving workers among diverse occupations. Further, their markets are relatively small, so they rely heavily on trade and foreign direct investment as sources of goods, demand, and expertise.

Previous studies such as those by Little, Mazumdar, and Page (1987) and Pack (1987) recognize the importance of producer heterogeneity in developing countries and analyze some of its implications. What distinguishes this volume from earlier work is that the research is based on comprehensive data from panels of producers surveyed in five semi-industrialized countries: Chile, Colombia, Mexico, Morocco, and Venezuela.[1] These data allow us to quantify several dimensions of producer heterogeneity and to follow plants over time as they enter the market, grow, and exit. The result is a new set of stylized facts on plant-level heterogeneity and dynamics in the semi-industrialized countries.[2]

Findings on Producer Heterogeneity, Turnover, and Economic Performance

Entry, exit, and market share reallocations reflect three forces. The first involves long-run shifts in technology and demand patterns that generate expansion of output and net entry of producers in some sectors, while generating contraction of output and net exit of producers in others. The entry and exit that result as a developing country shifts from the assembly of low-technology manufactured goods to the production of higher-quality differentiated ones are an example of this long-run adjustment. The second force is short-run or cyclical fluctuations in demand, such as might arise from changing macroeconomic conditions or trade policy. These could be an important source of entry and exit variation in industries where sunk costs are small so that short-term or hit-and-run entry may be profitable. The third factor contributing to turnover is the replacement of less-efficient producers by more-efficient ones in the same industry. If producers in an industry are heterogeneous in their levels of profit or productivity, market forces are likely to generate continual entry and exit, even if demand remains stable. Our first objective in this volume is to quantify and distinguish these three types of resource reallocation.

Each type of flux is potentially beneficial. If the level of efficiency differs across plants, the resource reallocations induced by these processes can be a source of sectoral productivity growth. Similarly, if changes in demand reduce profitability in one sector relative to another, the associated movement of resources is likely to improve welfare. Even if resources are not shifted between sectors, the phenomena of entry, exit, and reallocation of market share constitute a source of competitive pressure and can improve allocative efficiency by limiting the market power of incumbent producers. Against all of these benefits, one must weigh the transaction costs of moving resources and the income lost as a result of factors that are temporarily idled in the process. The second objective of this volume is to shed light on these various benefits and costs.

Patterns of Turnover

Given our first objective, we devote considerable attention to describing the patterns of entry, exit, and market share reallocation found in our sample of semi-industrialized countries. Very little is known about these processes, because comprehensive micro panels are needed to study them, and confidentiality problems have made such data inaccessible to researchers. Nonetheless, for purposes of this project, the statistical agencies of Chile, Colombia, and Morocco granted the World Bank access to their annual data on the *population* of manufacturing plants with at least ten workers.

COUNTRY BACKGROUND. The macroeconomic conditions that prevailed in these countries during our sample years (1979–86 for Chile, 1977–89 for Colombia, and 1984–89 for Morocco) typify the experiences of semi-industrialized countries in the 1980s, so our findings are probably representative of a broader group of nations. Each country began the decade with an overvalued currency and was forced to devalue and contract during the debt crisis. By the end of the sample period, each country had undergone some degree of structural adjustment and resumed growing.

There are nonetheless important differences among countries. Chile suffered a major financial crisis, because its manufacturing sector had become heavily indebted in dollars. Its contraction was severe, with unemployment reaching almost 30 percent and many manufacturing plants closing. Nonetheless, Chilean policies remained laissez-faire, with low tariffs, almost no nontariff barriers, very little public ownership in manufacturing, and little intervention in the labor market. Colombia underwent a much milder recession and recovery but remained more protectionist in its commercial policy. Finally, the Moroccan data base does not begin until after the recession, so we observe only the prolonged recovery that followed. During that time, the government promoted manufactured exports with various tax exemptions but kept some degree of protection from imports. These contrasts in experience help to explain cross-country differences in patterns of industrial evolution.

EMPLOYMENT FLOWS. The first way we quantify entry, exit, and changes in the size of continuing producers is by studying the gross flows of jobs (chapter 2). Several facts emerge. The annual average rate of job creation in new and expanding plants varies from 13 to 19 percent of manufacturing employment in Chile, Colombia, and Morocco, while the average rate of job destruction in contracting and closing plants varies from 12 to 14 percent (see figure 1.1). The magnitude of these job creation and destruction rates is remarkably similar across the three countries, in spite of their very different macroeconomic conditions.

These flows, when combined, indicate that the number of new manufacturing positions added and existing positions lost in the semi-industrialized countries amounts to 26 to 30 percent of total manufacturing employment in an average year, implying somewhat greater volatility than one finds in Canada and the United States (figure 1.1). This pattern may reflect macroeconomic instability in the South, such as

Figure 1.1 Job Creation and Destruction

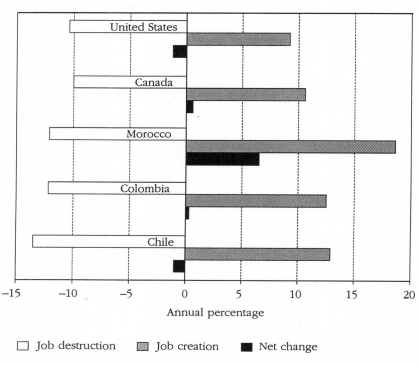

□ Job destruction   ▨ Job creation   ■ Net change

Note: Sample periods are Chile, 1979–86; Colombia, 1977–89; Morocco, 1984–89; Canada, 1973–86; and United States, 1973–86.
Source: Table 2.1.

the Chilean recession, or differences in the product mix across regions, or both. For example, the relative emphasis on light manufacturing in semi-industrialized countries may mean that sunk entry costs are relatively low and that producer turnover is high. If the costs of changing employers are similar for workers in both regions, the burden of adjustment to industrial evolution is typically greater for workers in semi-industrialized countries than in the North. However, these costs may be somewhat offset by the high geographic concentration of manufacturing activity, which makes it less likely that workers will need to relocate their residence in response to shifts in employment demand.

Although figure 1.1 depicts averages over several years, it would look rather similar if we focused on any one year. That is, substantial job creation and job destruction take place simultaneously at all phases of the business cycle. This pattern of turnover implies that producers respond in diverse ways to changes in their common economic environment. It also challenges the belief that fragmentation of the financial market, labor severance laws, and a propensity to prop up "sick" enterprises inhibit resource mobility and create stagnant industrial sectors in semi-industrialized countries.

The industrialization process typically involves structural transformation, as simple labor-intensive industries are displaced by more sophisticated manufactured products (Chenery, Robinson, and Syrquin 1986). Nonetheless, we find that interindustry shifting of jobs is no greater in the semi-industrialized countries than in the United States. After controlling for the net expansion or contraction of total manufacturing employment, more than 80 percent of employment reallocation occurs within, rather than across, four-digit International Standard Industrial Classification (ISIC) industries. Thus changes in the mix of products are not the main reason for changes in the allocation of resources, contrary to the traditional focus of the trade and development literature. Also, if worker skills are industry-specific rather than employer-specific, the dominance of job turnover *within* an industry implies less retraining per displaced worker than do comparable shifts between sectors.

Industries differ substantially in the magnitude of within-industry turnover, but the ranking of industries from low to high turnover tends to be very similar across countries. Table 1.1 presents average rates of employment turnover by industry, after controlling for the net change in the sector's employment. High-turnover industries, such as furniture, apparel, food processing, and wood products, all have relatively small-scale production and low capital intensity, while low-turnover industries, such as steel, chemicals, glass, and paper, have the opposite. Technology is thus an important determinant of industry-level turnover rates, and the prominence of industries like food and apparel in the manufacturing sectors of semi-industrialized countries helps to explain the high aggregate turnover rates documented in figure 1.1.

Although business cycle effects are not the dominant source of job creation and destruction, they are not negligible. Studies of Canada and the United States find that employment turnover is countercyclical, because job creation is more stable than job destruction. The semi-industrialized countries exhibit the opposite pattern: job creation rates are more sensitive than job destruction rates to fluctuations in aggregate economic activity. One interpretation is that plants in semi-industrialized countries have limited access to financial markets, which forces them to rely heavily on internal finance and makes expansion and entry more sensitive to demand conditions.

PLANT ENTRY AND EXIT. Our findings on employment flows imply substantial, continual resource reallocation among different plants. In the country studies for Chile (chapter 9), Colombia (chapter 10), and

Table 1.1 Average Annual Employment Turnover Rates, by ISIC Industry
(percentages)

Product	Employment turnover rate
Iron and steel	11
Industrial chemicals	12
Glass	12
Ceramic products	12
Paper	13
Rubber	14
Beverages	14
Nonferrous metal refining	14
Electrical machinery	16
Transport equipment	16
Other chemical products	16
Textiles	18
Professional and scientific equipment	19
Printing	20
Nonmetallic mineral products	20
Leather	20
Plastic products	20
Footwear	21
Fabricated metal products	22
Nonelectrical machinery	22
Furniture	24
Apparel	24
Food processing	24
Wood products	28

Source: Authors' calculations based on Chilean data for 1979–86, Colombian data for 1977–91, and Moroccan data for 1984–89. The turnover variable is defined in chapter 2, equation 2.5.

Morocco (chapter 12), more detailed analysis is undertaken to distinguish resource flows due to plant expansion and contraction from those due to entry and exit. The focus of these chapters is on the contribution of entering and exiting plants to sectorwide production and the extent to which turnover patterns at the industry level reflect technology or demand conditions.

Despite the diverse macroeconomic conditions in these three countries, several robust patterns of turnover emerge. In the manufacturing sector, overall rates of plant entry and exit are substantial in each country. Average annual entry rates are 6.1, 12.2, and 13.0 percent in Chile, Colombia, and Morocco, respectively, while average exit rates are 10.8, 11.1, and 6.0 percent. Fluctuations in the business cycle are important in

explaining entry and exit patterns. For example, during the Chilean recession, the plant exit rate rose as high as 13.0 percent in one year, but
during the subsequent recovery, it fell as low as 5.3 percent. Nonetheless, even during the depths of the Chilean recession, the new plant entry
rate exceeded 4 percent a year. Similarly, during the Moroccan expansion, the exit rate remained above 6 percent a year. Hence in the semi-
industrialized countries, as in the industrial countries, simultaneous
plant entry and exit at all phases of the business cycle are the norm.

Like employment flows, plant entry and exit patterns exhibit strong
industry effects. The average amount of plant turnover varies dramatically across industries, but the ranking of industries by average turnover
is similar across countries. We interpret this to mean that technology—
embodied in fixed operating costs and sunk entry costs—differs substantially across industries but is similar across countries for a given industry
and changes only slowly over time.[3] The pace at which efficient firms replace inefficient ones may thus naturally be more rapid in industries like
food processing and apparel than in industries like steel and chemicals,
which require greater investments in capital.

In addition to industry effects, year dummy variables help to explain
entry and exit rates. Presumably these dummies capture aggregate demand and credit market conditions, but once industry effects and common macroeconomic shocks are controlled for, fluctuations in trade patterns contribute no additional explanatory power. That is, exposure to
foreign competition or exporting opportunities typically has no special
effect on turnover, beyond its effect on aggregate demand. The one exception is Morocco, where export promotion programs appear to have
tilted entry patterns toward export-oriented sectors throughout the
sample period.

Since a large fraction of turnover reflects the simultaneous expansion
and contraction of different producers in the same industry, it is important to examine the differences between entering, exiting, and surviving
plants. The country studies identify several patterns. Not surprisingly,
entrants are small, averaging only about one-fourth the size of incumbent producers. They are thus responsible for more modest shares of
industrial production than their numbers would suggest. Nonetheless,
their size relative to that of incumbents and their rates of turnover are as
large in the semi-industrialized countries as they are in the United States.
If the ease of small-scale entry is indicative of competitive pressures, this
finding is further evidence against the popular perception that the higher
concentration rates observed in many developing countries reflect less
product market competition than in industrial countries (Rodrik 1988;
Krugman 1989).

Failure is not randomly distributed across the population of plants but
rather is concentrated among smaller plants, particularly younger ones.

Figure 1.2 Survival Rate of Plants by Age of Cohort, Chile and Colombia

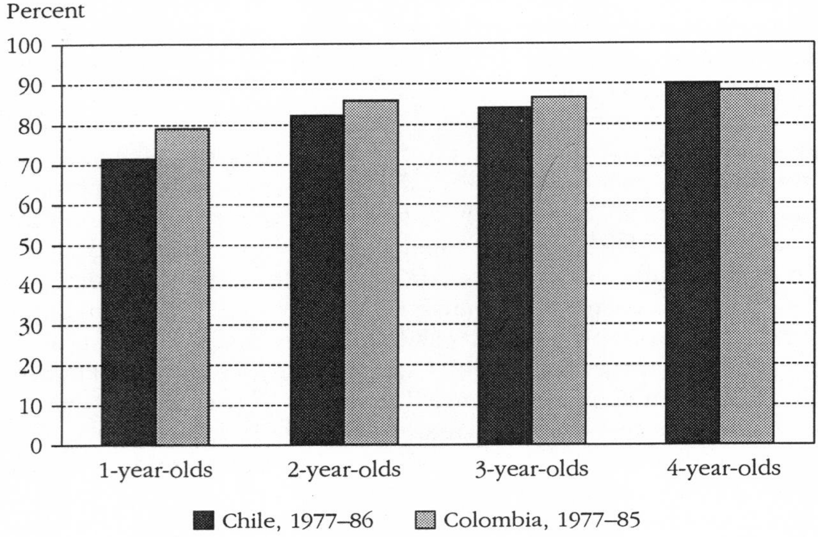

Percent

■ Chile, 1977–86   ▨ Colombia, 1977–85

Source: Chapters 9 and 10.

As a cohort of new plants ages, there is a clear increase in the proportion of plants that survive (see figure 1.2). For example, in Colombia the one-year survival rate increases from 79 percent for one-year-old plants to approximately 87 percent for plants more than three years old. In Chile, first-year survival rates average 73 percent, while four-year survival rates average 89 percent. This age pattern characterizes many studies of plants in industrial countries and is consistent with the view that heterogeneous producers are learning about their efficiency or profitability in the market. Firms that learn that they are relatively inefficient exit the market, and over time the cohort becomes increasingly composed of efficient producers with high probabilities of survival. Alternatively, the age pattern could reflect an increase in the fitness of the cohort, as learning-by-doing takes place or as new firms make productivity-improving investments.

Overall, the qualitative patterns of plant turnover are similar to those found in the manufacturing sectors of industrial countries: continual waves of small-scale producers enter the market, and many of them exit within the first few years of their existence. Theory suggests that heterogeneity in the level of profit or efficiency and uncertainty on the part of entrants about their future ranking relative to industry norms lie behind these phenomena. In addition, industries differ in the magnitude of turnover, with high-entry industries generally characterized by high exit.

Simultaneous entry and exit would be expected if sunk entry and exit costs were low. At a minimum, the turnover patterns found in the semi-industrialized countries—whether measured in terms of employment positions or number of plants—imply substantial resource mobility, much of it occurring between producers within the same industry.

Turnover and Productivity

As new products or technologies emerge, market share reallocations that favor the innovating producers generate gains in sectoral efficiency. Similarly, reallocations away from wasteful plants improve aggregate performance. If the intraindustry turnover patterns discussed in the last section are driven by this type of reallocation, there is a payoff in productivity growth. Indeed, as others have noted concerning India (Little, Mazumdar, and Page 1987; Pursell 1990), policies that prop up sick plants to maintain jobs are grossly inefficient. Chapters 3 and 4 assess the contribution of producer turnover to sectoral productivity growth by focusing on differences in the productivity of entering, expanding, contracting, and failing plants.

Chapter 3 reviews the evidence from industrial and developing countries on the importance of entry, exit, and interplant market share reallocations as sources of sectoral productivity growth. These processes do not appear to be the dominant source of productivity growth in the short run, but neither are they negligible. They can account for up to several percentage points of annual growth or shrinkage, depending on the time period, industry, and country.

Nonetheless, the productivity effects of turnover and share reallocations are no larger in the semi-industrialized countries than in the United States. Hence the rapid rates of job turnover do not obviously yield higher productivity. This result cannot be traced to limited cross-plant variation in productivity among the semi-industrialized countries: within most three-digit industries, one finds tremendous heterogeneity. Rather, it obtains because the potential productivity gains from market share reallocations are largely unexploited.

Chapter 4 presents new, detailed findings on the role of entry, exit, and market share reallocations in generating productivity growth among Chilean and Colombian manufacturers. In Colombia, turnover and share reallocations among incumbent plants often contribute more than 1 percentage point a year to total factor productivity growth, but their effect is sometimes negative and over the long run averages close to 0. The small year-to-year average impact of turnover does not occur because exiting plants are as productive as plants that survive—in fact, in most periods, they get 10 to 20 percent less output per unit of input bundle (see figure 1.3). Rather, turnover has a small impact on productivity for two reasons. First, exiting plants account for only 3 to 5 percent of the

Figure 1.3 Productivity of Plants by Age of Cohort, Colombia, 1982–86

Total factor productivity

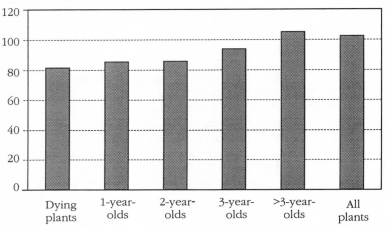

Note: Data are cohort-specific weighted averages of plant-level total factor productivity.
Source: Table 4.2.

market in a typical year. Second, plants in their first year of operation (entering plants) are only slightly more productive than exiting plants.

Nonetheless, the cumulative gains in productivity from turnover are far greater than the difference in productivity between dying plants in their last year and entering plants in their first year. As each new cohort of plants matures, some of its least productive members drop out, and its surviving members learn to be more efficient. So dying plants are eventually replaced with plants that are substantially more productive. (This pattern provides further evidence that the decline in failure rates documented in figure 1.2 reflects improvements in cohort efficiency.) Further, dying plants that exit are in the process of getting worse, and these plants might well become even less productive if they are not replaced (chapter 3). Finally, although turnover in any one year is small, after only four years, 20 to 30 percent of the initial population of plants typically turns over. For all of these reasons, policies that distort turnover patterns— either by subsidizing entry, by limiting entry, or by propping up less efficient producers that would otherwise exit—probably dampen productivity substantially in the long run.

Macroeconomic fluctuations can also create strong productivity effects, even in the short run. Because entry and exit rates vary over the business cycle, so do the market shares of incumbent producers. During upswings, incumbents lose market share as new plants enter more rapidly than incumbents fail. This can exert a countercyclical influence on productivity, because new and dying firms are typically less productive than continuing producers. Plant closures during the major recession did significantly improve labor productivity in Chile, and the rapid entry of inexperienced plants during the boom period did significantly hurt labor productivity in Morocco (chapter 3).

Plant-Level Determinants of Productivity

The scope for improving productivity depends not only on turnover patterns but also on the cross-plant distribution of efficiency levels and the response of this distribution to changes in economic conditions. Why does productivity differ across plants or grow within plants over time? In addition to the learning effects mentioned above, technology transfers, exploitation of economies of scale, managerial heterogeneity, and externalities are all possible causes that are explored in varying degrees in the remainder of this volume.

Chapter 7 assesses the role of foreign direct investment and finds that plants owned by multinational companies are typically more efficient than domestically owned establishments. Technology transfer from parent companies is one interpretation. However, contrary to earlier studies based on cross-sectional data, foreign direct investment does *not* appear to generate positive spillover effects for domestic firms in the same industry or region. At least in the short run, multinational corporations apparently siphon off demand or high-quality labor from domestically owned competitors.

The distinction between private and public ownership is also a relevant dimension of producer heterogeneity. The study of Turkey reported in chapter 13 finds that public ownership has a significant depressing effect on productivity and that public and private firms have qualitatively different responses to trade liberalization. This is consistent with the common belief that public sector managers, lacking the disciplining influence of shareholders, emphasize objectives like job security and compensation rather than efficiency.

If there are economies of scale, large plants are more efficient than small ones, so policies that influence the size distribution also affect productivity. For example, it is often observed that outward-oriented development strategies may increase the size of export-oriented producers by expanding the market. However, to the extent that scale economies are present, the same policies may *reduce* scale efficiency among import-competing firms (Rodrik 1988). These producers typically contract when trade liberalization increases import penetration in the domestic market (chapters 5 and 6).

In any event, as a source of productivity growth, changes in scale efficiency have probably been overemphasized relative to the other dimensions of performance (chapter 5). The largest plants in most industries typically have attained minimum efficient scale, and these plants dominate industrywide measures of performance. One implication is that computable general equilibrium models, which do not recognize size heterogeneity within a given industry, often overstate the potential gains from the exploitation of economies of scale that accompany trade liberalization.

The degree to which the domestic industry is exposed to international markets may affect productivity through other channels. Productivity dispersion is typically greater in industries protected from international competition, and higher productivity growth is often associated with the production of tradable products (chapter 3). These patterns may reflect limited access to foreign technology and expertise as well as difficulty acquiring imported intermediate and capital goods under protectionist trade regimes. However, there are plausible alternative explanations for the negative association between protection and productivity. For example, theory suggests that sectors with large start-up costs exhibit relatively little turnover and tend not to weed out low-productivity firms (Hopenhayn 1992). These sectors may also be relatively protected, because they are not in the comparative advantage of the semi-industrialized countries.

Plant-Level Determinants of Pricing Behavior

The country studies also provide some direct evidence on the variation in price-cost margins, both across industries and across plants within the same industry, as one way of assessing the extent of heterogeneity. Within industries, large plants do appear to be more profitable than their smaller competitors. But once size is controlled for, little systematic interindustry variation in margins remains, suggesting that entry barriers are small and that differences in industry margins largely reflect selection effects that cause efficient plants to gain market share within each industry.

Trade exposure does appear to exert additional competitive pressure on markups in Mexico (chapter 11), Morocco (chapter 12), and Turkey (chapter 13), either because it reduces the economywide returns to capital (as in the Hecksher-Ohlin model) or because it "disciplines" noncompetitive pricing behavior. The finding that openness reduces markups the most among large plants and concentrated industries suggests that market power is at least part of the story. This effect is particularly strong in Mexico, which went from being very protectionist to being very outward-oriented during the sample period (1985–90). In contrast, there is no correlation between trade flows and margins in the relatively open countries of Chile (chapter 10) and Morocco.

Conclusions

Industrial product markets in the semi-industrialized countries are relatively small, and they often are sheltered from international competition. Further, credit markets are poorly developed. Hence it is sometimes argued that incumbent producers are comfortably entrenched in the semi-industrialized countries and that turnover takes place among fringe producers who do not seriously discipline the pricing behavior of large firms. The research collected herein challenges that perception. The degree of flux in the manufacturing sectors of semi-industrialized countries is on average *greater* than that found in the North, so the competitive pressures are probably at least as great. Indeed, the relatively open countries in our sample show no evidence that imports contribute additional pressure at the margin.

In the short run, the replacement of dying plants with entering plants does not create dramatic productivity gains, since neither type of plant is very efficient on average, and neither accounts for large market shares. But dying plants become progressively less productive in their final years, while new plants that survive improve rapidly. Also, a large fraction of the manufacturing sector turns over within five to ten years. As a result, policies that inhibit this replacement process probably have substantial medium- and long-term detrimental effects on productivity.

The productivity gains from turnover are not costless. They are offset, in some measure, by the transaction costs of moving resources and by the income lost when factors are temporarily idled in the process. Indeed, if the costs of moving resources between two plants are comparable across countries, it appears that the semi-industrialized countries bear relatively more cost per unit of output than do Canada and the United States. We find no evidence that the productivity gains in the semi-industrialized countries are correspondingly larger. Hence, the high turnover among producers may reflect a greater degree of entrepreneurial groping for the right product or balance sheet in rapidly changing and highly unpredictable economies.

Notes

1. Details of these data bases may be found in the appendixes to the country studies in part II of this volume.

2. Additional findings based on these data have already been published in de Melo and Roland-Holst 1991; Haddad and Harrison 1993; Harrison 1994; Levinsohn 1993; Liu 1993; Roberts and Tybout 1991; Tybout 1992a and

1992b; Tybout, de Melo, and Corbo 1991; Tybout and Westbrook 1995; and Westbrook and Tybout 1993.

3. Chapter 3 reviews the theory linking technology and turnover patterns. Hopenhayn's (1992) model bears most directly on the results cited in this paragraph.

References

Chenery, Hollis, Sherman Robinson, and Moshe Syrquin. 1986. *Industrialization and Growth: A Comparative Study.* New York: Oxford University Press for the World Bank.

de Melo, Jaime, and David Roland-Holst. 1991. "Industrial Organization and Trade Liberalization: Evidence from Korea." In Robert E. Baldwin, ed., *Empirical Studies of Commercial Policy.* Chicago: University of Chicago Press for the National Bureau of Economic Research.

Haddad, Mona, and Ann Harrison. 1993. "Are There Productivity Spillovers from Direct Foreign Investment? Evidence from Panel Data for Morocco." *Journal of Development Economics* 42: 51–74.

Harrison, Ann. 1994. "Productivity, Imperfect Competition, and Trade Reform: Theory and Evidence." *Journal of International Economics* 36: 53–73.

Hopenhayn, Hugo. 1992. "Entry, Exit, and Firm Dynamics in Long-Run Equilibrium." *Econometrica* 60: 1127–50.

Krugman, Paul. 1989. "New Trade Theory and the Less Developed Countries." In Guillermo Calvo, ed., *Debt, Stabilization, and Development: Essays in Honor of Carlos Díaz-Alejandro.* New York: Basil Blackwell.

Levinsohn, James. 1993. "Testing the Imports-as-Market-Discipline Hypothesis." *Journal of International Economics* 35: 1–22.

Little, Ian M. D., Dipak Mazumdar, and John M. Page, Jr. 1987. *Small Manufacturing Enterprises: A Comparative Analysis of India and Other Economies.* New York: Oxford University Press for the World Bank.

Liu, Lili. 1993. "Entry, Exit, Learning and Productivity Change in Chilean Manufacturing." *Journal of Development Economics* 42: 217–42.

Pack, Howard. 1987. *Productivity, Technology, and Industrial Development: A Case Study in Textiles.* New York: Oxford University Press for the World Bank.

Pursell, Gary. 1990. "Industrial Sickness, Primary and Secondary: The Effects of Exit Constraints on Industrial Performance." *World Bank Economic Review* 4 (1): 103–14.

Roberts, Mark J., and James R. Tybout. 1991. "Size Rationalization and Trade Exposure in Developing Countries." In Robert E. Baldwin, ed., *Empirical Studies of Commercial Policy.* Chicago: University of Chicago Press for the National Bureau of Economic Research.

Rodrik, Dani. 1988. "Imperfect Competition, Scale Economies, and Trade Policy in Developing Countries." In Robert E. Baldwin, ed., *Trade Policy Issues and Empirical Analysis.* Chicago: University of Chicago Press for the National Bureau of Economic Research.

Tybout, James R. 1992a. "Linking Trade and Productivity: New Research Directions." *World Bank Economic Review* 6 (2): 189–211.

———. 1992b. "Making Noisy Data Sing: Estimating Production Technologies in Developing Countries." *Journal of Econometrics* 53: 25–44.

Tybout, James, Jaime de Melo, and Vittorio Corbo. 1991. "The Effects of Trade Reforms on Scale and Technical Efficiency: New Evidence from Chile." *Journal of International Economics* 31:231–50.

Tybout, James R., and M. Daniel Westbrook. 1995. "Trade Liberalization and the Dimensions of Efficiency Change in Mexican Manufacturing Industries." *Journal of International Economics* 39 (August): 53–78.

Westbrook, M. Daniel, and James R. Tybout. 1993. "Estimating Returns to Scale with Large, Imperfect Panels: An Application to Chilean Manufacturing Industries." *World Bank Economic Review* 7 (1): 85–112.

PART I

Heterogeneity, Productivity, and Employment Dynamics

2

Employment Flows
and Producer Turnover

Mark J. Roberts

The process of growth and development necessarily involves the replacement of outdated production methods with new technologies, the creation of new products, the opening of new markets, and the discovery of new applications for existing products. In most countries, these changes are accomplished by a continual, ongoing process of creative destruction that results in the gradual shifting of resources from contracting and failing producers to new and expanding ones.

When producers within a sector are identical, changes in demand and cost conditions lead to the shifts of resources across sectors that have been the focus of much empirical study by development economists. However, when producers within a sector vary enormously in size, input mix, and productivity, the evolutionary process also generates resource movements within sectors, even without changes in demand or cost conditions, as more profitable producers replace less profitable ones. It is these flows at the level of the individual plant or worker that are most likely to reflect both the adjustment costs associated with change and the potential benefits, such as higher productivity, more product diversity, and higher living standards.

This chapter focuses on the extent of micro-level resource reallocation in the manufacturing sectors of Chile, Colombia, and Morocco by quantifying the turnover in employment positions at the level of the individual manufacturing plant. By using plant-level panel data sets to track the employment level of individual plants over time, we distinguish the flow of jobs created in new and expanding plants from the simultaneous flow of jobs lost in plants that contract or close.

Recent studies of employment reallocation in Canada, the United States, and several European countries find that the gross flows of employment positions resulting from the entry, expansion, contraction, and exit of plants are several times larger than the net change in employment (Dunne, Roberts, and Samuelson 1989; Davis and Haltiwanger 1990, 1992; Davis, Haltiwanger, and Schuh 1994; Baldwin, Dunne, and Haltiwanger 1994). Thus, in these industrialized countries, a substantial amount of resource reallocation is continually occurring at the micro level even when there is little change in sectoral or aggregate totals.[1] This chapter provides complementary evidence on the extent of resource reallocation in three semi-industrialized countries.

There are reasons to expect less producer turnover in developing countries than in industrial countries. One is that government policies can directly interfere with the turnover process by subsidizing inefficient plants or industries. Government policies may also constrain the entry of new firms, through direct prohibition, credit rationing, or imperfections in capital markets that make it difficult for new firms to borrow. Trade policies that protect high-cost domestic producers or that slow the entry and expansion of new export producers also influence the process. Finally, uncertainty of future market conditions, such as can result from destabilizing macroeconomic policy, can also depress turnover in the presence of sunk entry or exit costs (Dixit 1989). Adjustments in the size of existing producers can also be affected by policy. Mandated severance payments for workers, for example, can lead to more costly adjustment and less turnover in employment. In contrast, developing countries may have higher rates of turnover than industrial countries, since a higher proportion of their employment, particularly in the manufacturing sector, is concentrated in smaller producers whose survival may be more sensitive to cyclical fluctuations.

Producer turnover can be costly if it requires the movement of workers either in and out of unemployment or between geographic regions. It can also be a beneficial source of change in sectoral and aggregate productivity if producers are not equally productive, because entry, growth, and exit alter the mix of efficient and inefficient firms. Tybout (1992) finds that the net exit of producers following the Chilean recession in the early 1980s contributed to an increase in productivity, because of the exit of inefficient plants, while the net entry of firms during the Moroccan expansion of the late 1980s contributed to a decline in productivity. Similarly, in chapter 4, Liu and Tybout find that exiting plants in Colombia are generally less efficient than incumbents, so that exit improves sectoral productivity.[2] Finally, high turnover rates can also provide competitive pressure in markets that are characterized by a small number of producers.

The goal of this chapter is to gauge the extent of resource reallocation at the micro level and to quantify the role of plant entry and exit as a contributing factor. To that end, employment reallocations that result from the entry and exit of plants are distinguished from employment changes that occur as continuing producers expand or contract. The focus is on employment change, the flow of new positions created by entering and expanding establishments, and the flow of positions destroyed by downsizing and exiting plants. The use of employment flows avoids the problems of differing output deflators across countries and allows direct comparison with recent studies for Canada and the United States.

The empirical findings are remarkably similar across the three developing countries and, in many ways, replicate patterns found in industrial-country data. Net changes in aggregate or sectoral employment mask large offsetting flows of new jobs created through plant entry and expansion and old jobs lost through the contraction and closing of other plants. Annual rates of job turnover are larger than comparable figures for Canada and the United States, averaging 24 to 30 percent of the manufacturing employment base in the three countries. Expansions and contractions of existing plants account for the majority of turnover in employment positions, but the entry and exit of producers are a larger component of the total in the developing countries.

Examining employment flows at the sectoral level reveals that more than 80 percent of total employment turnover occurs as a result of the entry, growth, and exit of plants *within the same industry* rather than from shifts in employment between industries. The rank correlation of industries on the basis of employment turnover rates is positive across the three countries, suggesting that technological factors, such as the magnitude of sunk entry costs or adjustment costs for existing producers, may play a large role in generating differences in average employment turnover rates among sectors. Contrary to the findings for Canada and the United States, cyclical fluctuations in the rates of job creation are larger than fluctuations in the rates of job loss, suggesting that major periods of employment restructuring are periods of high growth that are accompanied by substantial entry of new producers.

The next section defines the turnover variables that are quantified in this chapter. The following section summarizes the aggregate time-series patterns for the three countries with emphasis on the role of plant entry and exit as a source of employment turnover. The final section examines the cross-sectional and time-series patterns of turnover at the industry level.

Measurement Issues

Using the panel data sets for each country, which cover the population of manufacturing plants in operation in each of several years, it is possible to identify each plant as an entering, exiting, or surviving plant between each pair of years. Between year t and year $t + 1$, a plant is classified as a birth if it first appears in $t + 1$, as a death if it appears in year t but not in year $t + 1$, or as an incumbent survivor if it operates in both periods.[3] For each plant, the manufacturing censuses report the total employment in each year. By summing plant employment over the plants in each of these groups, the following employment totals can be defined: B_{t+1} is the number of employees in plants that begin operation in period $t + 1$. E_t, E_{t+1} are the number of employees in periods t and $t + 1$ in all surviving plants that expand employment or do not change employment between the two periods, so that E_{t+1} is greater than or equal to E_t. C_t, C_{t+1} are the number of employees in periods t and $t + 1$ in all surviving plants that contract employment between the two periods, so that C_{t+1} is less than C_t. D_t is the number of employees in period t in all plants that died in period t.

The level of employment (L) in each of the two periods is denoted L_t and L_{t+1} and can be defined as:

$$(2.1) \qquad\qquad L_t = E_t + C_t + D_t$$

$$(2.2) \qquad\qquad L_{t+1} = E_{t+1} + C_{t+1} + B_{t+1}.$$

The four components of the gross flow of employment positions are defined as B_{t+1} equals births; $\Delta E_t = E_{t+1} - E_t$ equals expansions; $\Delta C_t = -(C_{t+1} - C_t)$ equals contractions; and D_t equals deaths. These four components summarize the change in the number of occupied positions or employment opportunities within each group of plants. Because the underlying data are plant employment totals, it is not possible to tell if the actual jobs, or the individuals occupying the jobs, are the same ones over time. These components are used to define three other summary measures of employment turnover.

Net employment change between t and $t + 1$ is the difference between gross additions and gross losses:

$$(2.3) \qquad\qquad \Delta L_t = B_{t+1} + \Delta E_t - \Delta C_t - D_t.$$

Employment turnover is defined as the sum of the four components:

$$(2.4) \qquad\qquad T_t = B_{t+1} + \Delta E_t + \Delta C_t + D_t$$

and measures the total number of employment positions added or lost between the two years. The lower bound on the amount of turnover is the net employment change between the two years ($T_t \geq \Delta L_t$). Total employment turnover can also be divided into a component due to plant

Table 2.1 *Average Annual Job Growth and Turnover Rates in the Manufacturing Sector*
(percentages)

Country and period	Total manufacturing job growth rate	Gross job additions	Gross job losses	Turnover rate	Volatility rate
Average over entire period					
Chile, 1979–86	-1.0	12.9	-13.9	26.8	18.4
Colombia, 1977–91	0.3	12.5	-12.2	24.6	22.2
Morocco, 1984–89	6.5	18.6	12.1	30.7	24.2
Canada, 1973–86	0.6	10.6	10.0	20.5	17.8
United States, 1973–86	-1.2	9.2	-10.4	19.6	15.3
Average during years of employment expansion					
Chile	8.7	17.6	-8.9	26.6	17.8
Colombia	2.8	13.7	-11.0	24.7	21.9
Morocco	6.5	18.6	-12.1	30.7	24.2
Canada	2.4	11.4	-8.8	20.2	17.5
United States	3.2	11.1	-7.9	19.0	15.8
Average during years of employment contraction					
Chile	-8.2	9.4	-17.6	27.0	18.8
Colombia	-2.2	11.2	-13.3	24.5	22.4
Morocco	n.a.	n.a.	n.a.	n.a.	n.a.
Canada	-3.0	9.1	-12.1	21.1	18.1
United States	-5.5	7.4	-12.9	20.2	14.7

n.a. Not applicable (no periods of contraction).
Note: For the United States and Canada, the denominator in each rate is average employment in periods $t + 1$ and t; for developing countries, the denominator is employment at the start of each interval.
Source: For Canada and the United States, constructed from Baldwin, Dunne, and Haltiwanger 1994, table 1; for Chile, Colombia, and Morocco, author's calculations.

turnover (births plus deaths) and a component due to the turnover of positions in ongoing plants (expansions plus contractions).

Finally, the amount of employment turnover beyond that needed to account for the net change in the number of positions—referred to as the level of volatility—is defined as:[4]

$$(2.5) \qquad\qquad V_t = T_t - |\Delta L_t|.$$

In general, these summary measures are expressed as a proportion of employment in year t. The measures can be constructed for the whole manufacturing sector or for individual industries.

Aggregate Gross Flows of Employment Positions

Average annual employment growth and turnover rates were computed for the manufacturing sector in each of the three countries and, for comparison, Canada and the United States (see table 2.1; annual gross flow components for the three developing countries are reported in table 2.2). Averages were calculated over all the available years and then for periods of net expansion and net decline of manufacturing employment. For Colombia the data cover 1977–91, which includes two periods of manufacturing sector expansion (1977–79 and 1985–91) and a long period of employment contraction (1979–85). Net employment growth averaged only 0.3 percent a year over the whole period but rose to 2.8 percent a year during the expansions and dropped to –2.2 percent a year during the contractions. Although the Colombian manufacturing sector clearly experienced cyclical fluctuations, there is no pattern of long-term secular growth or decline in employment positions.

Long-term changes in the size of the manufacturing sector are more evident in Chile, Morocco, and the United States. Employment in Chile's manufacturing sector contracted by an average of 1.0 percent a year over 1979–86, a period encompassing both a massive recession and a subsequent expansion. Employment shrank 8.2 percent a year during the 1979–83 recession and grew 8.7 percent a year during the 1983–86 recovery. Morocco experienced positive employment growth in each sample year from 1984 to 1989. Employment growth ranged from 1.6 percent a year to 10.1 percent and averaged 6.5 percent over the period. The United States also experienced a secular decline in manufacturing employment over the 1973–86 period, averaging a loss of 1.2 percent a year. Again, cyclical fluctuations are important, with average annual employment growth rates of 3.2 percent during expansions and losses of 5.5 percent during contractions. In Canada the manufacturing sector grew at an average rate of 0.6 percent a year during 1973–86, including

Table 2.2 Gross Annual Employment Flows in Chile, Colombia, and Morocco
(percentages)

Country and year (t, t + 1)	L(t)	B / L	ΔE / L	ΔC / L	D / L	ΔL / L	T / L	V / L
Chile								
1979–80	310.1	0.022	0.083	−0.084	−0.087	−0.065	0.277	0.212
1980–81	289.9	0.032	0.064	−0.090	−0.078	−0.072	0.264	0.192
1981–82	269.1	0.021	0.033	−0.159	−0.066	−0.171	0.279	0.109
1982–83	223.1	0.043	0.076	−0.075	−0.065	−0.021	0.260	0.239
1983–84	218.5	0.078	0.120	−0.055	−0.041	0.102	0.294	0.192
1984–85	240.9	0.026	0.109	−0.050	−0.021	0.064	0.206	0.142
1985–86	256.3	0.047	0.149	−0.046	−0.054	0.095	0.297	0.201
Colombia								
1977–78	458.2	0.083	0.079	−0.057	−0.079	0.027	0.298	0.271
1978–79	470.5	0.101	0.077	−0.053	−0.091	0.034	0.322	0.288
1979–80	486.6	0.075	0.059	−0.063	−0.073	−0.002	0.270	0.269
1980–81	485.8	0.069	0.052	−0.072	−0.078	−0.029	0.271	0.242
1981–82	471.6	0.056	0.057	−0.089	−0.051	−0.026	0.252	0.226
1982–83	459.3	0.057	0.052	−0.081	−0.047	−0.023	0.232	0.209
1983–84	448.9	0.042	0.061	−0.069	−0.050	−0.017	0.222	0.205
1984–85	441.3	0.051	0.051	−0.089	−0.049	−0.036	0.239	0.204
1985–86	425.5	0.065	0.067	−0.053	−0.057	0.023	0.242	0.219
1986–87	435.4	0.064	0.098	−0.048	−0.037	0.077	0.247	0.170
1987–88	468.9	0.042	0.064	−0.070	−0.055	−0.020	0.231	0.210
1988–89	459.6	0.047	0.065	−0.052	−0.040	0.020	0.204	0.185
1989–90	468.7	0.031	0.064	−0.054	−0.037	0.004	0.187	0.182
1990–91	470.7	0.045	0.073	−0.052	−0.058	0.007	0.228	0.221
Morocco								
1984–85	220.8	0.071	0.098	−0.125	−0.027	0.016	0.322	0.306
1985–86	224.4	0.076	0.129	−0.099	−0.029	0.078	0.333	0.255
1986–87	241.8	0.064	0.122	−0.086	−0.022	0.078	0.294	0.217
1987–88	260.5	0.049	0.114	−0.089	−0.021	0.054	0.274	0.220
1988–89	274.4	0.069	0.138	−0.091	−0.014	0.101	0.312	0.211

Source: Author's calculations.

an average growth rate of 2.4 percent during expansions and a loss of 3.0 percent during contractions. Except for Morocco, each country experienced modest average changes in employment overall, varying from −1.2 to 0.6 percent a year, while also experiencing periods of more substantial growth and decline in employment.

Of primary interest to this study is the amount of micro-level turnover or reallocation in employment positions that lies behind these net changes in employment. Average rates of gross additions and losses of positions for the three developing countries show, as do all empirical studies for industrial countries, that the gross flows of positions were many times larger than the net change in employment (table 2.1, columns 2 and 3).[5] There were large flows of new jobs even during periods of overall manufacturing contraction and large flows of jobs lost during periods of substantial growth. The average annual rate of new job creation during Chile's massive recession of 1979–83 was 9.4 percent, although total manufacturing sector employment fell 8.2 percent a year. Morocco's overall manufacturing sector expansion of 6.5 percent a year was accompanied by an average annual job loss of 12.1 percent.

There are some differences in the rates of job creation and destruction between developing and industrial countries. For Canada and the United States, gross job additions and losses averaged approximately 10 percent a year. For Chile and Colombia, they averaged 12.2 to 13.9 percent a year; for Morocco, they were higher still. The main source of difference between the two groups of countries is the rate of gross job additions during expansionary periods, which averaged 11.1 and 11.4 percent a year for the United States and Canada, respectively, but varied from 13.7 to 18.6 percent a year for the three developing countries.[6] Throughout this chapter, the sensitivity of the job creation process to cyclical fluctuations is one of the main sources of difference between the industrialized and semi-industrialized countries.

Turnover and Volatility

Combining gross additions and losses yields average turnover in employment positions, which is the proportion of initial-year employment positions added through plant openings or expansions plus those lost through plant closings or cutbacks (table 2.1, column 4). Employment turnover rates were large for all five countries, but the three developing countries had underlying rates of plant-level employment reallocation that were some 25 to 50 percent *larger* than those found in Canada and the United States. The same pattern holds for expansionary and contractionary periods as well. In addition, there is little difference in the average rate of employment turnover for each country between growing and contracting periods. Employment turnover rates were always smallest in the United States and Canada, averaging 19.6 percent in the United States and 20.5 percent in Canada during both expansions and contractions. For Colombia and Chile, average turnover rates were 24.7 and 26.6 percent, respectively, during periods of employment growth and 24.5 and 27.0 percent during periods of contraction. For Morocco, which had no contractionary periods, the turnover rate averaged 30.7 percent.

An important and much discussed finding for the United States concerns the cyclical pattern of total employment reallocation. Davis and

Haltiwanger (1992) show that employment reallocation in the U.S. manufacturing sector is countercyclical, with higher rates of job turnover occurring during recessions. The simple correlation between the net growth rate and the turnover rate is −0.56.[7] This occurs because the time-series variation in job destruction rates is much larger than the time-series variation in job creation rates. Baldwin, Dunne, and Haltiwanger (1994) report that the ratio Var($\Delta C + D$) / Var($B + \Delta E$) equals 2.17 in the United States. This implies that job loss is much more sensitive to the business cycle than is job creation, so that recessions are periods of increased job destruction, with a much smaller decrease in job addition rates, while expansions are periods of decreased job destruction, with a much smaller increase in job addition rates. Baldwin, Dunne, and Haltiwanger (1994) also find a negative correlation between net change and turnover for the Canadian manufacturing sector, but the magnitude is smaller at −0.25 and not significantly different than 0. The ratio of the variance of job destruction to job creation in Canada is 1.54. These findings are consistent with the view that recessions are times of cleansing of the production structure as employers close or scale back inefficient plants.[8]

A countercyclical pattern of employment reallocation is not evident in the three developing countries. The simple correlation between net employment change and turnover is 0.21 in Colombia, −0.03 in Chile, and 0.01 in Morocco.[9] Corresponding to this, the ratio of the variance of job destruction to job creation is 0.65 in Colombia, 1.04 in Chile, and 0.995 in Morocco. Two of the three countries show no evidence of cyclical employment reallocation, while the third, Colombia, has a procyclical pattern. The pattern for Colombia arises primarily from the large variation in plant births over time and from the positive correlation between births and expansions. This suggests that the major periods of employment reallocation were not recessions, as in Canada and the United States, but rather periods of high growth that were accompanied by substantial entry of new producers.

One reason for the differences in cyclical patterns of the industrial and developing countries may be the differences in the size and age distribution of producers between the countries.[10] Davis and Haltiwanger (1992) and Davis, Haltiwanger, and Schuh (1994, section 4.3) provide some evidence for the United States on the sources of cyclical variation by plant type. They find that smaller, younger plants have higher rates of job turnover than larger, older plants and that they are also much less cyclically sensitive. The countercyclical reallocation pattern in the United States is driven by the adjustment, particularly the downsizing during recessions, of large, old manufacturing plants. The patterns observed in the three developing countries are much more similar to those found for small, young plants in the United States.

The final summary measure of employment flows presented in table 2.1 is the volatility rate. Because the net employment change in manufacturing is generally considerably smaller than the turnover rate, most of the micro-level employment reallocation observed in the three developing countries cannot be attributed simply to changes in the size of the manufacturing sector. As a result, the aggregate volatility rates parallel the turnover rates, and the rankings of the countries are the same (table 2.1, column 5). For Chile and Morocco, however, the large annual changes in employment did contribute to an increase in the magnitude of employment turnover. When measured by the volatility rate, employment reallocation in Morocco drops to the level for Colombia, approximately 24.0 percent, and that for Chile, at 18.4 percent, drops close to the level observed in the United States.

Overall, aggregate flows for the three countries reveal high turnover of positions, with average turnover rates that differ more across countries than between periods of growth and contraction within a country. The rate of turnover in employment positions is larger in Chile, Colombia, and Morocco than in Canada and the United States, a difference that persists even after controlling for the larger rates of net employment change in the developing countries. This suggests that country-specific factors such as the mix of industries and plant sizes, among other things, may have contributed to the differences in turnover. The three developing countries apparently do not have the countercyclical pattern of aggregate employment turnover that characterizes Canada and the United States but do have the cyclical patterns that characterize the subset of small, young producers in the industrial countries.

Contribution of Plant Entry and Exit

The turnover rates reported above represent a combination of size adjustments among ongoing establishments (ΔE_t and ΔC_t) and the entry and exit of establishments (B_t and D_t). The heavier concentration of industrial-country manufacturing employment in large, capital-intensive plants and in durable goods industries is likely to result in differences across industrial and developing countries in the importance of the sunk costs of entry and exit relative to the adjustment costs incurred in changing plant output.[11] This, in turn, should result in differences in the relative importance of plant entry and exit versus changes in the scale of continuing establishments as a source of employment turnover. If adjustment costs are small and sunk costs of entry are large, as is likely when the technology used is very capital intensive, most variation in demand should be met by changes in the size of continuing plants. Large or permanent increases in demand would be required to boost profits sufficiently to cover the sunk costs of entry and thus to induce entry.

Table 2.3 *Employment Reallocation Arising from Plant Entry and Exit and Expansion and Contraction*
(percentages)

Country and period	Net change		Turnover		Volatility	
	Entry and exit	Expansion and contraction	Entry and exit	Expansion and contraction	Entry and exit	Expansion and contraction
Average over entire period						
Chile, 1979–86	-2.0	1.1	9.8	17.1	6.5	11.6
Colombia, 1977–91	0.2	0.1	11.6	13.0	10.7	10.9
Morocco, 1984–89	4.3	2.2	8.9	21.8	4.6	18.5
United States, 1973–86	-1.1	-0.1	3.7	15.9	2.7	11.8
Average during years of						
employment expansion						
Chile	1.1	7.6	8.9	17.6	7.3	10.1
Colombia	0.6	2.2	11.9	12.8	10.8	10.6
Morocco	4.3	2.2	8.9	21.8	4.6	18.5
United States	-0.8	4.0	3.5	15.5	2.7	11.6
Average during years of						
employment contraction						
Chile	-4.4	-3.8	10.4	16.6	6.0	12.8
Colombia	-0.2	-2.0	11.3	13.2	10.6	11.3
Morocco	n.a.	n.a.	n.a.	n.a.	n.a.	n.a.
United States	-1.4	-4.1	4.0	16.3	2.6	12.1

n.a. Not applicable (no periods of contraction).
Source: For the United States, constructed from Baldwin, Dunne, and Haltiwanger 1994, table 1; for Chile, Colombia, and Morocco, author's calculations.

Conversely, if marginal adjustment costs increase rapidly with changes in plant size, then entry and exit should play a larger role as a source of changes in supply.

To assess the importance of plant entry and exit relative to the size adjustments of ongoing establishments, measures of net change, turnover, and volatility are constructed using employment flows from entering and exiting plants (B_t and D_t) and are then compared with comparable figures for continuing plants (ΔE_t and ΔC_t).

In Colombia, which experienced virtually no net employment growth over the whole period, the net change in employment positions was approximately 0.0 on average both for plant entry and exit and for adjustment in continuing plants (see table 2.3). In Chile and the United States, however, the net decline in manufacturing positions was accompanied by the loss of a substantial number of positions through plant exit. On average, the entry and exit of plants were responsible for a 2.0 percent decline in positions in Chile and a 1.1 percent decline in the United States per year. Similarly, the net growth in manufacturing employment in Morocco was accompanied by the creation of a substantial number of positions through plant entry. The net entry of new plants was responsible for a 4.3 percent average annual increase in positions. Somewhat surprisingly, over the entire period for all four countries, entry and exit apparently contributed more to the net change in positions than did the expansion and contraction of continuing plants. However, by disaggregating the years into those with positive and negative net growth, it can be seen that this result is driven by the periods of enormous economic change—the continuing economic expansion in Morocco throughout the sample period, accompanied by substantial new entry, and the large recession in Chile in the early part of the sample period, when plant exit was enormous.[12] For the other countries (Colombia and the United States) or time periods (Chilean expansion), continuing plants contributed a larger proportion of the net change in positions. The conclusion to be drawn from these simple time period averages is that plant entry and exit increase in importance as a source of the net change in positions during periods with large changes in demand.

In all four countries, expansions and contractions in continuing plants were the major source of turnover in the number of positions (table 2.3, columns 3 and 4), although in Colombia plant entry/exit and the expansion/contraction of existing plants were much closer than in the other countries.[13] The average turnover rates reveal a systematic difference in the importance of entry and exit in the developing countries relative to the United States: in both the expansionary and contractionary periods, plant entry and exit were responsible for a larger proportion of total turnover in the three developing countries. The ratio of entry/exit turnover to expansion/contraction turnover over all time periods (table 2.3, column 3 divided by column 4) was 0.41 for Morocco, 0.57 in Chile, and 0.89 in Colombia, compared with 0.23 for the United States.

The volatility rates indicate a substantial amount of reallocation in employment positions within each of the two groups of plants.[14] Two of the volatility measures stand out. One is the high volatility rate generated by entering and exiting plants in Colombia. For reasons explained in detail in chapter 10, the tracking of individual plants over time is most problematic in the Colombian data set, and the high volatility rate suggests the presence of errors in the time-series linkages.[15] If plants are not accurately followed over time in the panel data, breaks in a plant's data are counted as the exit of an existing plant and the entry of a new plant. In addition, if the plant's employment is stable across the two years, little net change in positions is generated by this incorrectly identified exit/entry pattern. This measurement error then results in an upward bias in all the turnover measures, with the largest effect likely to be on the volatility rate of entering and exiting plants. The second unusual observation is the volatility rate of 18.5 percent for continuing plants in Morocco. The other three countries had rates between 10.9 and 11.8 percent overall and between 10.1 and 12.8 for expansionary and contractionary periods.[16] The likely cause of the high rate for Morocco was the simultaneous expansion of one subset of manufacturing industries and contraction of another.

Based on the disaggregation in table 2.3, the entry and exit of manufacturing plants clearly played a larger role as a source of employment fluctuations in the three developing countries than in the United States. They accounted for a larger proportion of total employment turnover in both expansionary and contractionary periods. They were also responsible for the majority of net employment growth during periods of substantial structural change in Chile and Morocco.

Sectoral Gross Flows of Employment Positions

The aggregate flows described in the preceding section can also arise from expansion in some industries and simultaneous contraction in others, from employment shifts across geographic areas, and from changes within a sector or geographic region.[17] Using U.S. manufacturing data, Dunne, Roberts, and Samuelson (1989) find that shifts in the sectoral or geographic mix of plants contribute little to the overall flows of employment positions, while plant-level changes within the same sector and geographic region account for 74 percent of the gross flows of positions. To examine the relative importance of within- and across-industry job flows in Chile, Colombia, and Morocco, aggregate turnover (T) was decomposed following the method used by Dunne, Roberts, and Samuelson (1989):

$$(2.6) \qquad T_t = |\Delta L_t| + [\Sigma_j |\Delta L_{jt}| - |\Delta L_t|] + \Sigma_j [T_{jt} - |\Delta L_{jt}|].$$

L is the level of employment, j is the industry subscript, and t is the time period. The first term at the right side of the equation is the net change in manufacturing sector employment. The second term is the employment turnover arising from shifts across industries minus the employment turnover resulting from the net change in manufacturing employment and is referred to as across-industry turnover. The final term is the sum of the industry-level volatility or the excess of turn-over above the net change in sectoral employment and is referred to as within-industry reallocation. Because of substantial differences in the net growth of manufacturing sector employment among the three developing countries, decomposition of the volatility rate is likely to be more informative about the importance of within- and across-industry reallocations than is decomposition of aggregate turnover. The aggregate volatility rate can be decomposed into across-industry and within-industry components by subtracting the absolute value of aggregate net employment change from both sides of equation 2.6:

$$(2.7) \qquad V_t = [\Sigma_j |\Delta L_{jt}| - |\Delta L_t|] + \Sigma_j [T_{jt} - |\Delta L_{jt}|].$$

For all three countries, the largest contribution to the average aggregate turnover rate came from plant-level shifts within the same industry—from 59.4 percent to 78.0 percent—rather than from the net change in the size of the manufacturing sector or shifts of positions across sectors (see table 2.4). Decomposition of the volatility rate shows an even more striking similarity across countries. Once the net change in the level

Table 2.4 Decomposition of Aggregate Turnover and Volatility in Chile, Colombia, and Morocco
(average shares over time; percentages)

Country and period	Turnover			Volatility	
	Net change	*Across industry*	*Within industry*	*Across industry*	*Within industry*
Chile, 1979–86	31.1	9.5	59.4	12.2	87.8
Colombia, 1977–91	09.9	12.1	78.0	13.2	86.8
Morocco, 1984–89	21.3	13.5	65.1	16.9	83.1

Note: Data are for sixty-nine four-digit industries in Chile, seventy-three in Colombia, and sixty-one in Morocco.
Source: Author's calculations.

of manufacturing employment is accounted for, some 83.1 to 87.8 percent of total turnover in employment positions arose within the same industry.

Thus, as in industrial countries, the vast majority of job flows in these three developing countries was the result of the entry, expansion, contraction, and closing of plants *within the same industry*. But what accounts for the fact that while some producers in an industry were entering or expanding employment, others in the same industry were contracting or shutting down? Simple explanations based on the response of homogeneous producers to common shocks to sectoral demand are clearly not consistent with this pattern of simultaneous expansion and contraction in the same industry. In recent years, several theoretical models of industry-level dynamics have been developed that rely on underlying producer heterogeneity in demand or cost structures combined with a market selection process that sorts inefficient from efficient producers.[18] Of particular interest for developing countries is whether the selection process successfully isolates and rewards the efficient, more productive plants. Liu and Tybout (chapter 4) report evidence on differences in productivity among continuing and exiting plants that are consistent with differences in efficiency that affect turnover.

Differences in Turnover Patterns across Sectors

The last section demonstrated that most of the turnover in manufacturing employment positions occurs within industries, as one group of producers is replaced by another. The level of turnover in an industry will be determined by the interaction of market-level demand and cost shocks, plant-specific demand or productivity shocks, and underlying technological conditions, such as the capital intensity of the production process, the magnitude of sunk entry or exit costs, and the ease with which output levels of continuing producers can be adjusted. Each of these forces will contribute to both cross-industry and time-series variation in turnover rates. If technological conditions vary across industries but change only slowly over time for a given industry, they will generate permanent, systematic cross-sectional differences in turnover. Industries with low sunk entry costs, for example, should have higher turnover rates than industries with high sunk costs (Hopenhayn 1992).

In this section, we examine the turnover patterns by industry and year in the three developing countries for common industry-level factors. Several robust patterns have been noted in firm entry, growth, and exit data for industrial countries. One of the most common findings is that entry and exit are positively correlated at the industry level—industries with higher-than-average entry rates also have higher-than-average exit rates, and thus turnover rates tend to vary systematically across industries.

To examine this issue, average gross flow rates were computed for each industry in each country over time, and rank correlations were calculated for average industry-level values (see table 2.5). The rank correlation between employment growth due to plant births and employment loss due to plant deaths is high (from 0.565 for Morocco to 0.802 for Colombia), indicating that industries with high rates of employment creation from plant entry also have high rates of employment loss from plant exit.

This finding suggests that technological factors such as the magnitude of sunk entry costs are more important than changes in demand for understanding the average rates of industry-level entry and exit. If shifts in demand were the driving force behind the changes in industrial employment, we would expect to see high average rates of entry and low average rates of exit during periods of industry growth and the reverse pattern during periods of industry contraction. This would not produce the strong positive correlation observed in the data. In contrast, the positive correlation between birth and exit rates observed in the data could be produced by a combination of some industries with low entry costs, small-scale, non-capital intensive technologies—making both entry and exit relatively easy—and some industries with larger-scale, capital-intensive production methods and high entry costs—making entry and exit harder.

This technology-based explanation can be taken one step further. If the cost of adjusting production and employment levels varies systematically across industries, high rates of employment expansion and contraction would be expected in industries with low adjustment costs and low rates in industries with high adjustment costs. Positive rank correlations from 0.206 in Chile to 0.507 in Morocco among average rates of industry expansion (ΔE_t) and contraction (ΔC_t) in all three countries support that supposition (see table 2.5, column 2). Again, differences in production technologies across industries appear to be a major contributor to these patterns. In addition, reflecting the patterns of entry and exit and expansion and contraction already discussed, rank correlations between rates of gross job creation and gross job loss are strongly posi-

Table 2.5 Rank Correlations among Average Industry Variables in Chile, Colombia, and Morocco

Country	Entry and exit	Expansion and contractions	Gross job additions and gross job losses
Chile	0.644	0.206	0.546
Colombia	0.802	0.449	0.711
Morocco	0.565	0.507	0.535

Source: Author's calculations.

tive in all three countries (table 2.5, column 3). In each country, industries with the highest average rates of job creation have the highest average rates of job loss.[19]

If these average industry-level patterns are driven by technological differences, and if the technology for each industry is similar across countries, the ranking of industries with high and low turnover should be consistent in the three countries. More precisely, average industry-level rates of net employment change, turnover, and volatility should systematically reflect different combinations of changes in demand and differences in technology. If rates of sectoral demand growth are not highly correlated across countries, while technologies are, there should be different patterns of correlation in the three variables across countries.

The average rate of net employment growth in an industry is likely to reflect long-term changes in demand for the industry's output and should show the lowest correlation across countries. Turnover rates also reflect long-term changes in demand but, as discussed above, are also likely to reflect differences in entry costs and the capital intensity of the production process and thus should be more highly correlated across countries than rates of net employment growth. Finally, an industry's volatility rate nets out the employment turnover needed to account for the net employment change in the industry and thus is the most likely to reflect differences in technology.

The rank correlations for these three variables show this expected pattern: for each pair of countries, the rate of net employment change has the lowest correlation, the volatility rate has the highest, and the turnover rate falls in between (see table 2.6). Although this pattern of correlations is consistent with the fact that entry and adjustment costs differ with an industry's technologies, the magnitude of the correlations is not as high as the correlations within each country (reported in table 2.5). This difference is not surprising, since a large number of country-specific factors can affect an industry's pattern of base turnover, including credit market constraints and trade or industrial policies that affect specific sectors. The correlations for each of the variables are also highest between Chile and Colombia, which have the most similar industrial sectors among the three countries.[20]

Time-Series Patterns of Turnover within Sectors

The previous section identified several empirical regularities in the patterns of average gross flows and turnover across industries and countries. This section examines variations in employment reallocation within individual sectors over time. These would be expected to show a more prominent role for fluctuations in demand of the type, for example, that might arise from variations in trade policy. The interesting question is

Table 2.6 Rank Correlations of Average Industry Variables
across Countries

Variable	Chile and Colombia	Colombia and Morocco	Chile and Morocco
Rate of net employment change	0.310	−0.115	0.080
Rate of employment turnover	0.444	0.197	0.134
Rate of employment volatility	0.549	0.429	0.403

Note: Data are for 1979–86 in Chile, 1977–91 in Colombia, and 1984–89 in Morocco.
Source: Author's calculations.

the effect of cyclical fluctuations in industry-level demand on the magnitude and source of employment reallocations.

To isolate the time-series variation and remove the effect of differences in technology, each variable was expressed as a deviation from its industry-country mean over time. This normalization removes all industry- and country-specific effects that are fixed over time and thus controls for much of the likely variation in technology across sectors.[21] Then the standard deviation—summarizing the time-series variation in the industry-level measures—was computed for gross job additions and losses and for four components of gross flows.

The main finding is that the variance of gross job additions exceeded the variance of gross job losses in all three countries (see table 2.7). The ratio $Var(\Delta C + D) / Var(B + \Delta E)$ equals 0.642, 0.411, and 0.232 for Chile, Colombia, and Morocco, respectively. This implies that, at the industry level, net employment expansion was positively correlated with turnover, so that total industry-level employment turnover was procyclical.[22] This finding is contrary to that for industrial countries and is a much stronger pattern than found in the aggregate data discussed above. It suggests that as industry-level employment fluctuated over time, the amount of new job creation was the main source of variation, whereas job losses due to plant contraction and exit were relatively stable.

Table 2.7 Variance of Within-Industry Employment Flows in Chile,
Colombia, and Morocco

Rate	Chile	Colombia	Morocco
Gross job additions	0.0173	0.0112	0.0246
Gross job losses	0.0111	0.0046	0.0057
Birth rate	0.0069	0.0090	0.0144
Death rate	0.0066	0.0036	0.0016
Expansion rate	0.0088	0.0020	0.0096
Contraction rate	0.0042	0.0015	0.0037

Source: Author's calculations.

Disaggregating gross job creation and job loss into their entry, exit, expansion, and contraction components shows clearly that both plant turnover and change in the size of continuing plants contributed to the procyclical turnover in job positions (table 2.7). The variance of job creation due to plant entry exceeds that of job loss due to plant exit, and the variance of the rate of job expansion exceeds that due to contraction for all the countries. Only in the case of Chile, which experienced a major recession and partial recovery, does the time-series variation for job losses due to plant exit approach that for job creation due to plant entry. These numbers suggest that in all three countries, the job losses due to plant contraction and failure were relatively stable compared with the job gains due to plant expansion and entry, and they reinforce the conclusion from the aggregate data that job creation played a major role in restructuring employment.

Conclusions

In many ways, the patterns of employment gains and losses resulting from the entry, growth, and exit of manufacturing plants are remarkably similar for Chile, Colombia, and Morocco, although these three developing countries experienced very different patterns of growth in the manufacturing sector. First, as has been found in all studies for industrial countries, the net change in manufacturing employment between any two time periods masks substantial offsetting flows of new jobs created through plant entry and expansion and old jobs lost through plant contraction and closing. The annual rate of turnover in employment positions averaged between 24.6 and 30.7 percent of the total number of positions in the three countries, which is substantially higher than turnover figures for Canada and the United States. Second, there is no evidence at the aggregate level, as there is for Canada and the United States, of countercyclical employment turnover in the three developing countries. Chile and Morocco had no cyclical pattern, and Colombia had procyclical turnover, arising primarily from high variability in the rate of job creation. Third, employment flows arising from the entry and exit of plants were more important as a source of employment turnover in the developing countries than in the United States. This is true in both expansionary and contractionary periods.

The findings are also very similar for the three countries at the sectoral level. By far the largest share of the turnover in employment positions occurred within industries as plants entered, grew, contracted, and exited rather than across industries as demand, cost, and production patterns changed. Once the net change in the size of the manufacturing sector is controlled for, between 83.1 and 87.8 percent of annual employment turnover, on average, resulted from the turnover of positions within the same industry. This process of simultaneous entry and exit and expansion and contraction of plants is inconsistent with the view of homogeneous producers adjusting production in response to common demand shocks. Rather, it emphasizes the importance of producer heterogeneity, on either the demand or the cost side, in the adjustment process.

Several similarities in the magnitude of sectoral employment turnover across countries suggest that common technological factors, such as the importance of sunk entry costs, the capital intensity of the technology, or the extent of adjustment costs, played a large role in explaining differences in employment turnover at the industry level. This pattern closely mirrors findings for industrial countries. In contrast to the findings for Canada and the United States, however, there are strong patterns of procyclical turnover at the industry level. Industries with high rates of total job growth had higher rates of job turnover because of the increased magnitude of job creation by both new and existing plants. The overall picture is one of a relatively stable process of job loss with a more cyclically sensitive process of job creation.

The findings that producer turnover was a common phenomenon in these three developing countries and that it arose primarily from the simultaneous entry, growth, and exit of producers within the same industry are consistent with underlying heterogeneity in the costs or demands faced by individual producers. Once this within-industry heterogeneity is recognized, it is clear that policies that attempt to reduce turnover, by preventing exit for example, are likely to slow the process by which inefficient producers are replaced by more efficient ones. Particularly relevant here are policies that raise the fixed costs of entry or exit for producers. Theoretical results by Dixit (1989) illustrate that the presence of fixed entry or exit costs, particularly when combined with uncertainty about future market conditions, has a significant depressing effect on entry and exit and requires much larger shifts in market conditions to generate structural adjustment. In simulation exercises that emphasize the importance of producer heterogeneity and fixed exit costs, Hopenhayn and Rogerson (1993) illustrate that an increase in mandated severance payments to laid off workers actually reduces employment and labor productivity by distorting the turnover process.

Caballero and Hammour (1994b) provide a basis for examining the efficiency of the job reallocation process. In a model with fixed creation (or entry) costs, continual technological improvement embodied in new jobs, and cyclical demand fluctuations, they show that an efficient economy concentrates both job creation and destruction, and hence turnover, in recessions, because the opportunity cost of reallocation is lowest in periods of low demand. In contrast, labor market imperfections, which they model as resulting from bargaining between the worker and the firm, reduce the incentives to scrap outdated production units, resulting in too little turnover and an inefficient "decoupling" of the processes of job creation and destruction. The empirical implication of their model is that the efficient reallocation process results in a positive time-series correlation between gross job creation and destruction. The correlation for both Canada and the United States is negative, primarily resulting from high rates of job loss but low rates of job creation in recessions (Baldwin, Dunne, and Haltiwanger 1994, table 1). Caballero and Hammour (1994a) interpret this as reflecting cleansing of the production structure in recessions rather than increased reallocation activity.[23]

At the sectoral level, the correlation between gross job creation and destruction is also negative for two of the three developing countries, -0.361 for Chile and -0.148 for Morocco, but 0.044 for Colombia. The first two cases suggest a nonsynchronized process of creation and destruction, while the positive correlation for Colombia is consistent with a process that is more likely to reemploy labor resources quickly following job destruction.[24]

A common belief about developing countries is that their small, highly concentrated domestic markets, frequent use of restrictive commercial policy, and poorly developed credit markets are likely to constrain the dynamic reallocation of resources from old to new products or production techniques or from inefficient to efficient producers. The empirical results presented here do not support a view of a stagnant manufacturing sector in any of the three countries but rather indicate substantial micro-level reallocation of employment among producers with levels of turnover that exceed those found in Canada and the United States.

What remains to be examined in future research is how this turnover translates into benefits, such as the productivity gain from replacing inefficient with efficient producers, or generates costs, such as longer spells of unemployment or geographic relocation. Initial evidence on the productivity gains, presented in chapter 4, suggests that output reallocations among incumbents in Colombia have had little long-run effect on sectoral productivity. Productivity differences among entering, incumbent, and exiting plants do exist, however, so that significant benefits may accrue only after new producers have had sufficient time to grow and become a substantial source of sectoral output. This suggests that, although the costs of producer turnover may be felt in the short run, the benefits may only become evident over longer time horizons.

Notes

1. A related body of literature in industrial organization has focused on the patterns of net entry and gross entry and exit (Dunne, Roberts, and Samuelson 1988; Baldwin and Gorecki 1991; Geroski and Schwalbach 1991).

2. In contrast, however, market share reallocations among incumbent producers in Colombia appear to contribute little to changes in sectoral productivity. Baily, Hulten, and Campbell (1992) report that market share reallocations are an important source of productivity improvement in the U.S. manufacturing sector.

3. Since the micro data sets generally cover all manufacturing plants with ten or more employees in a given year, plant births and deaths will be generated by plants crossing the ten-employee threshold as well as by plants entering or exiting. The data for Colombia include several years in which all plants were surveyed, and we find that, because plants with fewer than ten employees account for so little employment, their exclusion has no effect on the gross flow rates for those years.

4. This measure is used by Dunne and Roberts (1991) in their study of entry and exit in U.S. manufacturing industries. It is equivalent to "excess employment reallocation" in Davis and Haltiwanger (1990, 1992).

5. Davis, Haltiwanger, and Schuh (1994, table 2.2) summarize gross and net flow studies for Canada, France, Germany, Israel, Italy, Sweden, and the United States.

6. For Chile and Morocco, some of this difference may arise because of the large net growth rates during expansionary periods, but for Colombia, the average growth rate during expansions is similar to that in the United States.

7. The $\text{Cov}(\Delta L, T) = \text{Var}(B + \Delta E) - \text{Var}(\Delta C + D)$, so that if job additions due to births and expansions have a larger time-series variance than job losses, the correlation will be positive; if the variance is smaller, the correlation will be negative.

8. Caballero and Hammour (1994a) explain these findings using a model of producers with heterogeneous technologies, increasing marginal entry costs, and cyclical demand movements. The need to smooth entry results in job loss as the important margin on which demand fluctuations, particularly sharp declines in demand, are accommodated. Thus recessions result in a cleansing of outdated production units.

9. These correlations are based on very few time-series observations: fourteen in Colombia, seven in Chile, and five in Morocco, so the conclusions must be carefully qualified. It is most accurate to say that there is no evidence of the countercyclical effect in these data. The next section examines the time-series patterns at the industry level, where a wider range of demand fluctuations are present.

10. The country studies for Chile and Colombia (chapters 9 and 10) summarize the size distribution of manufacturing plants with 10 or more employees. In Chile, approximately 85 percent of these plants have fewer than 50 employees, and only 4 percent have more than 200 employees. The corresponding numbers for Colombia are approximately 70 percent and 7.5 percent. In contrast, the size distribution of manufacturing plants in the United States is characterized by much larger plants. Of the approximately 162,000 U.S. plants with 10 or more workers in 1977, 62 percent had fewer than 50 employees and 9 percent had more than 250 employees. Also although extremely large plants, those with more than 1,000 employees, are rare in Chile and Colombia, in the United States they account for approximately 3.5 percent of plants with more than 10 employees. This gives large manufacturing plants a much more significant role as a source of employment flows in the United States than in Chile or Colombia.

11. Hause and DuRietz (1984) examine this tradeoff using Swedish manufacturing data and find that the share of employment attributable to entering plants is an increasing quadratic function of the industry's growth rate. Thus entrants

are responsible for a larger share of employment in industries with high growth rates.

12. Tybout (chapter 9) summarizes the magnitude of plant exit during the Chilean recession.

13. It is important to recognize that continuing plants are responsible for most employment positions in any year. If the gross flow of positions from plant deaths between years t and $t + 1$ is 6 percent, then 94 percent of the positions in year t are in plants that will survive until $t + 1$. Thus the finding that continuing plant turnover was higher than entry and exit turnover is not surprising.

14. Volatility resulting from entering and exiting plants is defined as $V_t = (B_{t+1} + D_t) - |B_{t+1} - D_t|$. Note that only the absolute value of net employment change from entering and exiting plants is subtracted. Employment volatility resulting from continuing plants is defined analogously using ΔE and ΔC in place of B and D, respectively.

15. The magnitude of the problem is difficult to determine. In chapter 10, I find that plant exit rates decline systematically with increases in plant age and size, as many other empirical studies have found. If the matching errors, which are unlikely to be related to plant size or age, were pervasive, then these size and age patterns would be obscured.

16. As with the overall volatility rates reported in table 2.1, the differences across expansionary and contractionary regimes appear small when compared with the differences across countries or plant types. For this reason, I do not discuss the time-series variation in detail.

17. Although regional reallocation is often discussed as a reason for job flows in the United States, it is unlikely to be of much consequence in the three developing countries over time. In all three countries, manufacturing production is highly concentrated in a small number of major cities, and the geographic distribution of employment changes little over time. Even in the United States, Dunne, Roberts, and Samuelson (1989) find that regional shifts account for very little of the total job flows.

18. Theoretical models have adopted a number of sources of producer heterogeneity including innate abilities (Jovanovic 1982), productivity of new investment (Pakes and Ericson 1990), idiosyncratic productivity shocks (Hopenhayn 1992), knowledge of demand (Jovanovic and Rob 1987), and vintage of capital stock (Lambson 1991).

19. Baldwin, Dunne, and Haltiwanger (1994) also report high rank correlations between an industry's gross job additions and gross job losses. For the United States, the correlation is 0.672, and for Canada, it is 0.831.

20. In a similar exercise, Baldwin, Dunne, and Haltiwanger (1994) compare patterns of industry-level turnover at the two-digit standard industrial code level for the United States and Canada and find that the high- and low-turnover industries are very similar in the two countries. They report that the rank correlation between the U.S. and Canadian industry-level turnover rates is 0.815, suggesting that differences in technology are important in explaining differences in turnover across industries and that the United States and Canada have very similar industrial structures. They also find that, unlike the pattern for the three developing countries, industry-level net employment growth is also highly correlated across the two countries with a rank correlation of 0.778. This suggests, not surprisingly, that sectoral demand shocks are much more highly correlated in Canada and the United States than in Chile, Colombia, and Morocco.

21. The total number of industry-year observations is 876 for Colombia, 483 for Chile, and 312 for Morocco.

22. The correlation between net change and turnover at the industry level is 0.235, 0.416, and 0.629 in Chile, Colombia, and Morocco, respectively.

23. Caballero and Hammour (1994b) also discuss the policy options available to a country with inefficiently low turnover resulting from labor market imperfections. They show that production subsidies alone do not restore the incentive to scrap outdated technologies but that, when combined with creation subsidies, such as tax credits for investment, they can restore efficiency to the reallocation process.

24. Unfortunately, it is also consistent with measurement error in the matching of plants over time.

References

Baily, Martin Neil, Charles Hulten, and David Campbell. 1992. "Productivity Dynamics in Manufacturing Plants." *Brookings Papers on Economic Activity: Microeconomics* 187–267.

Baldwin, John, Timothy Dunne, and John Haltiwanger. 1994. "A Comparison of Job Creation and Destruction between Canada and the United States." Working Paper 94-2. Center for Economic Studies, Bureau of the Census, U.S. Department of Commerce, Washington, D.C.

Baldwin, John, and Paul Gorecki. 1991. "Firm Entry and Exit in the Canadian Manufacturing Sector." *Canadian Journal of Economics* 24: 300–23.

Caballero, Ricardo J., and Mohamad L. Hammour. 1994a. "The Cleansing Effect of Recessions." *American Economic Review* 84: 1350–68.

———. 1994b. "On the Timing and Efficiency of Creative Destruction." Department of Economics, Massachusetts Institute of Technology, Cambridge, Mass.

Davis, Steven, and John Haltiwanger. 1990. "Gross Job Creation and Destruction: Microeconomic Evidence and Macroeconomic Implications." NBER *Macroeconomics Annual* 5: 123–8.

———. 1992. "Gross Job Creation, Gross Job Destruction, and Employment Reallocation." *Quarterly Journal of Economics* 107 (3): 819–63.

Davis, Steven, John Haltiwanger, and Scott Schuh. 1994. "Gross Job Flows in U.S. Manufacturing." Center for Economic Studies, Bureau of the Census, U.S. Department of Commerce, Washington, D.C.

Dixit, Avinash. 1989. "Entry and Exit Decisions under Uncertainty." *Journal of Political Economy* 97: 620–38.

Dunne, Timothy, and Mark J. Roberts. 1991. "Variation in Producer Turnover across United States Manufacturing Industries." In Paul A. Geroski and Joachim Schwalbach, eds., *Entry and Market Contestability.* New York: Basil Blackwell.

Dunne, Timothy, Mark J. Roberts, and Larry Samuelson. 1988. "Patterns of Firm Entry and Exit in U.S. Manufacturing Industries." *Rand Journal of Economics* 19 (4): 495–515.

————. 1989. "Plant Turnover and Gross Employment Flows in the U.S. Manufacturing Sector." *Journal of Labor Economics* 7 (1): 48–71.

Geroski, Paul, and Joachim Schwalbach, eds. 1991. *Entry and Market Contestability.* New York: Basil Blackwell.

Hause, John C., and Gunnar DuRietz. 1984. "Entry, Industry Growth, and the Microdynamics of Industry Supply." *Journal of Political Economy* 92: 733–57.

Hopenhayn, Hugo. 1992. "Entry, Exit, and Firm Dynamics in Long-Run Equilibrium." *Econometrica* 60 (5): 1127–50.

Hopenhayn, Hugo, and Richard Rogerson. 1993. "Job Turnover and Policy Evaluation: A General Equilibrium Analysis." *Journal of Political Economy* 101: 915–38.

Jovanovic, Boyan. 1982. "Selection and the Evolution of Industry." *Econometrica* 50: 649–70.

Jovanovic, Boyan, and Rafael Rob. 1987. "Demand-Driven Innovation and Spatial Competition over Time." *Review of Economic Studies* 54: 63–72.

Lambson, Val Eugene. 1991. "Industry Evolution with Sunk Costs and Uncertain Market Conditions." *International Journal of Industrial Organization* 9: 171–96.

Pakes, Ariel, and Richard Ericson. 1990. "Empirical Implications of Alternative Models of Firm Dynamics." Department of Economics, Yale University, New Haven, Conn.

Tybout, James R. 1992. "Linking Trade and Productivity: New Research Directions." *World Bank Economic Review* 6 (2): 189–211.

3

Heterogeneity and Productivity Growth: Assessing the Evidence

James R. Tybout

O ne of the most obvious features of industrial censuses is the tremendous diversity among plants producing similar goods. Even within narrowly defined industries, the range of output levels, capital-labor ratios, capital stock vintages, and profitability is wide (Berry 1992; Little, Mazumdar, and Page 1987). If the dispersion in these plant characteristics reflects an underlying dispersion in productivity and if entry, exit, or differential growth rates are continually altering market shares, then heterogeneity can be a basis for significant productivity change.

This chapter reviews the evidence on heterogeneity-based productivity growth in semi-industrialized countries and its relation to policy. The first section provides a brief overview of the ways in which productivity has been endogenized in analytical models. The next section contrasts traditional techniques for measuring industrywide productivity with methodologies that isolate the contributions of turnover, changing market shares, and changes in intraplant efficiency to growth in sectoral productivity. The third and fourth sections present evidence on the magnitude of these effects in industrial and semi-industrialized countries, respectively. Finally, the remaining sections relate each effect to the macroeconomic environment and policy.

The Theory of Productivity Growth

The analytical literature on productivity growth provides a diverse set of possible explanations for observed changes in productivity. Prior to discussing empirical findings, it is useful to review some of these theories.

43

In doing so, I distinguish two approaches to productivity analysis. One approach begins from the presumption that all plants in an industry or sector share a single, well-behaved production function. Productivity growth must thus occur through an orderly shift in the production technology common to all plants or through some general improvement in the quality of inputs. This characterization of productivity growth is easily the most common among empirical studies of productivity in developing countries. A second approach emphasizes cross-plant differences in productivity. Changes in market shares, entry and exit, or idiosyncratic improvements in performance at individual plants that are due to learning effects and the diffusion of technology explain growth in aggregate productivity.

The Representative Plant Approach to Productivity Modeling

There are many models of productivity determination in the representative plant tradition. One type links entrepreneurial effort or expenditures on process innovation to the intensity of product market competition (Corden 1974; Hart 1983; Martin and Page 1983; Scharfstein 1988; Rodrik 1991). This approach establishes a link between any policy that affects market structure—especially trade policy—and output per input bundle. Another strand of the literature links productivity and policy through exploitation of scale economies. Any policy that shifts the plant-specific demand schedules in an imperfectly competitive industry affects production levels and scale efficiency (see chapters 5 and 6). Again, trade policy is a favorite demand shifter. A third mechanism is posited by the "big push" models of economic development. These are based on externalities that make piecemeal modernization unprofitable, even when coordinated industrialization is better for everyone. The externalities may be pecuniary, through market size effects (Rosenstein-Rodan 1943; Murphy, Schleifer, and Vishny 1989), or they may take the form of productivity spillovers (Krugman 1991; Matsuyama 1991). To move the economy from a "backward" to a "modern" Nash equilibrium may require government intervention.

Representative plant models in the endogenous growth literature also link productivity and policy with externalities at the sector level. For example, Krugman (1987) and Lucas (1988) use learning-by-doing spillovers to link trade policy and sectoral growth patterns. These externalities ensure that any policy-induced shift in the composition of output will change sectoral learning rates and productivity growth. Grossman and Helpman (1991) and Rivera-Batiz and Romer (1991) obtain endogenous productivity growth by combining learning externalities with an explicit research and development sector. Policies that affect the allocation of resources to this sector or the access of producers to foreign technologies affect steady state growth rates.

Heterogeneity, Diffusion, and Innovation

If technological innovation takes place through a gradual process of efficient plants displacing inefficient ones, or through plant-specific innovation and learning by doing, the representative plant assumption embedded in the literature mentioned above is at best misleading (Nelson 1981). There is no single production function, and it is a mistake to think of productivity growth as an orderly shift in technology. Rather, the processes of learning, innovation, investment, entry, and exit are what matter.

The endogenous growth literature has recently begun to make producer or worker heterogeneity an integral part of the explanation of productivity growth. Some models have assumed a continuum of products, each of which is subject to learning-by-doing effects when it first appears (Young 1991; Lucas 1993). This makes productivity growth product-specific and links aggregate performance to the rate at which the economy shifts toward new goods. Other analysts have posited heterogeneous labor and corresponding heterogeneity in product quality. This leads to representations of productivity growth as a process of dropping low-quality goods and adding high-quality goods, while human capital levels drift upward to accommodate the transformation (Stokey 1991).

These models provide general equilibrium representations of productivity growth and thus are necessarily terse in their representation of production. Partial equilibrium approaches to productivity growth permit analysts to focus more on the micro details of industrial evolution and to recognize uncertainty. Jovanovic (1982) provides one of the key contributions. In his model, heterogeneous producers continually learn about their relative costs through market participation. As these forward-looking firms acquire experience, they become more certain of their "type" and eventually expand or exit. Although product markets are assumed to be perfectly competitive, firms of varying efficiency coexist at any point in time, and there can be simultaneous entry and exit. Young firms are relatively small, heterogeneous, and less cost-efficient on average than older firms. Sunk entry costs and the degree of uncertainty affect exit patterns and efficiency, inter alia, but policy intervention cannot improve social welfare.

In a recent variant on Jovanovic's (1982) model, Hopenhayn (1992) lets productivity shocks at each firm follow an exogenous Markov process and performs comparative statics on stationary equilibria. Most of Jovanovic's results still hold, but Hopenhayn goes beyond them to describe the long-run effects of changes in fixed costs, aggregate demand, and sunk costs, inter alia, on industry characteristics. For example, with sufficiently small fixed costs per period, he shows that simultaneous entry and exit will occur in stationary equilibria. And if technological change is disembodied, increases in fixed costs keep more firms at the low end of the productivity distribution out of the market. Under the same technology assumption, "changes in aggregate demand are neutral on all life cycle properties and on the rate of turnover in the industry, causing only changes in the total number of firms and the market price for the good in the industry" (p. 1143). Finally, an increase in sunk entry costs lowers entry and exit rates, keeps more firms with low productivity in the market, and increases the expected profits and market shares of large firms. So policies that inhibit entry reduce average productivity through selectivity effects, and they can appear to exacerbate market power in a setting where all plants are price takers.

Other partial equilibrium models treat production costs as *endogenously* determined by firms' investments in productivity enhancement.[1] This literature dates back to Griliches (1957) and Mansfield (1961), who model technological diffusion as reflecting firm-level decisions regarding the optimal timing for adopting new technology. At any point in time, the probability that a given firm will modernize depends on the costs of doing so, the productivity enhancement that results, and the proportion of firms that have already modernized. (The third factor matters because of information costs, competitive pressures, and risk considerations.)

This approach to explaining diffusion has been revised and extended in various ways. For example, taking Arrow's (1962) learning-by-doing model as a point of departure, Jovanovic and Lach (1989) model firms' timing decisions as reflecting two considerations: early adopters of new techniques earn high revenue per unit of output, but late adopters free-ride on technical refinements made by early users and enjoy low cost per unit of output. "These advantages are balanced off in a continuous-time, perfect-foresight equilibrium. Competition generates S-shaped diffusion and staggered entry and exit" (p. 690).

Taking a different tack, Pakes and Ericson (1987) and Pakes and McGuire (1994) deemphasize learning externalities but allow imperfect competition. In their representation of industrial evolution, each firm can spend resources to develop profit opportunities (improved goods, better production techniques, or larger stocks of fixed inputs). The outcomes of the investment process are uncertain and combine with the outcomes for competing firms to determine whether it is optimal for each firm to invest, operate with existing capital, or exit (Pakes and McGuire 1994, p. 556). Young firms are more likely to invest in improvements than old firms, so a firm's rate of productivity growth is correlated with its stage in the life cycle. The Pakes-Ericson-McGuire framework is too complex to generate many analytical results, but simulations show that turnover, markups, and welfare can depend critically on market size, entry barriers, and policies such as limits on market share. The main effects of policy tend to be redistributive between producers and consumers (through markups); net social welfare is relatively insensitive to policy changes.

Finally, some recent work has focused on the relation between uncertainty about market conditions and investments in technology. For example, when the incentive structure changes frequently and unpredictably, managers are reluctant to repeatedly incur the sunk costs of retooling (Dixit 1989). So plants created at different times using different technologies may coexist indefinitely. Further, when possibilities for substitution exist, managers may react to uncertainty by choosing labor-intensive technologies, even though more capital-intensive technologies would be less costly under stable market conditions (Lambson 1991). Rapid and efficient adjustments in productive capacity are likely only when governments establish a credible, stable policy regime.

In all of the evolution, diffusion, and learning models surveyed here, competitive product markets are consistent with the existence of heterogeneous technologies at any point in time. Further, the position of the demand curve affects the set of plants in the market and their characteristics, so policies acting on the product market generally affect rates of productivity growth. Finally, any policy that influences entrepreneurial ability to monitor new technological developments or that changes the expected returns from innovation has implications for the rate at which technology is diffused.[2] And of course, government interventions are potentially welfare improving whenever externalities are present.

Representative Plant versus Heterogeneity-Based Productivity Measurement

Clearly there are many potential links between policy and productivity, but it is not obvious which ones are empirically relevant, much less what their net effect will be in a particular context. Accordingly, considerable attention has focused on empirical research.

The Representative Plant Approach

The most common approach to productivity measurement is in the tradition of representative plant analysis and dates back to Solow (1957). It begins by assuming a neoclassical production function at the sectoral or industry level:

$$(3.1) \qquad\qquad Y = f(v, t).$$

Total output (Y) is a concave function of the vector of inputs $(v_{k \times 1})$ and a time index (t) that allows the function to shift with technological innovations or improvements in the efficiency of technologies. The elasticity of output with respect to time, $\varepsilon_{Y,t} = (\partial f / \partial t) / Y$, is referred to as total factor productivity (TFP) growth. Clearly this productivity measure has nothing to say about the role of heterogeneity in productivity growth; indeed, the assumptions that lie behind it are inappropriate if technology varies across plants.

The role of TFP growth is typically isolated empirically by expressing equation 3.1 in terms of growth and rearranging it so that:

$$(3.2) \qquad \varepsilon_{Y,t} = \dot{Y} / Y - \sum_{j=1}^{k} \eta_j \, (\dot{v}_j / v_j)$$

where a dot over a variable denotes its total derivative with respect to time, and $\eta_j = (\partial f / \partial v_j) \, (v_j / Y)$ is the elasticity of output with respect to the jth factor input. Then, after making the critical assumption that each factor is paid the value of its marginal product, output elasticities (η_j) may be replaced with factor shares (s_j) and TFP growth may be estimated using a Divisia index:

$$(3.3) \qquad \hat{\varepsilon}_{Y,t} = \dot{Y} / Y - \sum_{j=1}^{k} s_j \, (\dot{v}_j / v_j)$$

where the carat on $\varepsilon_{Y,t}$ indicates that the term is an estimator, and implementation requires that instantaneous time derivatives be replaced with discrete changes. The shares become averages of current and previous period shares, and the resultant measure of TFP growth is known as a Tornqvist index. More involved applications aggregate diverse types of labor, capital, and intermediates using Tornqvist indexes and analyze changes in the quality of each factor (for example, Jorgenson, Gollop, and Fraumeni 1987). Examples of this approach abound in the development literature; surveys include those of Chenery, Robinson, and Syrquin (1986) and Pack (1988).

Approaches That Recognize Heterogeneity

The representative plant approach to productivity analysis is popular because it can be executed at the sectoral or macro level with easily available data. But it is based on some unrealistic assumptions, including frictionless adjustment in factor stocks, competitive product and factor markets, and identical constant returns technologies at all plants. Violation of any of these conditions can lead to procyclical bias in measured productivity growth and systematic under- or over-statements (see, for example, Nelson 1981; Berndt and Fuss 1986; Hall 1988; Morrison 1989).

Further, the representative plant approach leaves a number of issues unresolved. Even if one discounts the problems above, it is incapable of distinguishing the contributions of productivity improvements common to all plants—due, for example, to economywide externalities or improvements in exploitation of scale economies—from the contributions of heterogeneity effects—due to entry, exit, diffusion, and plant-specific scale effects or learning. Doing so requires examining comprehensive plant-level data. Plant-level data also provide greater flexibility for dealing with measurement problems.

For these reasons, as comprehensive micro data bases have become available, a number of analysts have turned their attention to less restrictive approaches to studying productivity growth. Though the resultant studies differ in their specifics, each begins from plant-specific productivity trajectories for all plants in the industry and decomposes industry-wide productivity growth into the effects of intraplant efficiency changes, market share reallocations among plants with different levels of efficiency, and changes in the population of plants. Obviously this approach reveals more than sectoral analysis does about dimensions of adjustment, but it also is less sensitive to aggregation bias, because each plant is allowed to have its own technology and factor mix. Thus sectorwide productivity figures generated with the micro panel approach do not typically coincide with sectorwide productivity figures based on the representative plant approach described above.

Two approaches have been used to measure productivity at the plant level. One simply amounts to constructing output-to-labor ratios or level-form variants of the Tornqvist index, plant by plant. The other begins by using the micro data to estimate a production function, $Y^* = f(v,t)$. Depending on the application, Y^* may represent either the average or the maximum amount of output attained at the input vector v in period t, and the production function may be estimated either econometrically or as a nonparametric envelope of data points. Given $f(\cdot)$, the efficiency of the ith plant in year t is then imputed as $E_{it} = Y_{it} / f(v_{it}, t_0)$, where Y_{it} is the realized output of the ith plant, v_{it} is its input vector, and the denominator is a benchmark productivity level in period t_0.[3] Analogous exercises can be performed with cost functions.

Once the plant-specific productivity trajectories are calculated, these are used as building blocks to construct industrywide productivity series that can be decomposed into terms describing the effects of entry, exit, and market share reallocations. Defining E_t as a share-weighted average of the individual E_{it} values, Baily, Hulten, and Campbell (1992) report a typical decomposition:

$$(3.4) \qquad \Delta \ln E_t = \Sigma_{i \epsilon c} \, \theta_{it - \tau} \, \Delta \ln E_{it} + \Sigma_{i \epsilon c} \, (\theta_{it} - \theta_{it - \tau}) \ln E_{it}$$

$$+ (\Sigma_{i \epsilon b} \theta_{it} \ln E_{it} - \Sigma_{i \epsilon d} \theta_{it - \tau} \ln E_{it - \tau}).$$

Here $\Delta \ln E_t$ is industrywide productivity growth between periods $t - \tau$ and t, θ_{it} is the market share of the ith plant, and the plant subscript distinguishes continuing plants $(i \in c)$, beginning plants $(i \in c)$, and dying plants $(i \in d)$.[4] The first term on the right-hand side can be thought of as measuring the intraplant productivity growth effects that are the focus of representative plant analysis. The other two terms—share and turnover effects, respectively—pick up the role of heterogeneity and industrial evolution. More precisely, the former describes the effects of market share reallocations among incumbent plants, and the latter describes the net effects of entry and exit.

Once the components of productivity growth have been measured, the analysis can be taken further by correlating them with proxies for economic conditions such as trade protection measures and growth in gross domestic product. Similarly, the individual trajectories can be related to producer characteristics like age, product type, or size. Finally, alternative decompositions can be constructed to reveal the industrywide implications of cohort-specific performance (see chapter 4).

Empirical Evidence on the Role of Heterogeneity in Productivity Growth

What does recent evidence on the link between heterogeneity and productivity show? Independent of the research project reported in this volume, several other researchers have recently measured the effects of turnover and heterogeneity on productivity in the United States (Baily, Hulten, and Campbell 1992; Olley and Pakes 1992), Canada (Baldwin and Gorecki 1991), and Israel (Griliches and Regev 1992).

Baily, Hulten, and Campbell (1992) examine the evolution of industrial productivity over the period 1972–87, using the U.S. Bureau of the Census's Longitudinal Research Database. They implement equation 3.4 using a level-form variant of the Tornqvist index to impute E_{it} values. They find that "entry and exit play only a very small role in industry growth over five-year periods and that the increasing output shares in high-productivity plants are very important to the growth of manufacturing productivity" (p. 189). Increases in their market share account for annualized rates of productivity growth of between 0.4 percent and 1 percent, while plant turnover never accounts for more than 0.2 percent and is often a net drag (table 1, p. 207). Finally, tracking plants through time, they find a strong persistence in productivity rankings: "Being at the top often conveys advantages that allow the leading plants to stay there" (p. 189). The growth in market share of high-productivity plants and the persistence in plant rankings over time are both consistent with the partial equilibrium models of industrial evolution described in the first section of this chapter.

Using the same data base but limiting attention to producers of telecommunications equipment, Olley and Pakes (1992) perform related exercises. Their analysis is econometric rather than descriptive and is based on a variant of the Pakes and Ericson (1987) framework. They estimate each firm's productivity trajectory by fitting a production function in an econometric framework where factor demands depend on productivity. Using an expression such as equation 3.4 to summarize their results, Olley and Pakes find that productivity improved in the telecommunications industry because of "a reallocation of capital from less to more productive plants. Note that since this reallocation process seems to be greatly facilitated by entry and exit, an important part of it would not be picked up from the analysis of balanced panels" (p. 37). So, while they confirm the importance of share effects, their results differ from those of Baily, Hulten, and Campbell (1992) in that entry and exit *are* important. They also differ in that levels of *unweighted* average productivity changed little, implying that intraplant improvements are small on average. That is, turnover and changing market shares among incumbents are the main reason for growth in sectoral productivity.

Also using a variant of equation 3.4, Griliches and Regev (1992) analyze Israeli data spanning the period 1979–88. Limitations of the data base force them to focus on output per person-year as their measure of productivity (E_{it}). Unlike the two U.S. studies, they find that "The bulk of the growth in labor productivity . . . occurs within firms. . . . [In particular,] the sum of the replacement effect (differences in the productivity of entering versus exiting firms) and the weight-shift (the movement of employment from low productivity to higher productivity firms) [account] for only about a tenth of the overall growth in value added productivity" (pp. 8–9). In itself, this suggests that little is to be gained by abandoning the representative plant framework. But entering plants typically (but not always) have higher productivity than exiting plants, although the effect of turnover on aggregate productivity is small. Griliches and Regev also report a "shadow of death" effect: "Firms that are going to die, to exit in the future, are significantly less productive currently" (p. 12). As do the two U.S. studies, Griliches and Regev find substantial persistence in firm-specific productivity levels.

Finally, also using value added per worker, Baldwin and Gorecki (1991) study the relation between turnover and productivity in Canadian manufacturing for 1970–79. On average among industries showing positive productivity growth, turnover is found to account for about 30 percent of the total improvement. Among continuing plants those gaining market share over the decade were more productive than those losing market share. Also, on the basis of medians used to summarize the performance of subgroups, exiting plants were less productive than continuing plants, and entering plants were *more* productive than continuing plants.

Taken together, these four studies generally support the industrial evolution models described in the first section of this chapter, and they confirm that heterogeneity can be important. They also highlight the diversity of possible patterns. Aside from the finding that productivity rankings tend to persist through time, few results appear to be robust across countries. Do the results of the World Bank research project on industrial competition and productivity in semi-industrialized countries—reported in this volume and elsewhere—provide a better basis for generalization?

The least sophisticated attempt to quantify the role of heterogeneity and turnover is reported in Tybout (1992). Tybout, like Baldwin and Gorecki (1991), decomposes growth in sectorwide output per worker ($E = Y / L$) into the effect of productivity change among incumbents ΔE_c, changes in incumbent shares of total output $\Delta \alpha_c$, and the turnover effect caused by differences in productivity between dying and entering plants $(E_b - E_d)$:[5]

$$(3.5) \quad \left(\frac{\Delta E}{E} \right) = \left(\frac{\Delta E_c}{E} \right) \overline{\alpha}_c + \left[\overline{E}_c - \frac{(E_b + E_d)}{2} \right] \left(\frac{\Delta \alpha_c}{E} \right) + (E_b - E_d) \left(\frac{1 - \overline{\alpha}_c}{E} \right)$$

where a bar above a variable indicates an average of last period's and this period's value, and time subscripts have been suppressed. This expression is similar to equation 3.4 in general structure, although productivity growth for incumbents is not decomposed into intraplant and share effects.

Equation 3.5 is applied to data from Chile for 1979–85, Colombia for 1977–87, and Morocco for 1984–87 (see table 3.1). Unlike the findings of Baily, Hulten, and Campbell (1992) for the United States and Griliches and Regev (1992) for Israel, the effects of net entry or exit turn out to be important in both Chile and Morocco. During Chile's severe recession of the early 1980s, net exit increased the market share of incumbents, improving aggregate productivity. For importables and nontradables, net exit was the *main* component of productivity change (results not reproduced here). Net entry did the opposite in Morocco, where macroeconomic expansion was associated with rapid net entry, falling market shares for incumbents, and lower aggregate productivity. Both results reflect two facts: most entry and exit took place among small young plants, and these tended to be less productive on average.

Differences in productivity between entering and exiting plants sometimes account for changes in sectoral aggregates that are significant, but these changes are smaller than those due to productivity gaps between incumbents and others (table 3.1, column 3). As in Griliches and Regev

Table 3.1 Decomposition of Rates of Change in Sectorwide Output per Worker in Chile, Colombia, and Morocco

Country and period	Incumbents $\left(\dfrac{\Delta E_c}{E}\right)\overline{\alpha}_c$	Net entry $\left(\dfrac{\Delta \alpha_c}{E}\right)\left[\overline{E}_c - \dfrac{E_d + E_b}{2}\right]$	Turnover $\left(\dfrac{E_b - E_d}{E}\right)(1 - \overline{\alpha}_c)$
Chile, 1979–85	0.030	0.012	0.002
Colombia, 1977–87	0.040	0.003	0.004
Morocco, 1984–87	−0.021	−0.017	0.001

Source: Tybout 1992, table 4.

(1992), exiting plants tend to be less productive than the entering plants that displace them, but the contribution of this effect is small.

Liu (1993) takes a more detailed look at the role of entry and exit using the Chilean panel data. She uses an econometrically estimated total factor productivity measure developed by Cornwell, Schmidt, and Sickles (1990) to construct plant-specific E_{it} trajectories. Because time-series data on capital stocks could not be constructed for plants that first appeared after 1981, her analysis is limited to comparing plants that had entered by that year. Like Tybout (1992), she finds that (unweighted) mean productivity levels were lower among exiting plants than among plants surviving the 1979–85 period. Moreover, she finds the same "shadow of death" phenomenon that Griliches and Regev (1992) detected in Israel: plants about to exit are typically unproductive. Finally, the productivity of young cohorts systematically rises as they mature, reflecting the combined effect of weak plants dropping out and surviving plants improving.

Liu (1993) makes no attempt to decompose aggregate effects into intraplant and heterogeneity terms. To explore this issue and others, Liu and Tybout (chapter 4) reexamine heterogeneity and productivity change in Chile, adding Colombia to the analysis. Like Liu (1993), they exploit the methodology of Cornwell, Schmidt, and Sickles (1990) to obtain plant-specific productivity trajectories (E_{it}). They depart from Liu (1993) in several respects, however. First, they use *weighted* averages of plant-level productivity trajectories to construct the productivity growth components in equation 3.4 and to examine cohort-specific productivity growth. Second, because the data for Colombia include capital stock figures for all plants, Liu and Tybout are able to compare entering and exiting plants more thoroughly.

Several findings emerge on the role of heterogeneity effects in these countries. For Colombia, most of the long-run growth in technical efficiency can be attributed to intraplant improvements, although the influence of both plant turnover and share reallocations among incumbents is substantial in the short run. Each of the latter generated more than 3 percentage points of productivity growth in some years and industries but averaged close to 0 over the sample period. (It is not possible to look at the effects of turnover on total factor productivity for Chile.) These findings contrast with those for the United States, where share effects are almost always positive, and their cumulative effect is substantial.[6] So despite relatively large costs imposed on the work force in the form of high rates of job turnover in Colombia (chapter 2), the associated payoff in efficiency gains is not correspondingly large. Put differently, entry, exit, and market share reallocations appear to be driven by much more than cross-plant differences in productivity.

Nonetheless, the cumulative impact of turnover on productivity is probably substantial. The "shadow of death" effect implies that exiting plants are in a downward spiral, and they might well get worse if they were to hang around. Further, as new plants mature, their weighted average productivity rises rapidly: one-year-old and two-year-old plants are nearly as unproductive as exiting plants, but plants that survive to be four-year-olds match or exceed industry norms (chapter 4).[7] Both phenomena are consistent with the industrial evolution models surveyed earlier. If this shakedown process were thwarted by institutional barriers to entry, severance pay laws, or attempts to prop up sick firms, the eventual effects on industrywide productivity would probably be much larger than the productivity differential between exiting plants in their last year and entering plants in their first year.

Sources of Heterogeneity

The evidence reviewed so far suggests that market share reallocations and turnover can have significant effects on productivity growth. Also, intraplant efficiency gains are often plant-specific rather than part of an orderly industrywide shift in productivity. But *why* do some plants perform better than others, and how are plants able to change their productivity over time?

The Role of Scale Economies

One possibility is that both phenomena reflect internal economies of scale. Obviously, if incumbent plants face significant returns to scale at the margin, they can improve their productivity by expanding. Further, when market shares are shifted between plants of different sizes, sector-wide productivity changes because of changes in the exploitation of scale economies. Similarly, since incumbents are much larger than entering or exiting plants (see part II of this volume), turnover should create a *counter*cyclical tendency in sectoral productivity growth, because net exit of small plants occurs during downturns, perhaps dominating the direct scale effects of size adjustments among continuing plants. For example, the increase in productivity that accompanied the net exit of plants in Chile might have occurred because exiting plants were smaller than the minimum efficient scale. The same mechanism might have worked in reverse for Morocco, where rapid net entry of small plants took place during the sample years (table 3.1).

Nonetheless, econometric and engineering studies suggest that internal economies of scale are neither the main source of productivity dispersion across plants nor the main source of productivity growth within plants. As discussed in chapter 5, panel-based econometric studies typically find that returns to scale in manufacturing are close to unity, and engineering studies bear them out. Hence most of the variation in productivity across plants remains after scale effects have been netted out.[8] The fact that entering and exiting plants are typically less efficient than continuing ones appears to be a consequence more of their relative newness than of their relative size. Each entering cohort is inexperienced and includes producers destined to learn that their operations are unprofitable. Each exiting cohort includes producers who have just learned.

Other Sources of Differences in Efficiency

If scale economies do not explain the bulk of productivity growth within plants or productivity differences across plants, what does? We know that plant-level productivity is typically procyclical (see chapter 4), so it is likely that capacity utilization is part of the story. Further, there is considerable evidence that successful new firms improve their productivity as they mature—this phenomenon points to learning effects (see chapter 4 and the references in note 7). Plants also tend to maintain their productivity rankings over time, implying that managerial skill or persistent productivity shocks are a large part of the story. Evidence of this phenomenon is reported in Baily, Hulten, and Campbell (1992) and is implicit in all panel-based productivity studies that find significant plant-specific serial correlation in the production or cost function residual.[9]

Finally, externalities may be an important part of the story, but because they are difficult to isolate empirically, we know little about them. Caballero and Lyons (1991) find that productivity in individual manufacturing industries in European countries tends to rise when aggregate economic activity picks up, and Bartelsman, Caballero, and Lyons (1994) obtain similar results using industry-level data from the United States. (The latter authors also find that cross-industry productivity patterns correlate positively with activity levels among upstream suppliers of intermediate goods.) Finally, Krizan (1995) confirms the positive correlation between regional economic activity—measured either with output or employment—and plant-level productivity using panel data from Chile, Mexico, and Morocco.[10] The problem with all of these studies is that industry or plant-specific productivity is procyclical because of adjustment costs, which mean that capacity is underused in recession. Hence these performance measures naturally correlate with aggregate activity levels, even when no true externalities are present.

The Correlates of Productivity Growth Components

The review of micro studies in the previous section showed that aggregate productivity growth amounts to much more than a general increase in output levels per unit of input bundle: entry, exit, share effects, and plant-specific learning can all be important. But to what do these evolutionary processes respond? Is there a role for government intervention? Quantitative studies that directly address these issues are unfortunately scarce. Nonetheless, it is worth reviewing the available evidence on the correlates of heterogeneity-based productivity growth.

Although the components of productivity growth discussed above are jointly dependent processes, each is treated below in a separate subsection. First, the extent of cross-plant dispersion of productivity and its possible determinants are assessed. The larger the dispersion, the greater the potential effects of market share reallocations and turnover on sectoral productivity. Next, the circumstances under which market share reallocations and turnover take place are reviewed. Given that there *is* dispersion in productivity, these processes generate the sectorwide changes in performance that are represented by the second and third terms of equation 3.4. Finally, the correlates of improvements in intra-plant productivity are considered. This type of productivity change affects sectoral performance directly, as indicated by the first term on the right side of equation 3.4.

Productivity Dispersion

Evidence was reviewed earlier suggesting that young plants are systematically less productive than mature plants and that dying plants are often (but not always) less productive than continuing plants. Much more can be inferred about the nature of productivity dispersion by drawing on the "efficiency frontier" literature.[11]

Table 3.2 presents a sampling of cross-sectional studies of manufacturing industries in developing countries. (Studies of industrialized countries are too numerous to survey here.) Most fundamentally, these studies and those in table 3.3 (discussed later) typically find that measured dispersion is very large (specifics are not reported in table 3.2). For example, in Tybout, de Melo, and Corbo (1991), the *majority* of the

Table 3.2 Cross-Plant Correlates of Productivity

Study	Plant-specific productivity measure	Policy proxy and correlation with productivity (+ or −)	Other variables and correlation with productivity (+ or −)	Country, period, and industry
Pitt and Lee 1981	Econometrically estimated productivity residual	None directly examined	Age (−); size (+); foreign ownership (−)	Indonesia, 1972–75: weaving
Page 1984	Cross-sectional deviation from deterministic frontier	None directly examined; indirect inferences can be based on other variables (next column)	Firm size (0); worker experience (+); entrepreneur experience (+ or 0) and literacy (+); age (+); capacity utilization (+); labor turnover (0)	India, 1980: soap, printing, footwear, machine tools
Pack 1984 and 1987	Deviation from deterministic frontier and from minimum cost	None directly examined; indirect inferences based on other variables (next column)	Length of production run (+); task-level efficiency (+)	Philippines and Kenya, 1980: spinning and weaving
Chen and Tang 1987	Econometrically estimated productivity residual	Firm-specific export requirements (+)	Age (+); foreign ownership (0); size (0)	Taiwan (China), 1980: electronics
Suh 1992	Econometrically estimated productivity residual	Effective rate of protection (−)	None	Rep. of Korea, 1981–88: eight industries

(Table continues on the following page.)

Table 3.2 (continued)

Study	Plant-specific productivity measure	Policy proxy and correlation with productivity (+ or −)	Other variables and correlation with productivity (+ or −)	Country, period, and industry
Haddad 1993	Econometrically estimated productivity residual	Export intensity of production (+); sector import penetration (+)	Public ownership (+ or −); foreign ownership (+); age (+); product diversity (+)	Morocco, 1984–89: all two-digit manufacturing industries
Haddad and Harrison 1993	Econometrically estimated productivity residual	Share of fixed direct investment in plant (+) and in sector (0); tariffs (−)	Firm size (+); Herfindahl index (+)	Morocco, 1984–89: all manufacturing sectors
Aitken and Harrison 1994	Econometrically estimated productivity residual	Share of fixed direct investment in plant (+), in sector (−), and in region (mixed)	None	Venezuela, 1983–88: all manufacturing sectors
Aw and Hwang 1995	Cross-subsample comparison of econometrically estimated production function parameters	Whether firm is export oriented (+)	None	Taiwan (China), 1986: electronics

58

cross-plant variation in logarithmic output is not explained by factor stocks. Some of the unexplained variation reflects measurement problems, especially due to heterogeneous factor stocks. But even when labor is measured in efficiency units (that is, in terms of its market value), tremendous heterogeneity remains. One implication is that the *potential* for productivity gains through entry, exit, and market share reallocation is quite substantial. Nonetheless, as theory suggests (Hopenhayn 1992), sunk costs, factor market frictions, and uncertainty combine to limit the realization of these gains.

On the correlates of productivity, it is common to find that export-oriented firms and firms owned by multinational corporations are closer to the efficient frontier than other plants (see, however, Pitt and Lee 1981). There is also some evidence that productivity dispersion is greater in protected industries. Given the diversity of theoretical possibilities, it is remarkable that these patterns of association are as stable as they are. In the present context, they could be interpreted to mean that the scope for efficiency gains through share reallocations is greatest in protected industries and in industries where a subset of plants are exporters or foreign-owned. Alternatively, one might infer that the potential for *intra*-plant improvements is greatest under these conditions, a hypothesis I will return to later.

Caution is warranted, however. Both interpretations presume a causal relationship running from policy to performance, but firms are not randomly assigned the role of exporter or multinational. Generally, they self-select, and their productivity has a bearing on their decision: high-productivity firms may be better able to break into foreign markets, for example. Also, exporting industries tend to be more labor-intensive and involve relatively low entry costs. One should expect to find little productivity dispersion under these conditions (Hopenhayn 1992). So there is no guarantee that policies to encourage exports or foreign direct investment would reduce the market share of low-productivity firms or move them toward the efficient frontier.

Entry and Exit

Given that incumbents are different from new and dying plants, turnover generally affects sectoral productivity growth. But what affects turnover? In addition to technological factors, turnover appears to vary with the business cycle. Net entry increases with economywide expansion and with the lagged profitability of incumbents (see, for example, Geroski and Schwalbach 1991). Hence, the market share of incumbents shrinks during expansionary periods, as new firms crowd into the market more rapidly than others fail. This often exerts a countercyclical influence on productivity, because new and dying firms are typically less productive than continuing producers. Such countercyclical effects are noted in connection with Tybout's (1992) decomposition of sectorwide productivity per worker in Chile, Colombia, and Morocco (table 3.1); Olley and Pakes (1992) report a similar result for telecommunications, and Baily, Hulten, and Campbell (1992, p. 209) cite this phenomenon in U.S. manufacturing data. Also consistent with this pattern, Liu and Tybout (chapter 4) find that the market share of incumbents is typically somewhat higher in Chile—which underwent a massive recession during the sample period—than in Colombia (table 4.1 versus table 4.2). Nonetheless, in these countries, dying plants are occasionally *more* productive than incumbents, so the direction of the net entry effect is not guaranteed.

Some researchers have empirically distinguished macro conditions from industry-specific factors as determinants of entry and exit. In this regard, the chapters in part II of this volume generally find that macroeconomic shocks correlate through time with net entry or exit, while persistent industry characteristics explain *average* turnover rates. (Chapter 8 provides a more detailed summary.) In the long run, therefore, the rate at which efficient firms replace inefficient ones may be largely dictated by entry costs, fixed costs, and the stochastic processes that govern firm-specific productivity growth (see the earlier discussion of Hopenhayn 1992). For example, the high entry costs associated with steel production probably hold down turnover and reduce average efficiency in that sector relatively more than in low-cost industries like apparel or food processing.

The link between trade-related variables and turnover is not well established, although several descriptive regressions were run for the countries in part II of this volume (chapter 8 provides more details). For Morocco, entry is found to be more likely into export-oriented sectors than into other sectors, perhaps reflecting export promotion schemes during the sample years (chapter 12). However, in neither Chile (chapter 9) nor Colombia (chapter 10) is trade orientation significantly associated with entry-exit patterns. These findings are consistent with Hopenhayn's (1992) result that in the long run, industrywide demand shifts "are neutral on all life cycle properties and on the rate of turnover" (p. 1143).[12]

Of course, decisions about entry and exit are heavily dependent on expectations about future market conditions, and static regression models are inadequate to describe transition dynamics. Hence the country studies mentioned above have only begun to document the relation between turnover and policy. The only empirical attempts I know of to link policy directly with turnover in a forward-looking optimizing framework have been simulations (Hopenhayn and Rogerson 1993; Pakes and McGuire 1994).

Share Reallocation Effects

Even without entry and exit, share reallocations among incumbent producers can influence productivity growth. Several studies quantify this effect and relate it to the economic environment. They find that share effects are *not* systematically related to the business cycle in Colombia (Liu and Tybout in chapter 4), Mexico (Tybout and Westbrook 1995), or the United States (Baily, Hulten, and Campbell 1992). Nevertheless, market orientation can matter: tradable goods sectors showed significantly higher share-based productivity gains during Mexico's recent trade liberalization (Tybout and Westbrook 1995). Regulatory policy can matter too: Olley and Pakes (1992) report that deregulation of the U.S. telecommunications industry is associated with a significant reallocation of capital toward more productive establishments, an effect that more than offsets a slight decline in *intra*plant productivity and leads to industrywide improvements in productivity.

Finally, if scale economies matter, reallocations of market shares between small and large plants will influence sectoral productivity. Analytical frameworks that link such scale effects back to policy include Dutz (chapter 6 of this volume) and Roberts and Tybout (1991). Empirically, Tybout, de Melo, and Corbo (1991) find that reductions in the effective rate of protection are associated with larger market shares for smaller plants in Chile, although percentiles along the entire distribution of plant sizes appear to correlate negatively with protection. (The results for employment shares are somewhat different.) In contrast, Dutz (chapter 6) finds that import penetration is associated with relatively large reductions in output among small plants, and Roberts and Tybout (1991) find various measures of openness to be negatively associated with plant size, most significantly at the low end of the size distribution. These findings suggest that trade liberalization *reduces* exploitation of scale economies among import-competing producers. However, if small firms have relatively high marginal costs, the findings also imply desirable market share reallocation effects.

Intraplant Productivity Growth through Scale Effects

What are the correlates of *intra*plant productivity growth? I have already argued that internal scale effects are probably not a dominant source of efficiency gain because big plants, which dominate the behavior of sector aggregates, are typically scale efficient (see also chapter 5). Nonetheless, general differences in the average size of plants may account for some of the differences in productivity across countries or time, so I will begin by quickly reviewing what is known about the determinants of average plant size.

There is little doubt that bigger economies tend to have bigger plants (Banerji 1978, for example). Beyond that, it is hard to generalize about the determinants of plant size distributions. Several approaches to the issue may be distinguished. First, and least rigorously, a number of descriptive studies base their inferences on simple cross-country comparisons. These seem predisposed to find that open trade policies allow the exploitation of scale economies (Caves 1984; Conlon 1980).[13] A second group of studies relates various measures of scale efficiency to measures of foreign competition, controlling for a variety of factors (Caves, Porter, and Spence 1980; Saunders 1980; Caves 1984; Schwalbach 1988). Typically, the efficiency measure is regressed on export ratios, import penetration rates, measures of minimum efficient scale, and other control variables.[14] Most of these studies also conclude that foreign competition improves scale efficiency, although their usefulness is limited by methodological problems.[15] Finally, a third group of studies uses ad hoc regression models to look for correlations between trade policy proxies and plant size.[16] In contrast to the work cited above, these studies typically find that import penetration is associated with *smaller* plants, so the positive effects of openness on demand elasticities emphasized in the trade literature may be dominated by other factors, such as leftward shifts in the demand schedules with the removal of trade barriers (refer back to the first section). Findings on the correlation between export rates or effective protection rates and plant sizes are mixed.

In short, we know that big domestic markets tend to breed big plants, import penetration is associated with relatively small plants, and exporting plants tend to be bigger than others within an industry. Combined with the fact that most output is produced at plants with nearly constant returns to scale, these findings provide little support for the popular notion that trade liberalization generates significant gains in scale efficiency (chapter 5 and Tybout 1993 provide details).

Other Intraplant Effects

To assess the correlates of changes in intraplant productivity that are not related to scale economies, time-varying productivity measures are needed. A sampling of studies from the development literature that do this is presented in table 3.3. These studies, like those in table 3.2, measure plant-specific productivity (E_{it}) using one of the methods mentioned earlier in this chapter. However, instead of simply focusing on cross-plant variation, they correlate changes in performance with policy changes and plant characteristics.

Very briefly, as detailed in the third column, there is some evidence that reductions in protection are associated with improvements in productivity (Tybout, de Melo, and Corbo 1991; Suh 1992; Harrison 1994), but some studies find no effect (Tybout and Westbrook 1995). Similarly, the evidence is mixed on the relation between foreign ownership and productivity growth (chapter 7 of this volume).

Table 3.3 *Correlates of Intraplant Changes in Productivity*

Study	Productivity measure	Policy proxy and temporal correlation with productivity (+ or –)	Other variables and temporal correlation with productivity (+ or –)	Country, period, and industry
Nishimizu and Page 1982	Change in deviation from deterministic frontier and change in frontier	Priority in economic plans (+), quantitative import restrictions (–)	Comparative advantage (+)	Yugoslavia, 1965–78: all manufacturing sectors
Handoussa, Nishimizu, and Page 1986	Deterministic frontier and associated average efficiency levels	Degree of access to imported intermediate goods (+)	Output growth	Egypt, 1973–79: public sector manufacturing firms
Tybout, de Melo, and Corbo 1991	Intercept of econometrically estimated production function and its residual variation	Change in effective rate of protection (–)	None	Chile, 1967 vs. 1979: all three-digit manufacturing industries
Suh 1992	Time-varying efficiency residuals, econometrically estimated	Effective rate of protection (–, both cross-sectional and through time)	None	Rep. of Korea, 1981–88: food, textiles, industrial chemicals, pharmaceuticals, cement, iron/steel, electrical machinery

(Table continues on the following page.)

Table 3.3 (continued)

Study	Productivity measure	Policy proxy and temporal correlation with productivity (+ or −)	Other variables and temporal correlation with productivity (+ or −)	Country, period, and industry
Haddad and Harrison 1993	Time-varying efficiency residuals, econometrically estimated	Share of foreign ownership in firm (0) and sector (0)	Protection measures interacted with foreign direct investment (0)	Morocco, 1984–89
Aitken and Harrison 1994	Time-varying efficiency residuals, econometrically estimated	Share of foreign ownership at the sector level (−)	Region-specific fixed direct investment (0); skilled wages (0); electricity prices (0)	Venezuela, 1983–88
Tybout and Westbrook 1995	Time-varying efficiency residuals, econometrically estimated	Openness proxies (+), changes in openness proxies (0)	None	Mexico, 1984–90: all manufacturing industries
Chapter 7 of this volume; Harrison 1994	Tornqvist indexes, econometrically adjusted using Hall methodology	Dummy for trade reform years (+, foreign firms only); import penetration rates (0);	None	Côte d'Ivoire, 1979–87 : pooled manufacturing sector

One might conclude, at worst, that trade liberalization and foreign ownership do not hurt intraplant productivity, and at best they help, but many problems complicate this inference. To cite one example, trade reforms are typically accompanied by changes in the exchange rate, which affect the measured productivity of firms in direct proportion to their reliance on imported inputs. Exporters often import a relatively large share of their inputs and so enjoy relatively large reductions in input costs when protection for intermediate goods is reduced. This effect looks like reduced input use to the econometrician, who constructs "intermediate input use" as the cost of materials deflated by a general price index.[17] Changes in the rate of inflation also typically accompany changes in trade policy, so the inflation bias in capital stock measures and inventories will lead to spurious correlation between measured productivity and policy (see Tybout 1988). Definitive findings are probably impossible except where extensive plant interviews accompany the econometric analysis.

Conclusions

Productivity growth can be viewed as taking place through several channels: general improvements in productivity that are common to all producers, idiosyncratic improvements attributable to learning and technological diffusion within individual plants, and changes in the set of plants or their market shares. Because "representative plant" approaches to productivity analysis deal only with the first channel, a number of less restrictive approaches to theory and measurement have been deployed recently as plant-level panel data have become widely available. This chapter has taken stock of the evidence these approaches have generated, with special emphasis on studies of semi-industrialized countries undertaken for a recent World Bank project.[18]

Although productivity improvements within individual plants are typically the largest component of aggregate productivity growth, heterogeneity, share reallocations, and turnover are often also important. In some contexts, the shifting of market shares among incumbent producers is dominant; in others, it is the net entry or exit of plants that differ from incumbents. One clear pattern is that recessions tend to improve average productivity, since the least efficient producers exit when demand contracts. Similarly, recovery dampens productivity growth, because inefficient producers tend to remain in the market, and many new, inexperienced producers enter.

Compared with the United States, the relatively high average rates of job turnover in the semi-industrialized countries (documented in chapter 2) have *not* paid off in terms of relatively large average efficiency gains through plant turnover and market share reallocations. Nonetheless, it would be a mistake to assume that the cumulative effect of entry and exit on productivity in the semi-industrialized countries is small. As each new cohort of plants matures, inefficient plants are weeded out, and the survivors learn to be more efficient. After four years, the surviving new plants have achieved average levels of productivity that match industry norms. Further, plants that exit have exhibited a downward trend in productivity during the years prior to their departure. So if governments were to inhibit entry and exit, the efficiency loss over time would amount to much more than the impact of such policies in their first year.

In addition to age effects, cross-plant differences in productivity are correlated with exposure to foreign competition and the presence of direct foreign investment, although causal relationships are difficult to establish. Scale effects related to plant size do not appear to be the main reason that some plants do better than others.

Much of the cross-industry variation in turnover is persistent, suggesting that technology largely determines whether a sector exhibits strong productivity effects from turnover. In the long run, therefore, the rate at which efficient firms replace inefficient ones may be largely dictated by entry costs, fixed costs, and the stochastic processes that govern firm-specific productivity growth. Yet policy can matter too. For example, Olley and Pakes (1992) find that deregulation was associated with net entry in the U.S. telecommunications industry and that shifting market shares after deregulation improved productivity. Also, relatively high entry rates in exporting industries were associated with export promotion programs in Morocco.

These findings are intriguing, but we are far from an integrated framework that links policy with all the dimensions of industrial evolution. Given the central role of productivity gains in economic growth and development, the returns to research efforts in this domain are potentially high.

Notes

1. In developing countries, investments in productivity enhancement usually involve adapting an existing technology to local conditions. For an authoritative survey of what is known about these investments, see Evanson and Westphal 1995.

2. Evanson and Westphal (1995) survey the literature linking policy and diffusion in developing countries.

3. In cases where the production technology is econometrically estimated, the ratio E_{it} is typically represented as a "noisy" productivity measure. For broad surveys of this type of analysis, see Greene 1993 and Schmidt 1985.

4. $e_{Y,t}$ corresponds to $\Delta \ln E_t$ only when the entire sector shares a single, homothetic constant-returns technology.

5. Ideally, entry and exit would reflect the births and deaths of plants, respectively, but in practice they also reflect firms that cross the ten-worker threshold.

6. Similar findings on share effects emerge from a related study on Mexican manufacturing (Tybout and Westbrook 1995). That study is not surveyed here, because the data do not permit entry-exit analysis.

7. The existence of significant age effects is also well established for industrial countries. Pack (1991) surveys the literature on learning for developing countries; Malerba (1992) does likewise for industrial countries and reports some new evidence.

8. For example, scale effects prove to be a small part of measured productivity change in panel analysis of Mexico (Tybout and Westbrook 1995).

9. Studies for developing countries include Suh 1992, Haddad 1993, Haddad and Harrison 1993, Tybout and Westbrook 1995, and chapter 4 of this volume.

10. These data bases are documented in the appendixes to chapters 9, 11, and 12.

11. In this literature, plant-specific productivity levels, E_{it}, are obtained as deviations from the industry production function. The second subsection of this chapter provides further details.

12. This result is obtained for stationary equilibria under the assumption that exogenous firm-specific productivity shocks are disembodied.

13. Caves (1984, p. 316) reports data on manufacturing employment by size category for Australia, Canada, the United Kingdom, and the United States, concluding that, "The most interesting comparison is between Australia and Canada, nations of similar size. Canada has 70.3 percent of its manufacturing employment in plants employing 100 or more, whereas Australia has only 61.9; comparable figures for the United Kingdom and the United States are 79.8 and 74.6. . . . Conlon's (1980) investigation of matched Australian and Canadian industries confirms this difference." The pattern is attributed to Australia's commercial policy and the natural protection created by transportation costs.

14. Sometimes the link from productivity to scale is even more tenuous. For example, Pratten (1988) simply compares worker productivity across countries and finds that productivity is highest in the United States, then rather remarkably leaps to the conclusion that the higher productivity is a consequence of higher scale efficiency in the relatively large U.S. markets.

15. Most fundamentally, the usual simultaneity issues arise: the motivation for cross-industry regressions must be that the observations describe some kind of long-run equilibrium. But in the long run, all industry characteristics are endogenous, and no valid instruments are available to help to isolate structural relationships (Schmalensee 1989). Second, except in Caves, Porter, and Spence 1980, spurious positive correlation is probably present since domestic value added per worker is converted to world prices using the domestic rate of effective protection. Finally, labor productivity is not monotonically related to scale efficiency.

16. Cross-sectional studies include Scherer and others 1975, Owen 1983, Caves 1984, Muller and Owen 1985, Baldwin and Gorecki 1986, table 7.1, Schwalbach 1988, and Roberts and Tybout 1991. Temporal studies include Tybout, de Melo, and Corbo 1991 and Dutz, chapter 6 of this volume.

17. Most of these studies use a single intermediate goods price deflator for all producers in a given industry. Suh 1992 is an exception.

18. The project was "Industrial Competition, Productive Efficiency, and Their Relation to Trade Regimes," RPO 674-46.

References

Aitken, Brian, and Ann Harrison. 1994. "Do Domestic Firms Benefit from Foreign Direct Investment: Evidence from Panel Data." Policy Research Working Paper 1248. Policy Research Department, World Bank, Washington, D.C.

Arrow, Kenneth. 1962. "The Economic Implications of Learning by Doing." *Review of Economic Studies* 29: 155–73.

Aw, Bee-Yan, and Amy Hwang. 1995. "Productivity and the Export Market: A Firm-Level Analysis." *Journal of Development Economics* 47: 277–89.

Baily, Martin Neil, Charles Hulten, and David Campbell. 1992. "Productivity Dynamics in Manufacturing Plants." *Brookings Papers on Economic Activity: Microeconomics* 187–267.

Baldwin, John, and Paul Gorecki. 1986. *The Role of Scale in Canada–U.S. Productivity Differences in the Manufacturing Sector: 1970–1979.* Toronto: University of Toronto Press.

———. 1991. "Firm Entry and Exit in the Canadian Manufacturing Sector, 1970–1982." *Canadian Journal of Economics* 24: 300–23.

Banerji, Randev. 1978. "Average Size of Plants in Manufacturing and Capital Intensity: A Cross-Country Analysis by Industry." *Journal of Development Economics* 5: 155–66.

Bartelsman, Eric, Ricardo Caballero, and Richard Lyons. 1994. "Customer and Supplier-Driven Externalities." *American Economic Review* 84: 1075–84.

Berndt, Ernst, and Melvyn Fuss. 1986. "Productivity Measurement with Adjustments for Variations in Capacity Utilization and Other Forms of Temporary Equilibrium." *Journal of Econometrics* 33: 7–29.

Berry, Albert. 1992. "Firm or Plant Size in the Analysis of Trade and Development." In Gerald K. Helleiner, ed., *Trade Policy, Industrialization, and Development: New Perspectives.* Oxford: Clarendon Press.

Caballero, Ricardo, and Richard Lyons. 1991. "Internal Versus External Economies in European Industry." *European Economic Review* 34: 805–26.

Caves, Richard. 1984. "Scale, Openness, and Productivity in Manufacturing." In Richard E. Caves and Lawrence B. Krause, eds., *The Australian Economy: A View from the North.* Washington D.C.: Brookings Institution.

Caves, Richard, Richard Porter, and Michael Spence. 1980. *Competition in the Open Economy: A Model Applied to Canada.* Cambridge, Mass.: Harvard University Press.

Chen, Tain-jy, and De-piao Tang. 1987. "Comparing Technical Efficiency between Import-Substituting and Export-Oriented Foreign Firms in a Developing Country." *Journal of Development Economics* 26: 277–89.

Chenery, Hollis, Sherman Robinson, and Moshe Syrquin. 1986. *Industrialization and Growth: A Comparative Study.* New York: Oxford University Press.

Conlon, R. M. 1980. "International Transport Costs and Tariffs: Their Influence on Australian and Canadian Manufacturing." University of New South Wales, Kensington, Australia.

Corden, W. Max. 1974. *Trade Policy and Economic Welfare.* Oxford: Clarendon Press.

Cornwell, C. R., Peter Schmidt, and Robin Sickles. 1990. "Production Frontiers with Cross-Sectional and Time-Series Variation in Efficiency Levels." *Journal of Econometrics* 46: 185–200.

Dixit, Avinash. 1989. "Entry and Exit Decisions under Uncertainty." *Journal of Political Economy* 97: 620–38.

Evanson, Robert, and Larry Westphal. 1995. "Technological Change and Technology Strategy." In T. N. Srinivasan and Jere Behrman, eds., *Handbook of Development Economics,* vol. 3. Amsterdam: North-Holland.

Geroski, Paul, and Joachim Schwalbach. 1991. *Entry and Market Contestability: An International Comparison.* Oxford: Basil Blackwell.

Greene, William. 1993. "Efficiency Frontiers." Discussion Paper EC 93-20. Stern School of Business, New York University, New York.

Griliches, Zvi. 1957. "Hybrid Corn: An Exploration in the Economics of Technological Change." *Econometrica* 25: 501–522.

Griliches, Zvi, and Haim Regev. 1992. "Productivity and Firm Turnover in Israeli Industry." NBER Working Paper 4059. National Bureau of Economic Research, Cambridge, Mass.

Grossman, Gene, and Elhanan Helpman. 1991. *Innovation and Growth in the Global Economy.* Cambridge, Mass.: MIT Press.

Haddad, Mona. 1993. "How Trade Liberalization Affected Productivity in Morocco." Policy Research Working Paper 1096. Policy Research Department, World Bank, Washington, D.C.

Haddad, Mona, and Ann Harrison. 1993. "Are There Positive Spillovers from Direct Foreign Investment? Evidence from Panel Data for Morocco." *Journal of Development Economics* 42: 51–74.

Hall, Robert E. 1988. "The Relation between Price and Marginal Cost in U.S. Industry." *Journal of Political Economy* 96 (5): 921–47.

Handoussa, Heba, Mieko Nishimizu, and John Page. 1986. "Productivity Change in Egyptian Public Sector Industries after the 'Opening.' " *Journal of Development Economics* 20: 53–74.

Harrison, Ann. 1994. "Productivity, Imperfect Competition, and Trade Reform: Theory and Evidence." *Journal of International Economics* 36: 53–73.

Hart, Oliver. 1983. "The Market Mechanism as an Incentive Structure." *Bell Journal of Economics* 14 (autumn): 366–82.

Hopenhayn, Hugo. 1992. "Entry, Exit, and Firm Dynamics in Long-Run Equilibrium." *Econometrica* 60: 1127–50.

Hopenhayn, Hugo, and Richard Rogerson. 1993. "Job Turnover and Policy Evaluation: A General Equilibrium Analysis." *Journal of Political Economy* 101: 915–38.

Jorgenson, Dale, Frank Gollop, and Barbara Fraumeni. 1987. *Productivity and U.S. Economic Growth.* Cambridge, Mass.: Harvard University Press.

Jovanovic, Boyan. 1982. "Selection and the Evolution of Industry." *Econometrica* 50: 649–70.

Jovanovic, Boyan, and Saul Lach. 1989. "Entry, Exit, and Diffusion with Learning by Doing." *American Economic Review* 79: 690–99.

Krizan, C. J. 1995. "External Economies of Scale in Chile, Mexico, and Morocco: Evidence from Plant-Level Panel Data." Georgetown University, Washington, D.C.

Krugman, Paul. 1987. "The Narrow Moving Bank, the Dutch Disease, and the Competitive Consequences of Mrs. Thatcher: Notes on Trade in the Presence of Dynamic Scale Economies." *Journal of Development Economics* 27: 41–55.

———. 1991. "History versus Expectations." *Quarterly Journal of Economics* 106: 651–67.

———. 1992. *Geography and Trade.* Cambridge, Mass.: MIT Press.

Lambson, Val. 1991. "Industry Evolution with Sunk Costs and Uncertain Market Conditions." *International Journal of Industrial Organization* 9: 171–96.

Little, Ian M. D., Dipak Mazumdar, and John M. Page, Jr. 1987. *Small Manufacturing Enterprises: A Comparative Analysis of India and Other Economies.* New York: Oxford University Press for the World Bank.

Liu, Lili. 1993. "Entry-Exit, Learning, and Productivity Change: Evidence from Chile." *Journal of Development Economics* 42: 217–42.

Lucas, Robert. 1988. "On the Mechanics of Economic Development." *Journal of Monetary Economics* 22: 3–42.

———. 1993. "Making a Miracle." *Econometrica* 61: 251–72.

Malerba, Franco. 1992. "Learning by Doing and Incremental Technical Change." *Economic Journal* 102: 845–59.

Mansfield, Edwin. 1961. "Technical Change and the Rate of Diffusion." *Econometrica* 29: 741–66.

Martin, John P., and John M. Page, Jr. 1983. "The Impact of Subsidies on X-Efficiency in LDC Industry: Theory and an Empirical Test." *Review of Economics and Statistics* 65: 608–17.

Matsuyama, Kiminori. 1991. "Increasing Returns, Industrialization, and Indeterminacy of Equilibrium." *Quarterly Journal of Economics* 106: 617–50.

Morrison, Catherine. 1989. "Unraveling the Productivity Growth Slowdown in the U.S., Canada, and Japan: The Effects of Subequilibrium, Scale Economies, and Markups." NBER Working Paper 2993. National Bureau of Economic Research, Cambridge, Mass.

Muller, Jurgen, and Nicholas Owen. 1985. "The Effect of Trade on Plant Size." In Joachim Schwalbach, ed., *Industry Structure and Performance.* Berlin: Edition Sigma.

Murphy, Kevin M., Andrei Schleifer, and Robert W. Vishny. 1989. "Industrialization and the Big Push." *Journal of Political Economy* 97: 1003–126.

Nelson, Richard. 1981. "Research on Productivity Growth and Productivity Differences: Dead Ends and New Departures." *Journal of Economic Literature* 19 (September): 1029–64.

Nishimizu, Mieko, and John Page. 1982. "Total Factor Productivity Growth, Technological Progress, and Technical Efficiency Change: Dimensions of Productivity Change in Yugoslavia." *Economic Journal* 92: 920–36.

Olley, G. Steven, and Ariel Pakes. 1992. "The Dynamics of Productivity in the Telecommunications Equipment Industry." NBER Working Paper 3977. National Bureau of Economic Research, Cambridge, Mass.

Owen, Nicholas. 1983. *Economies of Scale, Competitiveness, and Trade Patterns within the European Community.* Oxford: Clarendon Press.

Pack, Howard. 1984. "Productivity and Technical Choice: Applications to the Textile Industry." *Journal of Development Economics* 16: 153–76.

———. 1987. *Productivity, Technology, and Industrial Development.* New York: Oxford University Press.

———. 1988. "Industrialization and Trade." In Hollis Chenery and T. N. Srinivasan, eds., *Handbook of Development Economics,* vol. 1. Amsterdam: North-Holland.

———. 1991. "Learning and Productivity Change in Developing Countries." In Gerald K. Helleiner, ed., *Trade Policy, Industrialization, and Development: New Perspectives.* Oxford: Clarendon Press.

Page, John. 1984. "Firm Size and Technical Efficiency: Application of Production Frontiers to Indian Survey Data." *Oxford Economic Papers* 32: 19–39.

Pakes, Ariel, and Richard Ericson. 1987. "Empirical Implications of Alternative Models of Firm Dynamics." SSRI Working Paper 8803. Social Science Research Institute, University of Wisconsin, Madison.

Pakes, Ariel, and Paul McGuire. 1994. "Computing Markov-Perfect Nash Equilibria: Numerical Implications of a Dynamic Product-Differentiated Model." *Rand Journal of Economics* 25: 555–89.

Pitt, Mark, and Lee-Fung Lee. 1981. "The Measurement and Sources of Technical Inefficiency in the Indonesian Weaving Industry." *Journal of Development Economics* 9: 43–64.

Pratten, Cliff. 1988. "A Survey of the Economies of Scale." In Commission of the European Communities, *Research on the "Cost" of Non-Europe.* Vol. 2: *Basic Findings.* Brussels: Commission of the European Communities.

Rivera-Batiz, Luis A., and Paul Romer. 1991. "International Trade with Endogenous Technological Change." *European Economic Review* 35: 971–1001.

Roberts, Mark, and James R. Tybout. 1991. "Size Rationalization and Trade Exposure in Developing Countries." In Robert E. Baldwin, ed., *Empirical Studies of Commercial Policy.* Chicago: University of Chicago Press for the National Bureau of Economic Research.

Rodrik, Dani. 1991. "Closing the Technology Gap: Does Trade Liberalization Really Help?" In G. Helleiner, ed., *Trade Policy, Industrialization, and Development: New Perspectives.* Oxford: Clarendon Press.

Rosenstein-Rodan, Paul N. 1943. "Problems of Industrialization of Eastern and South-Eastern Europe." *Economic Journal* 53: 202–11.

Saunders, Ronald. 1980. "The Determinants of Productivity in Canadian Manufacturing Industries." *Journal of Industrial Economics* 29: 167–84.

Scharfstein, David. 1988. "Product-Market Competition and Managerial Slack." *Rand Journal of Economics* 19 (spring): 147–55.

Scherer, F. M., and others. 1975. *The Economies of Multi-Plant Operation: An International Comparison Study.* Cambridge, Mass.: Harvard University Press.

Schmalensee, Richard. 1989. "Inter-Industry Studies of Structure and Performance." In Richard Schmalensee and Robert Willig, eds., *Handbook of Industrial Organization.* Amsterdam: North-Holland.

Schmidt, Peter. 1985. "Frontier Production Functions." *Econometric Reviews* 4: 289–328.

Schwalbach, Joachim. 1988. "Economies of Scale and Intra-Community Trade." In Commission of the European Communities, *Research on the "Cost" of Non-Europe.* Vol. 2: *Basic Findings.* Brussels: Commission of the European Communities.

Solow, Robert. 1957. "Technical Change and the Aggregate Production Function." *Review of Economics and Statistics* 29: 312–20.

Stokey, Nancy. 1991. "Human Capital, Product Quality, and Growth." *Quarterly Journal of Economics* 56: 587–616.

Suh, Dongsuk. 1992. "Trade Liberalization and Productive Efficiency in Korean Manufacturing: Evidence from Panel Data," Ph.D. diss., Georgetown University, Washington, D.C.

Tybout, James R. 1988. "The Algebra of Inflation Accounting." *International Economic Journal* 2: 83–100.

———. 1992. "Linking Trade and Productivity: New Research Directions." *World Bank Economic Review* 6 (2): 189–211.

———. 1993. "Internal Returns to Scale as a Source of Comparative Advantage: The Evidence." *American Economic Review: Papers and Proceedings* 83 (May): 440–43.

Tybout, James R., Jaime de Melo, and Vittorio Corbo. 1991. "The Effect of Trade Reforms on Scale and Technical Efficiency: New Evidence from Chile." *Journal of International Economics* 31: 231–50.

Tybout, James R., and M. Daniel Westbrook. 1995. "Trade Liberalization and the Dimensions of Efficiency Change in Mexican Manufacturing Industries." *Journal of International Economics* 39 (August): 53–78.

Young, Alwyn. 1991. "Learning by Doing and the Dynamic Effects of International Trade." *Quarterly Journal of Economics* 56: 369–405.

4

Productivity Growth in Chile and Colombia: The Role of Entry, Exit, and Learning

Lili Liu and James R. Tybout

As noted in chapter 3, manufacturing plants span a wide range of sizes and technologies. The distribution of these characteristics continually evolves as new producers enter, others exit, and still others expand, contract, or retool. Although these micro processes provide a basic source of efficiency growth, most attempts to measure changes in productivity in the semi-industrialized countries rely on aggregate data and thus begin from the assumption that each industry can be characterized by a representative plant. This chapter exploits comprehensive data on a panel of plants in Chile and Colombia to assess the consequences of ignoring cross-plant heterogeneity and to generate new evidence on the relation between productivity growth and industrial evolution in the semi-industrialized countries.

The findings shed light on several issues. Most fundamentally, by decomposing sectorwide measures of productivity, we isolate the roles of entry, exit, and within-plant productivity growth. For example, we find that new plants are typically 10 percent more productive in their first year than dying plants but are 15 to 20 percent less productive than the industrywide average. Those new plants that survive reach industry norms after roughly three years.[1] Turnover in any one year accounts for only a small fraction of productivity growth, but the cumulative effects over longer horizons can be substantial.

In addition, by comparing the microeconomic determinants of productivity in two very different economies in the late 1970s and early 1980s—Chile, a laissez-faire economy undergoing a financial crisis and severe recession, and Colombia, a relatively protected and regulated economy experiencing mild business cycles—we generate evidence on how policy regimes and macroeconomic shocks affect the sources of productivity growth. For example, although entering plants typically outperform dying plants in both countries, Chile broke from this pattern in the mid-1980s. This is probably because survival during that period depended more on the structure of the firm's balance sheet and access to subsidized credit than on its real-side performance.

Finally, to set the stage for these exercises, this chapter addresses some methodological issues. We develop and discuss two alternative micro-based productivity indexes, contrasting them with each other and with standard Divisia indexes based on aggregate data. Then we calculate all three indexes using the same data and compare their performance. Among other things, the analysis reveals that traditional measures of productivity are quite sensitive to aggregation bias, measurement error in intermediate inputs, and the assumption of long-run equilibrium.

Measuring Productivity Growth

Measures of factor productivity describe output per unit of input. *Total* factor productivity describes the joint productivity of all inputs, so a means of aggregation across the individual factors and plants is required.

The Traditional Measure of Productivity

One approach amounts to using the prices of inputs as weights. The popular Divisia index of sectoral productivity is based on this weighting scheme. If all markets are competitive and producers are in long-run equilibrium, the jth factor share matches the elasticity of output with respect to the jth factor, and growth in the Divisia index can be interpreted as a Hicks-neutral shift in productivity (Solow 1957). When these assumptions are violated, the Divisia index is likely to exhibit substantial procyclical bias (Berndt and Fuss 1986; Morrison 1989). Further, indexes based on industrywide data are subject to aggregation bias unless all producers share the same homothetic constant-returns technology.

An Alternative Measure

To relax these assumptions, we adopt an alternative approach to measuring sectoral productivity that is based in the literature on efficiency frontiers. This measure amounts to evaluating an estimated production function at the observed bundle of factor inputs and comparing the predicted output with the observed output. So long as an appropriate production function can be identified, this approach does not depend on assumptions of competitive profit maximization and long-run equilibrium for its validity.[2]

For each of n plants in our panel, we assume the following production function:

$$(4.1) \qquad Y_{it} = e^{\alpha_{0i} + \alpha_{1i}t + \alpha_{2i}t^2 + \eta_{it}} \prod_{j=1}^{J} X_{jit}^{\beta_j}$$

where Y_{it} is the output of the ith plant $(i = 1,n)$ in year t $(t = 1,T)$, X_{jit} is the ith plant's use of factor j $(j = 1,J)$ in year t, β_j is the elasticity of output with respect to factor j, and η_{it} is an error term. This production function employs a simple Cobb-Douglas technology to aggregate inputs, but unlike most empirical specifications, it allows each plant to have its own parabolic time trajectory for Hicks-neutral technological progress. The parameter vectors that describe these plant-specific trajectories, $\alpha_i = (\alpha_{0i}, \alpha_{1i}, \alpha_{2i})$, are the basic building blocks for our analysis of industrial evolution.[3] Estimation of all $3n + J$ parameters follows Cornwell, Schmidt, and Sickles 1990 (details are discussed in the appendix to this chapter).

The productivity of the ith plant in period t is measured by $E_{it} = \hat{Y}_{it} / \hat{V}_{it} = e^{\hat{\alpha}_{it}}$, where carats denote fitted values and V_{it} is the factor input index:

$$\hat{V}_{it} = \prod_{j=1}^{J} X_{jit}^{\hat{\beta}_j}$$

$$(4.2) \qquad \hat{\alpha}_{it} = \hat{\alpha}_{0i} + \hat{\alpha}_{1i}t + \hat{\alpha}_{2i}t^2.$$

$$\hat{Y}_{it} = e^{\hat{\alpha}_{it}} \hat{V}_{it}$$

Here, as in the literature on efficiency frontiers, predicted rather than actual output values are used in the numerator under the assumption that η_{it} represents measurement error in output (Schmidt 1985). But unlike the literature on efficiency frontiers, our comprehensive panel data allow us to construct a plant size–weighted average of predicted values that describes factor aggregate productivity at the industry level:[4]

$$(4.3) \qquad E_t = \left(\sum_{i=1}^{n} \hat{Y}_{it} \right) \Big/ \left(\sum_{i=1}^{n} \hat{V}_{it} \right) = \sum_{i=1}^{n} \left(\frac{\hat{V}_{it}}{\hat{V}_t} \right) E_{it}$$

where $\hat{V}_t = \Sigma_{i=1}^{n} \hat{V}_{it}$. To distinguish E_t from Divisia indexes, we refer to it as a technical efficiency measure.

In some contexts, it is necessary to distinguish two versions of E_t that differ in their underlying production technology. The first, which we call total factor technical efficiency and denote $E1_t$, is constructed using an expression for $\hat{V}_{it}$ that aggregates over three factor inputs: capital, labor, and intermediate goods. The second, which we call primary factor technical efficiency and denote $E2_t$, is constructed using an expression for $\hat{V}_{it}$ that aggregates only capital and labor. If producers can substitute smoothly between intermediate goods and other inputs, the $E1_t$ measure is more appropriate; if intermediate goods are used in fixed proportion to output, the $E2_t$ measure is preferred. Further discussion is provided in the appendix.

Divisia Indexes Compared with Technical Efficiency Measures

Most analyses of productivity in the semi-industrialized countries are based on sector-level Divisia indexes (hereafter B_t). As a prelude to our analysis of heterogeneity-based productivity growth, we investigate whether these traditional performance measures behave differently from E_t. If not, our decompositions simply help to explain why B_t changes. But if B_t and E_t are substantially different, it is worth exploring why and whether one performance measure should be preferred over another.

There are several reasons why the Divisia index *might* differ from both variants of E_t. One is that, unlike the E_t technical efficiency measures, the sector-level Divisia index is sensitive to allocative inefficiency. To see this, write the Divisia index in level form as

$$(4.4) \qquad B_t = \left(\sum_{i=1}^{n} \hat{Y}_{it} \right) \Big/ \prod_{j=1}^{J} \left(\sum_{i=1}^{n} X_{jit} \right)^{s_{jt}} = \left(\sum_{i=1}^{n} Y_{it} \right) \Big/ D_t$$

where s_j is the share of the jth factor's income in total factor income at the sectoral level. Clearly, the input aggregator D_t is independent of the allocation of factors across plants, so when any factor has different marginal products at different establishments—perhaps because of adjustment costs, uncertainty, or fragmented factor markets—factor reallocations exist that increase B_t by increasing its numerator. In contrast, factor reallocations between plants with equal technical efficiency (E_{it}) do not affect the productivity index E_t, even when the marginal product of a factor varies across plants (due, for example, to variation in factor proportions).[5]

A second distinction between the measures arises because the econometrically estimated factor weights β_j do not coincide with the factor shares s_{jt}. Changes in market conditions or technology may cause s_{jt} values to shift over time, while β_j values are fixed by assumption. If technology is evolving, changing factor weights *should* be recognized, so the time invariance of β_j values induces bias in E_t. But other forces are likely to be at least as important and to bias Divisia indexes through undesired variation in the s_{jt} terms. For example, factors often are not paid the value of their marginal product because there are adjustment costs. Similarly, if firms have monopsony power, s_{jt} values may consistently understate the marginal product of labor. (In most microeconomic data from developing countries, labor's coefficient considerably exceeds its share of costs.) Discrepancies between β_j and s_{it} also arise when factor stocks are measured with error; this makes standard estimators for the coefficients β_j inconsistent.[6]

Isolating Exit, Learning, and Market Share Effects

Because the sectorwide productivity trajectory E_t is a weighted sum of the productivity trajectories of plants, it is amenable to decomposition. After constructing E_t series for each country and comparing them with Divisia indexes (B_t), we exploit this feature of our efficiency measure. Our first decomposition of changes in sectoral productivity distinguishes the contributions of dying plants in their last year of operation from those of ongoing plants. Imagine that the plants in year t have been sorted into two groups: continuing plants, which remain in the data base in year $t + 1$ (denoted by $i \in c$), and dying plants that exit the data base in year $t + 1$ (denoted by $i \in d$). Then

(4.5)
$$E_t = \lambda_t^c \sum_{i \in c} \left(\frac{\theta_{it}}{\lambda_t^c} \right) E_{it} + (1 - \lambda_t^c) \sum_{i \in d} \left(\frac{\theta_{it}}{1 - \lambda_t^c} \right) E_{it}$$
$$= \lambda_t^c E_t^c + (1 - \lambda_t^c) E_t^d$$

where $\theta_{it} = \hat{V}_{it} / \Sigma_{k=1}^{n} \hat{V}_{kt}$ and $\lambda_t^c = \Sigma_{i \in c} \theta_{it}$. Comparisons of E^c and E^d reveal whether the short-run effect of plants exiting the industry is to improve aggregate productivity, and $1 - \lambda^c$ reveals what share of total factor use is attributable to exiting plants.

Productivity among continuing plants can be further decomposed by cohort. We do so by writing E_t as

(4.6)
$$E_t = \sum_{j=1}^{J} \lambda_t^{jc} E_t^{jc} + (1 - \lambda_t^c) E_t^d$$

where E_t^{jc} is the level of weighted average productivity among continuing plants in cohort j, and $\lambda_t^{jc} = \Sigma_{i \in cohort\, j} \theta_{it}$. Cohort j includes plants with exactly j years of experience if j is smaller than J and *at least J* years of experience if j is equal to J. This generalization of equation 4.5 recognizes that all plants in the "continuing" group may not be comparable and that young plants may differ systematically from old ones. For example, new plants may always be less productive than older ones because of start-up problems, even if the new plants are destined to become leaders in the industry. If this is the case, equation 4.5 will understate the long-run productivity gains from turnover.

In addition to revealing the speed with which efficiency improves among new plants, equation 4.6 can be used to identify the years that produce the "best" and the "worst" new plants, albeit using an ex post performance criterion. This type of exercise amounts to constructing the productivity trajectory describing the first k periods of operation for the cohort entering in period t_0 and comparing it to analogous trajectories for the cohorts entering in periods $t_0 + 1$, $t_0 + 2$, and so on.

Several studies have found that the reallocation of market shares among continuing plants can be an important source of productivity growth (Baily, Hulten, and Campbell 1992; Olley and Pakes 1992; Tybout and Westbrook 1995). To see if this holds true in Chile and Colombia, our final exercise isolates share effects. We begin by converting equation 4.5 to growth rates, so that aggregate productivity growth reflects growth among continuing plants and growth due to turnover:

$$(4.7) \quad \frac{\Delta E_t}{E_{t-1}} = \frac{\sum_{i \in c} (\theta_{it} E_{it} - \theta_{it-1} E_{it-1})}{E_{t-1}} + \frac{\sum_{i \in b} (\theta_{it} E_{it} - \sum_{i \in d} \theta_{it-1} E_{it-1})}{E_{t-1}}.$$

Then, we further decompose the continuing plant component of equation 4.7 into the effect of cross-plant reallocation of market shares and the effect of within-plant productivity growth, holding shares constant:

$$(4.8) \quad \frac{\sum_{i \in c} (\theta_{it} E_{it} - \theta_{it-1} E_{it-1})}{E_{t-1}} = \frac{\sum_{i \in c} \Delta \theta_{it} \, \overline{E}_i}{E_{t-1}} + \frac{\sum_{i \in c} \Delta E_{it} \overline{\theta}_i}{E_{t-1}}.$$

This expression is a variant of Baily, Hulten, and Campbell's (1992) equation 5, which is reproduced as equation 3.4 in chapter 3. Overbars indicate averages of period t and period $t - 1$ values.

Applying the Methodology to Chile and Colombia

Before presenting the findings on productivity, we briefly review the economic conditions that prevailed in Chile (1979–86) and Colombia (1977–85) during and preceding the sample periods. We also briefly describe the data (see chapters 9 and 10 for more detailed reviews).

Country Background: Chile

When General Augusto Pinochet overthrew the government in 1973, Chile's socialist economy was plagued by fiscal deficits, hyperinflation, foreign exchange shortages, and rationing. Average nominal tariff rates exceeded 100 percent, and a complex system of multiple exchange rates prevailed. Over the next five years, Pinochet's military government deregulated, privatized, and opened the economy to foreign markets.

After a deep recession, the industrial sector began to expand in 1976, and by 1981 it had surpassed 1973 production levels. However, manufacturing employment remained far below 1973 levels, implying that labor had been shed. Between 1979 and 1981, output continued to grow, but at a decreasing rate, constrained by an overvalued peso. Because this exchange rate policy squeezed profits, and because many firms and banks had become indebted in dollars during the expansion, Chile was in a poor position to weather the international credit crunch that precipitated the debt crisis. Thus, when the flow of foreign capital into Chile stopped in 1982, Chile plunged into financial crisis and recession, with unemployment rates approaching 30 percent. After large devaluations and various bailout measures, sustained recovery began in late 1983. This time employment expanded along with output.

Overall, then, 1979–81 was a period of industrial shakedown, characterized by decelerating growth and an increasingly overvalued currency. As the exchange regime collapsed, the country went into deep recession and financial crisis in 1982–83, causing many businesses to fail. The manufacturing sector began recovering in 1984–85 (see figure 4.1).

Figure 4.1 Output (Y), Total Factor Productivity (B), and Total Factor Technical Efficiency (E1), Chile, 1979–86

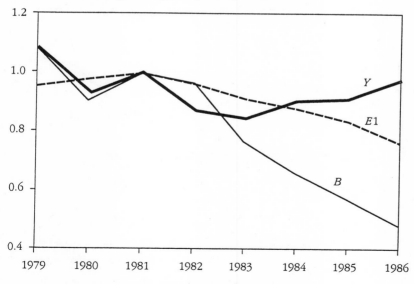

Note: All series are normalized to a value of 1.0 in 1981.
Source: Authors' calculations.

Country Background: Colombia

Between 1967 and 1973, real manufacturing output expanded rapidly, at an annual rate of almost 9 percent, and exports expanded at roughly 6 percent. This growth afforded policymakers some latitude for trade liberalization, and they gradually reduced quantitative trade restrictions on manufactured imports. Tariff reductions followed in 1974, bringing average nominal rates down from about 50 to 35 percent.

The beginning of the sample period in Colombia, 1976–85, was characterized by slower manufacturing growth, as high world prices for coffee in the late 1970s led to Dutch disease–induced appreciation in the real exchange rate. Stagnation followed in the early 1980s, with world recession and the debt crisis. Roughly speaking, Colombian authorities used commercial policy to soften the effects of falling demand. The movement toward trade liberalization slowed and was eventually reversed through rising protection during 1983–85. Beginning in 1986, trade policy became more liberal but did not return to 1980 levels.

Overall, the relative size of the industrial sector declined during 1976–85, but there was considerable fluctuation in manufacturing growth (see figure 4.2). During the first part of the period (1977–80), the

Figure 4.2 Output (Y), Total Factor Productivity (B), and Total Factor Technical Efficiency (E1), Colombia, 1977–87

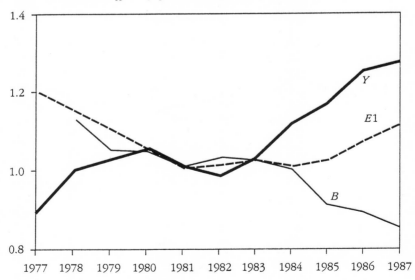

Note: All series are normalized to a value of 1.0 in 1981.
Source: Authors' calculations.

entire economy grew; during much of the second part (1981–83), it stagnated. Recovery began in 1984–85 and picked up speed during 1985–87.

Findings on the Productivity Aggregates

Before analyzing the effects of entry, exit, and learning on productivity in manufacturing, it is worthwhile to explore the empirical properties of the basic productivity measures used. Several issues are of concern. First, how and why do series based on Divisia indexes (B_t) differ from series based on econometrically estimated technical efficiency measures (E_t)? Second, does it matter much whether technical efficiency measures are estimated with intermediate inputs as an explanatory variable? Recall that leaving intermediate goods out of the equation amounts to assuming that they are used in fixed proportion to output, while including them amounts to assuming that firms face a unit elasticity of substitution between intermediate goods and primary inputs.

To address these questions, series on E_t and B_t were constructed for each manufacturing sector. In addition, the five largest industries (measured by the number of plants) were analyzed individually at the three-digit ISIC level: food, textiles, footwear, wood products, and metal products. Though the results of these analyses are too voluminous to report for every exercise, they are brought into the discussion when relevant.

Divisia Indexes Compared with the Total Factor Technical Efficiency Index

The contrast between the Divisia index (B_t) and the total factor technical efficiency index $(E1_t)$ for Chile and Colombia is striking, for both manufacturing aggregates (figures 4.1 and 4.2) and the industry-specific series (not reported). As expected, the fluctuation is more marked in B_t than in $E1_t$. But somewhat surprisingly, the Divisia index continues to deteriorate in both countries as they pull out of recession in the mid-1980s. In contrast, the technical efficiency index $E1_t$ improves with expansion in Colombia and declines much less than the Divisia series in Chile.

Several possible explanations for these diverging paths have already been identified. One is that Divisia indexes respond to factor reallocations across plants with different marginal products, while technical efficiency measures may not. This seems unlikely to be the entire explanation, however, since allocative efficiency is not expected to worsen dramatically with economic recovery. A second possibility is that differences in performance are attributable to the different weights that the two productivity measures place on factor inputs. Specifically, econometric estimates of the marginal product of labor are substantially higher than labor's share in factor payments, and the opposite is true for capital.[7] So expansions that involve substantial capital growth and little employment growth give the appearance of relatively rapid productivity growth when technical efficiency indexes are used in place of Divisia indexes. This explanation fits the Colombian data, which register a 7 percent decline in manufacturing employment but a 24 percent expansion in capital stock between 1982 and 1987.

The discrepancy in factor weights does *not* account for the divergence between Divisia and technical efficiency indexes in Chile, where employment grows more rapidly than capital during the recovery. Here the explanation is that Divisia indexes, by construction, allow the factor weights s_{jt} to shift over time, while the analogous weights β_j in technical efficiency indexes do not. This difference matters because the share of intermediate inputs jumps from 0.61 to 0.78 in Chile over the course of the recovery period, and use of intermediate inputs climbs about 65 percent. Together, these patterns pull down the Divisia index dramatically; the pull is much milder for the technical efficiency index, which does not allow the weight on material use to grow.

Whether one prefers Divisia or technical efficiency indexes therefore depends partly on whether one believes the data on intermediate inputs. If the data are trustworthy, the elasticity of substitution between intermediate and other inputs is clearly less than unity, so the Cobb-Douglas version of the technical efficiency model is inappropriate. The technical efficiency framework should either be abandoned or be salvaged by adapting a more flexible functional form like the translog. However, price deflators for intermediate inputs are relatively poor, so the rapid increase in the Chilean ratio of intermediates to output *may* largely reflect measurement problems.[8] If this is the case, neither the Divisia nor the total factor technical efficiency index is appropriate. But in the special case in which the ratio of physical output to each physical unit of intermediate inputs is inflexible and the quality of intermediates does not change much, it *is* appropriate to leave intermediates out of the analysis altogether and simply to express gross output as a function of primary inputs. The resultant measure $(E2_t)$ avoids the questionable set of premises on which Divisia indexes rest.

Primary Factor and Total Factor Technical Efficiency Indexes

To see how the exclusion of material inputs affects our technical efficiency measure, we next compare primary factor efficiency $(E2_t)$ with total factor efficiency $(E1_t)$. See figures 4.3 and 4.4. In Chile, dropping intermediate inputs is sufficient to reverse the downward trend in productivity during the recovery period; the series are now even more plausible than the traditional Divisia series. In Colombia, the effect is to

Figure 4.3 Total Factor (E1) and Primary Factor (E2) Technical Efficiency, Chile, 1979–86

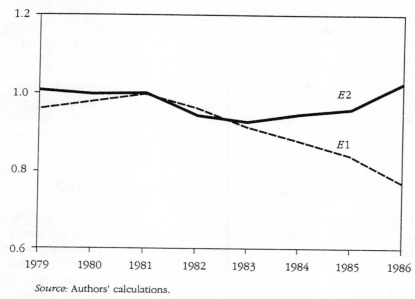

Source: Authors' calculations.

Figure 4.4 Total Factor (E1) and Primary Factor (E2) Technical Efficiency, Colombia, 1977–87

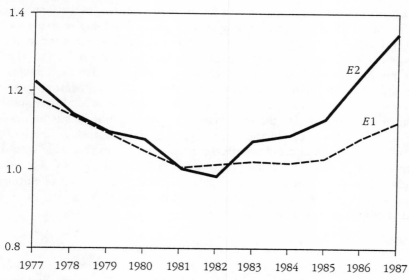

Note: All series are normalized to a value of 1.0 in 1981.
Source: Authors' calculations.

accentuate the upturn in productivity during the recovery period (1982–87) so that it reaches the questionable annualized rate of 7 percent. Primary and total productivity measures coincide in both countries until 1983, about the time when major devaluations took place that may cause valuation problems with imported intermediates thereafter.[9] Such valuation problems mean that the primary factor efficiency series may provide a better summary of performance and, more generally, that analysts of productivity in the semi-industrialized countries might find it revealing to check measures of primary factor productivity during periods of relative price volatility. In this spirit, in addition to reporting total factor technical efficiency series, we also report primary factor technical efficiency series for most of the exercises that follow.

Plant Heterogeneity and Aggregate Productivity

Having established that $E1$ and $E2$ are plausible—perhaps even superior—measures of productivity, we now use them to study the heterogeneity issues raised earlier. We first ask whether plant turnover tends to improve sectoral productivity in the sense that exiting plants are less efficient than plants remaining active. Our analysis is based on equation 4.5, which expresses sectoral productivity as a weighted average of productivity among plants that continue operating in the next period (E^c) and plants that do not (E^d). The weights λ^c and $1 - \lambda^c$ reflect each group's share of factor use.

For this exercise and those that follow, we focus on industry-specific series rather than manufacturingwide aggregates. By doing so, we avoid several types of aggregation bias that undermine inferences when the focus is on cross-plant comparisons. One bias arises from the fact that the production technology is estimated separately for each manufacturing industry. This makes the parameters of our input aggregator $\hat{V}_{it}$ vary across producers in different subsectors and renders cross-industry summations of this variable inappropriate. The other major bias is induced by measurement error in the output price deflators: *average* levels of productivity differ more dramatically across industries than one would expect with properly deflated output and capital stock series.[10] Accordingly, when using manufacturingwide aggregates, comparisons of exiting plants with other plants depend critically on which industries are expanding and which are contracting.

Chile

Table 4.1 reports series on $E1^c$, $E1^d$, and λ^c for each of the five major industries described earlier. (Series on $E2^c$ and $E2^d$ are qualitatively similar and thus are not reported.) The results here conform to earlier

Table 4.1 *Total Factor Technical Efficiency of Continuing and Exiting Plants in Chile, by Industry, 1980–85*

| Industry and year | Weighted average productivity | | Market share of continuing plants (λ^c) |
	Continuing plants ($E1^c$)	Exiting plants ($E1^d$)	
Food			
1980	0.989	0.710	0.978
1981	1.003	0.828	0.985
1982	0.998	0.947	0.970
1983	1.001	0.809	0.964
1984	1.015	0.934	0.986
1985	1.024	0.836	0.969
Average	1.005	0.844	0.975
Footwear			
1980	0.989	0.872	0.976
1981	0.992	1.066	0.941
1982	0.997	0.897	0.919
1983	1.034	0.730	0.938
1984	1.088	1.032	0.957
1985	1.143	1.213	0.940
Average	1.040	0.968	0.945
Metal products			
1980	0.985	1.017	0.971
1981	1.005	0.851	0.969
1982	1.021	0.823	0.941
1983	1.032	0.797	0.991
1984	1.025	0.817	0.997
1985	1.019	1.055	0.960
Average	1.014	0.893	0.972
Textiles			
1980	0.981	1.028	0.980
1981	1.008	0.840	0.950
1982	1.003	0.964	0.953
1983	0.999	1.062	0.981
1984	0.985	0.749	0.997
1985	0.973	0.809	0.989
Average	0.992	0.909	0.975
Wood products			
1980	0.999	1.135	0.943
1981	1.007	0.865	0.951
1982	1.029	0.915	0.940
1983	1.053	0.831	0.972
1984	1.053	0.590	0.986
1985	0.948	1.906	0.861
Average	1.015	1.040	0.942

(Table continues on the following page.)

Table 4.1   (continued)

| Industry and year | Weighted average productivity | | Market share of continuing plants (λ^c) |
	Continuing plants ($E1^c$)	Exiting plants ($E1^d$)	
Cross-industry average			
1980	0.989	0.952	0.970
1981	1.003	0.890	0.959
1982	1.010	0.909	0.945
1983	1.024	0.846	0.969
1984	1.033	0.824	0.985
1985	1.022	1.164	0.944
Average	1.013	0.931	0.962

Note: Both productivity series are expressed relative to the 1981 industrywide level of technical efficiency $E1$. Equation 4.5 provides algebraic definitions.
Source: Authors' calculations.

analyses of the Chilean data base (Tybout 1992; Liu 1993), although the methodology of the present study is distinct.[11] Specifically, within each industry dying plants are less efficient than continuing plants in most years, so a systematic shakedown is apparently at work. In a typical year, the margin of difference averages approximately 10 percent. Since value added is about one-third of gross output in manufacturing, this constitutes about a 30 percent shortfall in payments to primary factors, and—presuming that there is limited scope for wage reductions—a substantially larger shortfall in payments to capital. Hence, although the sample period spans several years of a severe financial crisis, cross-plant exit patterns are at least partly driven by *real-side* performance in Chile.

Notably, the exiting plants constitute a rather small share of total output $(1 - \lambda^c)$, even during Chile's deep recession of the early 1980s.[12] So the short-run effect of exit on productivity levels is typically small. This does not mean that turnover has a minor *long-run* effect on productivity. If the dying plants had been propped up rather than forced from the market, they would have gained market share, and their inefficiency would very likely have continued to worsen. (Liu 1993 documents that the productivity trajectory of dying Chilean plants systematically falls in the years prior to their exit.)

In some industries (footwear, metal products, and wood products), exiting plants were more efficient than incumbents during 1985, when Chile was pulling out of recession. At first glance, this appears to confirm the popular notion that recovery dampens the cleansing effects of recession. However, the efficiency gap between continuing and dying plants is closed because dying plants get better, not because continuing plants get worse. Hence a more plausible interpretation is that by the mid-1980s, business failures in Chile were induced largely by financial, rather than real-side, problems among small plants. Many of these plants relied heavily on expensive peso-denominated credit before the exchange regime collapsed, and their liquidity was drawn down during that period (Galvez and Tybout 1985; Tybout 1986). Thereafter, again because their debt was in pesos instead of dollars, they did not benefit much from the subsidized exchange rate or the special debt rescheduling that the government introduced to bail out large businesses. In short, real-side performance was of secondary importance for survival.[13]

Colombia

The Colombian results are qualitatively similar to the Chilean ones (see table 4.2).[14] Exiting plants are usually less productive than entering plants, although some industries go through periods when exiting plants perform better than incumbents. Further, with the exception of the years 1980 and 1985, the Colombian results are *quantitatively* quite similar. The discrepancy in 1985 is due to an unusual pattern in Chile that has already been discussed, but the discrepancy in 1980 is due to performance in Colombia: in all industries except wood products, dying plants are more efficient than continuing plants. We can only speculate about the reasons for this anomalous year; one possibility is that it was the culmination of a sustained period of appreciation and may have seen the exit of many efficient producers of tradable goods.

Overall, neither country exhibits a systematic tendency for the efficiency gap between continuing and exiting plants to covary with the business cycle. In regressions (not reported) explaining the efficiency gap, $E1_i^d / E1_i^c$, the t-ratio for the coefficient on output growth is less than 0.40 in both countries. Industry dummies are more significant, but there is no consistent pattern across countries. For example, the relative efficiency of dying producers of wood products is significantly lower than average in Colombia, but it is higher than average in Chile. Thus efficiency differentials reflect country-specific circumstances rather than technology and may respond to policy.

Exiting plants in Colombia account for a larger share of total factor use than their counterparts in Chile, even though Colombia's exit rates are substantially lower and its recession milder than Chile's (refer to chapters 9 and 10). Nonetheless, as in Chile, the short-run effect of exit on productivity in Colombia is small, since exiting plants never account for more than 7 percent of the market.

One is tempted to compare the gap between the efficiency of continuing and dying plants across countries and to draw some inferences regarding the ability of the market mechanism to weed out the least promising enterprises. Unfortunately, this is a more subtle exercise than it appears at first blush. Done correctly, it amounts to sorting plants on

Table 4.2 Total Factor Technical Efficiency of Continuing and Exiting Plants in Colombia, by Industry, 1978–86

| Industry and year | Weighted average productivity | | Market share of continuing plants (λ^c) |
	Continuing plants $(E1^c)$	Exiting plants $(E1^d)$	
Food			
1978	1.167	1.029	0.979
1979	1.093	1.102	0.973
1980	1.028	1.187	0.969
1981	1.008	0.867	0.944
1982	1.013	0.934	0.976
1983	1.028	0.933	0.982
1984	1.062	1.218	0.975
1985	1.126	1.227	0.944
1986	1.214	1.190	0.980
Average	1.082	1.076	0.969
Footwear			
1978	1.010	0.944	0.957
1979	1.033	1.155	0.940
1980	1.000	1.625	0.952
1981	1.007	0.856	0.954
1982	1.022	1.006	0.950
1983	1.032	0.910	0.938
1984	1.058	1.056	0.951
1985	1.118	0.930	0.948
1986	1.208	0.964	0.919
Average	1.054	1.050	0.945
Metal products			
1978	1.030	1.071	0.951
1979	1.039	0.976	0.971
1980	1.009	1.063	0.958
1981	1.007	0.808	0.967
1982	0.998	0.908	0.979
1983	0.988	0.823	0.964
1984	0.980	1.052	0.969
1985	0.967	0.854	0.970
1986	0.965	0.869	0.933
Average	0.998	0.936	0.962
Textiles			
1978	1.132	1.218	0.855
1979	1.112	0.803	0.979
1980	1.023	1.365	0.827
1981	1.004	0.825	0.976
1982	1.000	0.757	0.978
1983	0.995	0.903	0.978
1984	0.997	0.800	0.982

Table 4.2   (continued)

| Industry and year | Weighted average productivity | | Market share of continuing plants (λ^c) |
	Continuing plants ($E1^c$)	Exiting plants ($E1^d$)	
1985	1.022	0.782	0.866
1986	1.076	0.848	0.981
Average	1.040	0.922	0.936
Wood products			
1978	1.079	0.805	0.951
1979	1.039	0.733	0.954
1980	1.007	0.809	0.961
1981	1.010	0.839	0.942
1982	1.003	0.937	0.973
1983	0.995	0.857	0.952
1984	1.025	0.844	0.857
1985	1.048	0.846	0.978
1986	1.062	0.898	0.936
Average	1.030	0.841	0.945
Cross-industry average			
1978	1.083	1.014	0.939
1979	1.063	0.954	0.963
1980	1.013	1.210	0.933
1981	1.007	0.839	0.957
1982	1.007	0.908	0.971
1983	1.008	0.885	0.963
1984	1.024	0.994	0.947
1985	1.056	0.928	0.941
1986	1.105	0.954	0.950
Average	1.041	0.965	0.952

Note: Both productivity series are expressed relative to the 1981 industrywide level of productivity $E1$. Equation 4.5 provides algebraic definitions.

Source: Authors' calculations.

the basis of their ex ante expected profitability and examining the location of exiting plants in this distribution. Levels of current efficiency are presumably correlated with expected profitability, but many other factors also matter, especially during periods when the policy regime and macroeconomic conditions are changing. We therefore simply note that, except during 1980 and 1985, Chilean and Colombian efficiency gaps are remarkably similar.

Cohorts and Learning

We next further decompose productivity levels among continuing plants to determine whether new cohorts systematically improve as they mature, either through the attrition of low-productivity plants or through intraplant improvements in efficiency. The analysis is organized around equation 4.6, which allows total factor productivity to be expressed as a weighted average of cohort-specific productivity levels. Tables 4.1 and 4.2 report these levels and their associated weights for the two performance measures E1 and E2.

Unfortunately, separately tracking plants that are one, two, three, and four or more years old means that we have only five years of complete data for analysis. Nonetheless, some interesting patterns emerge. First, the plants that are one and two years old are almost *always* less productive than the plants with at least four years of experience. (The one slight exception occurs for one-year-old plants in 1986 as measured by E2; see table 4.3.) Even three-year-old plants are more efficient than older cohorts as a group in only three of ten possible comparisons. So a process of maturation and shakedown is clearly occurring that improves the performance of cohorts over time. The process is not automatic. For example, the cohort of plants first observed during 1984 got worse in

Table 4.3 Cohort-Specific Levels of Performance in Colombia, 1982–86

a. Total factor technical efficiency

Year	$E1^d$	$E1^{1c}$	$E1^{2c}$	$E1^{3c}$	$E1^{4c}$	$E1$
1982	0.838	0.814	0.899	1.155	1.015	1.006
1983	0.907	0.818	0.833	0.881	1.033	1.017
1984	0.891	1.025	1.038	0.841	1.043	1.009
1985	0.670	0.785	0.691	1.068	1.060	1.018
1986	0.773	0.845	0.833	0.752	1.104	1.070
Average	0.816	0.857	0.859	0.940	1.051	1.024

b. Primary factor technical efficiency

Year	$E2^d$	$E2^{1c}$	$E2^{2c}$	$E2^{3c}$	$E2^{4c}$	$E2$
1982	0.226	0.774	0.837	1.296	1.087	0.976
1983	0.643	0.821	0.867	0.865	1.138	1.071
1984	0.598	0.629	0.687	0.897	1.192	1.084
1985	0.895	0.483	0.438	0.757	1.213	1.125
1986	0.845	1.334	1.193	0.510	1.301	1.238
Average	0.641	0.808	0.805	0.865	1.186	1.099

Note: See discussion in the text for the definition of total factor (E1) and primary factor (E2) technical efficiency. Superscript *d* stands for dying cohort, *c* for continuing cohort, and the numbers for age of cohort in years. Equation 4.6 defines each element of the decomposition. All series are expressed relative to industrywide productivity levels (E1 or E2) in 1981.

Source: Authors' calculations.

1985 and only partly recovered during 1986. Also plants that were three years old during 1982 were exceptionally productive in that year but fell back toward sectoral levels of productivity in 1984. One question, which cannot be addressed with these data, is whether deviations from the "normal" maturation process are random or systematically related to macroeconomic conditions or the policy regime.

Second, exiting plants are always substantially below the productivity levels of surviving plants with four or more years of experience, although they occasionally do better than the one-year-old plants coming onstream to replace them. Here, too, we cannot conclude that the pattern is assured. As demonstrated in tables 4.1 and 4.2, many exceptionally efficient plants were part of the exiting cohort in 1980.

Together these patterns imply that the replacement of dying plants with one-year-old plants generates little productivity gain in the transition year: neither group of plants is very productive, and neither accounts for much output. But the new plants that survive improve quickly, and, as demonstrated elsewhere (Liu 1993), productivity among dying plants is typically in a downward spiral. So the longer-term implications of this turnover for productivity growth are significant, and policies that inhibit this process (such as bailout programs for unprofitable firms) probably significantly dampen productivity in the longer term. For example, in 1982, only 80 percent of the output came from plants that existed in 1977. In 1985, only 72 percent of the output came from such plants.

Market Share and Productivity Growth

Thus far, our discussion has focused on productivity levels. We now take up the role of heterogeneity and turnover in shaping productivity *growth*. First we isolate the portion of growth that is due to entry and exit; then we decompose the residual growth in the effects of gains in efficiency within plants and reallocation of shares among continuing plants.

Productivity Change and Turnover among Incumbent Plants

To isolate the role of entry and exit, we convert our level-form series E_t to a productivity growth series, as described by equation 4.7. Hereafter the focus is on Colombia, since productivity series cannot be calculated for plants that entered the Chilean data base after 1980.

Table 4.4 decomposes annual growth rates of total productivity (G_E) into the contribution of continuing (G_{EC}) and noncontinuing plants (G_{ET}), so that $G_E = G_{EC} + G_{ET}$ (refer to equation 4.7). No values are reported for 1977, 1978, and 1987 because at least one component of this identity cannot be calculated for these endpoint years. If the market shares of continuing, beginning, and exiting plants all remain stable,

Table 4.4 Industry-Specific Decomposition of Productivity Growth in Colombia, 1979–86

Industry and year	Industrywide growth in total factor efficiency (G_E)	Effect of incumbent plants (G_{EC})	Effect of plant-level turnover (G_{ET})
Food			
1979	−0.061	−0.068	0.007
1980	−0.055	−0.062	0.007
1981	−0.032	−0.043	0.011
1982	0.012	0.038	−0.026
1983	0.014	0.020	−0.006
1984	0.038	0.025	0.014
1985	0.062	0.026	0.036
1986	0.072	0.112	−0.040
Average	0.006	0.006	0.000
Footwear			
1979	0.033	0.004	0.029
1980	−0.010	−0.018	0.008
1981	−0.029	0.009	−0.038
1982	0.021	0.010	0.011
1983	0.004	−0.003	0.007
1984	0.032	0.037	−0.005
1985	0.048	0.051	−0.003
1986	0.072	0.045	0.027
Average	0.021	0.017	0.004
Metal products			
1979	0.005	0.028	−0.024
1980	−0.025	−0.041	0.016
1981	−0.011	0.007	−0.018
1982	−0.004	0.004	−0.008
1983	−0.014	−0.025	0.011
1984	0.000	−0.002	0.003
1985	−0.019	−0.012	−0.007
1986	−0.005	−0.040	0.034
Average	−0.009	−0.010	0.001
Textiles			
1979	−0.034	0.106	−0.140
1980	−0.021	−0.219	0.198
1981	−0.076	0.123	−0.199
1982	−0.005	−0.002	−0.003
1983	−0.002	−0.005	0.003
1984	0.000	0.006	−0.005
1985	−0.003	−0.094	0.091
1986	0.083	0.172	−0.090
Average	−0.007	0.011	−0.018
Wood products			
1979	−0.038	−0.032	−0.006
1980	−0.025	−0.023	−0.002
1981	0.000	−0.017	0.017

Table 4.4   (continued)

Industry and year	Industrywide growth in total factor efficiency (G_E)	Effect of incumbent plants (G_{EC})	Effect of plant-level turnover (G_{ET})
1982	0.001	0.024	−0.023
1983	−0.012	−0.028	0.016
1984	0.011	−0.069	0.080
1985	0.044	0.145	−0.101
1986	0.008	−0.029	0.037
Average	−0.001	−0.004	0.002
Cross-industry average			
1979	−0.012	0.005	−0.017
1980	−0.017	−0.045	0.028
1981	−0.018	0.010	−0.028
1982	0.003	0.009	−0.006
1983	−0.001	−0.005	0.004
1984	0.010	0.000	0.011
1985	0.016	0.014	0.002
1986	0.029	0.033	−0.004
Average	0.001	0.002	−0.001

Note: Precise expressions are provided in equation 4.7 of the text. Column 1 may differ slightly from the sum of columns 2 and 3 because of rounding.
Source: Authors' calculations.

these components simply reflect differences in the technical efficiency growth of each group of producers. However, to the extent that market shares fluctuate, our decomposition reflects that influence as well.

The cross-year average rate of growth in each component is small. For turnover, the reasons have already been discussed: entering plants in their first year are not much more productive than dying plants in their last year, and neither group accounts for much output. For incumbents, the explanation is apparent in figure 4.2. Our sample spans a business cycle, so there are productivity losses in the early years, offset by productivity gains as capacity utilization recovers in the later years.[15] Measured productivity gains are also limited by the fact that labor services are measured in efficiency units. This means that efficiency growth due to increases in the skill intensity of production or increases in the relative productivity of skilled workers are not picked up (see the appendix).

We expected to find a negative association between turnover-based gains in efficiency (G_{ET}) and output growth, since net exit by inefficient plants should bolster productivity during periods of contraction. This "cleansing effect of recessions" has been documented by Baily, Hulten, and Campbell (1992) using total factor productivity indexes for the United States and by Tybout (1992) using labor productivity series for

Chile and Morocco. But the G_{ET} series in table 4.4 do not covary negatively with output. That is, for reasons we have not isolated, relatively little weeding out occurred during the Colombian recession.

Finally, there is a surprisingly strong negative correlation between G_{EC} and G_{ET} (the Pearson correlation coefficient is −0.85). Algebraically, the reason is that the continuing plant effect is small and the turnover effect is large in years when many inefficient plants survive; see equation 4.7.[16] An unusually dramatic example is provided by the textile industry in Colombia, where, in both 1978 and 1980, many highly efficient producers left the market, while in 1979 almost all the inefficient producers stayed in (tables 4.2 and 4.3).

Decomposing Incumbent Productivity Change

Finally, we implement equation 4.8 to decompose technical efficiency growth among continuing plants (G_{EC}) into a within-plant effect and share reallocation effects. The results are reported in table 4.5.[17] Once

Table 4.5 *Industry-Specific Decomposition of Incumbent Effect in Colombia, 1979–86*

Industry and year	Total effect due to incumbent plants (G_{EC})	Share reallocation effect	Within-plant effect
Food			
1979	−0.068	−0.001	−0.066
1980	−0.062	−0.014	−0.048
1981	−0.043	−0.009	−0.033
1982	0.038	0.029	0.009
1983	0.020	0.000	0.020
1984	0.025	−0.007	0.032
1985	0.026	−0.014	0.040
1986	0.112	0.032	0.081
Average	0.006	0.002	0.004
Footwear			
1979	0.004	0.004	0.000
1980	−0.018	−0.025	0.007
1981	0.009	−0.003	0.011
1982	0.010	−0.009	0.019
1983	−0.003	−0.008	0.005
1984	0.037	0.005	0.032
1985	0.051	0.009	0.042
1986	0.045	0.003	0.042
Average	0.017	−0.003	0.020
Metal products			
1979	0.028	0.018	0.010
1980	−0.041	−0.015	−0.025

Table 4.5 (continued)

Industry and year	Total effect due to incumbent plants (G_{EC})	Share reallocation effect	Within-plant effect
1981	0.007	0.017	−0.010
1982	0.004	0.010	−0.005
1983	−0.025	−0.009	−0.017
1984	−0.002	0.018	−0.020
1985	−0.012	0.001	−0.013
1986	−0.040	−0.009	−0.031
Average	−0.010	0.004	−0.014
Textiles			
1979	0.106	0.079	0.027
1980	−0.219	−0.106	−0.113
1981	0.123	0.123	0.000
1982	−0.002	0.010	−0.012
1983	−0.005	−0.017	0.012
1984	0.006	0.005	0.000
1985	−0.094	−0.086	−0.009
1986	0.172	0.073	0.100
Average	0.011	0.010	0.001
Wood products			
1979	−0.032	−0.017	−0.015
1980	−0.023	−0.030	0.006
1981	−0.017	−0.025	0.009
1982	0.024	−0.007	0.032
1983	−0.028	−0.018	−0.010
1984	−0.069	0.011	−0.079
1985	0.145	0.099	0.046
1986	−0.029	−0.036	0.006
Average	−0.004	−0.003	−0.001
Cross-industry average			
1979	0.005	0.010	−0.005
1980	−0.045	−0.024	−0.022
1981	0.010	0.013	−0.003
1982	0.009	0.004	0.005
1983	−0.005	−0.006	0.001
1984	0.000	0.004	−0.004
1985	0.014	0.001	0.013
1986	0.033	0.008	0.025
Average	0.002	0.001	0.001

Note: The total effect is the column labeled G_{EC} from table 4.4. The share reallocation effect is growth in total factor efficiency due to the reallocation of market shares among incumbent plants, and the within-plant effect is growth in total factor efficiency due to intraplant improvements in efficiency. Equation 4.8 provides algebraic expressions. Column 1 may differ slightly from the sum of columns 2 and 3 because of rounding.

Source: Authors' calculations.

again, each component is small when averaged through time, but year-to-year growth rates can be substantial.

Our finding of a significant role for market share reallocation is consistent with that of Olley and Pakes 1992, Baily, Hulten, and Campbell 1992, and Tybout and Westbrook 1995. Nonetheless, it is noteworthy that cross-year averages suggest that share effects have little long-run effect on productivity. This runs counter to the findings for the United States and implies that, despite relatively high rates of job creation and job destruction, the technical efficiency gains from reallocation of workers among continuing plants are modest.

As expected, within-plant efficiency growth is strongly procyclical, probably because of capacity utilization effects and—less dramatically— the embodiment of new technologies during periods of rapid investment.[18] Share effects, in contrast, are negatively albeit weakly associated with output growth (the t-ratio is -1.68). This constitutes limited evidence for a version of the "cleansing effect of recessions" hypothesis: among incumbents, productive plants gain market share during contractionary periods.

Conclusions

It is worth repeating the central findings of the analysis. The differences between Divisia indexes and econometrically based technical efficiency indexes are important enough to create dramatically different pictures of productivity performance. These contrasts trace to differences in how the marginal products of factors are imputed: Divisia indexes assign a much larger weight to labor than do technical efficiency indexes and allow all weights to vary through time. Similarly, it matters a great deal whether intermediate inputs are assumed to substitute for primary inputs—in which case a total factor efficiency measure is appropriate—or must be used in fixed proportion to output—in which case some measurement error and aggregation problems can be avoided by studying primary factor efficiency. In our panels, the second approach appears to be the more sensible one. More generally, investigating the robustness of productivity series to assumptions and exploring the reasons for differences between alternative measures are critical to drawing conclusions about performance.

Looking across incumbent, entering, and exiting plants, we find evidence of significant heterogeneity. During most periods, exiting plants are about 10 percent less productive than incumbents, so their disappearance improves sectoral productivity. But exiting plants are occasionally *more* efficient, and when this occurs turnover has the opposite effect. Since exiting plants typically account for a small share of total factor use, and one-year-old plants are not much more efficient than exiting plants, the short-run effects of turnover are not dramatic. However, productivity typically drops among plants that exit and rises quickly among new plants that survive several years, so the cumulative effects of this cleansing process over a longer time horizon are probably substantial.

With the analysis limited to incumbent plants, heterogeneity still proves important. When we isolate the portion of change in sectoral productivity due to market share reallocations within this group, it often amounts to more than 1 percentage point of efficiency growth in absolute value. Nonetheless, unlike in the United States, the long-run average effect of share reallocations on industrywide technical efficiency is close to 0 in all Colombian industries we studied. One implication is that high rates of job creation and job destruction there (documented in chapter 2) do not produce strong efficiency gains.

Finally, when productivity is decomposed into the influence of different cohorts for the Colombian data, there is clear evidence of a maturation process. Plants with less than three years of market experience are, as a group, systematically less productive than those with four or more years of experience. The maturing process apparently approaches completion after three years, since plants with three years of experience can go either way. It is not possible to tell from these results how sensitive the patterns are to stages of the business cycle or to policy regime.

Overall, although the methodology deployed here has its own problems, it clearly indicates that heterogeneity is very important and that productivity analysis based on sectoral aggregates can mask as much as it reveals.

Appendix: Data and Estimation

The Estimator

To fit equation 4.2, we need not assume either long-run profit maximization or competitive product and factor markets. However, since all inputs are treated as independent of the error term, producers can have no advance knowledge of their η_{it} realizations at the time they choose their factor stocks for period t. With this assumption, consistent estimates of the vector $\beta = \beta_1, \beta_2, \ldots, \beta_J$ and unbiased estimates of the n vectors $\alpha = \alpha_{0i}, \alpha_{1i}, \alpha_{2i}$ can be obtained using the within estimator described in Cornwell, Schmidt, and Sickles 1990.[19] Effectively, this amounts to performing ordinary least squares of $\ln Y_{it}$ on the input vector $\ln X_{it} = (\ln X_{1it}, \ln X_{2it}, \ldots, \ln X_{Jit})$ and $(1, t, t^2)$, allowing the coefficients on 1, t, t^2 to vary plant by plant.[20]

We impose constant returns to scale when estimating the β_j values, thereby forcing all scale efficiency effects to show up through the term

$\hat{\alpha}_{it}$. (For example, when there are increasing returns, large plants exhibit high $\hat{\alpha}_{0i}$ values.) In principle, allowing nonconstant returns to scale permits us to decompose changes in intraplant efficiency into a term that reflects the volume of use and a term that reflects returns to scale.[21] In practice, however, deviations from constant returns are hard to pick up econometrically (see chapter 5).

For a handful of plants, the quadratic form for $\hat{\alpha}$ (equation 4.2) creates problems. Sharp reversals in productivity during the middle years of the sample period lead to extreme values of predicted productivity in the first or last sample year. Accordingly, plants whose predicted level of productivity is more than three standard deviations from the sectoral norm in any year are excluded from all figures on sectoral productivity and their associated decompositions.

Simultaneity Bias

Allowing entry and exit in the panel of plants brings up the possibility of simultaneity bias. Plants that are relatively efficient are more likely to survive and grow large. So if $\hat{\alpha}_{it}$ is treated as part of the disturbance term when fitting the production function, bias can arise from the correlation between factor stocks and the disturbance or from a nonrepresentative sample due to the exit of low-productivity plants.[22] However, the estimator described above effectively removes the systematic component of productivity growth from the residual. Hence, unless the transitory shock η_{it} is correlated with factor stocks, these biases are not likely to be a problem. We assume that such correlation is not present.[23]

Nonconstant Returns to Scale

The properties of our productivity series generally depend on whether we impose constant returns to scale. We have tried both approaches and found that unconstrained estimates generally exhibit *decreasing* returns. This implausible result is most likely due to measurement error; see chapter 6. Given that Westbrook and Tybout (1993) find constant returns in almost all sectors when they control for this bias, we adopt the constant returns estimates as our "preferred" β and α_i values.[24]

Treatment of Intermediate Inputs

We report two types of production functions. The first function expresses gross output as a Cobb-Douglas function of capital, labor (measured in efficiency units), and intermediate inputs, implicitly imposing unit elasticity of substitution between all three factors. Productivity series associated with this function are called total factor technical efficiency measures and denoted $E1_t$. The second function expresses gross output as a Cobb-Douglas function of capital and labor (measured in efficiency units), implicitly imposing fixed proportionality between intermediate inputs and gross output (Griliches and Mairese 1989 use this specification). Productivity series associated with this specification are called primary factor technical efficiency measures and denoted $E2_t$. We also experimented with value added production functions but found that the *percentage* increase in value added is tremendous among a handful of plants that start from levels of value added close to 0 and that these plants are highly influential in the sectoral aggregates.

Data

The panel data from each country cover nearly all plants with at least ten workers. Plant entry is the appearance of a plant in the data base, either because it has just started up or because it has crossed the ten-worker threshold. Similarly, dying or exiting plants drop out of the data base, either because they have shrunk below ten workers or because they have shut down altogether.

Capital stock figures for Chile are reported only for 1979 and 1980. To construct capital stock series for other years, we combine these stock data with gross investment figures. However, this cannot be done for plants that entered the data base in 1981 or thereafter, so there is a selectivity bias in the data for Chile, which describe only plants that were observed in 1979 or 1980. (Further details on construction of the data base are found in the appendixes to chapters 9 and 10.)

Finally, we want to control for cross-plant labor heterogeneity in our production function because plants that use a lot of skilled labor to produce a lot of output per worker are not necessarily more productive than those that rely on unskilled labor and produce less (controlling for capital stocks). Given that we do not observe detailed information on the employees of each establishment, we opt to control for labor heterogeneity by measuring the flow of labor services in "efficiency units" (Griliches and Ringstad 1971). At a given plant, this variable amounts to a weighted sum of the number of hours worked by each employee, the weights being proportional to his or her hourly wage. Since unskilled workers are normalized to have a wage of 1, the flow of labor services in efficiency units can be expressed as total labor costs divided by the wage of unskilled labor.[25] This approach implies that productivity growth due to the accumulation of skilled workers, or productivity growth that increases the wage premium for skilled labor, does *not* show up in our measured productivity series. Hence the figures we report probably understate productivity growth relative to alternative productivity series that measure labor services as total work hours.

Notes

1. In a previous study, Liu (1993) used Chilean data to construct average productivity differentials among entering, exiting, and continuing plants. This chapter goes beyond her work to examine how these differentials aggregate up to sector-level patterns of productivity in countries with different policy regimes.

2. Similar exercises can be done using cost functions and factor prices, but these require the assumption of profit maximization up to some parameterized deviation from optimality.

3. An alternative approach, used by Olley and Pakes (1992), is to assume that follows a first-order Markov process.

4. Equation 4.3 is similar to Baily, Hulten, and Campbell's (1992) equation 3. However, their equation is in logarithms.

5. Although we do not pursue it here, this distinction between input aggregates might be used as a basis for an allocative efficiency index: $\hat{V}_t / D_t$, or, perhaps better, $\hat{V}_t / [\Pi_{j=1}^{J} (\Sigma_{i=1}^{n} X_{jit})^{\beta_j}]$. Under constant returns to scale, it can be shown that this index is a weighted average of plant-specific deviations from the industrywide input ratio, with the weights reflecting the size of the associated plants. Limitations of this index are, first, that the industrywide mix of factor inputs may not minimize costs and, second, that it measures realized allocative efficiency rather than predicted efficiency, given uncertainty and adjustment costs.

6. Although it is not an issue in this chapter, E_t and B_t may differ if constant returns to scale are not imposed when estimating β_j values. Then, changes in scale efficiency show up in Divisia indexes, but not in E_t. The reason is that under increasing returns, the denominator of E_t expands more than proportionately with factor use, exactly offsetting output growth in the numerator due to scale effects, whereas the denominator of B_t is proportional to factor use. In Divisia indexes, constant returns are ensured because factor shares are used to estimate the elasticity of output with respect to factor inputs.

7. For example, in the Chilean food industry, labor's share of total costs is about 10 percent, and capital's share is about 22 percent. (The rest is materials.) But the estimated elasticity of output with respect to labor is 0.21, and the estimated elasticity of output with respect to capital is 0.08.

8. Material price deflators are constructed using dated and relatively aggregated input-output matrices. Moreover, they may not properly capture fluctuations in the price of imported inputs.

9. All of the patterns described here are robust in the sense that they emerge in our industry-by-industry figures too.

10. If variables are measured properly, one would expect to find that E_t series are similar in magnitude for most industries. Factor market arbitrage would shift resources toward those sectors where a bundle of inputs produces an unusually high value of output until discrepancies are roughly eliminated. But the calculated E1 and E2 series imply that some sectors systematically realize levels of productivity as much as *twice* as high as those of other sectors.

11. Tybout (1992) looks at labor productivity rather than total factor productivity. Liu (1993) bases her analysis on *unweighted* averages of technical efficiency, so big incumbent plants are given the same weight as small incumbent plants in the continuing plant aggregates. Also, Liu defines an exiting plant as one that leaves the data base *at some point* during the sample period, but not necessarily the next period. Therefore, incumbents include only plants that survived until 1986.

12. Although more than 15 percent of plants exited each year until 1984, the manufacturingwide market share of these plants never exceeded 3 percent—see chapter 9 for details.

13. Similar phenomena apparently drove survival patterns during Argentina's financial crisis of the early 1980s. Failure prediction models based on financial statements indicate that composition of a firm's balance sheet is a more important determinant of success than its earnings performance (Swanson and Tybout 1988).

14. Productivity among Colombian plants is quite volatile when primary factor efficiency ($E2$) is used as a measure of performance (figures not reported)—some especially unproductive establishments exited the data base in 1982 and 1983.

15. Pooling industries, a regression of G_E on the log of real industrial output yields a t-ratio of 3.94.

16. This selection process is not itself correlated with the business cycle, so it constitutes a source of noise in the regressions that predict G_{EC} and G_{ET} individually as a function of output growth. This is why the sum $G_E = G_{EC} + G_{ET}$ is strongly procyclical, while each component is not.

17. This is true regardless of whether productivity is measured with $E1$ or $E2$. Because these productivity concepts generate qualitatively similar results, only those based on the former are reported.

18. Pooling industries, the t-ratio is 2.95 in a regression of within-plant rates of efficiency growth on industrywide output growth.

19. Estimates of the α_i themselves are inconsistent as n goes to infinity (t fixed) because of the incidental parameters problem. Nonetheless, the E_t series we study are weighted *averages* of the α_i and are themselves consistent as n goes to infinity.

20. Operationally, the dimension of the computational problem is reduced by purging $\ln Y_{it}$ and the input vector $\ln X_{it} = (\ln X_{1it}, \ln X_{2it}, \ldots, \ln X_{Jit})$ of correlation with $(1, t, t^2)$, plant by plant, then performing ordinary least squares using the residual variation in each of these variables to obtain the coefficient vector $\beta = (\beta_1, \beta_2, \ldots, \beta_k)$. The coefficient vectors $\alpha_i = (\alpha_{0i}, \alpha_{1i}, \alpha_{2i})$ are then retrieved with plant-by-plant regressions of the residuals $\ln Y_{it} - \beta' \ln X_{it}$ on $(1, t, t^2)$.

21. Specifically, define
$$\hat{V}_{it} = \left(\prod_{j=1}^{J} X_{jit}^{\hat{\beta}_j / \hat{\mu}} \right) \left(\prod_{j=1}^{J} X_{jit}^{\hat{\beta}_j (1 - \hat{\mu}^{-1})} \right) = V_{it}^* \, \Gamma_{it}$$

where $\hat{\mu} = \Sigma_{j=1}^{J} \hat{\beta}_j$. Then an augmented measure of total factor productivity, E_t, can be defined as the product of a constant returns technical efficiency measure like E_{it} and the scale measure Γ_{it}. The appeal of this methodology is clear—scale effects can be isolated and compared with the unexplained efficiency residual as a source of productivity change. The main disadvantage of this approach is that returns to scale are difficult to identify econometrically with much accuracy (Westbrook and Tybout 1993).

22. More specifically, at least three years of data are needed to identify the vector α_i. Hence plants present in the data base for less than four years do not contribute to the identification of β, and the technology of these plants may differ systematically from that of plants present for four or more years. The potential for bias is most severe in Chile, where capital stock series are not available for plants that entered after 1981. Indeed, using a version of this specification in which productivity is time invariant, Liu (1993) rejects the null hypothesis that factor inputs are not correlated with productivity.

23. Formally testing this assumption would require maintaining the hypothesis that investment is a deterministic function of productivity, conditioned on observables (as in Olley and Pakes 1992) or reliance on asymptotic distributions as t goes to infinity. Neither approach seems promising, in our view.

24. It would be possible to use the returns to scale estimates of Westbrook and Tybout (1993) for input aggregates in Chile and Colombia. We leave this for future work.

25. Operationally, the flow of labor services measured in efficiency units is calculated as $L_u[1 + (Y_s/Y_u)]$ where L_u is the number of unskilled work hours, Y_s is the wage bill for skilled labor, and Y_u is the wage bill for unskilled workers. To see why this amounts to a weighted average of the different labor inputs, note that $Y_s = w_s L_s$ and $Y_u = w_u L_u$, where w_s and w_u are wage rates for skilled and unskilled workers, respectively. Although firms only report two types of labor, this calculation actually deals with heterogeneity across an arbitrary number of labor types, since Y_s is itself a weighted average.

References

Baily, Martin Neil, Charles Hulten, and David Campbell. 1992. "Productivity Dynamics in Manufacturing Plants." *Brookings Papers on Economic Activity: Microeconomics* 187–267.

Berndt, Ernst, and Melvyn Fuss. 1986. "Productivity Measurement with Adjustments for Variations in Capacity Utilization and Other Forms of Temporary Disequilibrium." *Journal of Econometrics* 33: 7–29.

Cornwell, Christopher R., Peter Schmidt, and Robin Sickles. 1990. "Production Frontiers with Cross-Sectional and Time-Series Variation in Efficiency Levels." *Journal of Econometrics* 46: 185–200.

Galvez, Julio, and James R. Tybout. 1985. "The Importance of Being a Grupo." *World Development* 13: 969–94.

Griliches, Zvi, and Jacques Mairese. 1989. "Heterogeneity in Panel Data: Are There Stable Production Functions?" NBER Working Paper 2619. National Bureau of Economic Research, Cambridge, Mass.

Griliches, Zvi, and Vidar Ringstad. 1971. *Economies of Scale and the Form of the Production Function: An Econometric Study of Norwegian Manufacturing Establishment Data.* In John Johnston, Dale W. Jorgenson, and Jean Waelbroeck, eds., *Contributions to Economic Analysis*, vol. 72. Amsterdam: North-Holland.

Liu, Lili. 1993. "Entry-Exit, Learning, and Productivity Change: Evidence from Chile." *Journal of Development Economics* 42: 217–42.

Morrison, Catherine. 1989. "Unraveling the Productivity Slowdown in the U.S., Canada, and Japan: The Effects of Subequilibrium, Scale Economies, and Mark-ups." NBER Working Paper 2993. National Bureau of Economic Research, Cambridge, Mass.

Olley, G. Steven, and Ariel Pakes. 1992. "The Dynamics of Productivity in the Telecommunications Equipment Industry." NBER Working Paper 3977. National Bureau of Economic Research, Cambridge, Mass.

Schmidt, Peter. 1985. "Frontier Production Functions." *Econometric Review* 4: 289–328.

Solow, Robert. 1957. "Technical Change and the Aggregate Production Function." *Review of Economics and Statistics* 39: 312–20.

Swanson, Eric, and James R. Tybout. 1988. "Industrial Bankruptcy Determinants in Argentina." *Studies in Banking and Finance (Annual Supplement to the Journal of Banking and Finance)*: 1–27.

Tybout, James R. 1986. "A Firm-Level Chronicle of Financial Crises in the Southern Cone." *Journal of Development Economics* 24: 371–400.

———. 1992. "Researching the Trade-Productivity Link: New Directions." PRE Discussion Paper 637. Policy Research Department, World Bank, Washington, D.C.

Tybout, James R., and M. Daniel Westbrook. 1995. "Trade Liberalization and the Dimensions of Efficiency Change in Mexican Manufacturing Industries." *Journal of International Economics* 39 (August): 53–78.

Westbrook, M. Daniel, and James R. Tybout. 1993. "Estimating Returns to Scale from Large, Imperfect Panels." *World Bank Economic Review* 7 (1): 85–112.

5

Scale Economies as a Source of Efficiency Gains

James R. Tybout and M. Daniel Westbrook

Internal returns to scale in developing countries are potentially important for two reasons. The first is that unexploited economies of scale open the possibility of gains in productivity. These gains might be reaped by making plants larger or, as emphasized in chapters 2 and 3, by reallocating market shares from smaller plants to larger ones. The second is that increasing internal returns to scale can lead to imperfectly competitive market structures and thereby influence how policy affects pricing behavior, product diversity, productivity, and growth.

Examples of models that embody the first consequence of scale economies abound in the recent trade literature.[1] Trade policy generally shifts the demand schedules facing domestic producers, who react by adjusting their levels of production.[2] Although the direction of adjustment depends on the particular model used and the trade orientation of the sector, numerous (highly stylized) simulation exercises have led economists to expect that trade liberalization will improve scale efficiency.

The trade literature also contains many examples in which the effects of policy depend on market structure, which in turn depends on the presence of increasing internal returns to scale. Among these examples, perhaps the most relevant for developing countries is the "import discipline" hypothesis: market power created by economies of scale is tempered by foreign competition, so trade liberalization moves domestic firms toward average cost pricing.[3] Although the role of scale economies is too indirect to be isolated empirically, various econometric studies have found that import competition does limit price-cost markups. (Chapters 1 and 8 provide details.)

The literature on endogenous growth (Romer 1990; Grossman and Helpman 1991) provides further examples of market structure effects based on increasing internal returns to scale; monopolistic competition allows modelers to endogenize the number of varieties of intermediate products and so the productivity of the final goods sector. Preliminary evidence suggests that these models are empirically relevant (Backus, Kehoe, and Kehoe 1992; Feenstra, Markusen, and Zeile 1992), but again, the importance of scale effects has not been quantified.

Models outside the trade literature have also incorporated scale economies to link policy and performance. The best known is by Rosenstein-Rodan (1943), who posits that traditional (cottage industry) production techniques exhibit constant returns, while modern (factory) techniques are characterized by scale economies and, beyond some threshold level of output, are more efficient. Modernization and scale efficiency thus depend on the level of demand for domestic output. But since demand depends on national income, which in turn depends on the prevalence of "modern" producers, he suggests that a coordination problem may inhibit development: no single producer in a traditional economy has an incentive to modernize first. This notion, later formalized by Murphy, Schliefer, and Vishny (1989), has been used to argue in favor of a "big push" by government to stimulate modernization. We know of no empirical research on the productivity gains from this type of scale effect, but many descriptive studies (for example, Banerji 1978) have found that plants are smaller in developing countries than in industrial ones.

In sum, internal returns to scale are heavily exploited in the literature on trade and development. The one effect that simulation modelers attempt to quantify—potential gains in productivity from the exploitation of scale economy—is often found to be substantial. Nonetheless, little effort is devoted to directly measuring returns to scale in developing countries, either to establish how extensive unexploited scale economies might be or to identify what gains in scale efficiency might be reaped through changes in policy. This chapter attempts to address both issues. In keeping with the orientation of this volume, we give special attention to the evidence gleaned from our large panels of manufacturing plants. The analysis begins with formal definitions of internal returns to scale, identifies their various sources, and reviews alternative approaches to measuring them. Estimates of returns to scale from selected studies are examined to see whether they provide any basis for generalization about the extent of internal returns to scale in various manufacturing industries. The evidence on the empirical significance of scale economies as a potential source of efficiency gain is also explored.

We conclude that internal returns to scale at the typical plant in a developing country are modest and that the scope for improving scale efficiency is more modest still. The reason is that large plants, which are close to minimum efficient scale, account for a disproportionate share of production. Simulation modelers have all ignored this fact and, accord-

ingly, have tended to overstate the gains from scale economy exploitation that are associated with trade liberalization.

A Taxonomy of Internal Returns to Scale

To interpret the empirical evidence on returns to scale, we must be precise about what we mean by scale economies and the technological and
economic forces that lie behind them. The analytical material draws
heavily on Panzar 1989; the description of sources, on Pratten 1988.

The Single-Product Case

In the case of a single output, returns to scale are often defined as the
percentage increase in output (Y) associated with a 1 percent increase in
all elements of the input vector (X). Or, writing the production function
as $Y = f(\lambda X)$, where λ is a scalar, the derivative $d\ln Y / d\ln\lambda$ evaluated at
$\lambda = 1$ is known as the scale elasticity of Y at X. Letting lower-case letters
denote logarithms, letting boldfaced letters indicate vectors, and index-
ing the elements of X with j, the scale elasticity can also be written

$$(5.1) \qquad S = \Sigma_j(\partial y / \partial x_j).$$

The scale elasticity is a purely technological construct that can be calculated without knowledge of the factor price vector (W). Nonetheless,
it is closely related to the firm's long-run cost function,

$$(5.2) \qquad C(Y, W) = \min_X[WX \mid Y = f(X)].$$

Specifically, if the firm employs a cost-minimizing input bundle X at each
level of output, the scale elasticity is the inverse of the elasticity of cost
with respect to output,

$$(5.3) \qquad S = 1 / (\partial c / \partial y),$$

which may also be written as the ratio of average cost to marginal cost.
The equivalence between the scale elasticity and the inverse of cost elasticity with respect to output obtains because cost minimization implies
that real factor prices are equal to the marginal revenue products of the
associated factors (Panzar 1989). If the firm is *not* operating at the cost-
minimizing input bundle (say, because of adjustment costs or uncertainty), there is no simple correspondence between the cost elasticity
with respect to output and the scale elasticity, except in the case of *short-
run* cost minimization in the presence of quasi-fixed inputs.[4]

There are a number of explanations for nonconstant returns to scale; we review the most commonly cited ones and relate them to the algebra above.

Sunk Costs

The first basic source of increasing returns to scale is the spreading of sunk costs that are associated with the initiation of production across longer or more intensive production runs. Examples of sunk costs include research for new product development, the retooling of production facilities, and the training of workers to operate new production lines.[5] Sunk costs differ from fixed costs, which are also incurred in initiating production, in that sunk costs cannot be retrieved and do not increase the scrap value of a liquidated firm.

Declining Marginal Costs

A second cause of returns to scale is higher productivity of the *non*sunk inputs at higher output levels. The most venerable explanation for this is the presence of economies of specialization, which allow firms operating on a larger scale to match inputs more closely to tasks. Economies of specialization are a consequence of indivisibilities.

Declining marginal costs also occur when large machines are more efficient than small ones for technological reasons. Pratten (1988) cites the example of container tanks, whose purchase cost is proportional to surface area, but whose productive capacity is determined by volume. He also notes that the amount of labor required to operate a machine does not always increase in proportion to its productive capacity.

Finally, the law of large numbers may help firms that mass-produce output. Although the breakdown of an individual machine is typically unpredictable, the *rate* of breakdown among a large number of machines may be highly predictable. Hence the need for stocks of replacement parts and repair crews may be proportionately less at large plants. A similar argument holds for inventory stocks and financial assets if large firms are able to diversify across individually unpredictable buyers and suppliers. For example, large corporations hold a relatively smaller fraction of their assets as cash than do small firms.

Several forces work *against* declining marginal costs. One is that large firms with specialized workers may find that the assembly line tasks are repetitive, monitoring is more difficult, and representatives of organized labor are relatively powerful. (Large firms pay workers more; these factors may help to explain why.) Large firms also tend to have more complex managerial structures, which may inhibit quick decisionmaking and create incentives to deviate from profit-maximizing behavior. Finally, supply schedules for some inputs may be upward sloping if the firm is big enough to influence prices in local factor markets.

Learning Effects

Dynamic scale economies are realized when a firm becomes more efficient as it accumulates experience in production. To reconcile this type of scale effect with the algebra of the previous section, one must interpret the input vector X as the *cumulative* total amount of inputs used and Y as cumulative output. Dynamic scale economies can derive from acquired familiarity with technology, improved dexterity among manual laborers, or process innovations that are developed along the way; accordingly, dynamic scale economies are typically irreversible.[6] Because learning effects describe the history of a plant rather than its size, they are conceptually distinct from scale effects, and we will treat them only tangentially hereafter.

Incentive Effects

Finally, by consolidating production vertically, firms may be able to avoid coordination problems that arise and to reduce the transaction costs associated with acquiring inputs and marketing output.

Multiple Outputs and Economies of Scale and Scope

When firms produce multiple products, the extent to which costs fall as firms grow depends not only on technology, but also on the expansion path of the output vector, so measurement of scale elasticities becomes more complex. Panzar (1989) describes generalizations of the expressions for scale elasticities at given product vectors and product-specific returns to scale for individual products or subsets of products. For our purposes, the practical implication of his expressions is that meaningful measures of scale economies at a multiproduct plant depend on the mix of goods being produced, not just the value of output.

Multiple products also allow for the possibility of *economies of scope*, which are said to occur when it is cheaper to produce a bundle of products together than individually. Diseconomies of scope can also occur if the production processes for different bundles get in each other's way. Panzar (1989, p. 16) notes that, when present, economies of scope "magnif[y] the extent of overall economies of scale beyond what would result from a simple weighted sum of product-specific scale economies."

Panzar and Willig (1975 and 1981) and Panzar (1989) identify several sources of economies of scope. One is when at least one factor is a pure public input. That is, once acquired, it can be costlessly used in the production of more than one type of output. Another is when two product lines can jointly satisfy the need for inputs more cheaply than either can in isolation.

Empirical Estimates of Returns to Scale

There are many approaches to estimating returns to scale in the literature, some quite rudimentary. For example, when better data are unavailable, the average size of large plants is often used as an estimate of the minimum efficient scale in each sector (for example, Jenny and Weber 1976; Jacquemin, de Ghellinck, and Huveneers 1980). Alternatively, Stigler (1958) suggests that plants that survive over some long period of time must be efficient and that the size of the smallest survivors marks the minimum efficient scale. Similarly, Lyons (1980) proposes that whenever a firm operates more than one plant, the first plant must have attained minimum efficient scale. These approaches have many obvious defects, so we limit our attention to the two methods that offer the best promise of revealing returns to scale: engineering studies and microeconometric studies. Since this volume is devoted to what we can learn from sets of plant-level panel data, we devote relatively more time to microeconometric studies.

The Engineering Approach

Engineering studies are generally carried out at the process or plant level. They estimate the hypothetical costs that would be incurred by plants of various capacities; output rates are typically set to be cost minimizing at the design scale. These studies are designed to capture the effects of economies associated with the spreading of sunk costs, length of production runs, and scope. Also by design, they often omit sources of economies that are external to the plant, as well as internal economies due to sources not directly technological, such as learning, marketing, and management. Pratten (1988, pp. 28–29) summarizes the engineering approach to measuring returns to scale as follows:

> In order to make engineering estimates the methods of production have to be broken down into individual processes and operations, and the technical basis for economies of scale has to be investigated. Usually it is not possible to describe processes in terms of engineering production functions which are based on scientific laws or experimental data, and so the estimates of the economies of scale for machines, process units, and operations are based on engineers', cost accountants', and managers' estimates of costs. Their estimates are based on operating experience for plants of varying size, the experience of planning and building new plants and expanding plant capacity and general experience of their industry. Estimates of the components of costs, capital, and operating costs for processes and/or for groups of processes, development, first copy or initial costs for products, etc. are assembled for each industry, and are

Table 5.1 Industries Ranked in Descending Order of Engineering Estimates of Returns to Scale

Industry	Scale economies due to			Cost disadvantage[a]		
	Production runs	Establishment size	Firm size	1/3 MES	1/2 MES	2/3 MES
Motor vehicles	x		x	10–15		
Other vehicles	x				8–20	
Chemicals	x			4–19	1–17	
Fibers	x				2.6–12	
Metals		x		11		
Office machinery	x				5–10	
Mechanical engineering	x				3–10	
Electrical engineering	x			4.6–15	4.5–15	
Instrument engineering	x					
Paper, printing, and publishing	x	x			8–36	
Nonmetallic minerals		x		8–11	25–26	
Metal goods	x				5–10	
Rubber and plastics	x			5–10	5–15	
Drinks and tobacco		x		2.2–10		
Food		x				2–21
Other manufacturing industries						
Textiles	x				5–10	
Timber and furniture	x					
Footwear and clothing	x				1.5	
Leather goods	x					

Note: Data are from forty-six studies covering various years. Each study uses only one measure of cost disadvantage.
a. Percentage increase in unit costs at the indicated fraction of minimum efficient scale. Ranges are due to variation over products, processes, countries, and plant size.
Source: Pratten 1988, tables 5.1 and 5.3b.

used to estimate the relationships between unit costs and the various dimensions of scale. . . . The weaknesses of engineering estimates . . . are that they are subject to a margin of error and that they lack rigour. . . . The main advantage of the engineering approach is that it is possible to hold other conditions, such as the state of the arts, . . . constant.

Pratten (1988) regards engineering estimates as reliable for development and production costs at the process or plant level but notes that they are much less well suited to investigating economies associated with multiproduct or multiplant firms. Scherer and Ross (1990, p. 114) echo Pratten's view:

> Substantial effort is required to enforce uniformity of technological assumptions. As with statistical cost function studies, cost and scale relationships may be complicated by product mix variations. Despite these difficulties, carefully executed engineering estimates undoubtedly provide the best single source of information on the cost-scale question.

Engineering studies typically do not report returns to scale in terms of the elasticities presented at the beginning of this chapter. Rather, they attempt to identify the minimum efficient scale and then calculate cost disadvantage ratios that describe the percentage increase in costs associated with reducing production to one-third, half, or two-thirds of that scale.[7]

As Berry (1992) notes, engineering studies are typically narrow in focus and expensive to execute, so many industries have not been systematically studied. That makes it difficult to assess the extent of unexploited scale economies in a particular country under a particular policy regime on the basis of engineering studies alone. Because the evidence is especially sketchy for developing countries, we direct our attention to what is known from engineering studies for industrial countries.

Pratten (1988) offers a recent comprehensive survey of these studies. Drawing on a variety of earlier papers and books, he provides extensive detail on the estimates available at what amounts to the five-digit International Standard Industrial Classification. Pratten reports estimates of cost disadvantage ratios from forty-six distinct studies. He then uses judgment to estimate returns to scale for other industries at the five-digit level that have technological similarities to the industries for which engineering estimates exist. Pratten aggregates up to twenty groups of industries at approximately the two-digit level and notes the main source of returns to scale in each case: production runs, establishment size, or firm size. Table 5.1 summarizes the information contained in his tables. The columns labeled cost disadvantage report the ranges that contain the estimated returns to scale of the forty-six studies cited by Pratten, with each five-digit industry assigned to one of the two-digit groups of industries. Industries are ranked in descending order of scale economies, according to Pratten's judgment.

Several findings displayed in table 5.1 bear notice. The cost disadvantage ranges are sometimes large, reflecting the fact that returns to scale may vary across product lines, technologies, and countries. Also, the rank ordering of cost disadvantages does not square well with the rank ordering that Pratten proposes (1988, table 5.3b). One reason is that he bases his qualitative assessments both on the minimum efficient scale (MES) as a percentage of the output of industries and on the cost gradient below the MES scale. The disparity in ranking of industries and estimated cost disadvantage may also reflect aggregation problems.

Pratten's summary also suggests that most increasing returns derive from the spreading of fixed costs over longer production runs—just the way returns to scale have usually been modeled by trade theorists. For single-product plants, there is no distinction between this source of scale efficiency gain and the spreading of fixed costs over higher levels of gross output. In industries where establishment size matters more than length of production run, there are likely to be start-up costs common to all products, so in these sectors economies of scope may be important.

Perhaps the most important finding is that, with several exceptions, the increases in unit cost associated with suboptimal scale are modest. Among the forty-five products covered by his survey, Pratten finds that at half the minimum efficient scale, costs average about 8 percent above minimum costs. Even this low figure appears to overstate the increase in median cost because the distribution is skewed to the right by a few outlying industries (motor vehicles, wide-body aircraft, and bricks). Eighteen product categories show cost increases of less than 5 percent, thirteen show increases between 5 and 10 percent, eleven show increases between 10 and 15 percent, and only three show more dramatic reductions in efficiency. Overall, then, the pattern confirms Scherer and Ross's (1990, pp. 114–15) conclusion that average cost curves are typically much flatter than they are drawn in textbooks.

The Microeconometric Approach

Econometric estimates of returns to scale are based on the observed association between cost and output or between output and inputs at the plant, firm, sector, or country level. Because studies at the sector or country level cannot distinguish scale economies from changes in market share allocation across heterogeneous plants, nor from technological progress, they are not considered in this chapter. While micro studies avoid some problems that plague aggregate studies, they still suffer from serious identification problems; at best, they identify a blend of scale economies and scope economies that Berry (1992) calls *returns to size*. Even returns to size may not be consistently estimated, depending on problems with measurement error, pooling bias, simultaneity bias, unobserved efficiency effects, and fluctuations in capacity utilization. Nonetheless, when appropriate data and techniques are used, econometric studies of the association between scale and average costs can be revealing.

ECONOMETRIC SPECIFICATIONS OF RETURNS TO SCALE. We organize our discussion by formulating a general stochastic representation of production technologies. Specifically, we assume that the *production and cost functions* for single-product plants in a particular industry take the forms

$$(5.4) \qquad y_{it} = f(x_{it}, z_{it}, t) + \mu_t + \varepsilon_{it}$$

and

$$(5.5) \qquad c_{it} = g(y_{it}, w_{it}, z_{it}, t) + \mu_{it}^* + \varepsilon_{it}^*.$$

The variables X, Y, C, and W were defined earlier (i and t index plants and time, respectively); z_{it} is a vector of exogenous plant characteristics such as location; μ_{it} and μ_{it}^* represent plant-specific efficiency effects known to managers but not observed by econometricians; and ε_{it} and ε_{it}^* are the usual stochastic disturbance terms that include measurement errors in variables on both sides of the equations as well as transitory productivity shocks that are not observed by anybody. For now, we need not specify particular functional forms for $f(\cdot)$ and $g(\cdot)$. Our first concern is to review some methodological issues related to the behavior of the stochastic disturbance terms.[8] This leads naturally to a discussion of alternative estimators and finally to a discussion of the evidence.

One methodological problem arises because managers base decisions concerning inputs and output on more information than is available to econometricians, leading to *simultaneity bias* because of the correlation between the explanatory variables and components of the stochastic disturbance terms (see Marschak and Andrews 1944; Fuss, McFadden, and Mundlak 1978; McElroy 1987; Mundlak 1996). Specifically, adjustment costs mean that changing factor inputs is not costless and that managers must plan ahead. So factor use observed in period t generally reflects managers' period $t - 1$ expectations of future trajectories for plant efficiency (μ_{it}^e), factor prices (w_{it}^e), and desired output levels (y_{it}^e).[9] Thus, ignoring risk considerations, managers' input demand functions might be expressed as the vector[10]

$$(5.6) \qquad x_{it} = h(w_{it}^e, y_{it}^e, z_{it}, x_{it-1}, \mu_{it}^e, t).$$

Simultaneity bias derives from the dependence of factor demands on expected plant efficiency, which is correlated with realized efficiency. In static representations of firm behavior, it is easy to show that $\partial x_i / \partial \mu_i > 0$ (Mundlak 1961; Zellner, Kmenta, and Dreze 1966); recent theories of industrial evolution establish that this result extends to dynamic contexts (Jovanovic 1982; Pakes and Ericson 1987). This positive correlation between μ_{it} and factor demands causes ordinary least squares (OLS) estimates of the production function to overstate returns to scale.

Similar problems arise with cost functions. Positive productivity shocks amount to negative cost function shocks, so in terms of our notation, $\text{cov}(\mu_{it}, \mu_{it}^*) < 0$ and $\text{cov}(\varepsilon_{it}, \varepsilon_{it}^*) < 0$. Hence output, y_{it}, being a function of $\mu_i + \varepsilon_{it}$, is negatively correlated with $\mu_i^* + \varepsilon_{it}^*$, and OLS estimates of cost elasticities with respect to output are biased downward. Again returns to scale estimates are overstated.

Measurement error is a second likely cause of correlation between explanatory variables and disturbances in both cost and production functions. For production functions, the main difficulty is that reported capital stock values are not accurate measures of the flow of capital services, a problem that may be acute when variations in capacity utilization are significant. For a production function in which capital stock is the only regressor measured with error, OLS understates the marginal product of capital and overstates the marginal product of labor; the net effect is understatement of returns to scale (Griliches and Ringstad 1971; Westbrook and Tybout 1993). In a more flexible model, say the translog, where capital stock, squared capital stock, and interactions between capital stock and other variables are present, the direction of the measurement error bias is indeterminate, but likely to go in the same direction.

In the cost function case, the measurement problem is different. Equation 5.5 is based on the assumption that firms minimize their costs over the input bundle, given knowledge of the *realized* w_{it} and y_{it} values. Put differently, this expression assumes that no adjustment costs are associated with changes in input use. But surely there *are* adjustment costs, so equation 5.6 provides a more realistic description of behavior: costs depend on *anticipated* factor prices and output levels. Measurement errors occur, because there is a discrepancy between the *realized* variables that enter the regression and the conceptually correct *expected* variables. In particular, if realized output is an imperfect proxy for the output anticipated when input choices are made, measurement errors may result in understatement of the output coefficient or, equivalently, in overstatement of returns to scale.[11] This type of measurement error is likely to be particularly severe during periods of economic uncertainty and when adjustment costs are significant.

Whether the production function or the cost function is more sensitive to measurement error depends on a variety of factors, including whether short-run or long-run equations are estimated and whether the noise-tosignal ratio is larger for observed capital stocks or for observed output and factor prices. If capital stocks were measured without error, we could argue that short-run cost functions might be less sensitive to measurement error than long-run cost functions, which presume that all factors freely adjust in each period. But even short-run functions are unlikely to avoid the problem entirely.

Finally, the relation between size and efficiency generally depends on the *mix of products* being produced. When the individual product lines are not reported, however, this dimension of plant size is unavoidably intertwined with others in the scale measure. Econometric techniques simply pick up the net effect of changes in the number of products and of changes in the length of the production run as plant size grows. Moreover, if product lines vary systematically with plant size, returns to scale that are product-specific could be masked by samples that span several product lines. This problem is represented by the scatter plots in figure 5.1, which shows several products with increasing returns pooled in a single sample. Of course, the direction of the bias could be reversed by assuming a different configuration for the product-specific scatters.

ALTERNATIVE ECONOMETRIC ESTIMATORS. The best approach to estimating plant-level returns to scale depends on many things: the relative strength of simultaneity bias and measurement error, the importance of sunk costs, the process generating plant-specific technical efficiency, the availability of instruments for addressing simultaneity bias and measurement errors, and the type of data (cross-sectional or panel). These issues may affect production functions and cost functions differently, so we discuss each separately.

We begin with *estimators for production functions.* As is well known, unobservable plant effects (represented by μ_{it}) in production functions introduce simultaneity bias. These effects can be controlled for in several ways. First, instrumental variables correlated with input demands but not with μ might be used. In principle, equation 5.6 provides the relevant instruments; in practice, however, it is difficult to find the data on w and z that are necessary to implement this strategy. Second, when panel data are available and the unobservable plant effects are fixed over time or are deterministic functions of time, the productivity effect can be swept out of the disturbance with one of several data transformations.[12] The first, known as "within" estimation, amounts to purging the explanatory variable matrix of correlation with μ_{it}. If μ is plant-specific but time invariant, purging simply amounts to expressing variables in plant-specific mean deviations. In a more general framework, Cornwell, Schmidt, and Sickles (1990) take μ_{it} to be a plant-specific quadratic function of time; this leads them to purge all right-side variables of correlation with t and t^2, plant by plant, prior to fitting the cost function.

Figure 5.1 Hypothetical Scatterplot Pooling Plants with Different Products

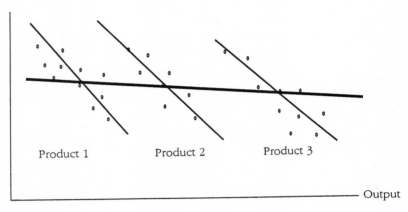

Alternatively, when μ values can be expressed as the sum of a time effect (common to all plants) and a time-invariant plant effect, "*j*th difference" estimation can be used. The *j*th difference estimator is the OLS estimator applied to the dependent and explanatory variables transformed as $d^j y_{it} = y_{it} - y_{it-j}$, and $d^j x_{it} = x_{it} - x_{it-j}$, where d^j is the *j*th difference operator. Differencing sweeps out the unobservable time-invariant plant effects just as the within transformation does.

Unfortunately, since both the within and the *j*th difference estimators exploit only temporal variation in the data, they may not adequately capture scale effects. One reason is that temporal variation identifies only the *marginal* productivity of the factors, so that fixed start-up costs are swept out with other unobservable plant characteristics.[13] If these costs are significant, returns to scale are understated. Second, during periods of changing capacity utilization, much of the variation in the flow of capital services goes unmeasured, introducing an additional source of measurement error. This latter problem highlights a particular drawback of the within and difference estimators, namely that the amount of variation in the data is reduced by the within and difference transformations and that the relative importance of measurement error may be heightened (Griliches and Hausman 1986). Under some fairly general assumptions, the longer difference estimators are subject to smaller measurement error bias than the within estimator. However, even the longest difference estimator ($j = T - 1$) does not eliminate measurement error bias entirely. In contrast, any estimator based exclusively on within-plant variation in the data is not subject to the bias (shown in figure 5.1) that results from pooling multiple products.

Instead of relying on temporal variation, one might exploit cross-plant variation in the data. OLS and between estimators are two simple ways to do so. The between estimates are obtained by performing OLS on the plant-specific means of the data, where the means are taken over all sample years. The OLS and between estimators do capture fixed start-up assets that are reported as part of the capital stock. Disadvantages of these estimators are that, first, they do not control for simultaneity bias due to unobserved plant effects (μ_{it}), and, second, although they are less sensitive to measurement error than temporal estimators (for reasons already discussed), they are not immune. (The between estimator is only sensitive to measurement error that persists over time, since it averages out cyclical errors while maintaining cross-plant variation in the data.)

Although *all* of the estimators mentioned are subject in varying degrees to measurement error bias, that bias can be removed asymptotically by using instrumental variables in each case. For production functions, instruments are required that reflect capacity utilization and are not correlated with transitory productivity shocks: usually no such instruments are available. Westbrook and Tybout (1993) construct long differences of a production function and instrument changes in capital with leads and lags of factor inputs using a generalized method of moments (GMM) estimator suggested by Griliches and Hausman (1986). However, since this approach identifies parameters on the basis of temporal variation only, it misses start-up costs. Moreover, the estimator performs poorly when short-run variation in the data is exploited, probably because measurement error due to the effects of capacity utilization remains.

As with production functions, one can base *estimators for cost functions* on within or difference transformations to eliminate the simultaneity bias in cost function estimators due to unobservable plant-specific efficiency effects. But, as with production functions, these transformations may well exacerbate the measurement error bias. In principle, measurement error bias can be eliminated by using instrumental variables. Unfortunately, the problem of finding appropriate instruments again arises. In the context of long-run cost functions, we require instruments that at once reflect firms' expected levels of output and that are not correlated with transitory productivity shocks and expectational errors. Capital stock may be a useful instrument under these circumstances, because it is a good proxy for firms' expectations regarding future demand, and measurement error in capital is unlikely to be correlated with expectational errors.[14]

It is common to augment econometric cost functions with systems of cost-share equations (from which input-demand equations can be derived) to enhance the efficiency of the estimators. As noted by Mundlak (1996), however, input-demand equations derived in this way do not actually reflect the plant managers' decisions embodied in equation 5.6, so the scale estimators are likely to be inconsistent.

Table 5.2 provides a summary of the biases that may affect the various estimators. We cannot predict whether cost functions or production functions will be more sensitive to any given bias, nor can we predict which source of bias will be more severe for any particular functional form or estimator. Estimators based only on temporal variation in the data (within and difference estimators) deal with the biases due to unobserved plant effects and pooling, but they exacerbate measurement error bias and miss sunk costs. Estimators (OLS and between) that include cross-plant variation do not eliminate the unobserved plant effect or the pooling bias. However, they are probably less sensitive to measurement error bias, and they pick up the start-up cost component of returns to scale. The between estimator is least subject to bias arising from cyclical fluctuations in capacity utilization, since it averages each variable over the entire sample period. Finally, although instrumental

Table 5.2 Sources of Bias in Estimating Production and Cost Functions with Plant-Level Panel Data

Estimator	Failure to capture sunk costs	Pooling across products	Unobserved plants effects	Measurement error
Based on cross-plant variation				
Ordinary least squares	No	Yes	Yes	Yes
Between estimators	No	Yes	Yes	Yes, but attenuated
Instrumental variables, untransformed data	No	Yes	No	No
Instrumental variables, between estimators	No	Yes	No	No
Based on within-plant temporal variation				
Within estimators	Yes	No[a]	No	Yes and likely exacerbated
jth difference	Yes	No[a]	No	Yes and likely exacerbated
Instrumental variables, within estimators	Yes	No[a]	No	No
Instrumental variables, jth difference	Yes	No[a]	No	No

a. Unless the mix of products varies within plants over the sample period.

variables estimators (including GMM estimators) are the solution in principle to the measurement error problems, it is usually impossible to find justifiable instruments that are strongly correlated with the relevant variables.

ECONOMETRIC FINDINGS. Much of the recent plant-level econometric work on returns to scale has focused on a few service network industries, especially electric power generation, telecommunications, and transportation services (air, rail, and trucking). This emphasis reflects the interest of regulators in economies of scale and scope; the greater heterogeneity of other products and the lack of carefully constructed data bases for other industries may also play a role. The work is methodologically interesting, but of little direct use for analyzing the manufacturing sector (see Panzar 1989 for a survey).

A more relevant strand of literature has applied various econometric techniques to estimation of cost and production functions for various manufacturing industries in several countries. This literature can be usefully subdivided into studies that exploit temporal variation in plant-level panels (Dhrymes 1991; Tybout and Westbrook 1992; Westbrook and Tybout 1993)[15] and studies that exploit cross-sectional variation in plant-level data (Griliches and Ringstad 1971; Ringstad 1978; Corbo and Meller 1979; Fuss and Gupta 1981; Baldwin and Gorecki 1986; Tybout, de Melo, and Corbo 1991; Baily, Hulten, and Campbell 1992).[16] Such a dichotomy reflects the susceptibility of alternative estimators to the sources of bias discussed in the previous sections. We review the results of several of these studies and examine them for generalizations about the seriousness of alternative biases, and we attempt to draw some conclusions about the ranking of industries by returns to scale.[17]

For *temporally identified returns to scale*, table 5.3 shows the within and long-difference estimators of translog production and cost functions for fourteen Mexican industries[18] and the within, long-difference, and GMM estimators for Chilean Cobb-Douglas production functions (Westbrook and Tybout 1993). The within estimators of the production functions are too low to be plausible. The long-difference production function estimators are also often low, and they have a high degree of variability. In contrast, the within and long-difference estimators of the cost functions for Mexico are implausibly high. In addition, the GMM estimates (which should be relatively free of measurement error) for Chile are very different from either the corresponding within or long-difference estimators. These observations, together with the fact that measurement error bias affects production and cost functions in opposite directions, suggest that measurement error is indeed a serious problem in both the Chilean and Mexican data sets.

Table 5.3 Within and Long-Difference Estimators of Returns to Scale for Mexico and Chile and Generalized Method of Moments Estimators for Chile

Industry	Mexico Translog production function		Mexico Translog long-run cost function		Chile, Cobb-Douglas production function		
	Within	Long difference	Within	Long difference	Within	Long difference	Generalized method of moments
Food	0.791	0.897	1.507	1.290	0.670	0.692	0.909
Beverages	0.606	0.575	1.840	1.880	0.659	1.381	1.294
Textiles	0.781	0.887	1.938	1.414	0.669	0.745	0.815
Apparel	0.815	0.917	1.380	1.557	0.744	1.077	1.034
Leather, footwear	0.842	0.970	1.425	1.396	0.829	1.110	1.033
Wood	0.963	1.111	1.705	1.266	0.803	0.537	0.890
Paper, printing	0.662	0.912	1.704	1.286	0.584	0.773	0.762
Basic chemicals	0.562	0.697	1.862	1.514	0.420	0.407	0.409
Tires and plastics	0.858	0.807	1.740	1.662	0.865	1.003	0.887
Other nonmetallic minerals	0.838	0.783	1.658	1.597	0.620	0.068	1.066
Metal products	0.780	0.611	1.902	1.983	0.599	0.877	1.166
Nonelectrical machinery	0.695	1.078	2.239	1.819	0.354	0.414	0.376
Electrical equipment	0.945	1.067	1.480	1.442	0.752	0.715	1.057
Transportation equipment	0.782	0.815	1.915	1.518	0.991	1.264	1.217

Note: Data for Mexico cover 1984–90: for Chile, 1979–86.
Source: For Mexico, authors' calculations; for Chile, Westbrook and Tybout 1993.

Table 5.4 contains *cross-sectionally identified* estimators of returns to scale for translog production and cost functions for Mexico (these figures are average returns to scale estimates over all plants in each sector; returns to scale for each plant are calculated at the logarithmic mean input and output levels for that plant over the sample period), nonlinear short-run cost functions for Canada (evaluated at half the minimum efficient scale), and Cobb-Douglas production functions for Canada, Chile, and Norway.[19] Instrumental variables estimates are included for the Canadian and Mexican cost functions. The estimates based on cross-sectional variation yield more sensible and stable results than those based solely on temporal variation: OLS and between estimators both give returns to scale estimates in the range of 0.963 to 1.300. Further, instrumenting the cost functions reduces returns to scale to almost exactly 1.0 in all but a few cases for both Canada and Mexico—the expected result when measurement error biases cost functions toward overstatement of returns to scale.

In our opinion, the cross-sectional estimators dominate the estimators based on temporal variation in the data (table 5.3) for several reasons. First, they appear to be much less sensitive to measurement error. Second, as already noted, cross-sectional estimators pick up the effect of spreading fixed start-up costs. Their main disadvantage is that they do not deal with the simultaneity bias induced by the unobservable plant-specific fixed effects. However, although this should lead to overstatement of returns to scale, the cross-sectional returns to scale do not appear to be implausibly large when the engineering studies are used as a benchmark (table 5.1). In fact, cross-sectional econometric estimators, like the engineering estimates, suggest that internal returns to scale at the "representative" plant are typically modest.

Generalizations across Specifications, Estimators, and Countries

We next investigate whether alternative studies yield returns to scale estimates that rank similarly across estimators, functional forms, or countries. There are several reasons for doing so. First, this exercise will help us to determine whether some sectors typically exhibit unexploited scale economies and whether the pattern of returns to scale differs between industrial countries and developing countries. Second, it will shed light on the magnitude of the biases in alternative estimators.

Correlations among Temporally Identified Estimates of Returns to Scale

Spearman rank correlation coefficients for pairs of temporally identified estimators show that there is no basis for generalizing about the rankings

Table 5.4 Ordinary Least Squares (OLS) and Between Estimators of Returns to Scale for Various Countries

Industry	Mexico[a]						Chile, Cobb-Douglas production function	Norway, Cobb-Douglas production function	Canada		
	Translog production function		Translog long-run cost function		Translog long-run cost function				Short-run cost-function (1965–68)[b]	Cobb-Douglas production function	
	OLS	Between	OLS	Between	OLS and instrumental variable	Between and instrumental variable	OLS	OLS	Instrumental variable	OLS 1970	OLS 1979
Food	1.022	1.013	1.072	1.056	0.966	0.984	1.190	1.034	1.04	1.277	1.269
Beverages	1.028	1.054	1.105	1.096	0.976	1.026	1.346	1.114	—	—	—
Textiles	0.996	0.970	1.085	1.079	0.963	1.016	0.986	1.043	1.01	1.129	1.098
Apparel	1.035	1.041	1.075	1.067	1.008	1.050	1.121	1.142	1.01	1.033	1.039
Leather, footwear	1.069	1.063	1.067	1.053	1.001	0.984	1.139	1.158		1.098	1.096
Wood	1.030	1.048	1.089	1.075	0.996	1.003	1.063	1.116	1.06	1.268	1.256
Paper, printing	1.029	1.016	1.039	1.026	0.992	0.997	1.021	0.980	1.02	1.218	1.222
Basic chemicals	1.047	1.051	1.054	1.057	0.993	1.013	1.105	0.921	1.02		
Tires and plastics	1.080	1.080	1.091	1.074	1.020	1.033	1.080	1.080	1.04		
Other nonmetallic minerals	1.033	1.060	1.053	1.035	0.240	0.950	1.068	1.104		1.161	1.101
Metal products	1.043	1.014	1.093	1.065	0.993	1.001	1.168	1.063	1.12	1.273	1.300
Nonelectrical machinery	1.070	1.089	1.178	1.176	0.993	1.013	1.084	1.091	1.01	1.139	1.135
Electrical equipment	1.079	1.024	1.098	1.077	0.988	0.993	1.048	1.056	1.02	1.048	1.072
Transportation equipment	1.036	1.038	1.061	1.064	1.009	1.025	1.112	1.124	1.11	1.127	1.131
Miscellaneous industries	1.110	1.112	1.113	1.058	1.233	1.049	—	—	1.01	1.083	1.042

— Not available.

Note: Data for Mexico cover 1984–90; for Chile, 1979–86; for Norway, 1963.

a. Average returns to scale estimates over all plants in each sector. Returns to scale for each plant are calculated at the logarithmic mean levels of input and output for that plant over the sample period.

b. Evaluated at half the minimum efficient scale.

Source: Griliches and Ringstad 1971; Fuss and Gupta 1981; Baldwin and Gorecki 1986; Tybout and Westbrook 1992; Westbrook and Tybout 1993.

of industries across countries or functional forms (see table 5.5). Only eleven of twenty-one coefficients are significant at the 20 percent level and ten are negative; four of the negative ones are significant at the 20 percent level. Since the within and long-difference estimators are particularly susceptible to measurement error, bias due to measurement error may be to blame for the lack of cross-country correlation among the rankings of alternative returns to scale estimates, insofar as the measurement errors associated with individual countries and specifications are different. Cross-country differences in the size distribution of plants may also be part of the explanation.

Within countries, these correlations reveal something about the different estimators (see the shaded boxes in table 5.5). For both Chile and Mexico, the within and long-difference production function estimators are significantly correlated, presumably because they both exploit temporal variation in the production data. Similar comments apply to the GMM estimator (which is available only for Chile). Mexican cost function and production function rankings based on temporal estimators are *negatively* correlated, which could result because measurement error bias pushes returns to scale estimates in opposite directions in cost and production functions.

Table 5.5 *Spearman Rank Correlation Coefficients for Pairs of Temporal Estimators*

Estimator	MPL	MCW	MCL	ChPW	ChPL	ChPG
MPW	0.52	-0.54	-0.31	0.73	0.05	0.18
	(0.06)	(0.05)	(0.27)	(0.003)	(0.85)	(0.55)
MPL				0.22	-0.38	-0.40
	(0.31)	(0.57)		(0.44)	(0.19)	(0.16)
MCW		(0.29)	(0.03)	-0.34	-0.18	-0.21
			0.38	(0.23)	(0.53)	(0.45)
MCL			(0.18)	-0.25	0.35	0.37
				(0.38)	(0.21)	(0.20)
ChPW					0.48	0.38
					(0.08)	(0.17)
ChPL						0.72
						(0.004)

Note: Shaded cells contain intracountry correlations; nonshaded cells contain intercountry correlations. Numbers in parentheses are p values. Estimators are defined as follows: *MPW:* Mexico, production function, within estimators; *MPL:* Mexico, production function, long-difference estimators; *MCW:* Mexico, cost function, within estimators; *MCL:* Mexico, cost function, long-difference estimators; *ChPW:* Chile, production function, within estimators; *ChPL:* Chile, production function, long-difference estimators; *ChPG:* Chile, production function, generalized method of moments.

Source: Authors' calculations based on table 5.3.

Table 5.6 Spearman Rank Correlation Coefficients for Pairs of Cross-Sectional Estimators

Estimator	MPB	MCO	MCB	MCO/IV	MCB/IV	ChPO	NPO	CaPO	CaCI
MPO	0.57 (0.03)	0.27 (0.35)	0.11 (0.71)	0.58 (0.03)	0.06 (0.85)	-0.01 (0.97)	0.15 (0.62)	-0.41 (0.19)	-0.27 (0.35)
MPB		0.17 (0.55)	0.13 (0.65)	0.37 (0.19)	0.14 (0.64)	0.13 (0.66)	0.45 (0.10)	-0.32 (0.31)	0.12 (0.70)
MCO			0.89 (0.0001)	0.05 (0.86)	0.34 (0.24)	0.17 (0.55)	0.14 (0.64)	-0.34 (0.28)	-0.42 (0.13)
MCB				0.02 (0.95)	0.55 (0.04)	-0.06 (0.84)	0.12 (0.68)	-0.48 (0.12)	-0.23 (0.42)
MCO/IV					0.50 (0.07)	0.17 (0.55)	0.48 (0.08)	-0.51 (0.09)	-0.10 (0.74)
MCB/IV						0.10 (0.74)	0.21 (0.46)	-0.63 (0.03)	-0.21 (0.48)
ChPO							0.32 (0.26)	-0.09 (0.78)	-0.05 (0.86)
NPO								-0.50 (0.10)	0.08 (0.80)
CaPO[a]									0.62 (0.02)

Note: Shaded cells contain intracountry correlations; unshaded cells contain intercountry correlations. Numbers in parentheses are p values. Estimators are defined as follows: MPO: Mexico, production function, ordinary least squares; MPB: Mexico, production function, between estimator; MCO: Mexico, cost function, ordinary least squares; MCB: Mexico, cost function, between estimator; MCO/IV: Mexico, cost function, ordinary least squares/instrumental variables; MCB/IV: Mexico, cost function, between estimator/instrumental variables; ChPO: Chile, production function, ordinary least squares; NPO: Norway, production function, ordinary least squares; CaPO: Canada, production function, ordinary least squares (1979 data); CaCI: Canada, short-run cost function, ordinary least squares/instrumental variables.

a. CaPO estimates based on 1970 and 1979 data are highly correlated (rank correlation coefficient = 0.96); CaPO estimates based on 1970 correlations with other estimators are qualitatively identical to those of CaPO based on 1979.

Source: Authors' calculations based on table 5.4.

124

Correlations among Cross-Sectionally Identified Estimates of Returns to Scale

Because the cross-sectionally identified estimators are less sensitive to measurement error, and because they better capture scale effects due to sunk costs, they may provide a sounder basis for generalizing about the rankings of industries by unexploited returns to scale (see table 5.6). Intercountry correlations show a weak positive association in rankings for the semi-industrialized countries, but not much. Rankings for Norway are also weakly positively correlated with the rankings of semi-industrialized countries, but Canadian rankings are *negatively* and sometimes significantly associated with the others. Intracountry correlations—which mainly pertain to Mexico—show that rankings of industries *are* always positively correlated across estimation techniques, but the correlations are disappointingly weak in most instances. Although poor cross-country correlations in rankings may partly reflect different plant-size distributions in different countries, poor intracountry correlation can only result from differences in the relative strengths of measurement error bias and simultaneity bias in the different estimators. The troubling message is that we cannot be sure of returns to scale rankings, even within countries. However, since all returns to scale estimators based on cross-plant variation yield figures in a small neighborhood of 1.0 (table 5.4), rankings may not matter much.

Correlations between Temporally and Cross-Sectionally Identified Estimates of Returns to Scale

Next, we ask whether any of the temporally identified estimators are significantly correlated with any of the cross-sectionally identified ones, again using Spearman rank correlation coefficients (see table 5.7). Within countries, most estimators show a weak positive correlation, just as with correlations among cross-sectionally identified estimates of returns to scale. Not surprisingly, correlations between estimators are stronger when both are for cost functions or both are for production functions. Across countries, there is not much association between rankings. The lack of positive intracountry correlation in rankings can be partly attributed to the different effects of the various biases on alternative estimators, and the lack of positive intercountry correlation for similar estimators partly reflects the fact that size distributions of plants are different across countries.

Comparing Engineering and Econometric Estimates of Returns to Scale

Engineering studies provide the most detailed assessment of returns to scale by sector, making them a useful reference point for evaluating

Table 5.7 Spearman Rank Correlation Coefficients for Pairs of Temporal and Cross-Sectional Estimators

Cross-sectional	Temporal						
	MPW	MPL	MCW	MCL	ChPW	ChPL	ChPG
MPO	0.27 (0.34)	0.16 (0.57)	−0.03 (0.91)	0.35 (0.23)	0.16 (0.57)	−0.03 (0.91)	−0.11 (0.71)
MPB	0.12 (0.69)	0.07 (0.82)	−0.00 (0.99)	0.37 (0.19)	0.02 (0.95)	0.11 (0.71)	−0.13 (0.67)
MCO	0.09 (0.77)	0.13 (0.67)	0.28 (0.33)	0.49 (0.08)	−0.00 (0.99)	−0.02 (0.95)	0.11 (0.71)
MCB	−0.00 (0.99)	0.16 (0.59)	0.45 (0.11)	0.37 (0.20)	0.00 (0.99)	−0.09 (0.75)	−0.03 (0.91)
MCO/IV	0.25 (0.38)	0.20 (0.49)	−0.02 (0.93)	0.09 (0.77)	0.52 (0.06)	0.29 (0.31)	−0.04 (0.90)
MCB/IV	−0.22 (0.45)	−0.19 (0.51)	0.36 (0.21)	0.39 (0.16)	0.18 (0.55)	0.31 (0.28)	−0.01 (0.97)
ChPO	−0.25 (0.39)	−0.39 (0.17)	−0.11 (0.71)	0.42 (0.14)	0.04 (0.89)	0.42 (0.13)	0.49 (0.08)
CaPO[a]	0.13 (0.68)	−0.28 (0.38)	−0.08 (0.81)	−0.32 (0.31)	−0.13 (0.68)	−0.29 (0.35)	0.23 (0.47)
NPO	0.43 (0.13)	0.23 (0.43)	−0.24 (0.40)	0.17 (0.55)	0.55 (0.04)	0.62 (0.02)	0.49 (0.07)
CaCI	0.14 (0.64)	−0.15 (0.64)	0.18 (0.56)	−0.05 (0.87)	0.17 (0.57)	−0.07 (0.82)	0.07 (0.81)

Note: Shaded cells contain intracountry correlations; unshaded cells contain intercountry correlations. Numbers in parentheses are p values. Estimators are defined as follows: *MPO:* Mexico, production function, ordinary least squares; *MPB:* Mexico, production function, between estimator; *MCO:* Mexico, cost function, ordinary least squares; *MCB:* Mexico, cost function, between estimator; *MCO/IV:* Mexico, cost function, ordinary least squares/instrumental variables; *MCB/IV:* Mexico, cost function, between estimator/instrumental variables; *ChPO:* Chile, production function, ordinary least squares; *NPO:* Norway, production function, ordinary least squares; *CaPO:* Canada, production function, ordinary least squares (1979 data); *CaCI:* Canada, short-run cost function, ordinary least squares/instrumental variables.

a. *CaPO* estimates based on 1970 and 1979 data are highly correlated (rank correlation coefficient = 0.96); *CaPO* estimates based on 1970 correlations with other estimators are qualitatively identical to those of *CaPO* based on 1979.

Source: Authors' calculations based on tables 5.3 and 5.4.

econometric estimates. Of course, a strong correspondence might not be expected: econometric estimates describe returns to scale for the observed size distribution of firms, but engineering studies measure returns to scale as if all firms were uniformly one-third or half the minimum efficient scale.

As we noted earlier, the engineering studies suggest returns to scale in the neighborhood of 1.05 to 1.10 for most sectors, values roughly consistent with the results for cross-sectional econometric cost and production functions. However, the engineering study figures are far below estimates based on temporally identified cost functions and far above estimates based on temporally identified production functions (unless instruments are used). This suggests that measurement error renders estimators based on simple temporal variation suspect.

Table 5.8 reports Spearman rank correlations between industry rankings based on econometric studies and those based on Pratten's (1988) survey of engineering studies (table 5.1). The associations are very weak, and the strongest ones are negative. We have already discussed two expla-

Table 5.8 Spearman Rank Correlation Coefficients for Pratten's Rankings Based on Engineering Studies with Time-Series and Cross-Sectional Econometric Estimates of Returns to Scale

Estimator	Spearman rank correlation coefficient
Based on cross-sectional variation	
MPO	−0.23 (0.42)
MPB	0.01 (0.96)
MCO	0.13 (0.66)
MCB	0.03 (0.92)
MCOI	0.13 (0.65)
MCBI	0.14 (0.63)
ChPO	0.18 (0.54)
CaPO[a]	−0.28 (0.35)
NPO	0.41 (0.15)
CaCI	−0.38 (0.19)
Based on temporal variation	
MPW	0.41 (0.14)
MPL	0.23 (0.43)
MCW	−0.49 (0.07)
MCL	−0.26 (0.36)
CPW	0.34 (0.24)
CPL	0.26 (0.38)
CPG	0.08 (0.78)

Note: Numbers in parentheses are p values. Estimators are defined as follows: MPO: Mexico, production function, ordinary least squares; MPB: Mexico, production function, between estimator; MCO: Mexico, cost function, ordinary least squares; MCB: Mexico, cost function, between estimator; MCO/IV: Mexico, cost function, ordinary least squares/instrumental variables; MCB/IV: Mexico, cost function, between estimators/instrumental variables; ChPO: Chile, production function, ordinary least squares; NPO: Norway, production function, ordinary least squares; CaPO: Canada, production function, ordinary least squares (1979 data); CaCI: Canada, short-run cost function, ordinary least squares/instrumental variables.

a. CaPO estimates based on 1970 and 1979 data are highly correlated (rank correlation coefficient = 0.96); CaPO estimates based on 1970 correlations with other estimators are qualitatively identical to those of CaPO based on 1979.

Source: Authors' calculations based on tables 5.3 and 5.4 and Pratten 1988.

nations for this finding. One is that each methodology is subject to various biases. Another is that engineering and econometric studies address conceptually distinct questions. A third complicating factor is that Pratten's classifications do not conform precisely with those used in table 5.4.

Conclusions

Two basic messages emerge from our review of empirical evidence on returns to scale. First, both engineering and econometric studies suggest that returns to scale are typically modest, rarely exceeding 1.05 in the relevant size range. Second, although it is hard to identify the sectors that exhibit the highest degree of unexploited scale economies in a particular country, it is even harder to establish stable cross-country ranking of industries by returns to scale. Perhaps these two findings are not surprising, since unexploited scale economies usually create incentives to expand or consolidate production. Nonetheless, they are often ignored, as we detail in the next section.

Evidence on Potential Gains in Scale Efficiency

The review of empirical evidence tells us something about the shape of cost curves. But describing the potential efficiency gains from exploiting scale economies requires complementary information on the size distribution of plants and its relation to policy. We now review the literature that attempts to quantify this link between policy and scale efficiency.[20]

Simulation Findings

By far the most common approach to measuring scale-based efficiency gains is to use computable general equilibrium (CGE) models. And by far the most common exercise performed considers the effects of trade liberalization on plant sizes through the analytical links mentioned at the beginning of the chapter. It is instructive to review briefly the methodologies applied in this literature and the findings they generate.[21] A quick preview of the discussion is presented in table 5.9.

Perhaps the best known attempt to assess the significance of these gains is the work of Harris (1984) and Cox and Harris (1985) on Canada, which builds on the econometric work of Baldwin and Gorecki (1986). They model each industrial sector as monopolistically competitive, with the representative plant characterized by increasing returns to scale.[22] Cost disadvantage ratios—based on averages of engineering and econometric estimates—range from 10 to 25 percent (Harris 1984, p. 1027), implying returns to scale of between 1.10 and 1.25 (see note 7). Trade liberalization forces plants to move down their average

Table 5.9 *Computable General Equilibrium Models of Trade with Internal Returns to Scale*

Study	Country	Scale elasticities in manufacturing[a]	Change in plant size	Change in welfare	Policy experiment
Harris 1984	Canada and rest of the world	1.10–1.25	Production runs increase by about 50 percent	2.7–4.1 percent (unilateral); 6.2–8.6 percent (multilateral)	Remove all protection unilaterally and multilaterally
Smith and Venables 1988 (a partial equilibrium study)	European Community	From Pratten 1988	Average cost falls by anywhere from 0.32 to 3 percent	0.70–2.3 percent	Reduce tariffs or integrate fully
Norman 1990	European Community and European Free Trade Association	European Community, 1.05–1.17; European Free Trade Association, 1.17–1.29	Not reported	European Community, −0.07 – −0.13; European Free Trade Association, 1.64–2.34	
Brown, Deardorff, and Stern 1991	Canada, Mexico, United States	Most sectors, 1.33	Average output per plant goes up from 0.2 to 5 percent in Mexico	Canada, 0 percent; Mexico, 1.6 percent; United States, 0.1 percent	Remove tariffs and nontariff barriers (no foreign direct investment effect)
Condon and de Melo 1991	Composite of Chile and Rep. of Korea	1.035–1.07		2–14 percent of base gross national product, depending on market structure assumptions	Remove quantitative restrictions on imports

(Table continues on the following page.)

Table 5.9 (continued)

Study	Country	Scale elasticities in manufacturing[a]	Change in plant size	Change in welfare	Policy experiment
de Melo and Roland-Holst 1991	Rep. of Korea	1.10–1.20 (depending on the exercise)	Plant size increases from 8 to 32 percent with contestable markets; shrinks slightly with monopolistic competition	Gain in scale efficiency ranges from –0.4 percent (monopolistic competition and low increasing internal returns to scale) to 5.8 percent with contestable markets	Remove all import protection
de Melo and Tarr 1991	Japan, United States, rest of the world	Constant returns except in steel, 1.04, autos 1.11	Not reported	0.5 percent of gross domestic product; scale effects a small fraction of this	Remove voluntary import restraints in steel, textiles, autos
Devarajan and Rodrik 1991	Cameroon	All sectors, 1.25	Not reported	2.0–2.2 percent, of which about 1 percent is scale effects (Cournot competition)	Remove tariffs
Gunasekera and Tyers 1991	Rep. of Korea	Not reported; said to come from several sources	Lengths of production runs increase from 40 and 100 percent	7 percent gain in gross national product (monopolistic competition)	Remove tariffs and export subsidies
Roland-Holst, Reinhardt, and Schiells 1992	Canada, Mexico, and United States	Canada, 1.02–1.25; Mexico, 1.09–1.27; United States, 1.02–1.25	For contestable markets: Canada, 1.2–83.0 percent; Mexico, 0.7–23.5 percent; United States, –0.9–25.0 percent	Canada, 6.75 percent; Mexico, 3.29 percent; United States, 2.55 percent	Remove tariffs and nontariff barriers (no foreign direct investment)

a. The relationship cited in text note 7 is used to convert all calibration information to returns to scale in this table.

130

cost curves because it induces reductions in the price of output according to Eastman and Stykolt (1967) pricing rules. In a typical experiment, the gains are found to be 3.49 percent of gross national product for unilateral tariff dismantling and 7.02 percent for multilateral trade liberalization (Cox and Harris 1985, table 1). Accompanying these improvements in productivity are 20 to 30 percent reductions in average fixed costs and 40 to 70 percent increases in the average length of production run. It is noteworthy that in most industries where net exports fall, output still rises because liberalization intensifies competition.

Less dramatic, but still substantial, scale effects have emerged from recent CGE models of the North America Free Trade Agreement (NAFTA). Roland-Holst, Reinhardt, and Schiells (1992) find that when constant returns are replaced with increasing returns, income gains increase from 4.87 to 6.75 percent for Canada, 2.28 to 3.29 percent for Mexico, and 1.67 to 2.55 percent for the United States (Brown 1992). Returns to scale range from 1.09 to 1.27 for Mexico and from 1.02 to 1.25 for Canada and the United States, depending on the sector. Brown, Deardorff, and Stern (1991) find smaller overall welfare gains of about 1.6 percent for Mexico, which they attribute mostly to the effects of improved scale efficiency. They impute scale economies in their model by assuming that for most manufacturing industries, one-third of total cost is fixed in each country, implying a whopping 33 percent cost disadvantage ratio at the margin. Like Harris (1984) and Cox and Harris (1985), Brown, Deardorff, and Stern (1991, p. 13) find that "Firm output rises in the United States and Canada in every industry." Similarly, it rises in all but four industries in Mexico, "and in all four cases the decline in firm output is trivially small."

Even larger gains have been found for other developing countries. De Melo and Roland-Holst (1991) calculate welfare improvements of up to 10 percent in simulations of trade liberalization for the Republic of Korea. These simulations are based on assumed cost disadvantage ratios of 20 percent. The largest gains come when markets are assumed to be contestable, since this allows the fullest exploitation of scale economies. Similar orders of magnitude are obtained by Gunasekera and Tyers (1991), who use a Harris-like model of Korea, which posits Chamberlinean competition and employs econometrically obtained returns to scale estimates to impute gains from trade liberalization amounting to 7 percent of gross national product. They attribute the gains largely to lengthened production runs and associated exploitation of scale economies. Condon and de Melo (1991) build a generic model of a semi-industrialized country and assume that returns to scale at the margin are about 1.07 in manufacturing industries. They find that quotas generate welfare costs on the order of 6 or 7 percent, depending on whether entry is free and whether there is collusive behavior behind the quota wall.

Finally, Devarajan and Rodrik (1991) assume a cost disadvantage ratio of 33 percent in Cameroonian manufacturing industries but find much smaller gains in scale efficiency from liberalization—on the order of 1 percent of gross national product. Again, plant size increases with liberalization in all imperfectly competitive sectors, even import-competing ones. Since increasing returns are typically limited to manufacturing industries, even these gains in scale are substantial when expressed as a fraction of industrial output.

We should caution that not *all* models with increasing internal returns to scale generate large-scale efficiency gains from liberalization.[23] For example, de Melo and Tarr (1991) assume that only two sectors have increasing returns—steel and autos—and find that most gains from liberalization are due to the transfer of rents from foreign suppliers to home consumers when quotas are removed. Mercenier (1992) and Smith and Venables (1991), studying European integration, also report modest gains in scale efficiency.

Pitfalls in Simulation Modeling

Unfortunately, this literature suffers from several methodological flaws that lead to overstated gains in scale efficiency. First, most of the models with internal returns to scale assume that *all* producers face cost disadvantage ratios averaging at least 10 percent—a figure toward the upper reaches of the engineering estimates and higher than most cross-sectionally based econometric estimates. Ratios this high may in fact describe the large number of small plants in a typical industry, but these plants account for only a small fraction of sectoral output. The bulk of production tends to come from large plants that are close to the minimum efficient scale.

Second, most of the simulations that find that trade liberalization improves scale efficiency have *all* plants expanding with liberalization, import competitors as well as exporters. But this built-in causality from policy to plant size is in doubt (Tybout 1993, pp. 441–43):

> Many studies report that exporters are typically larger than plants oriented toward the domestic market in the same industry [for example, Auguier 1980; Glejser, Jacquemin, and Petit 1980; Tyler 1976; Roberts and Tybout 1991]. Similarly, controlling for domestic market size, there appears to be a positive association between industry-wide plant-size measures and the amount of export activity [Schwalbach 1988; Owen 1983; Muller and Owen 1985; Scherer and others 1975]. These results could mean that bigness facilitates competitiveness in foreign markets. Further, bigger economies have bigger plants [Banerji 1978; Caves 1984; Baldwin and Gorecki 1986; Schwalbach 1988], so large domestic markets may confer a

competitive advantage on potential exporters through increasing internal returns to scale.

Even without increasing internal returns to scale, however, those plants with relatively low marginal costs are likely to be larger and export more (e.g., Krugman 1984); so the data may partly reflect cross-plant differences in learning-by-doing, R&D [research and development], region-specific externalities, capital-stock vintage [Jovanovic and Lach 1989], and luck [Jovanovic 1982]. In fact, I believe that much of the observed correlation between size and exports is due to these factors: in most industries, increasing internal returns to scale only explains a small fraction of measured productivity variation [Baily, Hulten, and Campbell 1992; Mody, Suri, and Sanders 1992; Olley and Pakes 1992; Tybout and Westbrook 1995]. . . .

[Further], trade liberalization also leads to heightened imports, and many econometric studies have found that import penetration is associated with *reduced* plant sizes, controlling for domestic demand [chapter 6 of this volume; Baldwin and Gorecki 1986; Schwalbach 1988; Roberts and Tybout 1991]. Studies correlating plant-size proxies with protection levels or intraindustry trade measures give conflicting messages.[24]

Other Evidence

To avoid the problems associated with the simulation literature, elsewhere we have used a different methodology to measure the gains in scale efficiency in Mexico during 1984–90, a period that spans extensive trade liberalization and so might show significant gains (Tybout and Westbrook 1995). Using econometrically estimated long-run cost functions (summarized in column 4 of table 5.4), the actual size distributions of plants, and actual plant-specific growth rates, we calculate the percentage change in average costs due to scale effects as:

$$(5.7) \qquad \sum_{i=1}^{n} g_i \alpha_i (\eta_i - 1)$$

where g_i is the cumulative growth rate in output for the ith plant between 1984 and 1990, α_i is its share in sectoral total cost, and η_i is its elasticity of cost with respect to output.

Although most industries registered substantial growth in output, in only three of twenty industries did the scale effect account for average cost reductions of more than 2 percent. Interestingly, substantial cost savings in most industries came from sources not related to scale, including the reallocation of market share away from high-cost plants and toward low-cost plants.[25]

Although this study pertains to only one country and time period, the results appear fairly robust. For example, they would not change much if we doubled or *tripled* the degree of scale economies at each plant. Accordingly, it is our impression that the simulation literature has created a mirage of large potential gains from unexploited scale economies by ignoring plant heterogeneity and, in some cases, by using market structure assumptions that lead to implausible adjustments in plant size. If internal scale economies *are* important in developing countries, it is most likely because they lead to imperfectly competitive market structures, which in turn condition pricing behavior, product diversity, and growth.

Conclusions

It is difficult to make decisive empirical statements about internal returns to scale. Results vary widely across studies, depending on the country and time period analyzed, whether cost functions or production functions are used, and whether cross-sectional or temporal variation in the data is exploited. Nonetheless, taking into account the various estimation problems and their severity in different contexts, we find several basic messages in the available evidence. The first is that, although many plants are inefficiently small, the cost disadvantage they suffer is typically modest, rarely exceeding 10 percent in the relevant size range. The second is that the bulk of production in most industries takes place at plants that are nearly scale efficient. Thus unexploited scale economies do not constitute a major source of potential gains in efficiency.

These findings lead us to doubt CGE-based simulation studies that conclude that trade liberalization causes large gains in scale efficiency. They presume returns to scale between 1.10 and 1.33 for the average plant, well above what the econometric and engineering literature suggests. Further, they model each industry as composed of identical plants, all inefficiently small. But as already noted, plants that are small enough to be markedly inefficient do not account for much production, even in developing countries. Finally, in many simulation studies, large gains in scale efficiency can be traced to expansions in plant size for virtually all industries—even those that compete with imports. Yet econometric evidence suggests that import-competing plants contract in the face of heightened foreign competition.

Of course, the finding that average cost curves are relatively flat in the observed plant-size ranges does not mean that scale economies can be ignored. They help to determine the observed size range itself and whether industries are composed of many competitive producers or a few oligopolistic ones. In so doing, they influence pricing behavior, product diversity, geographic concentration, innovation, and growth. Models that assume increasing returns in order to study these phenomena focus on the implications of increasing returns that we view as most important.

Notes

1. Relevant surveys include Helpman 1984, Helpman and Krugman 1985 and 1989, and Krugman 1989. Several collections of seminal papers are also available, for example, Kierzkowski 1984 and Grossman 1992.

2. This link has been explored under a variety of assumptions about market structure, including contestable markets (Helpman and Krugman 1985, chap. 4), monopolistic competition (for example, Krugman 1979), and Cournot oligopoly (for example, Helpman and Krugman 1985, chap. 5).

3. Note 1 provides references. The large literature on strategic trade policy is not particularly relevant to developing countries, because their output levels are typically small relative to global markets, and foreign producers are unlikely to respond to them.

4. Caves, Christensen, and Swanson (1981) obtained the following expression for S based on a short-run cost function: $S = [1 - (\Sigma_k \partial v / \partial z_k)] / (\partial v / \partial y)$, where v is variable costs and z_k is the kth quasi-fixed input. Morrison (1985) shows that this expression is correct only when the production function is homothetic. Oum, Tretheway, and Zhang (1991) propose a method for computing returns to scale from short-run cost functions related to production functions that are not homothetic; they demonstrate their method using airline and railroad data.

5. Sutton (1991) distinguishes between exogenous (technology-based) sunk costs and endogenous (research and development-based or advertising-based) sunk costs. The endogenous sunk costs are choice variables to the firm at the entry stage. To the extent that endogenous sunk costs are important, they can differ across plants and across market equilibria and so, therefore, can sunk cost–based returns to scale.

6. Arrow (1962) developed an early formalization of dynamic scale economies; Malerba (1992) provides a recent survey of the literature and some new empirical findings.

7. If costs take the form $C = F + \alpha Y$, where F is fixed cost and Y is output, then average costs are $(F / Y) + \alpha$, and minimum average cost is simply α. This implies that the cost disadvantage ratio is $F / \alpha Y$, and returns to scale (S) are $C / \alpha Y = (F + \alpha Y) / \alpha Y$, so returns to scale are 1 plus the cost disadvantage ratio.

8. After reading a draft of this section, Mark Roberts called our attention to Mairesse (1990), who makes a number of similar points. The reader may wish to consult his paper as well.

9. Expectations regarding desired level of output y_{it}^e are themselves dependent on the other arguments of the factor demand function, as well as on expectations regarding product market conditions.

10. Note that ε_{it} and ε_{it}^* do not appear as arguments of $h(\cdot)$, because we assume that they are unknown to managers at the time that decisions regarding inputs for period t are made.

11. Griliches and Hausman (1986) invoke a similar logic to explain why labor demand functions are often misspecified.

12. If μ_{it} follows a Markov process unknown to the econometrician, the problem becomes more difficult. Olley and Pakes (1992) develop one approach, but

it requires that investment (or some other observable choice variable to the firm) be a deterministic function of productivity, conditioning on other observables like age of plant.

13. The basic problem is as follows: capital stock consists of a component fixed at the initiation of production and a component that reflects accretions of capital over time, $K = F + S_t$. Temporal estimators relate ΔY to $\Delta K = \Delta S$, but ΔY generally depends on F.

14. Additional instruments are needed to estimate short-run cost functions, since these already contain capital stock as a regressor.

15. Dhrymes (1991) reports results for only three industries, so we do not include those in our tables.

16. Baily, Hulten, and Campbell (1992) focus on the entry, exit, and evolution of plants and on productivity gains due to reallocation of output from low- to high-productivity plants. See chapter 3 for more details.

17. Most of the studies we survey use functional forms too restrictive to allow variation in the degree of scale economies across the plant-size distribution. Hence a single number characterizes returns to scale at all plants.

18. These estimates were originally calculated for the working paper version of Tybout and Westbrook 1995 but were eventually dropped to conserve space: the working paper is Tybout and Westbrook 1992.

19. The Canadian cost function results are based on regression of the log of average variable cost on output and the inverse of output, with annual time dummies included and plant-size dummies used as instruments.

20. This section elaborates arguments made in Tybout 1993.

21. See Richardson 1989 for a more thorough survey and Brown 1992 for a recent analytical survey limited to simulations of the North American Free Trade Agreement.

22. "To account for the downward bias in the econometric estimates, the best-guess estimates of MES [minimum efficiency scale] and CDR [cost disadvantage ratio] used in the model were uniformly scaled up to a position approximately midway between the econometric estimates and the average engineering estimates" (Cox and Harris 1985, p. 124).

23. Much of the variation in percentage gains has to do with the extent to which potential gains in scale efficiency are exploited and, in particular, with the specification of international capital mobility, demand, and pricing rules. Brown (1992) provides an informative discussion of these specification issues.

24. Scherer and others (1975) and Baldwin and Gorecki (1986) find no effect; Caves (1984) finds a negative effect; Roberts and Tybout (1991) find a positive effect; and Tybout, de Melo, and Corbo (1991) find that the effect depends on the measure of size.

25. This finding broadly supports the vision of industrial evolution offered by Jovanovic (1982) and Pakes and McGuire (1992).

References

Arrow, Kenneth. 1962. "The Economic Implications of Learning by Doing." *Review of Economic Studies* 29: 155–74.

Auguier, Antione A. 1980. "Sizes of Firms, Exporting Behavior, and the Structure of French Industry." *Journal of Industrial Economics* 29: 203–18.

Backus, David, Patrick Kehoe, and Timothy Kehoe. 1992. "In Search of Scale Effects in Trade and Growth." Research Department Staff Report 152. Federal Reserve Bank of Minneapolis, Minneapolis, Minn.

Baily, Martin, Charles Hulten, and David Campbell. 1992. "Productivity Dynamics in Manufacturing Plants." *Brookings Papers on Economic Activity: Microeconomics* 187–267.

Baldwin, John, and Paul Gorecki. 1986. *The Role of Scale in Canada–U.S. Productivity Differences in the Manufacturing Sector: 1970–1979.* Toronto: University of Toronto Press.

Banerji, Randev. 1978. "Average Size of Plants in Manufacturing and Capital Intensity: A Cross-Country Analysis by Industry." *Journal of Development Economics* 5: 155–66.

Berry, Albert. 1992. "Firm or Plant Size in the Analysis of Trade and Development." In Gerald K. Helleiner, ed., *Trade Policy, Industrialization, and Development: New Perspectives.* Oxford: Clarendon Press.

Brown, Drucilla. 1992. "The Impact of a North American Free Trade Area: Applied General Equilibrium Models." In Nora Lustig, Barry Bosworth, and Robert Lawrence, eds., *Assessing the Impact of North American Free Trade.* Washington, D.C.: Brookings Institution.

Brown, Drucilla, Alan Deardorff, and Robert Stern. 1991. "A North American Free Trade Agreement: Analytical Issues and a Computational Assessment." Economics Department, Tufts University, Medford, Mass.

Caves, Douglas W., Laurits R. Christensen, and Joseph A. Swanson. 1981. "Productivity Growth, Scale Economies, and Capacity Utilization in U.S. Railroads, 1955–74." *American Economic Review* 71 (5): 994–1002.

Caves, Richard. 1984. "Scale, Openness, and Productivity in Manufacturing." In Richard E. Caves and Lawrence B. Krause, eds., *The Australian Economy: A View from the North.* Washington, D.C.: Brookings Institution.

Condon, Timothy, and Jaime de Melo. 1991. "Industrial Organization Implications of QR Trade Regimes in Developing Countries: Evidence and Welfare Costs." *Empirical Economics* 16: 139–53.

Corbo, Vittorio, and Patricio Meller. 1979. "The Translog Production Function: Some Evidence from Establishment Data." *Journal of Econometrics* 10: 193–99.

Cornwell, Christopher R., Peter Schmidt, and Robin Sickles. 1990. "Production Frontiers with Cross-Sectional and Time Series Variation in Efficiency Levels." *Journal of Econometrics* 46: 185–200.

Cox, David, and Richard Harris. 1985. "Trade Liberalization and Industrial Organization: Some Estimates for Canada." *Journal of Political Economy* 93: 115–45.

de Melo, Jaime, and David Roland-Holst. 1991. "Industrial Organization and Trade Liberalization: Evidence from Korea." In Robert E. Baldwin, ed., *Empirical Studies of Commercial Policy.* Chicago: University of Chicago Press for the National Bureau of Economic Research.

de Melo, Jaime, and David Tarr. 1991. *A General Equilibrium Analysis of Trade Policy.* Cambridge, Mass.: MIT Press.

Devarajan, Shanta, and Dani Rodrik. 1991. "Pro-competitive Effects of Trade Reform: Results from a CGE Model of Cameroon." *European Economic Review* 35: 1157–84.

Dhrymes, Phoebus. 1991. "The Structure of Production Technology Productivity and Aggregation Effects." Discussion Paper 91-5. Center for Economic Studies, Bureau of the Census, U.S. Department of Commerce, Washington, D.C.

Eastman, Harry, and Stefan Stykolt. 1967. *The Tariff and Competition in Canada.* Toronto: MacMillan.

Feenstra, Robert, James Markusen, and William Zeile. 1992. "Accounting for Growth with New Inputs: Theory and Evidence." *American Economic Review (Papers and Proceedings)* 82: 415–21.

Fuss, Melvyn, and V. K. Gupta. 1981. "A Cost Function Approach to Estimation of Minimum Efficient Scale, Returns to Scale, and Suboptimal Capacity: With an Application to Canadian Manufacturing." *European Economic Review* 15 (2): 123–35.

Fuss, Melvyn, Daniel McFadden, and Yair Mundlak. 1978. "Survey of Functional Forms in the Economic Analysis of Production." In Melvyn Fuss and Daniel McFadden, eds., *Production Economics: A Dual Approach to Theory and Applications,* vol. 1, pp. 219–68. Amsterdam: North-Holland.

Glejser, Herbert, Alexis Jacquemin, and Jean Petit. 1980. "Exports in an Imperfect Competition Framework: An Analysis of 1,446 Exporters." *Quarterly Journal of Economics* 94: 507–24.

Griliches, Zvi, and Jerry Hausman. 1986. "Errors in Variables in Panel Data." *Journal of Econometrics* 31 (1): 93–118.

Griliches, Zvi, and Vidar Ringstad. 1971. *Economies of Scale and the Form of the Production Function: An Econometric Study of Norwegian Manufacturing Establishment Data.* In John Johnston, Dale W. Jorgenson, and Jean Waelbroeck, eds., *Contributions to Economic Analysis,* vol. 72. Amsterdam: North-Holland.

Grossman, Gene. 1992. *Imperfect Competition and International Trade.* MIT Press Readings in Economics. Cambridge, Mass.: MIT Press.

Grossman, Gene, and Elhanan Helpman. 1991. *Innovation and Growth in the Global Economy.* Cambridge, Mass.: MIT Press.

Gunasekera, H. Don, and Rod Tyers. 1991. "Imperfect Competition and Returns to Scale in a Newly Industrializing Economy." *Journal of Development Economics* 34: 223–47.

Harris, Richard. 1984. "Applied General Equilibrium Analysis of Small Open Economies with Scale Economies and Imperfect Competition." *American Economic Review* 74: 1016–32.

Helpman, Elhanan. 1984. "Increasing Returns, Imperfect Markets, and Trade Theory." In Ronald Jones and Peter Kenen, eds., *Handbook of International Economics,* vol. 1. Amsterdam: North-Holland.

Helpman, Elhanan, and Paul Krugman. 1985. *Market Structure and Foreign Trade.* Cambridge, Mass.: MIT Press.

———. 1989. *Trade Policy and Market Structure.* Cambridge, Mass.: MIT Press.

Jacquemin, Alexis, Elisabeth de Ghellinck, and Christian Huveneers. 1980. "Concentration and Profitability in a Small, Open Economy." *Journal of Industrial Economics* 29: 131–44.

Jenny, Frederic, and Andre Paul Weber. 1976. "Profit Rates and Structural Variables in French Manufacturing Industries." *European Economic Review* 7: 187–206.

Jovanovic, Boyan. 1982. "Selection and the Evolution of Industry." *Econometrica* 50: 649–70.

Jovanovic, Boyan, and Saul Lach. 1989. "Entry, Exit, and Diffusion with Learning by Doing." *American Economic Review* 79: 690–99.

Kierzkowski, Henryk, ed. 1984. *Monopolistic Competition and International Trade.* Oxford: Oxford University Press.

Krugman, Paul. 1979. "Increasing Returns, Monopolistic Competition, and International Trade." *Journal of International Economics* 9: 469–79.

———. 1984. "Import Protection as Export Promotion." In Henryk Kierzkowski, ed., *Monopolistic Competition and International Trade.* Oxford: Oxford University Press.

———. 1989. "Industrial Organization and International Trade." In Richard Schmalensee and Robert Willig, eds., *Handbook of Industrial Economics,* vol. 2. Amsterdam: North-Holland.

Lyons, B. R. 1980. "A New Measure of Efficient Plant Size in U.K. Manufacturing Industry." *Economica* 47: 19–34.

Mairesse, Jacques. 1990. "Time-Series and Cross-Sectional Estimates on Panel Data: Why Are They Different and Why Should They Be Equal?" In J. Hartog, G. Ridder, and J. Theeuwes, eds., *Panel Data and Labor Market Studies.* Amsterdam: Elsevier Science Publishers B. V. (North-Holland).

Malerba, Franco. 1992. "Learning by Doing and Incremental Technical Change." *Economic Journal* 102: 845–59.

Marschak, Jacob, and W. H. Andrews. 1944. "Random Simultaneous Equations and the Theory of Production." *Econometrica* 12: 649–70.

McElroy, Marjorie B. 1987. "Additive General Error Models for Production, Cost, and Derived Demand or Share Equations." *Journal of Political Economy* 95 (4, August): 737–57.

Mercenier, Jean. 1992. "Can '1992' Reduce Unemployment in Europe: On Welfare and Employment Effects of Europe's Move to a Single Market." CRDE, University of Montreal, Montreal.

Mody, Ashoka, Rajan Suri, and Jerry Sanders. 1992. "Keeping Pace with Change: Organizational and Technological Imperatives." *World Development* 20 (2): 1797–816.

Morrison, Catherine J. 1985. "Primal and Dual Capacity Utilization: Application to Productivity Measurement in the U.S. Automobile Industry." *Journal of Business and Economic Statistics* 3: 312–24.

Muller, Jurgen, and Nicholas Owen. 1985. "The Effect of Trade on Plant Size." In Joachim Schwalbach, ed., *Industry Structure and Performance.* Berlin: Edition Sigma.

Mundlak, Yair. 1961. "Empirical Production Functions Free of Management Bias." *Journal of Farm Economics* 43: 44–56.

———. 1996. "Production Function Estimation: Reviving the Primal." *Econometrica* 64 (March): 431–38.

Murphy, Kevin M., Andrei Schliefer, and Robert W. Vishny. 1989. "Industrialization and the Big Push." *Journal of Political Economy* 97: 1003–26.

Norman, Victor. 1990. "Assessing Trade and Welfare Effects of Trade Liberalization." *European Economic Review* 34: 725–51.

Olley, G. Steven, and Ariel Pakes. 1992. "The Dynamics of Productivity in the Telecommunications Equipment Industry." NBER Working Paper 3977. National Bureau of Economic Research, Cambridge, Mass.

Oum, Tae H., Michael Tretheway, and Yimin Zhang. 1991. "A Note on Capacity Utilization and Measurement of Scale Economies." *Journal of Economic Business and Statistics* 9: 119–23.

Owen, Nicholas. 1983. *Economies of Scale, Competitiveness, and Trade Patterns within the European Community.* Oxford: Clarendon Press.

Pakes, Ariel, and Richard Ericson. 1987. "Empirical Implications of Alternative Models of Firm Dynamics." Social Science Research Institute Working Paper 8803. University of Wisconsin, Madison.

Pakes, Ariel, and Paul McGuire. 1992. "Computing Markov-Perfect Nash Equilibria: Numerical Implications of a Dynamic Product-Differentiated Model." Technical Working Paper 119. National Bureau of Economic Research, Cambridge, Mass.

Panzar, John. 1989. "Technological Determinants of Firm and Industry Structure." In Richard Schmalensee and Robert Willig, eds., *Handbook of Industrial Organization*, vol. 1. Amsterdam: North-Holland.

Panzar, John, and Robert Willig. 1975. "Economies of Scale and Economies of Scope in Multi-Product Production." Economic Discussion Paper 13. Bell Laboratories, Murray Hill, N.J.

———. 1981. "Economies of Scope." *American Economic Review* 71: 268–72.

Pratten, Cliff. 1988. "A Survey of the Economies of Scale." In Commission of the European Communities, *Research on the "Cost" of Non-Europe: Basic Findings,* vol. 2. Brussels: Commission of the European Communities.

Richardson, J. David. 1989. "Empirical Research on Trade Liberalization with Imperfect Competition: A Survey." OECD *Economic Studies* 12: 7–50.

Ringstad, Vidar. 1978. "Economies of Scale and the Form of the Production Function: Some New Estimates." *Scandinavian Journal of Economics* 80: 251–64.

Roberts, Mark J., and James R. Tybout. 1991. "Empirical Studies of Commercial Policy." In Robert E. Baldwin, ed., *Empirical Studies of Commercial Policy.* Chicago: University of Chicago Press for the National Bureau of Economic Research.

Roland-Holst, David, Kenneth Reinhardt, and Clinton Schiells. 1992. "North American Trade Liberalization and the Role of Non-Tariff Barriers." In U.S. International Trade Commission, *Economy-Wide Modeling of the Economic*

Implication of a FTA *with Mexico and a* NAFTA *with Canada and Mexico.* Publication 20436. Washington, D.C.: U.S. International Trade Commission.

Romer, Paul. 1990. "Endogenous Technological Change." *Journal of Political Economy* 98: S71–S102.

Rosenstein-Rodan, Paul N. 1943. "Problems of Industrialization of Eastern and South-Eastern Europe." *Economic Journal* 53: 202–11.

Scherer, Frederic M., and others. 1975. *The Economies of Multi-Plant Operation: An International Comparison Study.* Cambridge, Mass.: Harvard University Press.

Scherer, Frederic M., and David Ross. 1990. *Industrial Market Structure and Economic Performance.* Boston: Houghton-Mifflin.

Schwalbach, Joachim. 1988. "Economies of Scale and Intra-Community Trade." In Commission of the European Communities, *Research on the "Cost" of Non-Europe: Basic Findings,* vol. 2. Brussels: Commission of the European Communities.

Smith, Alistair, and Anthony Venables. 1988. "Completing the Internal Market in the European Community." *European Economic Review* 32: 1501–25.

———. 1991. "Economic Integration and Market Access." *European Economic Review* 35: 388–96.

Stigler, George. 1958. "The Economies of Scale." *Journal of Law and Economics* 54–71.

Sutton, John. 1991. *Sunk Costs and Market Structure: Price Competition, Advertising, and the Evolution of Concentration.* Cambridge, Mass.: MIT Press.

Tybout, James R. 1993. "Internal Returns to Scale as a Source of Comparative Advantage: The Evidence." *American Economic Review: Papers and Proceedings* 83 (May): 440–44.

Tybout, James R., Jaime de Melo, and Vittorio Corbo. 1991. "The Effect of Trade Reforms on Scale and Technical Efficiency: New Evidence from Chile." *Journal of International Economics* 31: 231–50.

Tybout, James R., and M. Daniel Westbrook. 1992. "Trade Liberalization and the Structure of Production in Mexican Manufacturing Industries." Georgetown University Working Paper 92-03. Washington, D.C.

———. 1995. "Trade Liberalization and the Dimensions of Efficiency Change in Mexican Manufacturing Industries." *Journal of International Economics* 39 (August): 53–78.

Tyler, William. 1976. *Manufactured Export Expansion and Industrialization in Brazil.* Tubingen, Germany: J. C. B. Mohr.

Westbrook, M. Daniel, and James R. Tybout. 1993. "Estimating Returns to Scale with Large, Imperfect Panels: An Application to Chilean Manufacturing Industries." *World Bank Economic Review* 7 (1): 85–112.

Zellner, Arnold, Jan Kmenta, and Jacques Dreze. 1966. "Specification and Estimation of Cobb-Douglas Production Function Models." *Econometrica* 34: 784–95.

6

Oligopolistic Firms' Adjustment to Quota Liberalization: Theory and Evidence

Mark A. Dutz

There has been rising agreement over the past few years that determining whether an economy gains from trade liberalization in an environment with imperfectly competitive markets is necessarily an *empirical* question (see the survey by Richardson 1988). That is so because the effects of trade liberalization on resource allocation depend not only on trade policies but also on the nature of oligopolistic interactions and the ease of entry and exit in particular industries. Economic theory alone does not provide a clear answer: whether domestic output and the equilibrium price fall or rise following trade liberalization depends on the assumptions underlying specific theoretical models.[1]

This study explores the extent to which incumbent firms actually adjust their output in response to trade liberalization. In particular, it explores the distribution of output adjustment to industry-specific shocks (here, a reduction in still-binding quota levels), both across asymmetrical firms within a given industry and among industries. Is there a systematic pattern in the output response of firms when import quotas are loosened? Does output contract more in larger firms than in smaller firms, or does it expand? If the size of a firm reflects cost efficiency and large firms are more cost-efficient, then output rationalization following trade reform may improve welfare if resources shift from smaller to larger, more cost-efficient users. At the level of the firm, competing theories explain how contraction differs by size of the firm.[2] At the level of the industry, there is a general presumption that the more competitive the industry, the larger the adjustment in output following an exogenous increase in imports. Highly concentrated industries with substantial rents have scope to compress these rents and may contract output only a little or not at all in response to trade liberalization. More competitive industries have to adjust their output more, since they have no margin of slack to compress rents. This perspective suggests that industry's output response to trade liberalization may reveal information about the degree of competition in the domestic market.[3]

The study is based on a sample of some 750 manufacturing firms drawn from surveys by Morocco's Ministry of Commerce and Industry for the years 1984 (the onset of trade liberalization) and 1987. Morocco was chosen from among industrializing countries that have recently implemented a major trade reform because the annual survey for those two years included a special supplement that collected a great deal of disaggregate data on production. Data were also collected on the value of imports and the degree of quota protection at the same level of disaggregation, which allow them to be matched to the industrial nomenclature. (See the appendix to this chapter for further discussion of the data.) Work at a more aggregate level would mask the simultaneous loosening of quotas on some products and tightening on other products within the same industrial sector. Significant changes in quotas across different industries provide a natural experiment that allows testing the responsiveness of firm-level output as a function of the firm's size before reform.

The evidence from the experience with trade reform in Morocco suggests that contraction of firm output is more pronounced the larger the increase in imports. Both the probability of exit and the percentage contraction in output among surviving firms are larger for small than for large firms. Both these forces provide evidence that resources may be shifting on average from smaller to larger firms in response to an increase in imports. If large firms are more cost-efficient, as both theory and data suggest, such a reallocation of output among firms is likely to be an additional source of welfare gain from trade liberalization.[4]

An Asymmetrical Oligopoly Model of Output Adjustment

The theoretical framework of this study is a domestic oligopoly model of output adjustment among competing firms that differ in their efficiency. Domestic firms in a given industry are assumed to produce a homogeneous good for the home market. A foreign good potentially competes with domestic goods, with a binding quota determining the actual level of imports.[5] In most of the theoretical analysis and in the empirical implementation, the foreign good is assumed to be a perfect substitute for the domestic good.[6] Trade liberalization acts like a shift parameter on the residual demand facing domestic suppliers. A higher level of imports as the quota is relaxed lowers the residual demand for domestic output,

$p(Q, M; \alpha)$, where p is domestic price in the industry, Q is total domestic output, M is the exogenously imposed binding import quota, and α is the shift variable representing an industrywide shock (for example, changes in the price of substitutes or in real national income). Residual demand is downward sloping ($p_Q < 0$) and clearly shifts in as the quota is relaxed ($p_M < 0$). It is assumed that $p_\alpha > 0$. With perfect substitutability between domestic and foreign output, $p_Q = p_M$ and $p_{QQ} = p_{QM}$.

Each domestic firm's technology is summarized by a quadratic cost function. Firms can differ in both the level of sunk capital invested, K_i, and an exogenous efficiency parameter, e_i (representing, for example, differing managerial ability). The general form of firm i's technology can be summarized by the cost function:

$$(6.1) \qquad C(w, q_i, e_i, K_i) = a(w, e_i, K_i) + b(w, e_i, K_i)q_i + f(w, e_i, K_i)q_i^2$$

where q_i is firm i's output and w is the vector of factor prices; $C_{qK}^i < 0$, so additional capital lowers the marginal cost curve, and nonsunk fixed costs are increasing in K. K_i is firm i's choice of equilibrium capacity given anticipated (before liberalization) market conditions. Total and marginal cost are also increasing in e: a better-managed firm is characterized by a lower e.

Firm i's profits are

$$(6.2) \qquad \pi^i(q_i, Q_{-i}, M) \equiv p(q_i + Q_{-i}, M; \alpha)q_i - C(q_i, e_i, K_i)$$

where $Q_{-i} \equiv Q - q_i$, the aggregate industry output of all firms other than firm i. Firms are assumed to behave as Cournot competitors, with the equilibrium being Nash in quantities.[7] Firm i's first-order condition, $\partial \pi^i / \partial q_i = 0$, is

$$(6.3) \qquad p(Q, M; \alpha) + q_i p_Q(Q, M; \alpha) - C_q^i = 0 \qquad i = 1, \ldots n.$$

It is instructive to rewrite equation 6.3 as

$$(6.4) \qquad q_i^*(M, \alpha; e_i, K_i) = \frac{p[Q^*(M, \alpha), M, \alpha] - C_q[q_i^*(M, \alpha), e_i, K_i]}{-p_Q[Q^*(M, \alpha), M, \alpha]}$$

where q_i^* denotes firm i's output at the noncooperative equilibrium, and Q^* is total equilibrium output of all domestic competitors. Firms with lower marginal cost (more capital, better management) have higher levels of equilibrium output. In equilibrium, size of the firm reflects cost-efficiency.

Determining the effect of a small loosening of the quota on firm-level output requires first determining the effect on aggregate output. Totally differentiating firm i's first-order condition (equation 6.3) given that $de_i = dK_i = 0$ yields

$$(6.5) \quad dq_i = -\left(\frac{-p_M - q_i p_{QM}}{C^i_{qq} - p_Q}\right)dM - \left(\frac{-p_Q - q_i p_{QQ}}{C^i_{qq} - p_Q}\right)dQ$$

$$+ \left(\frac{p_\alpha + q_i p_{Q\alpha}}{C^i_{qq} - p_Q}\right)d\alpha = -\gamma_i dM - \lambda_i dQ + \omega_i d\alpha.$$

Two effects arise from the loosening of quotas: a direct effect, as firm i adjusts to the increase in imports, and an indirect effect, as firm i adjusts to the aggregate response of domestic output to the rise in imports; γ_i measures firm i's output response to changes in imports, and λ_i measures its response to changes in aggregate domestic output. An industrywide shock α has an additional impact on firm-level output, captured by ω_i.

For the remainder of the analysis, let $p = p(Q + M; \alpha)$; under this assumption of perfect substitutability between domestic output and imports, $\gamma_i = \lambda_i$, so that $dq_i = -\lambda_i(dQ + dM) + \omega_i d\alpha$. Each firm's change in output therefore depends critically on its λ_i. How much each firm adjusts to the total change in the industry's output $(dQ + dM)$ depends on how these λ_i terms vary with the firm's size. For a given increase in imports, ceteris paribus, small firms bear the brunt of any contraction in the industry's output, if λ_i is decreasing in q_i (the likelihood of this happening is discussed below, in the context of the estimation equation). Note that under two standard assumptions on Cournot equilibrium (Shapiro 1989)—the industry's marginal revenue slopes downward (a weak condition for existence, implying $p_Q + q_i p_{QQ} < 0$), and each firm's residual demand curve intersects its marginal cost curve from above ($C^i_{qq} > p_Q$, a weak stability condition)—$\lambda_i > 0$ for all firms. The sign of ω_i depends on how the industrywide shock affects the slope of the inverse demand curve but is likely to be positive (unless $p_{Q\alpha}$ is sufficiently negative). Summing equation 6.5 across firms and letting $\Lambda \equiv \Sigma_i \lambda_i$ and $\Omega \equiv \Sigma_i \omega_i$ yields:

$$(6.6) \quad dQ = \left(\frac{-\Lambda}{1 + \Lambda}\right)dM + \left(\frac{\Omega}{1 + \Lambda}\right)d\alpha.$$

Ceteris paribus, aggregate domestic output falls in response to an exogenous increase in imports. The effect on aggregate output of a simultaneous industrywide shock $(d\alpha \neq 0)$ is more ambiguous. In the case of a growing economy, where $d\alpha > 0$ represents an increase in real national income, the response by individual firms to a positive aggregate shock (if $\omega_i > 0$ for sufficient firms such that $\Omega > 0$) tends to increase aggregate output. The adjustment of firms to such a positive industrywide shock tends to attenuate the aggregate contraction in response to the trade shock or may even result in a net increase in aggregate output.

The effect of a loosening of the quota on an individual domestic firm's output follows directly by substituting the industry's output response of equation 6.6 into equation 6.5:

$$(6.7) \quad dq_i = \left(\frac{-\lambda_i}{1+\Lambda}\right)dM + \left(\frac{(1+\Lambda)w_i - \lambda_i\Omega}{1+\Lambda}\right)$$

$$d\alpha = \left(\frac{[1/(1+\Lambda)][p_Q + q_i p_{QQ}]}{C^i_{qq} - p_Q}\right)dM$$

$$+ \left(\frac{p_\alpha + q_i p_{Q\alpha} + [(\Omega/1+\Lambda)][p_Q + q_i p_{QQ}]}{C^i_{qq} - p_Q}\right)d\alpha.$$

Each firm's adjustment of output to an increase in imports, ceteris paribus, depends on both industry-specific terms (the slope and curvature of demand functions) and firm-specific terms (equilibrium output before reform and the curvature of the firm's cost function).

In the empirical estimation of this relationship across industries, examining the impact of market share on the percentage adjustment of output, rather than examining the value of production on the level of adjustment, allows magnitudes to be compared across industries. In addition, since equilibrium output across firms depends only on cost variables, it is convenient to express the adjustment equation exclusively in terms of either cost parameters or output. Since the data set contains detailed information on output but limited information on costs, it is preferable to substitute out for C^i_{qq}. Given quadratic costs, C^i_{qq} equals $2f_i$; by substituting the assumed cost function (equation 6.1) for C^i_q in equation 6.3, $2f_i$ can be shown to equal $(p + q_i p_Q - b_i) / q_i$. Substituting this expression into equation 6.7 and expressing the relationship in proportional terms yields

$$(6.8) \quad \frac{dq_i}{q_i} = \left(\frac{[p_Q/(Q + s_i p_{QQ})]}{p - b_i}\frac{(QM)}{1+\Lambda}\right)\frac{dM}{M}$$

$$+ \left(\frac{[p_\alpha/(Q + s_i p_{Q\alpha})] + [\Omega/(1+\Lambda)][p_Q/(Q + s_i p_{QQ})]}{p - b_i}\right)d\alpha$$

where $s_i \equiv q_i/Q$, firm i's market share. This adjustment equation forms the basis of the empirical estimation.

For a given percentage increase in imports, ceteris paribus, a firm's adjustment of output is a function of the firm's size before reform.

Larger firms in Cournot equilibrium are characterized by lower levels of marginal cost, where $C_q^i = b(w, e_i, K_i) + 2f(w, e_i, K_i) q_i$; such firms have a lower e or a larger K. If big firms have lower b than small firms, then the denominator of the first term is larger for big firms. This effect suggests a smaller percentage contraction for big firms. Note that the numerator of the first term is negative if the industry's marginal revenue slopes downward. Therefore, for convex demand, the numerator is less negative for bigger firms, also suggesting a smaller percentage contraction for them.[8] Both effects reinforce each other: the numerator is less negative, and the denominator is larger, for big firms (assuming convex demand and a negative numerator). Under these conditions, *small firms are predicted to contract more in percentage terms than big firms in response to a given percentage increase in imports.*

In the presence of an industrywide shock (when $d\alpha \neq 0$), equation 6.8 highlights the existence of a relationship between firm size and firm adjustment that is independent of the trade shock. For a growing economy or an increase in the price of a substitute, the likely positive second term (unless $p_\alpha > 0$ is sufficiently small, and $p_{Q\alpha}$ is sufficiently negative) attenuates the contraction in firm-level output from the loosening of the quota. The magnitude of the firm-level adjustment to the industrywide shock also depends on the size of firms before reform. The relation between firm size and firm adjustment is more ambiguous here. Again, if big firms have lower b than small firms, then the denominator is larger for big firms. This effect suggests a smaller percentage expansion for big firms. Given that $p_\alpha > 0$, the numerator reinforces this tendency if $p_{Q\alpha} < 0$ (as long as the second part of the term is not significantly less negative for big firms). However, the numerator suggests a larger expansion for big firms if $p_{Q\alpha} > 0$. Although the extent of a firm's adjustment to an industrywide shock clearly depends on the firm's size before the reform, the direction of that dependence within this framework can be determined only at the empirical level. Equation 6.8 underlines the importance of controlling for a more general relationship between size and adjustment in the empirical implementation in order to isolate the import-related effect of size.

For larger changes in imports, the same set of variables that predicts that firms will contract their output also predicts that exit in response to reduced demand will be concentrated among small (high marginal cost) producers. Oligopolistic market structure is not crucial for the predicted relation between a firm's size and adjustment. If the domestic price is the tariff-inclusive world price, then increases in imports reflect reductions in tariffs or world prices. Under the assumption of price-taking behavior and linear marginal costs for firm i of the form in equation 6.1, all firms adjust their output by the same absolute amount, and so small, high a_i firms adjust by a larger proportion.[9]

One important extension to the comparative statics of equilibrium output in response to trade liberalization involves imported intermediate inputs. Typically, products used as inputs by a given industry are liberalized simultaneously with the lowering of trade barriers on the final good. This positive supply shock on the input side should be included in an assessment of the impact of trade liberalization on a particular industry. The simplest way to include concurrent liberalization of intermediate inputs is to consider the change in cost as reducing variable input costs uniformly across all firms within a given industry.[10] If the liberalization of imported inputs lowers costs, then adding such a term has an expansionary effect on the firm's output. The size of the cost-reduction effect also depends on the firm's size. To the extent that small firms are big users of inputs per unit of output, the percentage drop in their costs is larger than that for big firms. Therefore, adding the cost-reducing effect of the liberalization of imported inputs weakens the predicted relation between a firm's size and its adjustment in equation 6.8: a given percentage fall in cost as a result of the liberalization of imported inputs has a larger expansionary effect on smaller firms.[11] However, with convex demand, small firms are predicted to contract more in percentage terms in response to an increase in imports as long as the impact of the output adjustment term captured in equation 6.8 outweighs this additional liberalization effect.[12]

Statistical Framework and Empirical Results

The empirical work focuses on how incumbent firms adjust their output in response to changes in imports following an episode of trade liberalization. The theoretical model used here, with differences in cost explaining differences in size, predicts that firms will contract in response to an increase in imports (the expression multiplied by dM / M in equation 6.8 is negative for all firms) and that, with convex demand and larger firms characterized by a lower efficiency parameter e or a larger quantity of sunk assets K, smaller firms will contract more in percentage terms than larger firms. Under these conditions, a shift in resources from smaller to larger, more cost-efficient firms will improve welfare.

The proportional adjustment equation (equation 6.8) forms the basis of the empirical estimation. It expresses the percentage change in the output of a firm in response to a percentage change in imports as a function of the firm's market share. This effect is examined empirically by estimating a regression model that expresses a firm's growth rate as a function of its market share, the growth in industry imports, and controls for other industry-level changes in demand and cost. The estimated output adjustment equation is:

(6.9)
$$\Delta \ln q_{ij} = \beta_0 + \beta_1 \Delta \ln M_j + \beta_2 [(SH84_{ij})(\Delta \ln M_j)]$$
$$+ \beta_3 SH84_{ij} + \beta_4 F_{j+} \varepsilon_{ij}$$

where $\Delta \ln q_{ij}$ represents the percentage adjustment in the real value of production by firm i in industry j, $\Delta \ln M_j$ represents the percentage adjustment in real imports in industry j, $SH84_{ij}$ represents firm i's share of the value of aggregate domestic production for industry j before reform, and F_j represents a set of industry dummy variables to control for other demand and cost factors.

The model is used to test the two hypotheses mentioned above: (1) the larger the percentage increase in imports, the more significant the percentage contraction in firm-level output, and (2) for convex demand, the smaller the firm, the larger the percentage contraction. To test these hypotheses, equation 6.9 includes both $\Delta \ln M_j$ and an interaction term for $\Delta \ln M_j$ and $SH84_{ij}$. For convex demand, the theoretical model predicts a negative relation between $\Delta \ln q_{ij}$ and $\Delta \ln M_j$ that is less negative the larger the firm: the model therefore predicts a negative coefficient on $\Delta \ln M_j$, but a positive coefficient on the percentage change in imports interacted with the firm's market share. Market share $SH84_{ij}$ is also included by itself to control for the effects of cost heterogeneity on growth patterns, holding demand fixed. These effects are modeled formally by Jovanovic (1982), who shows that if producers have heterogeneous costs and market forces act to select out efficient from inefficient producers, then the size and age of the firm will be systematically correlated with its growth and failure rate.[13]

The industry dummy variables are used to control for other changes in industry-level demand besides imports and for industry-level changes in costs. In addition, a variable that represents the change in firm i's average cost between 1984 and 1987 in the production of product j (ΔAC_{ij}) should be included to capture the potential expansionary effect on output of lower-cost liberalized inputs. However, while the Moroccan industrial data set has detailed figures on production for 1984 and 1987, it contains very little data on costs and none on the costs of material inputs. To the extent that firms in closely related industries use a roughly similar basket of imported inputs, the impact of liberalized inputs on costs will vary systematically across broad groupings of industries. Sector-specific intercepts are included at progressively finer levels of disaggregation (from the two-digit sectoral level to the four-digit activity level).[14] Results are reported for the two-digit sectoral level, with the sample of eighty-two industries grouped into fourteen sectors, since finer levels of disaggregation result in insufficient observations for many groupings and so a loss of degrees of freedom. Although the inclusion of sectoral fixed effects is an imperfect way to control for the change in cost

Table 6.1 *Import-Related Firm-Level Adjustment*

Indicator	Survival equation (maximum likelihood)			Output adjustment equation (ordinary least squares)		
	1	2	3	4	5	6
Intercept	0.087 (0.063)	0.383 (0.288)	-0.064 (0.076)	-13.487 [5.166]	-3.204 [2.576]	-15.150 [3.398]
Percentage change in industry-level imports ($\Delta \ln Mj$)	-0.175 (0.044)	-0.144 (0.051)	-0.104 (0.048)	-2.133 [0.791]	-0.560 [0.421]	-1.419 [0.300]
Firm-level share of percentage change in imports ($SH84_{ij} \cdot \Delta \ln Mj$)	0.644 (0.177)	0.549 (0.181)	0.040 (0.245)	6.845 [2.742]	1.603 [1.462]	1.118 [0.334]
Firm-level market share ($SH84_{ij}$)			1.428 (0.406)			13.552 [3.168]
Inverse Mills's ratio (μ_{ij})				18.508 [6.964]	6.156 [4.393]	18.695 [4.106]
Sectoral fixed effects (F_j)	No	Yes	Yes	No	Yes	Yes

Note: Numbers in parentheses are ordinary least squares standard errors; numbers in brackets are White's (1980) heteroscedasticity-consistent standard errors. The sample consisted of 895 Moroccan firms for the survival equation and 429 for the output adjustment equation; data cover 1984–87.
Source: Author's calculations.

due to the concurrent liberalization of intermediate inputs, it is the only method available given the paucity of data on costs for 1984.

Although it seems most natural to estimate a separate relationship for each industry, the lack of degrees of freedom for industries with few firms and the attendant selection bias introduced by examining only industries with many firms suggest pooling the data across industries while controlling for industry effects. To assess where to allow coefficients to vary across industries and where it may be more efficient to estimate a single coefficient across all industries, a series of F-tests was performed on the various combinations of intercept and slope industry dummy variables for the first two right-hand-side variables in equation 6.9. The hypothesis that all industry coefficients are jointly insignificant cannot be rejected in any of these cases. The implication is that pooling the data and estimating one set of coefficients across industries may be appropriate.

A possibly important statistical issue in estimating equation 6.9 concerns sample censoring. The adjustment of firm-level output, here defined as the logarithmic change in real production value, can only be calculated for firms that did not exit from the data base between 1984 and 1987. More than half (52 percent) of the 895 firm-industry pairs operating in 1984 exited from their given industry at some time over the four years (recall that a given firm exiting from three different industries is recorded as three exits), for a loss of 38 percent of total 1984 production value in these industries.[15] These figures describe *movement out of the data base*. A firm with total sales revenue below DH100,000 employment below ten workers would be dropped from the survey (Morocco's currency is the dirham). A firm switching from one industry to another would appear as an exit from the first. An exiting firm may have been acquired by or merged with another firm. Finally, inconsistent reporting practices or recording errors may have resulted in a firm receiving a new identification code or product code between 1984 and 1987.[16] To correct for possible sample selection bias, Heckman's (1976) two-step estimation method is used.[17] The first step is to estimate a probit model (a *survival equation*), in which a qualitative dependent variable reflects whether $\Delta \ln q_{ij}$ is observed (estimation of this survival equation is of course informative in its own right). The second step is to estimate the *adjustment equation* (equation 6.9) on the censored sample, which now includes the information from the survival equation to correct for the sample selection bias. In this application, the variables in the survival and adjustment equations are the same.[18]

Estimates from the survival equation show that the probability of survival falls as imports rise, as predicted (see table 6.1). When the focus is exclusively on the relation between survival and change in imports (column 1), the coefficient on change in imports is negative and significant.

This negative coefficient together with the coefficient on the cross product of a firm's market share and the change in imports imply that, at the sample mean, a 1 percentage point increase in imports results in a 0.12 percentage point fall in the firm's probability of survival. The probability of exit is higher on average in industries with a larger percentage change in imports. The significant positive coefficient on the interaction term for a firm's market share and the change in imports, in contrast, implies that for a given increase in imports, larger firms have a higher probability of survival. With respect to the choice between surviving or exiting, small firms appear to bear the brunt of adjustment and to exit in greater numbers.

The results are robust to the inclusion of sectoral dummies (column 2). However, when firm size is also controlled for (column 3), the magnitude of the import coefficient is reduced. In that case, expansion of imports still acts to reduce the probability of survival, but the interaction term for the firm's market share and the change in imports is no longer significant. The main conclusion is that once the firm's market share is controlled for, expansion of imports reduces the likelihood of survival for all plants, but there is no evidence that the reduction falls more heavily on small producers.[19]

With respect to the impact of imports on the adjustment of surviving firms (columns 4–6), the estimated coefficient on the inverse Mills's ratio is positive in all three regressions and significantly different from 0 in two of them. These results imply that disturbances in the survival and adjustment equations are positively correlated. The coefficients are therefore expected to be biased, absent appropriate correction. The corrected adjustment equation forms the basis of the analysis. Although this equation exhibits multicollinearity, the estimates are precise enough.[20]

Focusing on the results in column 4, the negative coefficient on the change in imports implies that the percentage contraction in firm-level output is larger, on average, in firms in industries in which increases in imports are larger. The significant negative coefficient on the change in imports, together with the positive coefficient on the interaction term for change in imports and firm market share, implies that a 1 percentage point increase in imports results in a 1.51 percentage point contraction in firm output, when evaluated at the sample means. The positive coefficient on the interaction variable implies that, among surviving firms, small firms contract more in percentage terms than large ones.

The results for the adjustment of surviving firms are less robust to the inclusion of sector dummy variables (column 5) than the results on survival. One reason is that the sample is only half as large as that for the survival equation, so the addition of these dummies leads to less precise estimates; the size of the coefficient on the change in imports and on the interaction term for both the change in imports and firm market share falls once these industry dummies are included. The only variation as a result of imports now arises from intraindustry variation within a given sector rather than from variation across sectors.

However, the results on adjustment of surviving firms are more robust to the inclusion of controls for a firm's market share (column 6) than the results for survival. Size is a significant independent determinant of adjustment, with the positive coefficient implying that larger firms contract less in percentage terms than smaller firms. When a firm's market share is controlled for, the coefficient on the interaction term for market share and imports remains positive and statistically significant, implying, as predicted, that smaller firms contract more in percentage terms than larger firms in response to the increase in imports.[21]

The empirical evidence on within-industry shifts in resources following trade liberalization suggests that import expansion reduces the survival rate of domestic plants and the growth rate of surviving plants, with more of the adjustment among surviving plants falling on small producers. These results are consistent with the theoretical framework. The welfare implications of these within-industry shifts in resources following trade reform depend on the relationship between a firm's size and cost-efficiency.

Because of limited availability of data (particularly on input costs), the analysis of that issue is restricted to measuring the strength of the association between a firm's size and average variable cost (as a proxy for marginal cost). Spearman's rank correlation coefficient is calculated to measure whether smaller-than-average firms have larger-than-average costs:

$$(6.10) \qquad r_s \left[\frac{q84_{ij} - mq84_j}{mq84_j}, \frac{AC84_i - mAC84_j}{mAC84_j} \right]$$

where $q84_{ij}$ is firm i's physical production in 1984 in the six-digit product line j, $AC84_i$ is firm i's average variable cost (proxied by the firm's wage bill divided by the quantity of goods produced),[22] and m prefixes denote mean values for the product line. To the extent that firms within the same finely disaggregated six-digit classification produce goods of similar quality but with different price structures (different markups due to local market power), it is preferable to deflate a firm's wage bill by physical units. Since it is not possible to allocate a given firm's wage bill to its constituent products, it is appropriate to restrict the analysis to firms whose output of a single six-digit product constitutes its primary source of revenue.[23] The highly significant negative correlation coefficient estimated across product lines suggests that larger-than-average firms in a particular product line tend to have lower-than-average costs; the estimated correlation coefficient is −0.39 (significant at the 0.01

level). To estimate a relationship on a product-line by product-line basis, a smaller subsample of nine product lines is examined; all correlation coefficients from this subsample are negative, and three are significantly different from 0 (at the 0.05 confidence interval). Although an inference from this result to a positive relationship between size and efficiency must be very tentative, these findings suggest that larger firms are more cost-efficient, on average, than smaller firms.

Conclusions

As Morocco liberalized its restrictive trade policies over the period 1984 to 1987, the level of imports changed across industries according to the degree of liberalization of each industry. Such an exogenous trade liberalization provides a natural experiment that permits the testing of specific theories about the adjustment of output both across firms within a given industry and across industries. In addition, the relative adjustment of the output of individual firms within a given industry in response to these shocks provides evidence of the underlying shift in resources across firms. Such shifts may represent an additional source of welfare gain to the economy from trade liberalization, if resources shift from relatively less cost-efficient firms to more efficient ones.

The theoretical framework for the study is an oligopoly model in which competing firms are not equally efficient. Loosening a quota on elastically supplied imports will typically cause smaller firms with high marginal costs to contract more than larger firms with low costs (and to have a higher probability of exit), leading to lower industrywide average costs. This rationalization effect is an important component of the welfare impact of trade reform. The econometric studies focus on industries subject to binding import quotas before and after the trade reforms, using product-level data. Work at a more aggregate level would mask the simultaneous loosening of quotas on some products and tightening of quotas on others within the same industrial sector.

The empirical evidence supports the postulated links between imports and adjustment and between a firm's import-related adjustment of output and its size. The probability that a firm will exit an industry increases significantly with an increase in competing imports, although the magnitude of the change does not appear to fall disproportionately on small producers. Surviving firms contract their output in response to import expansion, but the strength of the adjustment varies inversely with their market share before the reform. The estimation of this effect corrects for the censored sample resulting from exit. These results suggest that small firms are more likely to bear the brunt of any aggregate contraction in output in response to an increase in imports. This finding, together with the finding of a positive relationship between a firm's size and efficiency, suggests that the trade reforms in Morocco had the rationalization effects that theory would predict.

These findings represent a first step in the analysis of how firms adjust to trade liberalization. Though it appears that, on average, smaller firms contract more in percentage terms than larger firms in response to a given increase in imports, the impact that adjustments in output between firms have on welfare depends on the aggregate level of shifts in resources within particular industries. One additional element essential to a full understanding of the direction of shifts in resources following trade liberalization would be a careful examination of entry behavior. It is clearly relevant whether entering firms have lower average costs than exiting firms. Detailed empirical analysis of the response of single-firm industries to import liberalization and analysis of export-oriented industries are also productive areas for future work.

Appendix: Data Description and Preparation

The empirical analysis is based on firm-level data collected by Morocco's Ministry of Commerce and Industry for 1984 and 1987 for manufacturing firms employing ten or more workers and for firms with fewer than ten workers but with total sales revenues exceeding DH100,000 (roughly US$10,000, at the average 1984–87 official exchange rate). The surveys contain standard statistics at the firm level by main activity (one observation per firm, where firms are classified according to a four-digit Moroccan industrial nomenclature), including total sales revenue, value of production, total wage bill, and year of establishment. The surveys for 1984 (at the onset of the trade liberalization) and 1987 also contain firm-level data by product (up to six observations per firm, depending on the number of products produced by each firm at the six-digit classification). These more detailed data include value of production, quantity produced, and capacity ("realizable" in terms of quantity). Employment data are not available at this very fine level of disaggregation. Consequently, this study uses production values as a measure of a firm's size and changes in production values (deflated) as a measure of a firm's adjustment. Since the analysis focuses on firm-level adjustment of output, the empirical analysis is limited to these two years. The level of aggregation is the five-digit level in the Moroccan industrial nomenclature (referred to as product groups in the Moroccan nomenclature and as industries in this chapter). This level was chosen because reporting is sometimes inconsistent for the same firm across different six-digit products within the same five-digit industry.

Data on the value of imports and degree of quota protection were collected and matched to the industrial nomenclature at the same level of

Table 6A.1 Summary Statistics, Industry- and Firm-Level Variables

Variable	Number of observations	Mean	Lower quartile	Median	Upper quartile
Industry-level variables					
Percentage change in imports [$\Delta \ln M_j = \ln(M87_j / M84_j)$]	82	1.091 (0.131)	0.136	0.605	1.822
Percentage change in production [$\Delta \ln Q_j = \ln(Q87_j / Q84_j)$]	82	0.016 (0.099)	-0.551	-0.031	0.406
Exit share ($\Sigma q84_{exit} / Q84_j$)	82	0.377 (0.033)	0.061	0.374	0.640
Entry share ($\Sigma q87_{new} / Q84_j$)	82	0.644 (0.196)	0.054	0.182	0.561
Number of firms, 1984	82	10.915 (1.299)	4	7	14
Herfindahl index, 1984 [$\Sigma_i (q84_{ij} / Q84_j)^2$]	82	0.346 (0.021)	0.187	0.294	0.501
Percentage change in Herfindahl index [$(H87_j - H84_j) / H84_j$]	82	0.192 (0.066)	-0.187	0.057	0.399
One-firm concentration, 1984 ($q84_{largest,j} / Q84_j$)	82	0.454	0.302	0.405	0.579
Percentage change in one-firm concentration [$(CR87_j - CR84_j) / CR84_j$]	82	0.190 (0.056)	-0.163	0.089	0.448
Firm-level variables					
Market share ($SH84_{ij} = q84_{ij} / Q84_j$)	895	0.092 (0.005)	0.005	0.022	0.109
Employment, 1984 ($TL84_{ij}$)	741	68.00 (4.60)	10	24	69.5
Adjustment [$\Delta \ln q_{ij} = \ln(q87_{ij} / q84_{ij})$]	429	0.166 (0.052)	-0.378	0.144	0.620

Note: Numbers in parentheses are standard errors.
Source: Author's calculations.

disaggregation.[24] Data on imports cover only one of the three import regimes in Morocco, goods imported directly for domestic use. Nonetheless, these data reflect the main impact of trade liberalization policies because a second category, goods imported under the temporary admission regime, benefited from free-trade status before the trade reforms and throughout the liberalization period, while goods in the third category, those imported under the industrial investment codes (specific capital goods), were exempt from customs duties. Nor is there any evidence of major shifts in the classification of goods between import regimes. The variable for degree of quota protection summarizes whether the products contained within a given industry could be imported freely (list A) or under some quantitative restriction (list B, importable under license authorization, or list C, prohibited). Unfortunately, no data are available on the actual quota per product. For each of the two years, the quota variable records the share of six-digit codes within a given industry that were under a controlled list (B or C). In practice, the correlation between a loosening of quotas as captured by this quota variable and a corresponding increase in imports is not as strong as would be expected since it is common for a larger or smaller number of import licenses to be granted with no corresponding movement between lists.

The study examines the behavior of firms in industries dominated by private ownership and not subject to heavy government regulation of prices.[25] Industries were selected on the basis of import and export behavior, with the focus on industries in which import competition appears to be important and to have increased. Industries in which the real value of imports fell between 1984 and 1987 were excluded, except where import quotas were concurrently tightened. Furthermore, the sample under consideration was restricted to industries that were domestically oriented, that is, whose exports accounted for less than 10 percent of production.[26] Since the study attempts to determine the variables affecting adjustment of incumbent firms within particular industries, industries that disappeared from the data set between 1984 and 1987 and those that appeared after 1984 were excluded. Finally, since the study focuses on a firm's size as an important determinant of adjustment, single-firm industries and industries in which the entire population of incumbents exited were also excluded. The sample under study, then, consists of eighty-two five-digit industries with 741 firms in 1984. Since more than 40 percent of the firms produced output in more than one industry, the number of observations is higher than the number of industries (if a given firm produced output in three industries, it is counted three times). There are 895 observations in the sample of eighty-two industries in 1984.

Some summary statistics on relevant firm and industry variables are reported in table 6A.1 (number of observations, sample mean, and quartiles for each variable). All percentage changes in production and imports are expressed in real terms, with 1987 values deflated by two-digit sectoral deflators for domestic production values and by three-digit subsectoral deflators for import values. The industries under consideration were characterized by increasing imports, with the median industry in 1987 experiencing a roughly 80 percent real increase over the 1984 level of imports (in a few instances, products were moved from the freely importable list to a more restricted list requiring licenses). While the aggregate domestic value of production declined in real terms for more than half the industries, domestic production expanded in the remaining industries. This effect can no doubt be attributed in part to the liberalization of inputs imported by these industries, though available data do not allow this effect to be isolated.

The exit share variable captures the value of 1984 domestic production in each industry accounted for by exiting firms (firms that were no longer recorded in a particular industry in the 1987 data set). The entry share variable captures the value of production accounted for by new entrants between 1984 and 1987 as a share of 1984 production. At the median, firms exiting the industry by 1987 accounted for slightly less than 40 percent of the value of the industry's output in 1984; concurrently, the production of new entrants at the median accounted for slightly less than 20 percent of the value of the industry's output in 1984 (see chapter 7 for further discussion of entry and exit patterns in Morocco). Industry-level statistics also reveal the concentrated structure of most industries in the sample. The median industry in 1984 consisted of seven firms, and concentration increased between 1984 and 1987, as measured by changes in the Herfindahl index and in the one-firm concentration index (the percentage of total sales in the industry accounted for by the largest firm in each year).

The firm adjustment variable, $\Delta \ln q_{ij} = \ln(q87_{ij} \,/\, q84_{ij})$, representing percentage adjustment in real value of production by firm i in industry j, is clearly only available for surviving firms. Firms below the twenty-fifth percentile were very small, as measured by firm-level market share and employment. One-quarter of firms in the sample hired between 1 and 10 employees, one-quarter hired between 10 and 25 employees, and another quarter hired between 25 and 70 employees. The largest firm hired roughly 1,400 employees.

Notes

This chapter is part of the World Bank research project "Industrial Competition, Productive Efficiency, and Their Relation to Trade Regimes." I am very grateful for helpful comments and discussions with Tim Besley, Tom Bogart, David Card, John DiNardo, Avinash Dixit, Gene Grossman, Guy Lacroix, Thomas Lemieux, Ceyla Pazarbasioglu, Mark Roberts, Daniel Sullivan, Jim Tybout, and Robert

Willig. I also thank participants at seminars at New York University's Stern School of Business, Princeton University, Queen's University, and the World Bank for comments. I appreciate the opportunity to use data from the Moroccan Ministry of Commerce and Industry. Financial support from the Social Sciences and Humanities Research Council of Canada and from a Sloan grant to the International Finance Section at Princeton University is gratefully acknowledged.

1. In a symmetric oligopoly model, Buffie and Spiller (1986) show that in the short run a rise in the output of domestic firms in response to an increase in imports is consistent with existence and stability conditions. For price to increase in the long run in their model, the degree of competition (as captured by a firm-specific conjectural variations parameter) must increase as the number of firms falls.

2. See Lieberman 1990 for a review of theoretical findings on divestment in declining industries. Differences in efficiency among firms, with larger firms being more cost-efficient than smaller ones, would cause smaller producers to exit earlier during a decline in demand. However, in a Cournot-Nash model where firms are equally efficient and under the assumption of an all-or-nothing reduction in capacity, larger firms exit first, since smaller firms can remain profitable over a longer period as demand falls to zero. Under a similar model but with continuous capacity adjustment, larger firms reduce capacity first; subsequent reductions in capacity as demand continues to fall are predicted to be identical across firms (see Ghemawat and Nalebuff 1987).

3. Roberts and Tybout (1991) examine patterns of rationalization using plant-level data for Chile and Colombia. They find that an increase in import competition reduces the size of all plants, particularly in the long run, but that conclusions about whether small or large producers reduce their size more depend on how import competition is measured. They do find that industries in which domestic producers have high rates of entry and exit adjust less in response to changes in imports.

4. This study provides evidence that rationalization (in the sense of a reallocation of output from smaller to larger incumbent firms) occurred following a particular episode of trade liberalization. Further work is needed to combine these results with the effect that the behavior of new entrants had on welfare.

5. What is crucial is that the international price be low enough so that the quota is always filled.

6. This assumption seems appropriate given the disaggregate data on production and imports that are available for the empirical study. If the imported good is an imperfect substitute for the domestic good within a given industry, domestic firms retain more market power as the quantitative trade barrier is relaxed than they do in the case of perfect substitutes.

7. The analysis can be generalized in a straightforward fashion to include conjectural variation equilibria, allowing for more or less aggressive behavior by firms.

8. The assumption of convex demand seems more appropriate than linear or concave demand as a working assumption to determine the likely direction of firm-level adjustment; isoelastic demand functions, for example, in general seem to fit data much better than linear functions.

9. More sophisticated, dynamic models are required for a detailed analysis of exit decisions given the irreversibility of asset dissolution. See Dixit 1989 for a

careful theoretical treatment of optimal inertia in investment decisions under
uncertainty. When the price of output follows a random walk, the exit trigger
price is less than the variable cost minus the interest on the exit cost; the entry
trigger price correspondingly exceeds variable cost. This band around the pre-
dictions of a static model suggests a forward-looking perspective on the variance
of cost and demand as they affect firm-level profitability. However, lacking such
proxies in the Moroccan data, this industry-specific noise is absorbed into industry dummies or the error term.

10. In practice, different firms within an industry may rely on imported inputs
to different degrees. The inclusion of data on changes in firm-level average unit
cost, if available, would control for these differences across firms in the empirical implementation.

11. For an illustrative example of the analytics of simultaneous liberalization
of intermediate inputs, see the appendix in Dutz 1991.

12. It is a plausible conjecture that small firms may be less involved in trade in
their role as importers of intermediate inputs. Such a conjecture would
strengthen the presumption that small firms contract more, in percentage terms.

13. In empirical studies based on the Jovanovic model, Dunne, Roberts, and
Samuelson (1989) and Evans (1987a and 1987b) find that the growth and failure rates of firms or plants are negatively correlated with size.

14. While the fixed effects capture the average change in unit cost for firms
within a given sector, they also capture differences in productivity and technology and changes in markups, among other effects, to the extent that they vary
across sectors.

15. These figures may seem high when compared with other empirical evidence on exiting firms. In a Wisconsin panel of industries, 45 percent of firms
active in 1978 exited over the subsequent eight-year period (Pakes and Ericson
1987, table 1). In Colombia over the period 1977–85, an average of almost 22
percent of new plants exited each year. The percentage of exiting plants
decreased as plants aged, stabilizing at approximately 13 percent a year for
plants more than three years old (chapter 10). However, in contrast to other
studies, the sample of industries under consideration here is restricted to import-
competing industries experiencing a substantial increase in imports over the
given four-year period.

16. Examination of the data reveals many such cases across different six-digit
products within the same five-digit level of aggregation. This was the main reason for choosing to work at the five-digit level of aggregation.

17. For an exposition, see Amemiya 1985, pp. 368–72, and Maddala 1983,
pp. 231–34; for recent applications to the relationship between the growth and
size of firms, see Evans 1987a and 1987b and Hall 1987. Evans and Hall find
that corrections for plant failure have little effect on the estimated coefficients in
the growth equation.

18. Absent certain firm-level financial variables (which are not available in the
present Moroccan data set), it is not clear which of the remaining real-side variables might explain the decision of firms to exit, but not the decision of surviving firms to adjust.

19. See Dutz 1991 for results on alternate specifications. When total employment is used to control for the general effect of a firm's size, the probability of
survival in response to the loosening of quotas is once again significantly lower
for smaller firms. Total employment as a measure of a firm's size is a much less

significant independent determinant of survival than of market share, perhaps because this variable is not disaggregated according to the different industries in which a given firm operates.

20. Collinearity diagnostics, including an examination of the eigenvalues of the first moments matrix and the principal components of estimate variances, highlight that the inverse Mills's ratio, μ_{ij}, is highly collinear with other regressors, in particular the constant term.

21. As in the survival equations, the impact of a firm's size on import-related adjustment (as captured by the interaction term for imports and size of the firm) is much stronger when the employment measure of size is used as a control (Dutz 1991).

22. Such a proxy is more appropriate the more likely it is that the firm's labor costs are proportional to total variable costs.

23. The correlation coefficient is estimated on 343 firm-product observations, where the firm's revenues from a single product account for at least 90 percent of total revenues.

24. Since a complete set of trade data from Morocco is not available, data used as an input to a World Bank study are used. Trade data for 1987 at this level of disaggregation are not available, so 1986 data are used. Data for 1986, however, seem to be a good instrument for 1987, since at a more aggregate level (the three-digit subsector), 1987 figures are very similar to 1986 figures; according to these aggregate figures, the largest changes in imports occurred between 1984 and 1986.

25. Due to the limited availability of data, the relevant industries satisfying this and the following criteria are chosen based on the more aggregate three-digit subsector classification. Subsectors with more than 50 percent state ownership or subject to major government price regulation include fertilizer, pulp and paper, sugar, tobacco, edible oils, grain processing, bakeries, milk, animal feed, cement, and chemicals.

26. The impact of trade liberalization is expected to be very different in export-oriented sectors that benefit from temporary admission schemes (duty-free import of all inputs, with no license required for imports otherwise subject to quota or prohibited).

References

Amemiya, Takeshi. 1985. *Advanced Econometrics*. Oxford: Basil Blackwell.

Buffie, Edward F., and Pablo T. Spiller. 1986. "Trade Liberalization in Oligopolistic Industries: The Quota Case." *Journal of International Economics* 20: 65–81.

Dixit, Avinash. 1989. "Entry and Exit Decisions under Uncertainty." *Journal of Political Economy* 97: 620–38.

Dunne, Timothy, Mark Roberts, and Larry Samuelson. 1989. "The Growth and Failure of U.S. Manufacturing Plants." *Quarterly Journal of Economics* 104: 671–98.

Dutz, Mark A. 1991. "Firm Output Adjustment to Trade Liberalization: Theory with Application to the Moroccan Experience." Policy Research Working

Paper 602. Trade Policy Division, Policy Research Department, World Bank, Washington, D.C.

Evans, David S. 1987a. "The Relationship between Firm Growth, Size, and Age: Estimates for 100 Manufacturing Industries." *Journal of Industrial Economics* 35: 567–82.

———. 1987b. "Tests of Alternative Theories of Firm Growth." *Journal of Political Economy* 95: 657–74.

Ghemawat, Pankaj, and Barry Nalebuff. 1987. "The Devolution of Declining Industries." Discussion Paper 120. Woodrow Wilson School, Princeton University, Princeton, N.J.

Hall, Bronwyn. 1987. "The Relationship between Firm Size and Firm Growth in the U.S. Manufacturing Sector." *Journal of Industrial Economics* 35: 583–606.

Heckman, James J. 1976. "The Common Structure of Statistical Models of Truncation, Sample Selection, and Limited Dependent Variables and a Simple Estimation for Such Models." *Annals of Economic and Social Measurement* 5: 475–92.

Jovanovic, Boyan. 1982. "Selection and Evolution of Industry." *Econometrica* 50: 649–70.

Lieberman, Marvin B. 1990. "Divestment in Declining Industries: Shakeout or Stakeout." *Rand Journal of Economics* 21: 538–54.

Maddala, G. S. 1983. *Limited-Dependent and Qualitative Variables in Econometrics*. Cambridge, U.K.: Cambridge University Press.

Pakes, Ariel, and Richard Ericson. 1987. "Empirical Implications of Alternative Models of Firm Dynamics." Social Science Research Institute Working Paper 8803. Social Science Research Institute, University of Wisconsin, Madison.

Richardson, J. David. 1988. "Empirical Research on Trade Liberalization with Imperfect Competition: A Survey." Department of Economics, University of Wisconsin, Madison.

Roberts, Mark J., and James R. Tybout. 1991. "Size Rationalization and Trade Exposure in Developing Countries." In Robert E. Baldwin, ed., *Empirical Studies of Commercial Policy*. Chicago: University of Chicago Press.

Shapiro, Carl. 1989. "Theories of Oligopoly Behavior." In Richard Schmalensee and Robert D. Willig, eds., *Handbook of Industrial Organization*. Amsterdam: North-Holland.

White, Halbert. 1980. "A Heteroscedasticity-Consistent Covariance Matrix Estimator and a Direct Test for Heteroscedasticity." *Econometrica* 48: 817–38.

7

Determinants and Effects of Direct Foreign Investment in Côte d'Ivoire, Morocco, and Venezuela

Ann Harrison

The virtual disappearance of commercial bank lending to developing countries in the 1980s created a resurgence of interest in direct foreign investment. The need for alternative sources of capital, combined with an increasing skepticism about import-substituting trade strategies, led many developing countries to liberalize restrictions on incoming foreign investment. Some countries even tilted the balance toward foreign firms by offering special incentives: in the Czech Republic, joint ventures pay lower income taxes than domestic enterprises; in much of the Caribbean, foreign firms receive income tax holidays, exemptions from import duties, and subsidies for infrastructure.

Are such subsidies justified? Foreign investment may generate a number of benefits for the host country: by financing the expansion of business or the creation of new firms, it increases employment; it may lead to the transfer of knowledge or new technologies from foreign to domestic firms; and it may provide critical know-how to enable domestic plants to enter export markets. If foreign firms introduce new products or processes to the domestic market, domestic firms may benefit from the accelerated diffusion of new technology (see Caves 1982 and Helleiner 1989 for surveys on the transfer of technology). In some cases, domestic firms may increase their productivity simply by observing foreign firms in the region. Diffusion may also occur through turnover of labor, as employees move from foreign to domestic firms. If this spillover benefit is not completely internalized by the incoming firm, some type of subsidy could be justified. The expectation that foreign investment may serve as a catalyst for domestic production rationalizes policies in economies as diverse as those of Bulgaria and Taiwan (China), whose governments offer special treatment for foreign firms in high-technology sectors.

Despite the voluminous literature on direct foreign investment in the 1960s and 1970s, the empirical evidence on spillovers from foreign sources of equity investment remains slim. This chapter draws on new data sources for Côte d'Ivoire, Morocco, and Venezuela to explore two related questions. To what extent do joint ventures or wholly owned foreign subsidiaries exhibit higher levels of productivity than their domestic counterparts? Does technology spill over from these foreign entrants to domestically owned firms?

The research reported here is the first to exploit panel data at the level of individual firms, which allows a more detailed comparison of foreign and domestic firms than was previously possible. The behavior of foreign and domestic firms can be compared by sector, controlling for firm-specific attributes such as size. The panel nature of the data also allows the analysis to go beyond the cross-sectional studies of the past, which compared partial measures of productivity (such as labor productivity) across sectors. The availability of data for several countries permits exploration of the extent to which the impact of foreign investment is a general or a country-specific phenomenon.

The analysis shows that in Morocco and Venezuela, firms with foreign equity participation pay higher wages, have significantly higher levels of productivity, and export and import more than their domestic counterparts. It also finds that the presence of foreign firms has no impact or a strong negative impact on the productivity of domestic plants in Morocco and Venezuela, in contrast to previous studies on the extent to which technology spills over from foreign to domestic firms. This negative effect is likely to be a short-run phenomenon, as foreign firms steal market share from domestic competitors and reduce their utilization of capacity. We also examine the response of domestic and foreign firms to trade liberalization in Côte d'Ivoire. The results suggest that productivity increases more in foreign than in domestic firms.

Characteristics of Foreign Direct Investment in Côte d'Ivoire, Morocco, and Venezuela

For 1987 the share of foreign direct investment in the manufacturing sector—defined as a weighted mean of foreign shares in the assets of a firm—was 7 percent in Venezuela, 14 percent in Morocco, and 38 percent in Côte d'Ivoire (see table 7.1). Though these shares may be overstated for Côte d'Ivoire and Morocco because the firm-level sample is incomplete (only the largest firms are included in the Côte d'Ivoire sample), they provide a notion of the magnitude of foreign investment.[1]

Table 7.1 Share of Foreign Direct Investment in Manufacturing in Côte d'Ivoire, Morocco, and Venezuela, 1975–89
(percentages)

Year	Côte d'Ivoire	Morocco	Venezuela
1975	67	—	—
1976	67	—	—
1977	61	—	—
1978	64	—	—
1979	54	—	—
1980	55	—	—
1981	54	—	—
1982	49	—	—
1983	49	—	4
1984	43	—	5
1985	42	13	7
1986	40	15	7
1987	38	14	7
1988	—	15	8
1989	—	15	—

— Not available.
Note: Foreign share is computed as a mean of foreign share in total assets, weighted by firm-level assets.
Source: Author's calculations.

Much of the temporal and cross-country variation in direct foreign investment appears to be induced by policy. Côte d'Ivoire has long encouraged foreign entry as a strategy for developing its manufacturing sector: foreign ownership accounted for as much as 67 percent of total assets in 1975. Morocco and Venezuela, however, restricted foreign investment in the 1970s and then reversed these policies in the 1980s. To reduce the dominant role of French firms in the Moroccan economy, the government passed the Moroccanization Decree of 1973, which restricted foreign ownership of certain industrial and commercial activities to no more than 49 percent. By the 1980s, however, Morocco was encouraging greater foreign investment by easing the restrictions on foreign investors, relaxing the rules on repatriation of capital, and simplifying the approval process for foreign investment. Venezuela discriminated against foreign firms in various ways between 1975 and 1989, including imposing higher income tax rates (50 percent compared with 35 percent for domestic firms), restricting the use of confidentiality and trade secrets in joint ventures, and restricting foreign exchange. In 1989 all of these discriminatory regulations were eliminated.

One important policy issue is the extent to which foreign investment gravitates toward oligopolistic markets or protected sectors. Helleiner

(1989, p. 1451), in reviewing the role of foreign investment in developing countries, claims that "The prospect of large and especially protected local markets are the key to most import-substituting manufacturing firms' foreign activities." To the extent that direct foreign investment is associated with protection, it can reduce national welfare by allowing rents from protected sectors to be siphoned off by foreign firms.

The literature on foreign direct investment typically also focuses on the following determinants: (1) lower wages, which make it more attractive to produce abroad, (2) intangible assets, such as managerial skills, that cannot be licensed abroad, and (3) potentially large domestic markets. Another important determinant of foreign investment is likely to be domestic regulations that restrict incoming investment to certain sectors of the economy.

To quantify the importance of these determinants for each of the three countries in our sample, the following empirical specification is adopted:

$$(7.1) \quad DFI_{jt} = f(IMP_{jt}, H_{jt}, IMP \cdot H_{jt}, LABOR / CAPITAL_{jt},$$
$$REGUL_{jt}, MARKET\ SIZE_{jt},\ WAGES_{jt},\ POLLUTION_{jt}).$$

Direct foreign investment (DFI) is defined in two ways. First, it is defined as the share of foreign investment in total assets within each sector j at time t. Thus the equation explains the determinants of the amount of foreign investment (0 to 100 percent) *within* any one sector. Second, it is defined as (the log of) the total stock of foreign investment in a particular sector.

The independent variables, which vary across sector j and time t, include (1) import penetration (IMP) as a proxy for trade protection, (2) the Herfindahl index (H), equal to the sum of the square of market share of firms in each sector, as a measure of concentration, (3) the labor-capital ratio in sector j, (4) a measure of regulations ($REGUL$), which varies from 0 (no restrictions are placed on direct foreign investment) to 2 (direct foreign investment is prohibited), (5) a measure of market size, which is defined as the lagged share of sales in sector j as a percentage of total sales in manufacturing during the previous period, (6) wages in sector j and time t in France (for Côte d'Ivoire and Morocco) and the United States (for Venezuela), and (7) the costs of pollution abatement. Pollution abatement costs, measured using U.S. data on the costs of pollution abatement by sector, are included to test for the possibility that sectors with higher costs of pollution abatement in industrial countries are attracted to developing countries, where environmental regulations are less restrictive.

Equation 7.1 is estimated as a pure "between" regression, by averaging each sector's variables over time and estimating equation 7.1 as a cross section. All standard errors are corrected for arbitrary heteroscedasticity. The results are reported in table 7.2. Statistically significant variables include the Herfindahl index, import penetration, market size, and pollution abatement costs. The single most important determinant of foreign investment appears to be the size of the market: foreign investment gravitates toward sectors with a larger share of aggregate sales. Foreign investment is also more likely to be located in less concentrated sectors and in markets with lower competition from imports. Finally, pollution abatement costs appear to play a significant role in foreign investment in Côte d'Ivoire and Morocco. Other factors, such as wages, regulations, and capital intensity in the host country, do not appear to be important. In part, the lack of statistical significance of the regulatory framework may stem from the fact that restrictions on foreign entry may only be imposed in sectors with large inflows of foreign investment.

Description of Domestic and Foreign Firms

If foreign investment is an avenue for the transfer of technology, plants with foreign equity should exhibit some type of technological superiority. This superiority should manifest itself through higher levels of productivity in firms with greater foreign participation in equity. The firm-level panel data sets permit total factor productivity to be compared across foreign and domestic firms, which is much less misleading than comparisons based on measures of partial productivity such as labor productivity (which typically varies with capital intensity).

The relative performance of foreign and domestically owned firms is measured using the following indicators: output per worker, exports as a percentage of total sales, imported inputs as a percentage of total sales, net exports (exports minus imports) as a percentage of total sales, real wages, and deviation from overall norms in the sector for multifactor productivity, as well as growth in total factor productivity. Foreign firms are defined as all firms with foreign equity that exceeds 5 percent of assets.[2] Wages are computed as the total value of remuneration to workers divided by the number of employees. The derivation of multifactor productivity and growth in total factor productivity are discussed in greater detail below.

Most performance measures in table 7.3 are reported as the ratio of the performance of foreign firms to that of domestic firms. Thus, for example, a value of 2.0 for output per worker in the food products industry in Morocco indicates that worker output is twice as high for foreign-owned firms as for domestic firms, a difference that is statistically significant at the 5 percent level. In general, the ratios of unweighted means show that foreign firms in Morocco pay higher

Table 7.2 Determinants of the Sectoral Distribution of Foreign Direct Investment in Côte d'Ivoire, Morocco, and Venezuela

Variable	Côte d'Ivoire		Morocco		Venezuela	
	Percent DFI	Log DFI	Percent DFI	Log DFI	Percent DFI	Log DFI
Herfindahl index (H)	-6.34 (2.95)**	-2.66 (1.99)	0.40 (3.51)	-6.69 (2.88)**	-3.76 (2.06)*	-0.04 (1.56)
Import penetration (Imp)	-0.25 (1.68)	-0.06 (0.90)	-1.32 (0.58)**	-2.93 (0.76)**	1.61 (2.31)	2.79 (1.26)**
Imp · H	6.33 (4.46)	5.05 (2.81)*	-24.96 (16.78)	-24.89 (10.14)**	1.67 (3.56)	-22.03 (8.61)**
Regulations on direct foreign investment	—	—	-0.09 (0.35)	-0.17 (0.33)	2.58 (2.58)	-0.06 (0.51)
Labor-capital ratio	0.003 (0.001)**	-0.01 (0.00)**	-0.02 (0.11)	-0.04 (0.10)	-0.74 (0.40)*	-1.78 (0.57)**
Market size	94.45 (8.59)**	32.14 (7.57)**	3.24 (19.23)	16.19 (10.46)	88.65 (26.26)**	56.59 (15.52)**
Source wage	0.00 (0.00)	0.00 (0.00)	0.00 (0.00)	0.0002 (0.0001)**	0.00 (0.00)	0.00 (0.00)
Cost of pollution abatement	0.54 (0.36)*	0.44 (0.19)**	2.89 (1.16)**	0.93 (0.26)**	-0.41 (0.49)	0.19 (0.19)
Number of observations	30	30	61	59	66	54
R^2	0.87	0.65	0.46	0.46	25	0.50

— Not available.
* Significant at the 10 percent level.
** Significant at the 5 percent level.
Note: Numbers in parentheses are standard errors. All standard errors were corrected for heteroscedasticity. Data for Côte d'Ivoire cover 1975–87; for Morocco, 1985–89; for Venezuela, 1983–88.
Source: Author's calculations.

Table 7.3 Productivity, Outward Orientation, and Wages: Ratios of Foreign-Owned Manufacturing Firms to Domestic Firms in Côte d'Ivoire, Morocco, and Venezuela

Country and industry	Output per worker	Real wages	Exports as a percentage of sales	Imported inputs as a percentage of sales	Net exports	Total factor productivity deviation[a]	Total factor productivity growth
Côte d'Ivoire							
Grain processing	0.7	0.8	8.6*	8.4*	-2.6	—	-0.4
Food processing	1.02	0.9	7.0*	1.9*	50.0*	—	-0.2
Oil	6.4*	1.9*	0.7	99.3*	-9.3	—	0.9
Other food	1.3	1.0	—	4.8*	-13.7*	—	5.1
Textiles, clothing	2.3*	1.4*	6.8*	2.0	1.6	—	-0.2
Wood products	1.6*	1.1	2.2*	—	21.0*	—	5.3
Chemicals	1.5*	0.9	0.7	1.9*	-15.4*	—	1.9
Rubber	0.5*	0.7	1.9	0.9	22.2	—	6.2
Cement	3.0	1.1*	5.5*	1.1*	-10.9*	—	-3.5
Transport	1.3	1.0	0.4	34.0	-12.1*	—	-2.2
Machinery	0.8	0.9	39.7	0.6	16.6*	—	-6.5
Paper products	1.3	1.0	2.5*	1.8*	-21.5*	—	2.6
All sectors	0.9	0.8*	3.1*	2.6*	0.0	—	-0.5
Morocco[b]							
Food products	2.0 (0.9)*	2.3 (1.2)*	15.2 (4.5)*	—	—	0.7 (0.7)*	-6.4
Other food	0.5 (0.5)	1.2 (1.1)	20.0 (2.7)*	—	—	1.0 (1.3)	-7.3
Beverages, tobacco	1.4 (0.6)*	2.2 (1.4)*	10.8 (9.6)*	—	—	0.9 (4.0)	-7.0
Textiles	1.1 (0.5)	0.9 (0.2)	1.5 (0.7)*	—	—	0.9 (1.0)	0.0
Apparel	0.8 (1.1)	1.3 (1.4)*	1.8 (1.1)*	—	—	0.9 (1.0)	-12.3*

(Table continues on the following page.)

169

Table 7.3 (continued)

Country and industry	Output per worker	Real wages	Exports as a percentage of sales	Imported inputs as a percentage of sales	Net exports	Total factor productivity deviation[a]	Total factor productivity growth
Morocco[b] (continued)							
Leather products	1.1 (0.6)	2.0 (1.8)*	2.3 (1.4)*	—	—	1.0 (1.0)	0.3
Wood products	1.2 (1.0)	1.6 (1.0)*	8.5 (6.3)*	—	—	0.8 (0.8)*	−64.7
Paper products	1.5 (0.6)*	1.7 (1.3)*	11.7 (30.7)*	—	—	0.9 (0.4)*	14.0
Nonmetallic minerals	2.3 (2.2)*	1.9 (2.2)*	6.1 (1.6)*	—	—	0.7 (0.5)*	4.4
Basic metals	1.0 (0.3)	1.9 (1.2)*	0.2 (0.1)*	—	—	1.3 (21.2)	−0.3
Metal products	0.6 (0.5)	1.1 (1.1)	4.0 (2.3)*	—	—	1.0 (0.8)	−1.5
Machinery	1.1 (2.2)	0.8 (1.8)	5.0 (0.2)*	—	—	0.9 (0.7)	−1.8
Transport equipment	1.6 (2.0)*	2.0 (2.1)*	1.6 (0.4)	—	—	0.8 (0.7)*	9.7
Electronics	1.5 (1.3)*	2.1 (2.0)*	4.5 (3.9)*	—	—	0.8 (0.8)*	0.3
Scientific instruments	1.3 (1.7)*	1.7 (1.8)*	0.3 (0.1)	—	—	1.0 (1.1)	16.2
Chemicals	2.0 (0.6)*	2.6 (1.8)*	1.9 (0.0)*	—	—	0.7 (1.9)*	1.1
Rubber	0.9 (1.8)	1.5 (3.8)	4.2 (3.6)*	—	—	0.9 (0.8)*	−1.3
Other manufacturing	0.9 (0.8)	0.6 (0.8)	0.6 (0.5)	—	—	1.1 (1.0)	−21.3
All sectors	1.2 (0.7)	1.7 (1.3)*	2.0 (0.7)*	—	—	0.9 (0.9)*	−6.7*

Venezuela

Food, beverages	2.0*	0.7	4.4*	10.2*	9.1*	—
Textiles, apparel, leather	1.4*	3.5	1.6	-0.2*	9.9*	—
Wood products	1.4*	0.0	1.7	-0.2*	9.5	—
Paper products	2.2*	5.5*	1.2	-7.1*	8.0*	—
Chemicals	1.4*	3.5*	1.6	-7.1*	—	—
Nonmetallic minerals	1.7*	7.0*	4.3*	-2.6*	14.7*	—
Basic metals	1.6*	8.3*	2.6*	18.8*	0.0	—
Machinery, metal products	1.7*	10.9*	3.2*	-10.3*	7.7*	—
Other manufacturing	1.6*	0.6	3.6*	-13.5*	—	—
All sectors	1.7*	8.4*	2.9*	6.9*	8.5*	2.7*

— Not available.

* Statistically significant at the 5 percent level.

Note: A firm is defined as foreign if more than 5 percent of total assets are foreign owned. Data for Côte d'Ivoire cover 1975–87; for Morocco, 1985–89; for Venezuela, 1983–88.

a. Data for Morocco are ratios of the average deviation of the productivity of foreign firms from best practice to average deviation of the productivity of domestic firms. A value of less than 1 indicates deviation from best practice among foreign firms. Data for Venezuela are coefficients on the participation of foreign equity in a production function specification. A positive coefficient indicates that foreign equity raises productivity.

b. For Morocco the first number in each cell is a ratio of unweighted means; the numbers in parentheses are weighted by size of the firm.

Source: Author's calculations.

wages, export a higher share of output, and exhibit higher labor productivity, although the difference in labor productivity is not significant in the aggregate.[3]

The pattern is similar for Côte d'Ivoire and Venezuela. Joint ventures in the two countries tend to export more than their domestic counterparts, but only in Venezuela do foreign firms exhibit higher labor productivity and pay higher wages. In both countries, foreign firms have a much higher propensity to import—their ratios of imports to sales are almost three times higher than those of domestic plants in the same sector. Differences in net exports (exports minus imports) are also compared as a share of total sales. The difference in net exports across foreign and domestic firms varies significantly in both size and magnitude across different sectors for Côte d'Ivoire and Venezuela. For all sectors together, however, there is no difference in net exports generated by foreign versus domestic firms in Côte d'Ivoire and a difference of only 6.9 percent in Venezuela. Foreign firms in Côte d'Ivoire also import significantly more than their domestic counterparts.

Deviations in total factor productivity—which takes into account the combined productivity of the firm when all inputs are included—are calculated from estimates of total factor productivity by Haddad and Harrison (1993) for Morocco and by Aitken and Harrison (1994) for Venezuela. Haddad and Harrison compute a firm-specific level of total factor productivity that is essentially the firm-level residual in a production function estimation. They then compute efficiency at the firm level relative to the most efficient firm in each sector. Given N firms, there will be N estimated productivity measures within each sector j, given by $\hat{a}_{1j}, \ldots, \hat{a}_{Nj}$. Relative efficiency for firm i is given by z_{ij}, where

(7.2)
$$\hat{a}_j = \max(\hat{a}_{ij})$$
$$z_{ij} = \hat{a}_{ij} - \hat{a}_j,$$
$$i = 1, 2, \ldots, N \text{ for each sector } j.$$

A large negative value for z_{ij} indicates that firm i is very inefficient relative to the most efficient firm in sector j. A ratio of less than unity in table 7.3 indicates that foreign firms are relatively more productive than their domestic counterparts, since the deviation z_{ij} from the best-practice firm is low. Both weighted and unweighted means for the deviations show that, on average, foreign firms in Morocco have achieved a higher level of productivity than domestic firms.

Aitken and Harrison (1994) also compare the level of total factor productivity across foreign and domestic firms in Venezuela, but the approach is slightly different. They estimate a Cobb-Douglas production function in levels for each sector: output is expressed as a function of materials, skilled labor, unskilled labor, dummy variables for each year, and foreign ownership. The coefficient on foreign ownership can be interpreted as the percentage difference in productivity between foreign and domestic firms. In Venezuela, as in Morocco, plants with foreign equity participation consistently exhibit higher levels of total factor productivity. These results suggest that firms with foreign equity participation exhibit some sort of technological superiority in these countries. They also suggest that a complete explanation of sectoral productivity must begin with a framework flexible enough to recognize heterogeneity among producers. (See chapter 3 of this volume for studies of this type.)

Do foreign firms also dominate the growth of productivity? Although firms with foreign equity exhibit faster growth of total factor productivity than domestic firms in Venezuela, the reverse is found in Morocco, and the difference is insignificant for firms in Côte d'Ivoire. This result is not particularly surprising. Although foreign firms are expected to exhibit higher levels of productivity, their rate of growth of productivity is expected to be lower than that of domestic firms that are catching up to the higher levels of productivity of their foreign counterparts.

Testing for Spillovers of Technology from Foreign Investment

The comparisons presented so far suggest that in Morocco and Venezuela firms with foreign ownership exhibit a technological edge. This section examines whether any of this technological advantage spills over to domestic firms. If the knowledge or new technology embodied in foreign firms or joint ventures is transmitted to domestic firms, then the productivity of domestic plants (measured in levels or growth rates) should be higher in sectors with a large foreign presence. We first turn to an examination of the relationship between spillovers of technology and the level of domestic productivity using Moroccan data. We then examine the impact, using both the Moroccan and Venezuelan data, of foreign investment on the growth rate of domestic productivity.

Spillovers and the Level of Productivity

Haddad and Harrison (1993) examine the impact of direct foreign investment on dispersion in the level of productivity for Morocco. The findings on spillover effects—the extent to which the presence of direct foreign investment increases the rate of productivity growth, after accounting for other factors—show some evidence that direct foreign investment moves domestic plants toward greater efficiency in Morocco. In Venezuela, plants in sectors with heavy direct foreign investment appear to do better. However, when industry effects are included, direct foreign investment no longer appears to generate positive spillovers; if anything, the effect is negative. Essentially, this means that short-run temporal variation in direct foreign investment does not improve the productivity of domestic plants, possibly because multinational corporations take market share from domestic plants, thereby reducing their capacity utilization.

Haddad and Harrison use a modified version of the z_{ij} term defined in equation 7.2. Normalizing the productivity terms so that they can be compared across different sectors requires one more step. Given N firms, there will be N estimated productivity terms within each sector j, given by $\hat{a}_{1j}, \ldots, \hat{a}_{Nj}$. Thus, u_{ij}, the deviation of firm-level productivity from the best-practice level for the sector, can be defined as follows:

(7.3) $$\hat{a}_j = \max(\hat{a}_{ij})$$

$$u_{ij} = (\hat{a}_{ij} - \hat{a}_j) / \hat{a}_j,$$

$i = 1, 2, \ldots, N$ for each sector j, where all $u_{ij} < 0$.

The dispersion of productivity across firms in sector j can then be examined, using the following equation, which controls for size of the firm:

(7.4) $$u_{ij} = f(DFI\text{-}Firm_{ij}, DFI\text{-}Sector_j, SIZE_{ij}).$$

DFI-Firm is the share of foreign assets in each firm's total assets, DFI-Sector is the share of foreign firms (as measured by firm-level assets) in the sector, and SIZE is a measure of the size of the firm, proxied by the ratio of firm-level sales to total sales for the largest firm in each sector.

The results show a positive and statistically significant coefficient on the share of each firm's assets that are foreign owned (see table 7.4), which is consistent with the results showing less deviation from levels of best-practice productivity in plants with foreign equity participation (table 7.3). The positive and significant coefficient on size also suggests that larger firms are more likely to achieve higher levels of productivity than smaller firms. The positive and significant coefficient on sectoral foreign investment—a measure of the impact of foreign presence on the deviation of productivity from best-practice levels—suggests a smaller deviation in sectors with more foreign investment. The coefficient of 0.17 on sectoral direct foreign investment (DFI-Sector) indicates that an increase by one standard deviation in foreign share would bring a firm 4 percent closer to best practices.

Market structure and trade policy variables are introduced to test the sensitivity of these results (column 3 in table 7.4). The Herfindahl index is included to capture the effects of industry-level concentration, and

Table 7.4 Impact of Foreign Ownership on Firm-Level Productivity in Morocco

Variable	All firms	Domestically owned firms	
		Without market structure variables	*With market structure and trade policy variables*
Intercept	−0.441 (0.004)	−0.444 (0.004)	−0.295 (0.023)
DFI-Firm	0.030 (0.008)	n.a.	n.a.
DFI-Sector	0.170 (0.019)	0.174 (0.022)	0.109 (0.023)
Size of firm	0.002 (0.00001)	0.002 (0.0001)	0.002 (0.0001)
Tariffs (*Tar*)	n.a.	n.a.	−0.092 (0.043)
Nontariff barriers (*NTB*)	n.a.	n.a.	−0.008 (0.001)
Tar · NTB	n.a.	n.a.	0.009 (0.001)
Herfindahl index	n.a.	n.a.	0.116 (0.021)
Number of firms	3,933	3,105	3,105
R^2	0.16	0.12	0.19

n.a. Not applicable.
Note: Numbers in parentheses are standard errors. The dependent variable is the deviation of firm-level productivity from sector-level best practices. Data cover 1985–89.
Source: Haddad and Harrison 1993, table 4. Reprinted with kind permission of Elsevier Science-NL, Amsterdam.

average tariffs and coverage of quantitative import restrictions by sector for 1984–87 are included to capture differences in protection across industries. When these variables are included, the coefficient on foreign share drops slightly but remains positive and statistically significant. The negative coefficients on tariffs and nontariff barriers suggest that greater protection is associated with a movement of plants away from best practices. An interaction term for trade policy variables is also included to allow for the possibility that the impact of any one trade policy instrument is mitigated if used in conjunction with another.

Extending to Venezuela the approach taken for Morocco provides a means of examining the robustness of the finding on spillovers in the level of productivity. Aitken and Harrison (1994) examine Venezuelan data for a panel of firms, employing a production function that is slightly different than the Moroccan one because the data are richer. Data for Venezuela include information on material inputs (*M*) and skill categories of workers (*SKL* and *UNSKL*).

(7.5) $$Y_{ijt} = A_{ijt} F(SKL_{ijt}, UNSKL_{ijt}, M_{ijt}, K_{ijt})$$

where *Y* is total production and *A* is level of productivity, which is assumed to vary across firms in each sector *j* over time *t*. The log-level specification is derived by assuming a Cobb-Douglas production function, yielding

$$(7.6) \qquad \log Y_{ijt} = \log A_{ijt} + a_1 \log SKL_{ijt} + a_2 \log UNSKL_{ijt}$$
$$+ a_4 \log M_{ijt} + a_5 \log K_{ijt}.$$

In contrast to the analysis for Morocco, the analysis for Venezuela examines only the impact of foreign investment on domestic firms, excluding from the sample all firms with some foreign ownership. The analysis imposes a common production technology across sectors (up to the intercept), rather than estimating coefficients on factor stock industry by industry.

To decompose productivity into several components, Aitken and Harrison assume that

$$(7.7) \qquad \log A_{ijt} = \text{Constant} + b \; DFI\text{-}Sector_{jt} + cC_j + dD_t + e_{it}$$

where C_j and D_t are dummy variables for sector and time. Combining equations 7.6 and 7.7 yields the estimating equation

$$(7.8) \; \log Y_{ijt} = \text{Constant} + b \; DFI\text{-}Sector_{jt} + cC_j + dD_t + a_1 \log SKL_{ijt}$$
$$+ a_2 \log UNSKL_{ijt} + a_4 \log M_{ijt} + a_5 \log K_{ijt} + e_{it}.$$

Some versions of this model omit the C_j dummy variable for sectors. When included, these dummies take out all time-invariant, industry-specific productivity effects. Any residual correlation between direct foreign investment and productivity is therefore due to industry-specific temporal fluctuations.

The estimations that omit industry-specific effects essentially replicate earlier tests of the spillover hypothesis (Globerman 1979; Blomstrom and Persson 1983). Because of data limitations, these studies estimate the impact of foreign investment using cross-sectional data, relying on differences across sectors to identify the effects of foreign investment. Without corrections for industry effects, the results for Venezuela yield plausible coefficients on all inputs, all of which are positive and statistically significant (see table 7.5). The coefficient on the share of foreign ownership in the sector (*DFI-Sector*) is also positive and significant, with a point estimate of 0.061 that is in the same range as results obtained in earlier work. That estimate suggests that if the share of labor employed by foreign-owned firms rises from 0 to 10 percent of the manufacturing sector, output increases 0.6 percent. Since the estimation controls for increases in inputs, this 0.6 percent increase is a pure gain in total factor productivity.

Table 7.5 Impact of Sectoral Foreign Investment on the Productivity
of Domestic Firms in Venezuela

Variable	Without industry dummy variables	With industry dummy variable	
		At two-digit level	At four-digit level
Material (M)	0.569 (0.002)	0.573 (0.002)	0.585 (0.002)
Capital (K)	0.084 (0.001)	0.076 (0.002)	0.060 (0.002)
Unskilled labor (UNSKL)	0.296 (0.003)	0.293 (0.003)	0.293 (0.003)
Skilled labor (SKL)	0.110 (0.002)	0.114 (0.003)	0.108 (0.003)
Foreign presence in sector (DFI-Sector)	0.061 (0.032)	−0.028 (0.031)	−0.223 (0.059)

Note: Numbers in parentheses are standard errors. The dependent variable is the log output produced by domestically owned firms, which are defined as firms that have no foreign ownership over the entire sample period. All regressions include annual time dummy variables. Data cover 35,514 observations during 1983–88.

Source: Aitken and Harrison 1994.

But if foreign firms tend to locate in the more productive sectors, estimates of the impact of foreign share are biased upward. One way to correct for this is to introduce sector dummy variables that control for differences in productivity across industries that are due to unobserved factors, using the variation over time within industries to identify the impact of foreign investment. When the model is estimated with dummy variables for industries at the two-digit level, the coefficient on direct foreign investment switches from positive to negative and becomes statistically insignificant. This change suggests that the positive and statistically significant impact of foreign investment that is obtained when using cross-industry data is not robust: it is impossible to distinguish the possibility that foreign investment has positive spillovers on productivity in domestic firms from the possibility that foreign firms simply locate in productive industries.

Including dummy variables at the two-digit industry level may not entirely remove the type of bias discussed above, because foreign investment may be attracted to the most productive subsectors within an industry. To test for this possible bias, Aitken and Harrison (1994) estimate the equation again with industry dummies at the four-digit level.[4]

The impact is dramatic. The coefficient on direct foreign investment becomes even more negative (from −0.028 to −0.22) and is significant at the 1 percent level. The coefficient of −0.22 suggests that an increase in the share of foreign investment from 0 to 10 percent of manufacturing would be accompanied by a *decline* in total factor productivity of 2.2 percent. This negative spillover is consistent with several alternative models of foreign entry. Aitken and Harrison (1994) present a model in which foreign entry reduces the demand for domestically owned production, driving up the average costs of domestic firms. Another possibility is that foreign firms draw away the best workers or locate in areas with the best infrastructure, restricting access to domestic competitors and thereby reducing their productivity. Another plausible explanation is that productive industries are also profitable industries, so that foreign direct investment simply fulfills an equilibrating role in the world economy. The demand-side interpretation is appealing, because correlations based on temporal variation in the data are likely to reflect movement along short-run cost curves, while cross-sectional correlations come closer to long-run effects.[5]

The finding of negative spillovers contrasts with earlier findings in the literature and calls into question the existence of a positive transfer of technology through foreign entry, at least in the Venezuelan case. Foreign investment could also be associated with declining productivity in the aggregate, while still conveying substantial benefits to nearby plants. To examine the impact of locating in an area with a high share of foreign investment, Aitken and Harrison depart from previous research by allowing foreign share to vary across both industries (j) and regions (s). The productivity term A can now be specified as:

$$(7.9) \quad \log A(s)_{ijt} = \text{Constant} + b_1 DFI\text{-}Sector_{jt} + b_2 DFI\text{-}Local(s)_{jt}$$
$$+ L(s)_t + cC_j + dD_t + e_{it}$$

where the location-specific productivity term $L(s)_t$ varies across regions and over time, but not across industries. If $L(s)_t$ is positively correlated with foreign share, the coefficient on $DFI\text{-}Local$ overestimates the impact of location-specific foreign investment on productivity. For example, if foreign firms are more attracted to regions that benefit from agglomeration economies, analysis shows a correlation between domestic productivity and foreign share in a particular location even in the absence of spillovers.

Variations in productivity due to agglomeration economies or other region-specific effects are captured by the log of the real wage for skilled labor ($\log Wage_{st}$) and region-specific price of electricity ($\log Elecp_{st}$). Rauch (1991) provides empirical evidence for the United States that variation in the accumulation of human capital across cities is reflected in higher wages for individuals. Energy prices are included here, because the government of Venezuela explicitly encourages firms to locate in some regions by offering special energy subsidies in those regions.

These variables are included as proxies for $L(s)_t$, which cannot be observed. Because foreign investment in any one four-digit industry is unlikely to affect significantly the skilled wage for all industries in the region, the skilled wage is independent of the $DFI\text{-}Local$ variable. Combining equations 7.9 and 7.6 yields

$$(7.10) \quad \log Y_{ijt} = \text{Constant} + a_1 \log SKL_{ijt} + a_2 \log UNSKL_{ijt}$$
$$+ a_4 \log M_{ijt} + a_5 \log K_{ijt} + b_1 DFI\text{-}Sector_{jt} + b_2 DFI\text{-}Local_{sjt}$$
$$+ b_3 \log Wage_{st} + b_4 \log Elecp_{st} + cC_j + dD_t + e_{it}.$$

Foreign share, electricity prices, and the wage for skilled labor are cal-culated at the district level. Venezuela's twenty-three regions together contain 220 districts covering an average of 1,600 square miles. If skilled wages and electricity prices can capture only imperfectly regional agglomeration economies that are fixed over time, estimates for coeffi-cients on foreign investment at the local level could still be inconsistent. Consequently, equation 7.10 is estimated using a within transformation of the data at the regional level, computed by subtracting from each vari-able its region-sector mean over time.

The results show that direct foreign investment at the sectoral level continues to have a negative and statistically significant impact on the productivity of domestic plants for both classes of plants (see table 7.6). This negative impact is consistent across subsectors. At the local level, however, there is some evidence of positive spillovers in sectors such as wood products and pottery and glass. Across all sectors, *DFI-Local* has essentially no impact on plant-level productivity.

Alternative specifications that allow for dynamic effects (by including lags of direct foreign investment) or that employ dummy variables as an alternative definition of foreign presence yield similar results. Sectoral for-eign investment has a negative and significant impact on productivity. At the local level, foreign investment generally has no positive spillover on domestic firms. Nevertheless, we must be cautious in interpreting these

Table 7.6 Combined Regressions of Sectoral and Regional Foreign Share for Venezuela: Within Estimates

Sector	Sectoral foreign share	Regional foreign share
Food products	−0.395 (0.096)	0.062 (0.077)
Textiles and clothing	−0.032 (0.320)	−0.196 (0.163)
Wood products	−1.511 (0.687)	0.637 (0.220)
Paper and publishing	0.179 (0.448)	0.007 (0.100)
Pottery and glass	−0.158 (0.198)	0.485 (0.167)
Basic metals	0.283 (0.236)	0.056 (0.187)
Machines and equipment	−0.132 (0.110)	−0.052 (0.087)
All industries	−0.217 (0.062)	−0.014 (0.047)

Note: The dependent variable is the log output produced by domestically owned firms, defined as firms that have no foreign ownership over the entire sample period. All regres-sions include annual time dummy variables, the overall skilled wage in the region, and price of electricity. Numbers in parentheses are standard errors. Data cover 34,236 observations during 1983–88.

Source: Aitken and Harrison 1994.

Table 7.7 *Impact of Foreign Investment on Productivity Growth in Morocco, by Level of Protection*

Variable	All firms	Tariffs		Quotas		Reduction in quotas	
		Low	High	Low	High	Low	High
$d \log L$	0.770	0.752	0.767	0.725	0.779	0.778	0.762
	(0.009)	(0.025)	(0.016)	(0.023)	(0.016)	(0.012)	(0.013)
$d \log K$	0.088	0.077	0.070	0.061	0.076	0.081	0.100
	(0.011)	(0.035)	(0.019)	(0.025)	(0.022)	(0.014)	(0.018)
DFI-Firm	-0.020	-0.011	-0.039	0.022	-0.073	-0.025	-0.011
	(0.023)	(0.054)	(0.041)	(0.044)	(0.048)	(0.028)	(0.040)
DFI-Sector	-0.039	-0.005	-0.139	-0.191	-0.012	-0.035	-0.083
	(0.061)	(0.134)	(0.127)	(0.135)	(0.128)	(0.077)	(0.100)
R^2	0.42	0.38	0.39	0.33	0.41	0.42	0.40
Number of observations	11,772	1,585	4,212	2,154	3,643	6,402	5,370

Note: The dependent variable is the change in log value added. All equations include time dummies and sector dummies at the two-digit level. Numbers in parentheses are standard errors. Data cover 1985–89.
Source: Haddad and Harrison 1993, table 7. Reprinted with kind permission of Elsevier Science-NL, Amsterdam.

findings. The results suggest that short-run temporal variation in direct foreign investment does not positively influence the productivity of domestic plants, possibly because multinational corporations take market share from domestic plants, thereby reducing their capacity utilization. The only exceptions are domestic firms that are foreign owned at some time during the sample period. For these firms, the positive impact of foreign presence can be large and significant, depending on the specification.

Spillovers and Productivity Growth

An alternative way to study temporal fluctuations is to convert the data on level of productivity to rate of productivity growth. Haddad and Harrison (1993) do this for the panel of Moroccan data, beginning with a production function, with value added Y as a function of two inputs, capital and labor:

$$(7.11) \qquad Y_{ijt} = A_{ijt}F(L_{ijt}, K_{ijt}).$$

The level of productivity is given by A_{ijt}, which is assumed to vary across firms within each sector j and across time t. Totally differentiating this equation and assuming that each factor is paid the value of its marginal product yields the following equation (in logs):

$$(7.12) \qquad d\log Y_{ijt} = (dA / A_{ijt}) + a_1 d\log L_{ijt} + a_k d\log K_{ijt}$$

where dA / A is growth in productivity. The coefficients on growth in labor and capital are simply their shares in value added. To test the hypothesis that growth in productivity is affected by the share of foreign investment, productivity growth is decomposed into the following components:

$$(7.13) \qquad dA / A_{ijt} = aDFI\text{-}Firm_{ijt} + bDFI\text{-}Sector_{jt} + cC_j + dD_t.$$

Productivity growth varies across sectors j and time t and as a function of the level of foreign investment in both firms and sectors. The coefficient on DFI-$Sector$ measures positive spillover. Combining equations 7.12 and 7.13 yields

$$(7.14) \qquad d\log Y_{ijt} = aDFI\text{-}Firm_{ijt} + bDFI\text{-}Sector_{jt} + cC_j + dD_t$$
$$+ a_1 d\log L_{ijt} + a_k d\log K_{ijt}.$$

At the firm level, the impact of foreign investment is negative but statistically insignificant, indicating that growth in productivity is lower among foreign firms than among domestically owned firms, although the difference is not significant (see table 7.7). If domestic firms exhibit higher growth of productivity than foreign-owned firms, could this catch-up be due to spillovers from foreign investment? The sign on *DFI-Sector* is negative, but insignificant, providing no evidence for positive spillovers from direct foreign investment.[6]

The lack of evidence on positive spillovers from foreign investment could be due to distortions in the trade policy regime. If foreign firms are attracted to highly protected domestic markets, the results presented in column 1 of table 7.7 could suffer from bias caused by omitted variables so that the coefficient on foreign investment is underestimated if protected sectors exhibit low productivity growth.

To examine the impact of protection on potential spillovers from foreign investment, the sample is split into low- and high-protection groups, using three measures of protection. The first measure of protection is the average tariff level by three-digit sector for the three years for which it is available (1984, 1987, and 1988). The second measure is the share of production subject to quantitative restrictions. The third is the change in quota coverage between 1984 and 1988. The coefficient on *DFI-Sector* is insignificant and negative, once again suggesting that positive spillovers of technology are absent in the short run. The coefficient on *DFI-Firm* is significantly negative only in the protected sectors, suggesting that foreign firms exhibit lower productivity growth relative to domestic firms only in protected sectors.

Trade Reform, Productivity, and Ownership in Côte d'Ivoire

The preceding section found little evidence that technology spills over from foreign to domestic firms in Morocco or Venezuela, although the participation of foreign equity conveys clear benefits to joint ventures in the form of higher productivity. These results suggest that whatever gains in technology occur through foreign investment are captured entirely by joint ventures. Another potential gain is that the participation of foreign equity may ease the transition to a more open economy. Firms with foreign equity may be better prepared, through easier access to information and outside capital, to make the transition under trade liberalization. This section tests that possibility using data for Côte d'Ivoire in an estimating equation that extends the approach taken by Hall (1988) and Domowitz, Hubbard, and Petersen (1988), as described by Harrison (1994).

A modified production function for firm i in sector j at time t is given by

$$(7.15) \qquad (dy - de)_{ijt} = B_{0j} + B_{1j} [dx - (a_l + a_m)de]_{ijt} +$$
$$B_{2j} \{D[dx - (a_l + a_m)de]\}_{ijt} +$$
$$B_{3j} D + B_{4j} dk_{ijt} + (df_{it} / f_{it}) + u_{it} .$$

Lower-case variables y, l, m, and e are equal to $\ln(Y / K)$, $\ln(L / K)$, $\ln(M / K)$, and $\ln(E / K)$; Y, L, M, E, and K are firm-specific output, labor, material inputs, energy consumption, and capital stock. The extent to which the coefficient B_1 exceeds unity is a measure of market power, while $1 - B_4$ measures returns to scale. The term df_{it} / f_t is a firm-specific effect in the growth rate.

A dummy variable D is included in equation 7.15 to account for changes in behavior and productivity during the trade reforms of 1985–87. If productivity increases during the reform, coefficient B_3 should be positive, while if trade reform increases the competitive behavior of firms, coefficient B_2 should be negative, reflecting the fall in markups when firms are exposed to international competition.

Three different measures of changes in trade policy are used: a simple before-and-after comparison (using the dummy variable D), import penetration, and tariffs. The sample is split into foreign, public sector, and private firms. When openness is measured using the before-and-after comparison, coefficient B_3 is positive and significant only for foreign firms, signifying that productivity in foreign firms reacts more positively to liberalization (see table 7.8). Results using import penetration and tariffs are generally insignificant.

The markups of foreign and domestic firms respond differently to changes in tariffs, but not much differently to greater import penetration. In markups, foreign firms do not gain as much from higher tariffs as do domestic public and private firms and gain only slightly more from greater import penetration. Overall, the results suggest that increased openness does not greatly affect the markup behavior of foreign firms, but it does encourage foreign firms to increase productivity more than other firms.

Conclusions

According to Helleiner (1989), the neoclassical approach to foreign investment stresses the possible benefits generated through favorable externalities, particularly through technological diffusion and training. Yet, as Helleiner points out, "Research upon the less direct provision of extra inputs to the host country—through training, the local diffusion of knowledge, and technology, etc.—has been fairly limited and anecdotal" (p. 1455). Other approaches to the analysis of foreign investment stress its presence in oligopolistic and protected markets, where multinational corporations can exploit their firm-specific assets. Until now, opportunities to test these theories have been extremely limited, primarily because of the paucity of disaggregate data. The empirical results presented here are a first step to research some of these issues with micro data.

Table 7.8 Comparison of Production Function Estimates across Public, Private, and Foreign Firms in Côte d'Ivoire

Indicator	Market power (B_1)	Markup (B_2)	Productivity (B_3)	Returns to scale (B_4)
Before-and-after comparisons				
Public	1.124 (0.108)	0.012 (0.202)	−0.049 (0.037)	0.933 (0.083)
Private	0.911 (0.055)	0.012 (0.074)	−0.020 (0.025)	0.840 (0.039)
Foreign	0.944 (0.024)	0.019 (0.031)	0.029 (0.011)	0.872 (0.017)
Import penetration				
Public	1.584 (0.180)	−0.815 (0.258)	0.002 (0.065)	1.044 (0.083)
Private	1.011 (0.077)	−0.209 (0.150)	0.074 (0.054)	0.868 (0.040)
Foreign	1.095 (0.036)	−0.226 (0.057)	0.004 (0.023)	0.894 (0.017)
Tariff				
Public	0.908 (0.140)	0.254 (0.108)	0.047 (0.027)	1.022 (0.088)
Private	0.549 (0.142)	0.631 (0.220)	−0.044 (0.045)	0.867 (0.039)
Foreign	0.993 (0.033)	−0.019 (0.037)	−0.019 (0.015)	0.898 (0.017)

Note: Numbers in parentheses are standard errors. Data cover 1975–87.
Source: Author's calculations.

For two out of the three countries studied, the evidence suggests that foreign investment tends to locate in more protected and less concentrated sectors. Yet more research on the direction of causation is warranted. All three case studies show a positive relationship between foreign ownership and exports and between import propensities and real wages. Firms with foreign ownership exhibit higher levels of total factor productivity, although the evidence on differences in growth of productivity is mixed. In addition, evidence for Côte d'Ivoire suggests that foreign firms are more likely than domestic firms to improve productivity in response to trade liberalization. Despite this superior performance, there is almost no evidence for Morocco or Venezuela of positive short-run spillovers of technology from foreign to domestic firms. Nevertheless, these findings must be interpreted with caution. The results emphasize year-to-year variations in the data, suggesting that short-run temporal variations in direct foreign investment negatively affect the productivity of domestic plants, possibly because multinational corporations take market share from domestic plants and lead to reduced capacity utilization. However, long-run positive spillovers may occur, particularly if the cross-sectional positive correlation between foreign investment and productivity of domestic plants is interpreted as indicating long-run effects.

Research needs to build on these results by examining the conditions under which inflows of foreign investment encourage technological change. Anecdotal evidence for Taiwan (China), for example, suggests that foreign firms play a positive role in transmitting new technology to domestic firms. Several factors could account for such transfers in Taiwan, including a policy environment that creates specific incentives for diffusion of technology and a better educated work force, greater openness to trade, more productive and newer foreign investment, or a smaller technological gap between domestic and foreign firms.

Notes

This chapter was prepared partly under World Bank RPO 678-29, "Technology Spillovers, Agglomeration, and Direct Foreign Investment." This chapter draws extensively on research results presented in Aitken and Harrison 1994 and Haddad and Harrison 1993.

1. For Venezuela, sample weights permit aggregating plant-level data up to industry-level totals even for those (smaller) plants where a complete census is not possible. Consequently, the share of direct foreign investment is not likely to be subject to the same bias in measurement.

2. Haddad and Harrison (1993) examine alternative definitions of foreign ownership for Morocco and find similar results for comparative performance across majority- and minority-owned joint ventures.

3. The results for means weighted by size of firm (shown in parentheses in table 7.3) reveal a slightly different story for Morocco. Foreign firms as a group

do not exhibit higher levels of labor productivity or a greater outward orientation in most sectors, although they still exhibit higher levels of total factor productivity and continue to pay higher wages than domestic firms.

4. The equation is also estimated using a within transformation of the data at the firm level, which transforms all variables by subtracting out the firm-specific mean over time. Because the results are not affected by the transformation, the within estimates are not reported here.

5. It should be noted, however, that negative spillovers (at the national level) are picked up even when the data are transformed to four-year changes. These results are not reported here.

6. Alternative specifications (reported in Haddad and Harrison 1993) that omit time or sector dummies and estimate the equation only for domestic firms yield the same results.

References

Aitken, Brian, and Ann Harrison. 1994. "Do Domestic Firms Benefit from Foreign Direct Investment? Evidence from Panel Data." Policy Research Working Paper 1248. Policy Research Department, World Bank, Washington, D.C.

Blomstrom, Magnus, and Hakan Persson. 1983. "Foreign Investment and Spillover Efficiency in an Underdeveloped Economy: Evidence from the Mexican Manufacturing Industry." *World Development* 11 (6): 493–501.

Caves, Richard. 1982. *Multinational Enterprise and Economic Analysis.* Cambridge, U.K.: Cambridge University Press.

Domowitz, Ian, R. Glenn Hubbard, and Bruce C. Petersen. 1988. "Market Structure and Cyclical Fluctuations in U.S. Manufacturing." *Review of Economics and Statistics* 70 (1): 55–66.

Globerman, Steven. 1979. "Foreign Direct Investment and 'Spillover' Efficiency Benefits in Canadian Manufacturing Industries." *Canadian Journal of Economics* 12 (1): 42–56.

Haddad, Mona, and Ann Harrison. 1993. "Are There Positive Spillovers from Direct Foreign Investment? Evidence from Panel Data for Morocco." *Journal of Development Economics* 42: 51–74.

Hall, Robert E. 1988. "The Relation between Price and Marginal Cost in U.S. Industry." *Journal of Political Economy* 96 (5): 921–47.

Harrison, Ann. 1994. "Productivity, Imperfect Competition, and Trade Reform: Theory and Evidence." *Journal of International Economics* 36: 53–73.

Helleiner, Gerald K. 1989. "Transnational Corporations and Direct Foreign Investment." In Hollis Chenery and T. N. Srinivasan, eds., *Handbook of Development Economics,* vol. 2, chap. 27. Amsterdam: North-Holland.

Rauch, James E. 1991. "Productivity Gains from Geographic Concentration of Human Capital: Evidence from the Cities." Department of Economics, University of California, San Diego.

PART
II

Markups and Producer Turnover: Case Studies of Five Countries

8

A Preview of the Country Studies

Mark J. Roberts and James R. Tybout

In the development literature, issues of market structure are typically analyzed using industrywide profitability proxies like price-cost margins and industrywide entry barrier proxies like the Herfindahl index. (Lee 1991 provides a survey.) In that tradition, the country studies in this volume attempt to link market structures with macroeconomic conditions and trade flows using data aggregated to the industry level. But this is not the main contribution of the country studies. Because they are based on plant-level panel data, they provide several types of information on market structure in developing countries that was not previously available. Perhaps most important, they report new facts on the processes of entry, exit, and maturation that characterize developing-country producers.[1] Further, in examining pricing behavior, they control for time-invariant technological factors and describe within-industry heterogeneity. Indeed, a common theme of chapters 9–13 is that producers within a manufacturing industry are heterogeneous and that working with aggregate data can mean missing much of what is important.

Aside from these contributions, the country studies serve several other purposes. One is to provide background information for other chapters in this volume. Accordingly, in addition to describing the data bases and discussing policy regimes, each chapter summarizes distributions and patterns of correlation for a standardized set of variables. Finally, depending on the special circumstances of the country and time period, most of the authors pursue a special issue in depth. For Chile this issue is the tracking of plants as they switch sectors in response to the new incentive structure. For Morocco it is the relation between performance, product diversity, and market orientation (domestic versus foreign). In the case of Mexico, relatively detailed information on commercial policy is available, so the issue is how the dimensions of protection are related to performance. For Turkey the issue is the contrast between public and private enterprises. Finally, for Chile and Colombia, cohort analysis is used to describe patterns of growth and survival.

This overview briefly outlines the common methodologies used in the country studies, summarizes the major findings, and describes their implications for industrial performance. The results of similar studies for industrial countries are also presented to provide a context for the findings.

Descriptive Overview

Each chapter provides background information on the country's macro-economic environment and trade policy during the sample period to sketch in some of the broad economic influences on industries. Each chapter also describes producers in the manufacturing sector, highlighting their diversity in size, age, geographic region, and industry, and provides information on differences in trade exposure and performance among industries, including productivity growth and price-cost margins.

Entry and Exit Analysis

A combination of small markets, scale economies, and institutional problems in developing countries is often blamed for limiting producer turnover and contributing to inefficient production and market power. Evaluating this claim is difficult, however, because there is little concrete evidence about how much producer turnover actually takes place.

Three of the case studies provide some of this information for developing countries. For Chile, Colombia, and Morocco, comprehensive data allow us to study the process by which plants (or firms) enter and exit the industry. For these countries, the studies quantify rates of entry and exit by industry and compare the size and share of output of entering and exiting plants with those of other producers in the same industry. Cross-sectional correlations of entry and exit rates are also presented.

The entry and exit statistics constructed for each industry follow those used by Dunne, Roberts, and Samuelson (1988), with plant entry rates between years $t-1$ and t defined as

$$(8.1a) \qquad ER_{jt} = NE_{jt} / NT_{jt-1}$$

and exit rates as

$$(8.1b) \qquad XR_{jt} = NX_{jt-1} / NT_{jt-1}$$

where NE_{jt} is the number of plants that enter industry j between years $t-1$ and t; NT_{jt} is the total number of plants in industry j in operation in year t (this includes plants that enter between years $t - 1$ and t; and NX_{jt-1} is the number of plants that exit industry j between years $t - 1$ and t.

The denominator in both equations is the total number of plants in year $t - 1$. The exit rate is the number of exiting plants as a proportion of the pool of possible exiting plants, $NT(t - 1)$. The entry rate is the number of entering plants as a proportion of the number of plants in operation in period $t - 1$, rather than as a proportion of the pool of possible entrants, which cannot be observed. Entry and exit amount to the appearance and disappearance of plants in the data base, respectively, rather than the birth and death of plants. Because the data bases are nearly comprehensive for plants with at least ten workers, entry and exit statistics describe the crossing of the ten-worker threshold.

To attribute the market share of total output to plants entering (ESH) or exiting (XSH) the industry between years $t - 1$ and t, we use

$$(8.2a) \qquad ESH_{jt} = QE_{jt} / QT_{jt}$$

and

$$(8.2b) \qquad XSH_{jt-1} = QX_{jt-1} / QT_{jt-1}$$

where QE_{jt} is the total output of plants that enter industry j between years $t - 1$ and t; QT_{jt} is the total output of all plants in industry j in year t; and QX_{jt-1} is the total output in year $t - 1$ of plants that exit industry j between years $t - 1$ and t. The market share of entering plants is accordingly a proportion of output in year t, while that of exiting plants is measured relative to output in year $t - 1$.

The average size of entering plants relative to incumbents (ERS) and the average size of exiting plants relative to remaining plants (XRS) are defined as

$$(8.3a) \qquad ERS_{jt} = \frac{QE_{jt} / NE_{jt}}{(QT_{jt} - QE_{jt}) / (NT_{jt} - NE_{jt})}$$

$$(8.3b) \qquad XRS_{jt-1} = \frac{QX_{jt-1} / NX_{jt-1}}{(QT_{jt-1} - QX_{jt-1}) / (NT_{jt-1} - NX_{jt-1})}$$

These measures permit comparisons between the average size of entering plants and incumbents and the average size of exiting and surviving plants at a particular time. Accordingly, the denominator of ERS_{jt} includes all plants present in year t except the entrants, and the denominator of XRS_{jt-1} includes all plants present in year $t - 1$ except those that exit before year t.

These statistics summarize the magnitude of plant turnover in the manufacturing sector, but they say nothing about what happens to plants following entry. To elucidate that performance, the studies of Chile and Colombia measure the patterns of growth and failure of plants for successive cohorts of entrants. They summarize these patterns using the share of manufacturing output held by the cohort, the average size of surviving members of the cohort (relative to all manufacturers), and the year-to-year survival rates as the cohort ages.

Findings on Entry and Exit Rates

Several general patterns of entry and exit are evident. First, entry and exit rates are substantial. In Colombia, (plant) entry rates average 12 percent a year; in Chile, during a major recession, they average 6 percent; and in Morocco, (firm) entry rates average 13 percent. Despite the popular perception that entry and the associated competitive pressures are relatively limited in developing countries, these entry figures *exceed* the comparable figures reported for industrial countries.[2] For the United States, Dunne, Roberts, and Samuelson (1988) report an average industry-level entry rate of 41 and 52 percent over a five-year period. For Canada, Baldwin and Gorecki (1991) find that 33 percent of the firms in operation in 1979 were not in operation in 1971 and that annual entry rates during 1971–84 ranged from a low of less than 2 percent to a high of 10 percent. For the United Kingdom, Geroski (1991) reports entry rates averaging almost 7 percent a year for 1974–79.

Second, in each year exit rates are close to entry rates. Exit rates average 11.1, 10.8, and 6.0 percent a year in Colombia, Chile, and Morocco, respectively. Similar results have been obtained for the industrial countries. For example, in the United States average industry-level exit rates range from 41.7 to 50.0 percent for a five-year interval. Entry and exit are therefore much more than adjustments in the number of plants as demand fluctuates. They reflect largely the continual replacement of one group of producers by another.

A third robust finding is that firms entering and exiting an industry are smaller than the incumbent producers. In Colombia, the average output of entering plants is 39 percent the average output of incumbents; in Chile, it is 26 percent; in Morocco, it is 24 percent. As a result, the high entry rates translate into modest shares of production. On average, entrants have market shares of 5, 2, and 3 percent in Colombia, Chile, and Morocco, respectively. This too is similar to the pattern in industrial countries. For example, in the United States, entrants average about one-quarter the size of incumbents.

The studies in this volume and those of industrial countries all find a positive cross-sectional correlation between industry-level entry and exit rates. This indicates that industries tend to differ systematically in their degree of turnover, probably because of technological factors like scale economies and sunk entry costs. Accordingly, average gross turnover rates may provide a good proxy for the exogenous determinants of market structure. However, because entry and exit figures covary positively, *net* entry figures are a poor indicator of overall turnover in an industry.

A final set of issues concerns what happens to new producers. Do they tend to fail quickly following entry or to expand and eventually become substantial producers? How long does the process take? Answers to these questions indicate whether production and employment tend to be concentrated in an older group of larger, stable plants or to turn over as young plants grow and older plants fail.

One robust finding is that the probability of failure declines as producers grow older. In Colombia, plants face a 21 percent probability of failure in their first year, but this declines to 13 percent after three years and stabilizes thereafter. In Chile the average first-year failure rate is 27 percent, and this declines to 15 percent after three years. Studies that have followed cohorts of entering plants or firms in industrial countries report similar declines in failure rates as producers age (Evans 1987a and 1987b; Dunne, Roberts, and Samuelson 1988, 1989a, and 1989b; Geroski 1991). Most entrants have very short lives and never become large producers. Over time, the output of a cohort of entrants tends to fall, because the loss of output from exiting producers is greater than the gain in output from survivors that are growing. The notion that new firms typically grow to become significant producers thus does not match the patterns found.

Correlates of Industry-Level Turnover

Patterns of plant turnover reflect three distinct processes. One involves long-run shifts in technology and patterns of demand. As new products and production techniques are developed, and as demand shifts across industries, producers enter expanding sectors and exit contracting ones. A second source of plant turnover is short-run cyclical fluctuations in demand, which can induce short-run deviations from long-term trends in gross entry and exit. A third source of turnover is the replacement of less-efficient producers by more-efficient ones, which can occur even in industries facing stable levels of demand. This turnover varies across industries with technology differences, especially those relating to sunk costs and different production processes. There is virtually no information on how important each of these sources of turnover is for developing countries.

To summarize the importance of these forces, each study reports summary regressions predicting industry-level entry and exit rates. The explanatory variables are dummies for time (DT_t) to serve as a proxy for changing macroeconomic conditions, the growth in industrial production (GRQ_{jt}), import penetration (IMP_{jt}), and export shares (EXP_{jt}) to summarize industry-level demand conditions, and industry dummies (DI_j) or other summary measures of industrial structure, including capital-output ratios (KQ_{jt}), and Herfindahl indexes (H_{jt}) to capture technology. In each case, the regressions are a variant on the following specification:

$$(8.4a) \qquad ER_{jt} = f(GRQ_{jt}, IMP_{jt}, EXP_{jt}, KQ_{jt}, H_{jt}, DT_t, DI_j)$$

$$(8.4b) \qquad XR_{jt} = f(GRQ_{jt}, IMP_{jt}, EXP_{jt}, KQ_{jt}, H_{jt}, DT_t, DI_j)$$

where subscripts j and t refer, respectively, to industry and time.

The empirical results from these regressions suggest that macroeconomic conditions and differences in technology across industries are the main determinants of the variation in industry-level entry and exit rates. Once time and industry effects are controlled for, the remaining variables, particularly those measuring time-series variations in industrial structure or imports, have little explanatory power. Variation in the growth of industry output, which is likely to reflect industry-level fluctuations in demand, is important in several of the countries, with higher growth being positively correlated with entry and negatively correlated with exit. The overall patterns of correlation suggest most strongly that entry and exit rates largely reflect differences in the nature of technology, presumably the importance of sunk costs, with some role for fluctuations in demand to affect the rates over time. Using U.S. data, Dunne and Roberts (1991) also find that once the technology is controlled for using industry fixed effects, remaining variation in entry and exit rates largely reflects fluctuations in output over time.

Price-Cost Margins

Traditionally, industry-level data have been used to describe the relationship between trade exposure and the performance of domestic manufacturing industries. In line with this literature, each country study examines the correlation between trade exposure and price-cost margins at the industry level, using import penetration (imports as a share of domestic sales, defined as domestic production plus imports minus exports) as the measure of trade exposure. One difficulty with this level of analysis is that it says nothing about whether the observed effects are common to all producers in the industry or are concentrated in a subset of producers. Thus the country studies also examine the correlation between trade exposure and price-cost margins at the plant level to see if it varies among different groups of producers.

Industry-Level Analysis

Several empirical studies have examined the cross-sectional correlation between industry-level price-cost margins and import competition.[3] Schmalensee (1989) summarizes findings for industrial countries in his stylized fact 4.6: "The ratio of imports to domestic competition tends to be negatively correlated with the profitability of domestic sellers, especially when domestic concentration is high."

The negative association between import penetration and price-cost margins is not in itself evidence of noncompetitive market structures. For example, the Hecksher-Ohlin model predicts that trade liberalization induces this type of correlation if import-competing sectors are capital-intensive. However, the stronger negative effect of import penetration in highly concentrated industries is consistent with the argument that imports are likely to affect average profits if some or all firms in the industry are earning above normal returns. Whether the excess profits result from differences in efficiency across plants or from noncompetitive behavior cannot be identified at this level of aggregation.

The country studies use the industry-level price-cost margin to measure industry-level performance. The price-cost margin is measured as the value of output minus expenditures on labor and materials over the value of output. This is equivalent to economic profits plus payments to fixed factors (capital) as a proportion of industry-level revenue: $PCM_{jt} = [\Pi_{jt} + (r_t + \delta)K_{jt}] / P_{jt}Q_{jt}$, where Π_{jt} is economic profits of industry j in year t, r_t is the competitive gross rate of return on capital, δ is the depreciation rate, K_{jt} is capital stock, and $P_{jt}Q_{jt}$ is industry-level revenue. (For further discussion on price-cost margins, see Fisher and McGowan 1983; Schmalensee 1989.) The price-cost margin varies across industries with variations in capital intensity and in the rate of economic profit.

Since industrial capital stocks change slowly over time, temporal variations in the margin are likely to reflect mostly fluctuations in output, while cross-sectional variations are likely to reflect variations in capital intensity and economic profits. Each country study uses the panel structure of the data to distinguish these sources of variation.

The basic model examined in the country studies is a variant of that of Domowitz, Hubbard, and Peterson (1986):

$$(8.5) \qquad PCM_{jt} = f(H_{jt}, IMP_{jt}, H_{jt} \cdot IMP_{jt}, KQ_{jt}, DI_j, DT_t).$$

The explanatory variables include two measures of industry structure—the Herfindahl index, H_{jt}, and the import penetration rate, IMP_{jt}—as well as the industry-level capital-output ratio, KQ_{jt}; industry dummy variables, DI_j; and time dummies, DT_t. (In the Mexican study, IMP_{jt} was replaced by variables that measure commercial policy more directly—tariff rates and import license coverage.)

How the estimated parameters are interpreted depends on the type of variation used to identify them. Specifically, if industry dummies are excluded, most of the variation is across industries, and the Herfindahl index and capital-output ratio pick up variations in technology and the degree of competition among domestic producers. The procompetitive effect of imports should show up as a negative correlation between import penetration and margins. Also, if high-concentration industries have economic profits, they should be relatively sensitive to competition from abroad, so the coefficient on an interaction term between import penetration rates and the Herfindahl index should be negative. Indeed, these relationships are typically found in both industrial and developing countries (Schmalensee 1989; Lee 1991). The studies in this volume, not surprisingly, pick up similar correlations. Studies of four of the five countries—Chile, Colombia, Mexico, and Morocco—find that proxies for trade exposure are negatively correlated with margins and that the effect is largest in highly concentrated industries. Some weak evidence of import discipline is found for the public sector plants in Turkey.

This version of the model, which does not include industry dummies, is based on the presumption that capital-output ratios effectively control for differences in technology and that, conditioned on this variable, a stable cross-industry empirical relationship exists. If this is not the case, then observed correlations may reflect unmeasured differences in technology. For example, relatively efficient industries may be both more profitable (high margins and high concentration) than others and better able to compete against potential imports (low import penetration).

With panel data, it is possible to control for persistent effects of technology and market structure by including dummy variables for industries in the regression. Then estimated coefficients reflect only temporal variations in the data. Because import penetration rates (and alternative measures of commercial policy) change through time, price-cost margin regressions with industry dummies are better suited to isolating the disciplining effects of foreign competition.

When industry dummies are included in the margin regressions, evidence of import discipline effects is found in Colombia and Mexico. This result is consistent with the conjecture that these countries were the least competitive before trade liberalization and therefore had the most to gain from import discipline. In both cases, these countries were characterized by inward-looking trade strategies for at least a portion of the sample years. Chile, in contrast, was already quite open by the time the sample period began. The results for Mexico are probably the most useful, because data on commercial policy are directly observable, and hence the results are less subject to simultaneity bias than those from the other country studies, which proxy exposure to foreign competition with rates of import penetration.

Plant-Level Analysis

Additional evidence on the extent of competition within a given industry can be generated by studying margins at the plant level. This exercise, taken from Schmalensee (1985), amounts to asking whether cross-plant variations are due to industrywide effects or to plant-specific market shares. Efficient plants should be larger and have higher profits, so a positive correlation is generally expected between market shares and price-cost margins, regardless of whether firms have market power (Demsetz 1973). If the degree of market power varies across product groups, industry dummies pick up this source of difference in plant-level profitability.[4] Tests of the null hypothesis that industry dummies are equal thus amount to tests for the absence of market power.[5]

The country studies use the following specification:

$$(8.6) \qquad PCM_{ijt} = f(S_{ijt}, S_{ijt}^2, KQ_{ijt}, IMP_{jt}, IMP_{jt} S_{ijt}, DI_j, DT_t)$$

where PCM_{ijt} is the price-cost margin of plant i in industry j and year t, S_{ijt} is the share of this plant's output in total domestic production, IMP_{jt} is the import penetration rate for industry j in year t, and DI_j and DT_t are dummy variables for industry and time, as before. The interaction term $IMP_{jt} S_{ijt}$ is included to allow for the possibility that the disciplining effect of import penetration is felt more heavily among large producers.

The importance of industry-level effects differs across countries. In most cases, industry dummies contribute virtually nothing to the explanation of margins, once market share, capital intensity, and import penetration rates are controlled for. In fact, as detailed in chapter 9, the case could be made that there is less evidence of market power in these countries than Schmalensee (1985) finds in his analysis of the United States.

Margins do correlate with market shares: they rise at a diminishing rate, perhaps partly reflecting the Demsetz effects described above. But there appears to be more to the story. In *every* country studied, relatively high industrywide exposure to foreign competition is associated with lower cost-price margins, and the effect is concentrated in large plants. This finding is much more systematic than the industry-level effects discussed earlier. It suggests the presence of an import discipline effect that acts on the larger producers.

Conclusions

The combination of small domestic markets and relatively concentrated domestic industries is often cited as prima facie evidence of substantial market power among manufacturers in developing countries. However, the studies in this volume point to two significant sources of competitive pressures. First, producer turnover rates in the countries studied match or exceed those in Canada, the United Kingdom, and the United States. These results suggest that entry barriers are low and that new producers provide a continual competitive threat to incumbents. Not only are young firms common, they are at least as large relative to older plants as they are in the industrial countries.

Second, imports exert additional competitive pressures. The strongest evidence of this comes from plant-level margin regressions, which suggest that, for all countries studied, margins among big plants are tempered by exposure to foreign competition. The most compelling case is that of Mexico, which went from being one of the most inward-looking countries to being one of the most outward-oriented. The Mexican results reveal a robust negative association between industry-specific tariffs and quotas, on the one hand, and markups among large plants, on the other. Competition from imports does not appear to correlate with the patterns of entry and exit, however, once aggregate demand shocks have been controlled for.

None of these basic findings could have been identified using industry-level data, which by construction aggregate out producer heterogeneity. There are, of course, many other ways in which the acknowledgment of heterogeneity could change industrial analysis; some of these are pursued in other chapters of this volume.

Notes

1. Further analysis of entry and exit is provided in chapters 2, 3, and 4.

2. The empirical evidence for a number of industrial countries is summarized in Geroski 1991, chap. 2; cross-country comparisons are available in Geroski and Schwalbach 1991.

3. For a recent survey of semi-industrialized countries, see Lee 1991. For a sampling of studies of industrial countries, see Jacquemin, de Ghellinck, and Huveneers 1980; Marvel 1980; Pugel 1980; Geroski 1982; and Domowitz, Hubbard, and Peterson 1986. Additional references are discussed in Caves 1989.

4. Schmalensee (1985) attempts to assess whether the positive correlation between industrial concentration and profitability arises from market power in concentrated industries or from cost heterogeneity, or efficiency differences, across producers. In the case of cost heterogeneity, the positive correlation arises because relatively efficient firms earn higher-than-average profits and also become the major producers in the industry. Schmalensee finds that profitability varies significantly across industries and positively with firm size. He concludes that, although both effects are present, the market share effects do not explain a sizable part of the variability in firm-level profits.

5. Of course, as Schmalensee acknowledges, cross-industry differences in profitability may be due to the short-run effects of sectoral shocks. This problem should not seriously affect panel studies covering time periods as long as those used in these studies.

References

Baldwin, John, and Paul Gorecki. 1991. "Firm Entry and Exit in the Canadian Manufacturing Sector." *Canadian Journal of Economics* 24: 300–23.

Caves, Richard. 1989. "International Differences in Industrial Organization." In Richard Schmalensee and Robert Willig, eds., *Handbook of Industrial Organization*. Amsterdam: North-Holland.

Demsetz, Harold. 1973. "Industry Structure, Market Rivalry, and Public Policy." *Journal of Law and Economics* 16: 1–10.

Domowitz, Ian, R. Glenn Hubbard, and Bruce C. Peterson. 1986. "Business Cycles and the Relationship between Concentration and Price-Cost Margins." *Rand Journal of Economics* 17: 1–17.

Dunne, Timothy, and Mark J. Roberts. 1991. "Variation in Producer Turnover across United States Manufacturing Industries." In Paul A. Geroski and Joachim Schwalbach, eds., *Entry and Market Contestability*. Oxford: Basil Blackwell.

Dunne, Timothy, Mark J. Roberts, and Larry Samuelson. 1988. "Patterns of Firm Entry and Exit in U.S. Manufacturing Industries." *Rand Journal of Economics* 19 (4): 495–515.

———. 1989a. "Firm Entry and Post-Entry Performance in the U.S. Chemicals Industries." *Journal of Law and Economics* 32: S233–71.

———. 1989b. "The Growth and Failure of U.S. Manufacturing Plants." *Quarterly Journal of Economics* 104: 671–98.

Evans, David. 1987a. "The Relationship between Firm Growth, Size, and Age: Estimates for the U.S. Manufacturing Sector." *Journal of Industrial Economics* 35: 567–82.

———. 1987b. "Tests of Alternative Theories of Firm Growth." *Journal of Political Economy* 95: 123–37.

Fisher, Franklin M., and John J. McGowan. 1983. "On the Misuse of Accounting Rate of Return to Infer Monopoly Profits." *American Economic Review* 73 (March): 82–97.

Geroski, Paul A. 1982. "Simultaneous Equation Models of the Structure-Performance Paradigm." *European Economic Review* 19: 145–58.

———. 1991. *Market Dynamics and Entry*. Oxford: Basil Blackwell.

Geroski, Paul A., and Joachim Schwalbach. 1991. *Entry and Market Contestability: An International Comparison*. Oxford: Basil Blackwell.

Jacquemin, Alexis, Elisabeth de Ghellinck, and Christian Huveneers. 1980. "Concentration and Profitability in a Small, Open Economy." *Journal of Industrial Economics* 29: 131–44.

Lee, Norman. 1991. "Market Structure and Trade in Developing Countries." In Gerald K. Helleiner, ed., *Trade Policy, Industrialization, and Development: New Perspectives*. Oxford: Clarendon Press.

Marvel, Howard P. 1980. "Foreign Trade and Domestic Competition." *Economic Inquiry* 18: 103–22.

Pugel, Thomas. 1980. "Foreign Trade and U.S. Market Performance." *Journal of Industrial Economics* 29: 119–29.

Schmalensee, Richard. 1985. "Do Markets Differ Much?" *American Economic Review* 75 (3): 341–51.

———. 1989. "Inter-Industry Studies of Structure and Performance." In Richard Schmalensee and Robert Willig, eds., *Handbook of Industrial Organization.* Amsterdam: North-Holland.

9

Chile, 1979–86: Trade Liberalization and Its Aftermath

James R. Tybout

Two aspects distinguish the performance of Chile's industrial sector during 1979–85 from the industrial performance of the other countries studied in this volume. First, prior to 1979 Chile had already adopted a very open trade regime. Second, the sample years include a period of severe recession and financial crisis and so offer some evidence on the impact of such shocks to the industrial sector and the consequences of government rescue attempts.

Several hypotheses concerning the effects of foreign competition are examined. First, because the sample period immediately followed a dramatic trade liberalization, evidence of market power and productive inefficiency among Chilean producers of tradable goods should be slight. Second, to the extent that a shakedown of the industrial sector was still unfolding in the early sample years, recent changes in patterns of exposure to international competition should be associated with patterns of entry and exit. Product lines should be realigning with the country's comparative advantage, and inefficient plants should be shaping up or shutting down. These hypotheses are explored by analyzing industry-specific entry and exit rates during the 1980s and comparing them with rates in other countries. The competitiveness of the industrial sector is assessed through an analysis of the factors that influence the degree of competition, focusing in particular on whether exposure to foreign trade affects competition. (See chapter 4 for a detailed treatment of manufacturing productivity during the sample years.)

Chile's Radical Reforms of the 1970s

As did much of Latin America during the 1960s, Chile pursued a strategy of inward-oriented development.[1] The system of incentives—including

200

tariffs, quotas, exchange rates, and domestic market regulations—favored manufacturing at the expense of agriculture and import-competing producers over exporters (Corbo 1985). This bias intensified under the populist-socialist orthodoxy of Salvador Allende's government of 1970–73. By 1973 average tariff rates exceeded 100 percent, prior deposit requirements for importers created heavy additional surcharges, and a complex system of multiple exchange rates had developed. Chronic fiscal deficits and the associated inflationary pressure (repressed through price controls) strained the economy.

The Augusto Pinochet government that took control in 1973 implemented radical changes in policy. Fiscal austerity and price stabilization programs to settle the macroeconomy were complemented by laissez-faire microeconomic policies. Public enterprises were sold, prices and interest rates were decontrolled, and trade protection was dismantled. The average nominal tariff rate plunged from 105 percent in 1974 to about 12 percent in 1979 (World Bank 1989).

After an initial period of recessionary shock, industry began to recover in 1976 (see figure 9.1). Several features of the recovery are noteworthy. The employment losses that accompanied the 1974–75 recession were

Figure 9.1 Employment and Production in Manufacturing in Chile, 1969–87

Index (1986 = 100)

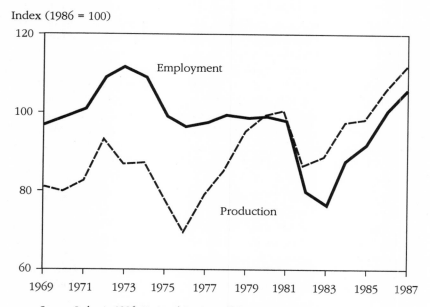

Source: Jadresic 1986; National Institute of Statistics, various years.

not reversed during the 1976–81 recovery in output; rather, labor productivity increased dramatically. The balance of trade in industrial products worsened considerably during the latter part of the recovery, in response partly to trade liberalization and partly to the considerable appreciation of the real exchange rate after 1979.[2] A third feature was the emergence of a handful of powerful conglomerates (*grupos*), which consolidated control over financial and industrial enterprises.

By the end of 1982, the Chilean economy was again in serious trouble. The exchange rate had been overvalued for some time, and producers in the tradable sector were experiencing a protracted profit squeeze. Large inflows of capital were needed to finance the current account deficit, yet international credit was evaporating, exacerbating the financial stress of firms as interest rates soared. The government finally devalued the peso, but the financial soundness of the economy had already been undermined, and a major recession followed. Unemployment reached roughly 30 percent in 1983.

To help the economy regain its footing, the government essentially took control of major private banks, purchased their nonperforming loans, and initiated a recapitalization program. Industrial loans were reprogrammed as long-term debt, with several years of grace granted before interest payments were to resume at controlled rates. Industry recovered quickly, thanks to these financial relief measures coupled with preferential exchange rates for foreign debt, devaluation, a mild increase in tariff protection, and a reduction in the corporate income tax rate from 38 to 10 percent. As the recovery gathered strength, average tariffs were gradually scaled down from a peak of 36 percent in September 1984 to a modest 15 percent by 1988.

The industrial sector in Chile is now popularly believed to be one of the most efficient in Latin America. Despite the government's essentially laissez-faire antitrust policy, it is commonly held that foreign competition prevents firms from exercising much market power and forces inefficient firms to reform or shut down. The *grupos* are still in evidence, but they too are considered to be efficient competitors.

Patterns of Entry and Exit

On average during the survey period of 1979–85, Chile had about 4,800 industrial plants with ten or more workers, 85 percent of which had less than fifty employees (see table 9.1).[3] About 60 percent of the plants were located in the Santiago area. Food industries (industrial classification 311–312) had by far the greatest concentration of plants, followed by wood products, textiles, apparel, and fabricated metal products. The number of plants declined dramatically between 1979 and 1983, rebounding slightly in 1984 and 1985.

Table 9.1 Characteristics of Plants in Chile, 1979–85
(percentage of total for each category unless otherwise specified)

Characteristic	1979	1980	1981	1982	1983	1984	1985
Number of plants	5,814	5,308	4,872	4,484	4,205	4,378	4,333
Type of business							
Collective	5.7	5.8	5.7	5.4	5.6	4.5	4.0
Cooperative	0.9	0.6	0.5	0.6	0.6	0.5	0.6
Corporation	17.6	18.4	18.8	19.8	20.3	20.5	20.7
Partnership	40.8	43.3	43.9	44.2	46.6	49.2	49.9
Proprietorship	29.5	27.5	26.7	25.8	23.8	22.4	22.1
Public	0.9	0.9	0.9	1.0	1.0	1.0	1.0
Other	4.6	3.5	3.4	3.2	2.2	1.8	1.7
Number of employees							
10–49	83.0	83.4	84.2	86.7	87.1	85.3	84.0
50–99	9.0	8.6	8.1	7.1	6.6	7.5	8.3
100–199	4.1	4.3	4.1	3.4	3.5	4.0	4.4
200 or more	3.9	3.7	3.5	2.8	2.8	3.1	3.3
Region							
Antofagasta	1.9	1.9	1.8	1.9	2.0	2.0	2.2
Araucana	2.9	2.5	2.5	2.4	2.4	2.4	2.4
Atacama	0.9	1.0	1.0	0.9	1.0	0.9	1.0
Bio-Bio	8.1	8.1	8.1	8.3	8.3	8.4	8.9
Coquimbo	1.7	1.8	1.9	1.9	1.9	1.7	1.7
Ibañes del Campo	0.4	0.4	0.3	0.4	0.4	0.5	0.4
Los Lagos	3.7	3.8	3.8	3.7	3.4	3.5	3.7
Magallanes y Antartica	1.1	1.1	1.1	1.2	1.5	1.5	1.4
Maule	4.4	4.0	3.8	3.8	4.4	4.0	4.1
O'Higgins	3.0	3.2	3.0	3.3	3.4	3.4	3.3
Santiago	61.2	61.3	61.2	60.3	59.5	60.3	59.3
Tarapaca	2.2	2.1	2.1	2.3	2.3	2.2	2.3
Valparaiso	8.6	8.8	9.3	9.5	9.6	9.1	9.3
Industry and ISIC number							
312 Food	27.7	28.4	29.2	30.8	32.2	32.0	32.2
313 Beverages	3.6	3.5	3.2	3.4	3.5	3.2	2.9
314 Tobacco	0.1	0.1	0.1	0.1	0.1	0.1	0.1
321 Textiles	8.7	8.4	8.3	7.8	7.8	7.7	7.8
322 Apparel	7.6	7.5	7.1	6.8	6.3	6.7	6.3
323 Leather products	1.5	1.4	1.4	1.3	1.3	1.2	1.2
324 Footwear	3.2	2.9	2.8	2.8	3.0	3.0	3.0
331 Wood products	9.0	8.5	8.3	8.0	8.0	7.7	7.9
332 Furniture	3.6	3.6	3.5	3.2	2.8	2.7	2.7
341 Paper	1.2	1.3	1.2	1.2	1.2	1.4	1.3
342 Printing	4.2	4.3	4.2	4.4	4.2	3.8	3.8
351 Industrial chemicals	1.1	1.1	1.2	1.2	1.2	1.3	1.4
352 Other chemicals	2.9	3.1	3.3	3.3	3.4	3.4	3.4
353 Petroleum refining	0.2	0.2	0.2	0.2	0.2	0.2	0.0
354 Petroleum derivatives	0.1	0.1	0.2	0.2	0.2	0.2	0.4
355 Rubber products	1.1	1.3	1.2	1.2	1.2	1.3	1.3
356 Plastics	2.9	3.1	3.1	3.2	3.4	3.7	3.7
361 Ceramics	0.2	0.2	0.2	0.2	0.3	0.3	0.3
362 Glass	0.6	0.5	0.6	0.5	0.5	0.5	0.5
369 Nonmetallic minerals	2.3	2.6	2.6	2.5	2.5	2.5	2.7
371 Iron and steel	1.1	0.9	0.9	0.8	0.9	0.7	0.7

(Table continues on the following page.)

Table 9.1   (continued)

Characteristic	1979	1980	1981	1982	1983	1984	1985
372 Nonferrous metals	0.6	0.6	0.6	0.6	0.5	0.5	0.6
381 Metal products	7.9	8.4	8.5	8.1	7.7	8.2	8.1
382 Nonelectrical machinery	2.9	2.6	3.0	3.1	3.0	3.0	2.9
383 Electrical machinery	1.5	1.4	1.3	1.3	1.3	1.3	1.3
384 Transport equipment	2.6	2.3	2.3	2.1	2.1	1.9	2.0
385 Professional equipment	0.3	0.1	0.3	0.3	0.1	0.3	0.4
390 Other manufacturing	1.3	1.2	1.3	1.2	1.0	1.1	1.2

Source: Author's calculations based on survey data from the National Institute of Statistics.

Even though more plants were exiting than were entering manufacturing, during the prosperous years preceding the 1982 crisis, total factor productivity was growing at a respectable pace (see table 9.2 and figure 4.1). This positive association between growth of productivity and net exit is unusual and may reflect a shakedown that eliminated inefficient producers.[4] During the recession years of 1982–83 and the nascent recovery years of 1984–85, both total factor productivity and net entry became procyclical, as might be expected. But considering the dramatic swings that occurred in output during the 1980s, measurements of total factor productivity should not be given undue weight, since much of the increase may reflect changing rates of capacity utilization.[5]

Entry Patterns

Entry rates include both new entrants—start-up plants and plants newly expanded to at least ten employees, bringing them into the data base for the first time—and switching plants—plants that simply changed product line (see the appendix for details). For the manufacturing industry as a whole, new plants entered at a rate of about 4 percent in a typical year, with rates spiking in 1983–84 after beginning to rise in 1982–83 (see table 9.3). Curiously, only the 1983–84 figure looks "normal" when placed beside comparable statistics for Colombia (see chapter 10) and the United States (Dunne, Roberts, and Samuelson 1988); rates for all other years look very low. New plants averaged about one-fourth the size of incumbent plants, but the relative size of the two groups varied considerably over time.

Plants that switched industries were, as expected, typically closer in size to incumbents than were new entrants. But, like new entrants, their relative size was unstable, falling from three-quarters the size of incumbents in 1981 to less than a third in 1982. This volatility apparently reflects a more rapid decline in output for switching plants than for incumbents at the onset of the recession. The switches may have been

Table 9.2 Growth in Productivity, Output, and Import Penetration in Chile, 1980–81 to 1984–85 (percentages)

Industry	Productivity growth (TFP5)			Growth in real output (GTGVO5)			Growth in import penetration (GIMP)		
	1980–81	1982–83	1984–85	1980–81	1982–83	1984–85	1980–81	1982–83	1984–85
Food	1.5	0.9	0.8	7.0	2.9	7.4	1.6	-6.4	-26.5
Beverages	-3.8	-1.5	-0.7	-3.2	-5.9	1.6	-1.3	-25.8	-11.3
Tobacco	-11.0	-8.3	5.5	-5.3	-14.4	-4.6	-35.8	-36.3	-43.0
Textiles	8.5	-4.9	2.1	0.8	-5.3	8.8	22.1	-16.9	-2.9
Apparel	3.2	-4.6	5.8	7.7	-11.2	16.0	26.9	-26.2	-9.7
Leather products	10.1	-10.2	2.1	14.8	-11.9	3.0	28.4	-67.6	25.4
Footwear	7.2	-8.0	2.6	9.1	-3.5	7.7	57.3	-67.5	-20.5
Wood products	-3.1	1.9	8.4	1.1	-8.0	20.4	34.1	-45.8	-10.7
Furniture	-4.7	-7.8	-0.5	0.5	-25.9	12.6	41.8	-72.9	-6.6
Paper	-15.2	7.8	-0.3	11.7	5.7	3.6	-5.3	-11.3	-6.1
Printing	4.4	-25.0	-1.9	-9.2	-22.5	-6.8	-0.4	-10.1	9.5
Industrial chemicals	3.4	3.0	-1.4	-14.5	11.6	14.4	11.7	-0.3	-0.9
Other chemicals	5.9	-6.5	-0.8	7.2	-8.9	2.9	0.0	2.3	0.9
Petroleum refining	8.1	-4.1	-0.2	3.2	-5.7	-2.9	44.1	13.9	-39.3
Petroleum derivatives	0.7	-15.9	11.2	27.5	-18.3	82.7	-15.4	-58.5	-26.4
Rubber products	-0.5	0.2	2.8	-1.0	-8.4	14.0	19.9	1.0	-2.5
Plastics	4.2	-12.4	7.8	13.7	-21.5	14.6	22.4	-5.9	-14.0
Ceramics	21.1	-23.1	-0.3	-9.2	-21.1	-9.6	74.1	-59.3	-18.0
Glass	3.6	-2.5	10.6	3.7	-10.5	17.8	15.0	-14.0	3.0
Nonmetallic minerals	11.6	-21.9	3.3	14.7	-22.6	6.3	-1.3	-5.3	-0.1
Iron and steel	9.1	-14.9	1.4	-32.3	-22.1	-0.2	13.1	-19.1	23.7
Nonferrous metals	3.1	1.3	-3.5	12.5	12.5	-4.0	-10.8	-31.2	6.0
Metal products	4.7	-8.2	-1.2	5.8	-11.2	5.3	16.3	-0.6	5.3
Nonelectrical machinery	3.8	-3.5	4.0	25.1	-31.3	17.2	-0.6	-5.0	10.1
Electrical machinery	21.5	-26.9	11.9	-22.2	-36.0	15.3	8.4	-1.0	0.9
Transport equipment	9.4	-12.9	2.7	23.4	-54.8	22.5	9.0	-5.9	-1.4
Professional equipment	2.0	-5.8	-2.0	23.5	-15.8	-14.8	-0.9	-1.5	2.2
Other manufacturing	-7.0	16.9	-24.3	5.5	-25.6	3.1	6.2	-2.8	-4.1
Average	3.6	-7.0	1.7	5.6	-13.9	10.1	16.2	-2.0	-5.6

Source: Author's calculations based on survey data from the National Institute of Statistics.

Table 9.3 *Aggregate Entry and Exit in the Manufacturing Sector in Chile, 1979–85*
(percentages)

Entry or exit statistic	1979–80	1980–81	1981–82	1982–83	1983–84	1984–85
Entry rates (ER)						
All entrants	9.5	7.1	7.5	9.6	15.0	6.0
New entrants	4.0	4.1	4.3	6.7	13.2	4.3
Switching plants	5.5	3.0	3.2	2.9	1.7	1.8
Entrants' share of output (ESH)						
All entrants	6.2	4.1	2.3	2.9	3.8	2.5
New entrants	1.2	1.6	1.2	2.1	2.7	1.0
Switching plants	5.0	2.5	1.1	0.7	1.0	1.5
Entrants' relative size (ERS)						
All entrants	56.8	51.1	26.6	25.6	23.3	39.1
New entrants	25.9	35.2	23.8	28.0	19.4	22.5
Switching plants	82.6	75.0	32.3	23.2	60.4	82.3
Exit rates (XR)						
All existing plants	18.2	15.3	15.5	15.9	10.8	7.1
Plants disappearing in the next year	12.7	12.3	12.3	13.0	9.1	5.3
Plants switching to another three-digit industry	5.5	3.0	3.2	2.9	1.7	1.8
Exiting plants' share of output (XSH)						
All existing plants	9.7	5.6	3.8	3.9	2.3	2.5
Plants disappearing in the next year	4.4	3.5	2.4	3.1	1.4	0.9
Plants switching to another three-digit industry	5.3	2.1	1.4	0.7	1.0	1.6
Exiting plants' relative size (XRS)						
All existing plants	48.4	32.9	21.4	21.3	19.7	33.9
Plants disappearing in the next year	31.8	25.7	17.2	21.8	13.9	16.7
Plants switching to another three-digit industry	96.4	69.9	43.7	24.0	55.3	89.8

Note: Plant switching is defined at the three-digit level of industrial classification.
Source: Author's calculations based on survey data from the National Institute of Statistics.

induced partly by a rapid decline in demand for the products of the switching plants. The fraction of plants that switched industries declined almost continuously during the sample period, perhaps reflecting a settling down of entrepreneurs into a stable mix of products following the reform years.[6]

Several simple regressions using entry rates decomposed into plants that switched industries and those that entered as new plants reveal differences between the two groups of producers (table 9.4, models 3 and 4).[7] Most of the explained variation in entry is due to switching plants. The sign of the coefficients for new and switching plants is the same, but the value is generally larger for switching plants. Also, the downward trend in gross entry rates in 1979–81 was essentially a downward trend in switching plants. The rates for new plants were generally as high during 1981–85 as they were in 1980, higher after controlling for factors such as growth in output. This confirms the impression given by aggregate entry rates that plants were settling into a stable product mix by the mid-1980s. Finally, all the significant industry-level effects are for switching firms, not new entrants.

Entrants' share of output reflects the interaction of entry rates and relative size. The high entry rates in 1983 and 1984 more than offset the drop in average size of entrants, causing the market share of new entrants to rise above 2 percent in those years. This finding suggests that new, small firms were an unusually significant part of the driving force behind Chile's industrial recovery in the mid-1980s.

Exit Patterns

Exit rates were well above entry rates for 1979–82, which explains the large drop in the total number of plants during this period. Exiting plants also accounted for a larger share of output than entering plants in those four years, so the patterns of turnover tended to shrink net output. Net output shrank not because exiting plants were *bigger* than entering plants—in fact they were smaller in all years for which comparisons can be made—but rather because so many plants exited. That many small exiting plants were replaced by a few large plants implies that turnover increased the average scale of production.

The regressions also show that plants exiting one industry to enter another are less predictable than plants leaving manufacturing entirely. The rate of plant disappearance is negatively correlated with growth in output, and the correlation is strong enough for the F-statistic to be significant at any reasonable confidence level.[8] The switching plants that exited, however, are completely unpredictable. So although we can predict which sectors attract switching plants, we cannot predict the sector from which switching plants will exit.

Table 9.4 Regression Coefficients with Entry Rate and Exit Rate as the Dependent Variable

Variable	Entry rate Model 1 (gross)	Model 2 (gross)	Model 3 (new)	Model 4 (switching)	Exit rate Model 1 (gross)	Model 2 (gross)	Model 3 (dying)	Model 4 (switching)
Independent variable								
Intercept	0.189 (0.078)*	0.113 (0.02)*	0.012 (0.051)	0.176 (0.064)*	0.256 (0.118)*	0.180 (0.025)*	0.157 (0.055)*	0.099 (0.091)
GTGVO	0.149 (0.029)*	0.209 (0.026)*	0.042 (0.019)*	0.106 (0.023)*	-0.032 (0.042)	-0.030 (0.037)	-0.049 (0.019)*	0.017 (0.032)
H	-1.036 (0.228)*	0.025 (0.033)	-0.057 (0.149)	-0.979 (0.186)*	-0.768 (0.376)*	-0.093 (0.044)*	-0.480 (0.174)*	-0.288 (0.288)
IMP	0.062 (0.095)	0.086 (0.024)*	0.060 (0.062)	0.002 (0.078)	-0.024 (0.145)	0.004 (0.032)	0.006 (0.067)	-0.030 (0.112)
KQR5	-0.016 (0.052)	0.001 (0.02)	-0.009 (0.034)	-0.007 (0.042)	-0.051 (0.08)	-0.024 (0.026)	-0.053 (0.037)	0.001 (0.062)
Year dummy variable								
1981	0.053 (0.019)*	-0.060 (0.021)*	-0.023 (0.013)	-0.030 (0.016)	0.010 (0.027)	0.006 (0.026)	0.007 (0.012)	0.003 (0.021)
1982	0.001 (0.02)	0.012 (0.022)	0.010 (0.013)	-0.009 (0.016)	0.023 (0.028)	0.020 (0.027)	0.017 (0.013)	0.006 (0.021)
1983	-0.032 (0.02)	-0.044 (0.021)*	0.017 (0.013)	-0.049 (0.016)*	-0.048 (0.027)	-0.055 (0.026)*	-0.023 (0.013)	-0.026 (0.021)
1984	-0.011 (0.02)*	-0.019 (0.021)	0.074 (0.013)*	-0.086 (0.016)*	-0.072 (0.027)*	-0.071 (0.027)*	-0.059 (0.012)*	-0.014 (0.021)
1985	-0.074 (0.019)*	-0.078 (0.021)*	-0.020 (0.012)	-0.054 (0.016)*	—	—	—	—
Industry dummy variable								
Food	0.091 (0.07)	—	0.041 (0.045)	-0.132 (0.057)*	-0.120 (0.107)	—	-0.033 (0.049)	-0.087 (0.082)
Beverages	-0.051 (0.074)	—	0.038 (0.048)	-0.089 (0.061)	-0.540 (0.114)	—	0.025 (0.053)	-0.078 (0.088)
Tobacco	0.901 (0.208)*	—	0.143 (0.135)	0.758 (0.170)*	0.521 (0.342)	—	0.348 (0.158)*	0.173 (0.262)
Textiles	-0.056 (0.056)	—	0.022 (0.036)	-0.078 (0.046)	-0.046 (0.086)	—	0.002 (0.040)	-0.048 (0.066)
Apparel	-0.055 (0.066)	—	0.031 (0.043)	-0.086 (0.054)	-0.050 (0.1)	—	-0.002 (0.046)	-0.047 (0.077)
Leather products	-0.037 (0.069)	—	0.024 (0.045)	-0.061 (0.056)	-0.035 (0.104)	—	0.028 (0.048)	-0.063 (0.080)
Footwear	-0.027 (0.072)	—	0.040 (0.047)	-0.067 (0.059)	-0.057 (0.108)	—	0.004 (0.050)	-0.061 (0.083)
Wood products	-0.020 (0.078)	—	0.072 (0.051)	-0.091 (0.064)	-0.003 (0.124)	—	0.071 (0.057)	-0.075 (0.095)
Furniture	0.022 (0.072)	—	0.053 (0.047)	-0.031 (0.059)	0.034 (0.11)	—	0.074 (0.051)	-0.040 (0.085)
Paper	0.037 (0.075)	—	0.043 (0.049)	0.021 (0.061)	0.027 (0.121)	—	0.060 (0.056)	-0.033 (0.093)

	(1)	(2)	(3)	(4)	(5)	(6)	(7)	(8)
Printing	0.014 (0.069)	—	0.026 (0.045)	-0.012 (0.057)	-0.020 (0.108)	—	0.032 (0.050)	-0.052 (0.083)
Industrial chemicals	-0.060 (0.041)	—	-0.011 (0.027)	0.005 (0.034)	-0.035 (0.062)	—	-0.039 (0.029)	0.004 (0.048)
Other chemicals	-0.070 (0.064)	—	0.002 (0.042)	-0.073 (0.052)	-0.117 (0.098)	—	-0.064 (0.045)	-0.053 (0.075)
Petroleum refining	0.320 (0.113)*	—	0.018 (0.074)	0.302 (0.093)*	0.264 (0.178)	—	0.088 (0.082)	0.176 (0.136)
Petroleum derivatives	0.388 (0.092)*	—	0.013 (0.060)	0.375 (0.075)*	0.141 (0.154)	—	0.072 (0.071)	0.069 (0.118)
Rubber products	0.097 (0.061)	—	0.023 (0.040)	0.074 (0.050)	0.037 (0.096)	—	0.032 (0.045)	0.005 (0.074)
Plastics	-0.007 (0.067)	—	0.051 (0.043)	-0.058 (0.055)	-0.066 (0.102)	—	-0.024 (0.047)	-0.043 (0.078)
Ceramics	0.393 (0.092)*	—	0.065 (0.060)	0.328 (0.075)*	0.237 (0.145)	—	0.150 (0.067)*	0.087 (0.111)
Glass	0.173 (0.081)*	—	0.010 (0.053)	0.163 (0.066)*	0.144 (0.136)	—	0.112 (0.063)	0.032 (0.104)
Nonmetallic minerals	0.049 (0.082)	—	0.067 (0.053)	-0.017 (0.067)	0.033 (0.13)	—	0.085 (0.060)	-0.052 (0.099)
Iron and steel	0.289 (0.081)*	—	0.025 (0.053)	0.264 (0.066)*	0.213 (0.128)	—	0.077 (0.059)	0.138 (0.098)
Nonferrous metals	0.158 (0.08)	—	0.013 (0.052)	0.142 (0.065)*	0.084 (0.124)	—	0.001 (0.057)	0.082 (0.095)
Metal products	-0.018 (0.057)	—	0.031 (0.037)	-0.049 (0.046)	-0.033 (0.087)	—	-0.009 (0.040)	-0.024 (0.067)
Nonelectrical machinery	0.061 (0.041)	—	-0.004 (0.027)	0.065 (0.034)	0.046 (0.063)	—	0.003 (0.029)	0.043 (0.048)
Electrical machinery	0.020 (0.041)	—	-0.008 (0.027)	0.028 (0.033)	0.012 (0.062)	—	-0.015 (0.029)	0.027 (0.047)
Transport equipment	0.068 (0.044)	—	0.0002 (0.029)	0.068 (0.036)	0.057 (0.065)	—	0.034 (0.030)	0.022 (0.050)
Professional equipment	0.074 (0.048)	—	-0.006 (0.031)	0.080 (0.039)*	0.024 (0.071)	—	-0.025 (0.033)	0.048 (0.055)
Dependent mean	0.108	0.108	0.055	0.054	0.136	0.136	0.090	0.047
σ^2	0.005	0.006	0.002	0.003	0.009	0.009	0.002	0.005
R^2	0.456	0.326	0.371	0.520	0.128	0.133	0.518	0.077
F-statistic	4.895	9.958	3.732	6.027	1.584	3.666	5.261	1.329

— Not available.

* Significant at the 5 percent level.

Note: GTGVO is real output growth, H is the Herfindahl index of industry concentration, IMP is the import penetration rate, and KQR is the industry capital-output ratio. Numbers in parentheses are standard errors.

Source: Author's calculations based on 1979–85 survey data from Chile's National Institute of Statistics.

Survival Patterns

The chances for survival can be reasonably expected to differ for recent entrants to the market and for older firms. On the one hand, given the adjustment costs of retooling a plant, recent entrants may enjoy more flexibility in reacting to the new rules of the game. On the other hand, older firms have survived more trials, and a process of natural selection should have eliminated many of the poor performers among them.

Following a typical pattern, the market share of firms already in place in 1979 gradually declined over the sample period (see table 9.5; Roberts, in chapter 10, finds the same pattern for Colombia; Dunne, Roberts, and Samuelson 1988 find it for the United States). Surprisingly, however, the pattern does not hold for cohorts that entered during 1983 and 1984.

Plants in both cohorts started small, but the 1983 entrants grew faster than others, so part of their increase in market share was due to rapid growth in output. Also, although younger cohorts typically have lower year-to-year survival rates than older ones (Dunne, Roberts, and Samuelson 1988; Evans 1987), plants entering in 1983 and 1984 survived the first year with unusually high frequency.[9] (The 1981 cohort also had unusually good survival skills.)

What explains these high rates of survival? One possibility is that the new economic regime was firmly in place by the 1980s, so entrants during this decade were able to invest in activities that were to be promoted in coming years (such as exportable goods based on natural resources). Another is that conditions were so harsh during the recession, especially in 1982 and 1983, that only the most promising ventures were initiated in those years. In support of this view that selectivity took place at the portal, recall that entry rates were remarkably low during all sample years except 1984.

Conclusion

Extremely low rates of entry in the Chilean manufacturing sector during the first half of the 1980s, coupled with more typical exit rates (comparable to those of Colombia), indicate that a major shakedown occurred in manufacturing. Plants that entered in 1983 and 1984 grew so rapidly that their market share expanded relative to that of older cohorts—perhaps because new plants were not burdened with the financial problems afflicting firms already in the market.[10] As expected, both entering and exiting plants tended to be much smaller than their incumbent counterparts. But, entering plants were larger than the exiting plants they replaced, so turnover increased average scale. Finally, when output growth and other factors are controlled for, the amount of industry-level switching among continuing plants shows a clear downward trend in the

*Table 9.5 Share of Output, Relative Size, and Survival Rates of
Entering Plants in Chile, 1979–85*
(percentages)

Cohort	1979	1980	1981	1982	1983	1984	1985
Share of manufacturing output							
Pre-1980 plants	1.0	93.8	91.3	90.2	87.7	84.3	81.9
1980 entrants	n.a.	6.2	4.6	3.9	3.8	3.1	3.1
1981 entrants	n.a.	n.a.	4.1	3.6	3.5	2.9	3.0
1982 entrants	n.a.	n.a.	n.a.	2.3	2.1	2.2	1.9
1983 entrants	n.a.	n.a.	n.a.	n.a.	2.9	3.7	3.8
1984 entrants	n.a.	n.a.	n.a.	n.a.	n.a.	3.8	3.8
1985 entrants	n.a.	n.a.	n.a.	n.a.	n.a.	n.a.	2.5
Size of surviving plants relative to that of all manufacturing plants							
Pre-1980 plants	1.0	10.2	10.8	11.3	11.8	12.9	13.0
1980 entrants	n.a.	59.5	58.3	57.4	69.0	68.2	72.9
1981 entrants	n.a.	n.a.	53.1	67.4	76.6	76.7	81.0
1982 entrants	n.a.	n.a.	n.a.	28.3	40.9	53.3	52.0
1983 entrants	n.a.	n.a.	n.a.	n.a.	27.8	49.2	56.9
1984 entrants	n.a.	n.a.	n.a.	n.a.	n.a.	26.1	30.3
1985 entrants	n.a.	n.a.	n.a.	n.a.	n.a.	n.a.	40.6
Year-to-year cohort survival rates							
Pre-1980 plants	1.0	81.8	86.4	87.1	87.4	91.9	95.1
1980 entrants	n.a.	1.0	70.4	77.8	77.2	86.3	92.0
1981 entrants	n.a.	n.a.	1.0	63.6	81.2	86.6	94.0
1982 entrants	n.a.	n.a.	n.a.	1.0	60.0	81.3	88.2
1983 entrants	n.a.	n.a.	n.a.	n.a.	1.0	76.2	88.1
1984 entrants	n.a.	n.a.	n.a.	n.a.	n.a.	1.0	87.1
1985 entrants	n.a.	n.a.	n.a.	n.a.	n.a.	n.a.	1.0

n.a. Not applicable.
Note: Entry is to industries at the three-digit level of industrial classification.
Source: Author's calculations based on survey data from the National Institute of
Statistics.

1980s, suggesting that producers were settling into a stable mix of products by 1984–85. Switching plants appear to have moved fairly pre-
dictably to sectors with high output growth and low concentration, but
sectors of origin for switching plants are completely unpredictable.

Competition

The analysis thus far sugests that Chile's trade liberalization and other
reforms systematically shifted resources among sectors. It remains to
investigate whether, once these reforms were accomplished, producers
still enjoyed market power in some manufacturing industries. This sec-

tion analyzes the issue using the models of price-cost margins summarized in chapter 8.

Price-Cost Margins at the Industry Level

Estimates of price-cost margins in Chilean manufacturing industries show that time and especially industry effects are very important (table 9.6). With dummy sets for industry (DI) and time (DT) included, the adjusted R^2 is about 0.85. Without the industry dummies, it is 0.28. Although the year effects appear higher late in the sample period, none of the coefficients for the time dummy variables is significantly different from 0, indicating that the trend toward increasing margins is mild.

The significance of industry dummies calls into question the validity of cross-industry regression models that explain markups. To the extent that industry dummies are correlated with the explanatory variables appearing in these models, the results are subject to omitted variable bias. For example, the role of capital-output ratios (KQ) depends strongly on whether industry effects are included. If industry effects are left out, capital-output ratios have positive and significant coefficients. If industry effects are controlled, temporal variation in capital intensity is not significantly related to fluctuations in price-cost margins within industries.

The role of import penetration (IMP) also depends on industry effects. A significant negative association between import penetration and price-cost margins emerges when industry effects are not controlled for, but when they are, the association becomes positive and marginally significant. There is more to the story. If industry effects are ignored and an interaction term is added between the industry structure term (H) and import penetration, then import penetration appears to reduce margins more in industries that are relatively concentrated. This result is familiar from previous studies (Jacquemin, de Ghellinck, and Huveneers 1980; Pugel 1980) and is typically interpreted as providing support for the import-discipline hypothesis.[11] The result disappears, however, if industry effects are controlled for. If anything, import penetration then tends to increase margins most in relatively concentrated industries. This finding implies that omitted factors such as entry barriers correlate with both price-cost margins and import penetration rates but are eliminated as a source of bias when industry effects are taken into account.

The effect of industrial concentration on margins appears to be positive, regardless of the specification used. This result squares with many other studies of the determinants of price-cost margins, with or without import penetration variables. The association is much weaker in this study, however, when industry effects are controlled for. Also, when the interaction term between concentration and import penetration is included, the effect of concentration on price-cost margins becomes

Table 9.6 *Regression Estimates with Industry-Based Price-Cost Margin as the Dependent Variable*

Variable	Model 1	Model 2	Model 3	Model 4
Independent variable				
Intercept	0.231 (0.046)*	0.333 (0.074)*	0.26 (0.026)*	0.236 (0.029)*
H	0.367 (0.135)*	0.184 (0.167)	0.312 (0.041)*	0.397 (0.050)*
IMP	0.114 (0.057)*	−0.032 (0.117)	−0.093 (0.029)*	0.026 (0.078)
KQR	−0.048 (0.032)	−0.029 (0.048)	0.083 (0.025)*	0.111 (0.037)*
$H \cdot IMP$	n.a.	0.531 (0.286)	n.a.	−0.682 (0.234)*
$KQR \cdot IMP$	n.a.	−0.074 (0.12)	n.a.	−0.073 (0.157)
Year dummy variable				
1980	−0.007 (0.013)	−0.005 (0.013)	−0.003 (0.028)	−0.004 (0.028)
1981	0.001 (0.014)	0.004 (0.014)	0.018 (0.028)	0.022 (0.028)
1982	0.018 (0.013)	0.024 (0.014)	0.015 (0.028)	0.010 (0.028)
1983	0.013 (0.013)	0.015 (0.013)	0.003 (0.028)	−0.003 (0.028)
1984	0.020 (0.013)	0.023 (0.013)	0.026 (0.028)	0.021 (0.028)
1985	0.026 (0.013)*	0.027 (0.013)*	0.025 (0.028)	0.020 (0.028)
Industry dummy variable				
Food	0.026 (0.042)	−0.068 (0.065)	n.a.	n.a.
Beverages	0.191 (0.045)	0.091 (0.070)	n.a.	n.a.
Tobacco	0.198 (0.131)	0.249 (0.133)	n.a.	n.a.
Textiles	0.027 (0.034)	−0.035 (0.048)	n.a.	n.a.
Apparel	0.008 (0.040)	−0.071 (0.059)	n.a.	n.a.
Leather products	−0.017 (0.042)	−0.101 (0.062)	n.a.	n.a.
Footwear	0.064 (0.044)	−0.023 (0.065)	n.a.	n.a.
Wood products	0.127 (0.047)	0.014 (0.077)	n.a.	n.a.
Furniture	0.049 (0.044)	−0.042 (0.066)	n.a.	n.a.

(Table continues on the following page.)

Table 9.6 (continued)

Variable	Model 1	Model 2	Model 3	Model 4
Industry dummy variable *(continued)*				
Paper	0.194 (0.045)	0.109 (0.064)	n.a.	n.a.
Printing	0.128 (0.043)	0.047 (0.061)	n.a.	n.a.
Industrial chemicals	0.048 (0.026)	0.037 (0.027)	n.a.	n.a.
Other chemicals	0.142 (0.039)	0.066 (0.057)	n.a.	n.a.
Petroleum refining	−0.257 (0.074)	−0.290 (0.076)*	n.a.	n.a.
Petroleum derivatives	−0.098 (0.057)	−0.150 (0.063)*	n.a.	n.a.
Rubber products	−0.030 (0.040)	−0.085 (0.049)	n.a.	n.a.
Plastics	0.054 (0.041)	−0.034 (0.062)	n.a.	n.a.
Ceramics	−0.084 (0.056)	−0.139 (0.063)*	n.a.	n.a.
Glass	0.116 (0.049)	0.068 (0.055)	n.a.	n.a.
Nonmetallic minerals	0.204 (0.049)	0.111 (0.071)	n.a.	n.a.
Iron and steel	−0.085 (0.053)	−0.143 (0.061)	n.a.	n.a.
Nonferrous metals	0.128 (0.051)	0.049 (0.067)	n.a.	n.a.
Metal products	0.031 (0.035)	−0.033 (0.049)	n.a.	n.a.
Nonelectric machinery	−0.203 (0.026)	−0.203 (0.026)*	n.a.	n.a.
Electric machinery	−0.020 (0.026)	−0.022 (0.026)	n.a.	n.a.
Transport equipment	−0.096 (0.028)	−0.116 (0.031)*	n.a.	n.a.
Professional equipment	−0.057 (0.029)	−0.052 (0.03)	n.a.	n.a.
Dependent mean	0.333	0.333	0.333	0.333
σ^2	0.002	0.002	0.011	0.011
R^2	0.847	0.848	0.276	0.302
F-statistic	30.973	29.725	9.271	8.665

n.a. Not applicable.
* Significant at the 5 percent level.
Note: H is the Herfindahl index of industry concentration, *IMP* is the import penetration rate, and *KQR* is the industry capital-output ratio. Because the results are insensitive to the capital stock measure used, results are reported for only one measure. Numbers in parentheses are standard errors.
Source: Author's calculations based on survey 1979–85 data from Chile's National Institute of Statistics.

insignificant. Here, too, the omission of industrial characteristics appears to be a significant part of the explanation for the oft-observed association between concentration and margins.

In short, there is little evidence that foreign competition disciplines market power in Chile. Although imports do tend to concentrate in industries with low margins, there is no evidence that allowing additional imports into a specific industry would affect these margins. It may be that the industrial sector is so competitive that intraindustry variations in import penetration are irrelevant. Less plausibly, these results may mean that market structures are not competitive and that imports do not affect market power. The plant-level analysis provides some evidence in support of the first interpretation.

Price-Cost Margins at the Plant Level

When price-cost margins are used to measure performance, any cross-plant variation may be due to industrywide effects or to plant-specific market shares. Schmalensee (1985) has argued that if industry effects are statistically insignificant, it is likely that markets are basically competitive. (Any correlation between market shares and profits can be explained by arguing that the most efficient firms are the most profitable and so have probably grown the fastest.) But if industry effects are empirically important, market structure—the ability of firms to restrict competition—is probably part of the explanation.

Unlike in the industry-level regressions, capital-output ratios account for most of the explained variation at the plant level (see table 9.7). When KQ and KQ^2 are omitted from the model, the R^2 drops from 0.447 to 0.002 in the regression with pooled data. Similarly, it drops to 0.065, 0.019, 0.005, and 0.278 for the subsamples including proprietorships, partnerships, corporations, and public enterprises, respectively. More often than not, coefficients on KQ and KQ^2 are negative, suggesting that temporal variation in output induces this strong association. (Recall that output appears in the numerator of the price-cost margin and the denominator of the capital-output ratio.)

In the regression with pooled data, industry dummy coefficients are significantly different from one another (the F-value is 19.38), but their exclusion only reduces R^2 by 0.013, to 0.434. This result stands in contrast to findings for the United States that industry effects account for "at least 75 percent of the variation of industry rates of return on assets" (Schmalensee 1985, p. 349). According to Schmalensee's logic, Chile's industrial sector appears to be *more* competitive than its U.S. counterpart.[12] Similar results emerge when each type of Chilean business is analyzed separately. This surprising finding challenges the commonly held belief that small product markets and poorly developed financial

Table 9.7 *Regression Coefficients with Plant-Level Price-Cost Margin (PCM) as the Dependent Variable*

Variable	All plants	Proprietorships	Partnerships	Corporations	Public enterprises
Independent variable					
S	2.469 (0.248)*	37.077 (4.464)*	6.177 (0.794)*	0.931 (0.178)*	74.561 (39.219)
$S \cdot S$	−3.225 (0.432)	−799.839 (140.583)*	−24.253 (5.841)*	−1.024 (0.286)*	−2,176.010 (1,162.608)
IMP	0.009 (0.053)	0.034 (0.112)	0.064 (0.058)	−0.094 (0.057)	−0.551 (9.243)
$IMP \cdot S$	−1.434 (0.415)*	−10.769 (11.814)	−1.343 (1.194)	−0.544 (0.303)	80.903 (115.212)
KQ	0.031 (0.002)*	−0.087 (0.005)*	−0.034 (0.003)*	−0.036 (0.003)*	−0.889 (0.299)
$KQ \cdot KQ$	−0.001 (0.000)*	0.002 (0.000)*	−0.002 (0.000)*	0.000 (0.000)*	0.109 (0.050)*
Year dummy variable					
1980	0.042 (0.009)*	0.004 (0.013)	0.017 (0.011)	0.015 (0.013)	−0.038 (0.542)
1981	0.030 (0.10)*	−0.027 (0.014)*	−0.001 (0.011)	−0.005 (0.013)	−0.078 (0.472)
1982	0.016 (0.010)	−0.047 (0.016)*	−0.018 (0.012)	0.025 (0.014)	−0.856 (0.612)
1983	0.017 (0.010)	−0.058 (0.015)*	−0.015 (0.012)	−0.006 (0.013)	−0.756 (0.499)
1984	0.025 (0.010)*	−0.047 (0.016)*	−0.019 (0.012)	−0.025 (0.014)	−0.655 (0.556)
1985	0.040 (0.010)*	−0.033 (0.016)*	−0.004 (0.012)	−0.028 (0.013)*	−0.574 (0.558)
Dependent mean	0.230	0.154	0.233	0.326	−0.169
R^2	0.447	0.115	0.814	0.101	0.865
R^2 without industry dummies	0.434	0.060	0.807	0.052	0.500
F-test					
H_0: industry dummies are the same	19.38*	13.46*	15.68*	8.93*	12.19*
H_0: model has no explanatory power	458.36*	18.95*	1,168.00*	12.94*	7.91*

* Significant at the 5 percent level.

Note: IMP is the import penetration rate, KQ is the plant-level capital-output ratio, and H is the Herfindahl index of industry concentration. Numbers in parentheses are standard errors. The number of observations is 22,174 for all plants, 5,451 for proprietorships, 10,167 for partnerships, 4,553 for corporations, and 35 for public enterprises. Data are for 1979–85.

Source: Chile's National Institute of Statistics.

markets enhance the monopoly power of industrialists in developing countries.

Although the effects of market share are not strong, they are significant.[13] Generally, increases in share improve price-cost margins, but at a decreasing rate. The association between margins and market share is at least as strong among proprietorships and limited partnerships as it is among corporations, even though the former tend to be the smaller companies. The findings may reflect cost heterogeneity rather than market power. For example, firms with high marginal costs have low price-cost margins and capture small market shares in a Cournot equilibrium (Roberts and Tybout 1991). An identical pattern emerges in the study of Colombia (chapter 10).

Import penetration appears to have an insignificant influence on price-cost margins for all types of business organization, a finding consistent with the industry-level analysis of margins once industry effects are controlled for. This result casts doubt on the conjecture that variations in the market power of industries are associated with variations in their degree of exposure to international competition. Overall, the results also cast doubt on the notion that Chilean industries are generally not very competitive yet are not influenced by import competition. Indeed, the findings suggest that Chilean manufacturing industries may be more competitive than U.S. industries. A tentative conclusion is that most sectors are sufficiently free of entry barriers or sufficiently exposed to foreign competition to eliminate significant monopoly profits, regardless of the level of imports.

Conclusions

Overall, the patterns of entry and exit reported here suggest that the Chilean industrial sector underwent a process of rationalization during the first half of the 1980s. Exposed to substantial new import competition with the dismantling of trade barriers in the late 1970s, the sector was then buffeted by a severe recession and widespread insolvency in the first years of the 1980s. The number of plants in operation dropped rapidly, as entry rates fell and exit rates did not. An unusually large portion of plants that remained active switched their product lines. Entering plants, though fewer, were larger than exiting plants, so scale efficiency may have improved somewhat.[14] Plants were attracted to industries experiencing rapid growth in output but did not necessarily leave industries experiencing slow growth.

The now smaller industrial sector responded positively to government rescue efforts, including debt relief measures, business tax reductions, devaluations, and other measures. New firms that entered in the early stages of the recovery, though small, were unusually dynamic and captured an increasing share of the domestic market. Switching between industries by continuing plants declined noticeably as the recovery progressed, suggesting the culmination of a process of rationalization.

Industries with high rates of import penetration appear to have been relatively competitive, with relatively high entry rates (suggesting the absence of entry barriers) and relatively low price-cost margins. However, there is no intraindustry correlation between import penetration and entry rates or margins, so it cannot be inferred that further trade liberalization would have reduced further the market power of domestic firms. Neither does it appear that import penetration was closely related to the size of entrants relative to incumbents.

Competition was apparently strong in Chile. Dummy variables for industry do not help much to predict plants' margins, given their market shares, as they do in studies for other countries. By Schmalensee's (1985) logic, this suggests that productive resources freely gravitated to high-return activities, equating the marginal product of capital across sectors. If this interpretation is correct, the absence of a correlation between import penetration and price-cost margins within industries need not imply that the import-discipline hypothesis is wrong. Rather, it may simply mean that, at the margin, there was little market power to discipline.

Appendix: Data Preparation

Annual plant-level data for 1979–85 on all manufacturing plants with at least ten workers were provided for this study by Chile's National Institute of Statistics. These data include various production, employment, overhead, investment, intermediate input, and balance sheet variables.

A Description of the Methodology

To distinguish plants that were in the data base in 1979 from plants that appeared in 1980, 1981, and so on, plants were assigned year-of-entry codes. Then the various entry and exit statistics defined in table 9A.1 were constructed. These statistics describe movement into or out of the *data base*, which includes only firms with at least ten workers. A plant appearing in the data base for the first time may have entered either by expanding its employment to ten or more workers or by undertaking "green field" construction (building a new plant as opposed to renovating or expanding an existing plant). There is also a third possibility for plants appearing in a particular *industry* for the first time: they may simply have switched product line. The first two types of entrants are referred to as new entrants and the third is referred to as switching plants. Together, entry rates for the two groups constitute the gross entry rate for an industry.

Table 9A.1 Definition of Entry- and Exit-Related Variables

Variable	Definition
$NE(j, t)$	Number of plants that enter industry j in year t; calculated as the number of plants that newly enter industry j in year t plus the number of plants that operate in industry i in year $t - 1$ and switch to industry j in year t
$NE_n(j, t)$	Number of plants that newly enter industry j in year t
$NE_s(j, t)$	Number of plants that operate in industry t in year $t - 1$ and switch to industry j in year t
$NX(j, t - 1)$	Number of plants that exit industry j between year $t - 1$; calculated as the number of plants that exit industry j between year $t - 1$ and do not enter another industry in year t plus the number of plants that exit industry j between year $t - 1$ and t and enter industry i in year t
$Nx_d(j, t - 1)$	Number of plants that exit industry j between year $t - 1$ and t and disappear in year t (that is, do not enter another industry in year t)
$NX_s(j, t - 1)$	Number of plants that exit industry j between year $t - 1$ and t but switch to another industry i in year t
$NT(j, t)$	Total number of plants in operation in industry j in year t
$QE(j, t)$	Total output of plants that enter industry j in year t
$QE_n(j, t)$	Total output of plants that newly enter industry j in year t
$QE_s(j, t)$	Total output of plants that switch to industry j in year t
$QX(j, t - 1)$	Total output of plants that exit industry j between year $t - 1$ and t
$QX_d(j, t - 1)$	Total output of plants that exit industry j between year $t - 1$ and t and disappear in year t
$QX_s(j, t - 1)$	Total output of plants that exit industry j year $t - 1$ and t and switch to industry i in year t
$QT(j, t)$	Total output of all plants in operation in industry j in year t
Entry / exit ratio	
$NE(t)/NT(t - 1)$	Aggregate entry rate
$NE_n(t)/NT(t - 1)$	Aggregate new entry rate
$NE_s(t)/NT(t - 1)$	Aggregate switching entry rate
$NX(t - 1)/NT(t - 1)$	Aggregate exit rate
$NX_d(t - 1)/NT(t - 1)$	Aggregate disappearing exit rate

(Table continues on the following page.)

Table 9A.1 (continued)

Variable	Definition
Entry/exit ratio *(continued)*	
$NX_s(t-1)/NT(t-1)$	Aggregate switching exit rate
$QE(t)/QT(t)$	Market share of entrants
$QE_n(t)/QT(t)$	Market share of new entrants
$QE_s(t)/QT(t)$	Market share of entrants that are switching
$QX(t-1)/NT(t-1)$	Market share of exiting plants
$QX_d(t-1)/NT(t-1)$	Market share of exiting plants that are disappearing
$QX_s(t-1)/NT(t-1)$	Market share of exiting plants that are switching

Size ratio

$$\frac{QE(t)\,/\,NE(t)}{[QT(t)-QE(t)]/[NT(t)-NE(t)]}$$

Average size of entrants relative to incumbents

$$\frac{QE_n(t)\,/\,NE_n(t)}{[QT(t)-QE_n(t)]/[NT(t)-NE_n(t)]}$$

Average size of new entrants relative to incumbents and entrants that are switching

$$\frac{QE_s(t)/NE_s(t)}{[T(t)-QE_s(t)]/[NT(t)-NE_s(t)]}$$

Average size of entrants that are switching relative to incumbents and new entrants

$$\frac{QX(t-1)/NX(t-1)}{[QT(t-1)-QX(t-1)]/[NT(t-1)-NX(t-1)]}$$

Average size of all exiting plants relative to continuing plants

$$\frac{QX_d(t-1)/NX_d(t-1)}{[QT(t-1)-QX_d(t-1)/[NT(t-1)-NX_d(t-1)]}$$

Average size of exiting plants that are disappearing relative to continuing plants and exiting plants that are switching

$$\frac{QX(t-1)/NX_s(t-1)}{[QT(t-1)-QX_s(t-1)]/[NT(t-1)-NX_s(t-1)]}$$

Average size of exiting plants that are switching relative to continuing plants and exiting plants

Standardizing Variables across Census Years

There were several inconsistencies in the original definitions of variables from one year to the next. For example, certain components of gross investment were omitted in all observations in 1979. These types of problems were uncovered through identity checks and were corrected by recalculating relevant variables. Identity checks also revealed a handful of randomly scattered inconsistencies that could not be explained as changes in definition. Observations exhibiting this type of problem were excluded from calculations and regressions.

Identifying Entering and Exiting Plants

The original data base consisted of seven annual cross-sectional files. On the basis of plant identification codes and standard industrial codes for each observation, the files were merged into a single-panel data base sorted by plant, year, and type of product. The intertemporal pattern of missing values for each plant was then used as the basis for the analysis of plant-level entry, exit, and switching. Finally, data on patterns of ownership (based on 1985) were merged with the sorted data base and used to analyze the behavior of multiplant firms.

Putting Data in Constant Prices

The data include both stock variables (like fixed capital), which are observed at a point in time, and flow variables (like total sales), which are recorded on a continuous basis. If inflation is substantial, stock and flow variables cannot be mixed, because flow variables are valued roughly at an annual average price and stock variables are valued at an end (or beginning) of year price. To convert from year-end to annual average prices, each stock variable was multiplied by the ratio of an annual average price index to a year-end price index, based on industry-specific output prices. Since Chilean accounting norms require that firms express their capital stocks and inventories in year-end prices, adjustment for further bias in stock variables—as would be necessary with first-in, first-out accounting, for example—was unnecessary. After all variables were expressed in mid-year prices, the data were put in constant 1979 prices using industry-specific price deflators.

The following expression was used to impute year-end prices for 1978 and 1985, since only average annual price indexes are available for each industry:[15]

(9A.1) $PE_{jt} = (P_{jt} P_{jt+1})^{1/2}$

where PE_{jt} is year-end price in industry j in year t, P_{jt} is mid-year price in industry j in year t, and P_{jt+1} is mid-year price in industry j in year $t+1$.

Constructing Capital Stock Variables

There are two problems with the reported capital stock figures. First, they were reported as part of plants' balance sheets, and balance sheet data were collected only for 1980 and 1981. For most firms, seven years of data on fixed investment and depreciation could be combined with 1980 or 1981 stock values to construct capital stock series. That could not be done, however, for plants that entered between 1982 and 1985.

The second problem concerns depreciation. Both data on investment and data on capital stock were reported by type of asset: buildings, machinery, and vehicles.[16] Identity checks revealed that each type of capital asset was expressed in gross terms in balance sheets and had not been adjusted for depreciation. Moreover, the accumulated depreciation figures had not been decomposed by type of asset, so that had to be estimated. This was done on the basis of current depreciation figures, which were observable by type of asset in each sample year. For the ith plant and the mth type of asset, cumulative depreciation on base year ($t_0 =$ 1980 or 1981) capital stock ($\text{CUM}_{im_{t_0}}$) was imputed as a fraction of total cumulative depreciation at the ith plant, CUM_{it_0}:

$$(9A.2) \qquad CUMD_{im_{t_0}} = \left(\frac{A_{im}}{B_i}\right) \cdot CUMD_{i,_{t_0}}.$$

Here D_{imt} is the current depreciation in asset m in year t for plant i, $B_i = \Sigma_{t=1979}^{1985} \Sigma_{m=1}^{5} D_{imt}$ is total depreciation for plant i from 1979 to 1985, $A_{im} = \Sigma_{t=1979}^{1985} D_{imt}$ is total depreciation in asset m from 1979 to 1985 for plant i. For plants for which *total* cumulative depreciation data were missing for the base year, $CUMD_{it_0}$, a total depreciation had to be imputed based on a regression of total $CUMD_{it_0}$ on gross base capital stock, K_{it_0}. The regression was fit using all plants for which both variables are observable:

$$(9A.3) \qquad \hat{C}UMD_{it_0} = \hat{\beta}_0 + \sum_{m=1}^{5} \hat{\beta}_m K_{im_{t_0}}$$

so for the plants with missing data, equation 9A.2 becomes

$$(9A.4) \qquad \hat{C}UMD_{im_{t_0}} = \left(\frac{A_{im}}{B_i}\right) \cdot \left(\hat{\beta}_0 + \sum_{m=1}^{5} \hat{\beta}_m K_{im_{t_0}}\right)$$

The imputed accumulated depreciation for each type of fixed asset in the base years (1980 and 1981) was subtracted from the associated gross stocks to get net base year stocks for each plant. Then annual data on plants' investment and depreciation were used to construct the series of net capital stock using the perpetual-inventory method.[17] This involved accumulating capital forward for 1982–85 and backward for 1979, using the following equation:

$$(9A.5) \qquad K_{imt} = (1 - \Delta_m)K_{imt-1}\left(\frac{P_t}{P_{t-1}}\right) + I_{imt}.$$

Here K_{imt} is net capital stock in asset m at the end of year t for plant i, Δ_m is the assumed rate of economic depreciation for asset m, I_{imt} is gross investment in asset m by plant i in year t, and P_t is the general industry (mid-year) price index in year t. Assumed annual rates of economic depreciation of 5 percent for buildings, 10 percent for machinery, and 20 percent for vehicles were used instead of book values. Once the capital stock series were constructed in mid-year prices, they were put in *constant* prices.

For some plants, capital stock values were missing for 1980 but were available for 1981. If 1980 were used as the unique base year, capital stock values would have been missing for these plants, so two sets of net capital stock variables were constructed, one based on 1980 and one on 1981. Similarly, two sets of *gross* capital stock variables were constructed. This construction followed the same logic as that for net capital stock except that K_{im} in the base year was the reported *gross* capital stock, not adjusted for depreciation.

Thus five different capital stock concepts were potentially available for use: K_1 equals plant-level net capital stock (1980 = base year), K_2 equals plant-level net capital stock (1981 = base year), K_3 equals plant-level gross capital stock (1980 = base year), K_4 equals plant-level gross capital stock (1981 = base year), and K_5 equals plant-level mixed capital stock (1980 or 1981 = base year).[18]

The number of plants for which data on capital stock could be constructed naturally depended on the concept of capital stock that was used. The following table summarizes these figures:

Capital stock concept	Number of observations	Percentage of total observations
K_1	21,861	65
K_2	22,586	68
K_3	28,156	84
K_4	27,515	82
K_5	19,985	60

An examination of the ratio of capital to value added in two sample industries showed ratios lower than expected. This is apparently because plants rented some of their assets: zero values were found for certain categories of assets, especially buildings. Excluding those plants yielded an aggregate ratio of capital to value added that appears reasonable and exhibits no time trend.

Series for capital stock were particularly important in the analysis of productivity reported in this chapter, in Liu 1993, and in chapter 4. In addition to choice of base year and depreciation rate, it was necessary to deal with plants that were missing figures for capital stock in *some* years. The convention chosen was to leave plants out of the analysis entirely if they did not have a complete series of capital stock for the seven-year sample period. For this chapter, figures for total factor productivity were thus constructed for each industry and year by aggregating K_5 figures over all plants with complete data for all years. Other series of total factor productivity were constructed using K_1, K_2, K_3, and K_4. Here, however, aggregations were done over all plants with complete data in the current year, so some fluctuations in capital (as well as output and employment) reflected entry and exit. The results from K_1 through K_4 were qualitatively similar.

Notes

1. This section draws on Corbo 1985, Galvez and Tybout 1985, and World Bank 1989.
2. The appreciation was a consequence of the government's attempt to stabilize prices by keeping the rate of devaluation below the rate of inflation (see, for example, Corbo 1985).
3. This analysis is based on plant-level industrial survey data collected for the period 1979–85 by Chile's National Institute of Statistics. In principle, the data cover all plants with at least ten workers.
4. For more detailed analyses of the shakedown process in Chile, see chapter 4; Liu 1993; Tybout, de Melo, and Corbo 1991.
5. In the short run, it is costly to adjust capital stocks, so per unit payments to owners of capital need not equal the value of capital's marginal product. But the weight assigned to capital in calculations of total factor productivity is only justified when such an equality holds. In particular, when an industry has excess capacity (and thus is not at minimum average cost), the weight assigned to the growth of capital stock is too large, and the implied growth rate of total factor productivity is too small. See chapter 3 for further details and references.
6. The same result emerges if one examines switches between four-digit industries.
7. Each is regressed on industry characteristics that vary through time, time dummies, and industry dummies. The sum of coefficient estimates across models 3 and 4 yields the vector of coefficients for the gross entry rate regression of model 1. An analogous relationship holds for disaggregate versus gross exit rates.
8. Although this correlation squares with intuition, it does not emerge in the other countries studied by this project.
9. Young firms also typically have higher growth rates (see, for example, Evans 1987). However, these higher growth rates are rarely sufficient to offset the relatively high failure rates of young firms, so the market share of young cohorts typically falls.
10. This occurred despite higher failure rates among young plants, a feature typical of cohort analysis in other countries.

11. In an analysis of Chilean industrial census data, de Melo and Urata (1986) find only weak support for this effect.

12. Schmalensee's dependent variable is operating earnings over assets, so this comparison is not strictly correct. To make the model more comparable, price-cost margins were replaced with operating earnings over the real value of capital stocks, and the exercise was repeated, omitting KQ and KQ^2 from the right-hand side. Then R^2 in the model with industry dummies is only 0.0069, and this falls to 0.0036 when industry dummies are excluded. (The associated F-statistic for the null that industry effects do not matter is 2.80.) So qualitatively the conclusion holds up, but it is weaker with the alternative measure of profitability.

13. A word of caution on statistical tests is in order. Because the data are from a panel survey, it is likely that there is plant-specific serial correlation in the disturbance term, but no correction was made. Although this does not destroy the consistency of coefficient estimators, it biases ordinary least squares estimators for standard errors.

14. See, however, chapter 4, which finds that the productivity gains were small.

15. Annual average (mid-year) price indexes, P_{jt}, for each industry were obtained from the Central Bank of Chile. Because these figures begin in 1979, it was necessary to impute a year-end price for 1978 and 1985 for each industry. This was done by assuming that each industry experienced inflation during 1978 at the rate of increase in the wholesale price index over the periods year-end 1978 to mid-1979 and mid-1985 to year-end 1985.

16. A fourth type of asset is reported in balance sheets—other fixed assets—but this was not part of the breakdown of investment. Treatment of this inconsistency is discussed later.

17. Figures on gross investment in "other fixed assets" were not included in the raw data. The base year value of net stocks of "other fixed assets" was thus carried over to other years, assuming no new investment, after adjusting for changes in price. This procedure does not bias the figures for total capital stock if the "other" category is distributed across types of reported investment.

18. If, for a given plant, a capital stock series could be constructed using either 1980 or 1981 as a base year, 1980 was chosen. Capital stock series for plants with only one viable base year were, of course, constructed using the available data. For K_5, *unlike* for K_1 through K_4, only plants with complete data on capital stock for all seven sample years were included.

References

Corbo, Vittorio. 1985. "Reforms and Macroeconomic Adjustments in Chile during 1974–84." *World Development* 13 (August): 893–916.

de Melo, Jaime, and Shujiro Urata. 1986. "The Influence of Increased Foreign Competition on Industrial Concentration and Profitability." *International Journal of Industrial Organization* 4 (3): 287–304.

Dunne, Timothy, Mark J. Roberts, and Larry Samuelson. 1988. "Patterns of Firm Entry and Exit in U.S. Manufacturing Industries." *Rand Journal of Economics* 19 (4): 495–515.

Evans, David S. 1987. "Tests of Alternative Theories of Firm Growth." *Journal of Political Economy* 95 (August): 657–74.

Galvez, Julio, and James R. Tybout. 1985. "Microeconomic Adjustments in Chile during 1977–81: The Importance of Being a *Grupo.*" *World Development* 13 (August): 969–94.

Jacquemin, Alexis, Elisabeth de Ghellinck, and Christian Huveneers. 1980. "Concentration and Profitability in a Small Open Economy." *Journal of Industrial Economics* 29: 131–44.

Jadresic, Esteban. 1986. "Evolución del empleo y desempleo en Chile, 1970–85." *Colección Estudios* CIEPLAN 20 (December): 147–93.

Liu, Lili. 1993. "Entry-Exit, Learning, and Productivity Change: Evidence from Chile." *Journal of Development Economics* 42: 217–42.

National Institute of Statistics. Various years. *Boletín Mensual.* Santiago.

Pugel, Thomas. 1980. "Foreign Trade and U.S. Market Performance." *Journal of Industrial Economics* 29: 119–29.

Roberts, Mark J., and James R. Tybout. 1991. "Size Rationalization and Trade Exposure in Developing Countries." In Robert E. Baldwin, ed., *Empirical Studies of Commercial Policy.* Chicago: University of Chicago Press for the National Bureau of Economic Research.

Schmalensee, Richard. 1985. "Do Markets Differ Much?" *American Economic Review* 75 (3): 341–51.

Tybout, James R., Jaime de Melo, and Vittorio Corbo. 1991. "The Effects of Trade Reforms on Scale and Technical Efficiency: New Evidence from Chile." *Journal of International Economics* 29: 231–50.

World Bank. 1989. "Chile: Industrial Finance Sector Report." Latin America and the Caribbean Department, Washington, D.C.

10

Colombia, 1977–85: Producer Turnover, Margins, and Trade Exposure

Mark J. Roberts

This chapter uses a panel of plant-level data to examine the industrial structure and market performance of Colombia's manufacturing sector for 1977–85. In summarizing market structure we focus on both the cross-sectional distributions of plant characteristics and the dynamic patterns of plant entry, growth, and exit over time. A unique strength of the panel data is that they allow us to follow cohorts of entering plants and to quantify the patterns of growth and failure as each cohort ages. In examining market performance we focus on variation in price-cost margins at the plant level. During the period covered by our data, Colombia underwent a liberalization and then a tightening of trade restrictions. A common theme throughout the chapter is the effect of these changes in the trade environment on market structure and producer performance.

Trade Policy in Colombia

From the late 1960s through the mid-1970s, Colombia gradually reduced import restrictions and increased the emphasis on exports. Between 1967 and 1975, real gross domestic product grew at an average annual rate of 6.3 percent, and manufacturing grew at an even more impressive 8.6 percent (World Bank 1991, table 1.2). The volume of exports expanded at about 6.1 percent a year. The volume of imports was erratic from year to year, but average growth between 1967 and 1975 was 8.4 percent a year (García García 1991).

Based on historical standards, the latter half of the 1970s was characterized by a fairly liberal trade environment. Quantitative restrictions were continually reduced as commodities were shifted from restricted or prior licensing categories to free import categories. This shift reached its high point in 1980, when approximately 69 percent of all commodities did not require import licenses (World Bank 1991, table 2.1). Nominal tariffs were reduced sharply from an average of 46 percent in 1973 to 31.8 percent in 1974 and then continued to fall gradually to reach 26.9 percent in 1980.

Throughout the late 1970s, soaring world prices for coffee and heavy foreign borrowing contributed to large inflows of foreign exchange. A declining real exchange rate hurt the growth of exports and increased domestic pressure to slow import liberalization. This contributed to the decision to reverse trade liberalization in 1981. In that year, only 36 percent of all commodities were classified in the free import category, and the number of products subject to quantitative restrictions continued to rise through 1984. By that time, only 0.5 percent of all commodities could be freely imported, 83 percent required licenses, and 16.5 percent were prohibited. Nominal tariffs were also increased, as the government shifted toward strengthening the protection from imports in 1982. The average nominal tariff equaled 33.7 percent in 1983. This substantial increase in import restrictions was again loosened significantly in 1985, but not enough to return them to 1980 levels. The basic system of export promotion established in 1967 remained in place throughout this period, however. Overall, Colombia's trade policy was largely a decision on how tightly to restrict imports, so the change in import penetration over time is likely to reflect the change in policy regime.

The shifts in trade policy in the late 1970s and early 1980s coincided with changes in output of the manufacturing sector and growth in productivity. Real growth in sectoral output averaged almost 8 percent a year from 1977 to 1980 for the manufacturing industries (see table 10.1), while growth of sectoral productivity averaged −0.7 percent. Growth of output and productivity declined to −1.3 and −2.6 percent, respectively, over 1980–83 but recovered after 1983.

In summary, the time period covered by this study captures the end of a period of gradual trade liberalization and output growth (1977–80) followed by considerably slower growth and increased import protection (1980–83). Although output grew after 1983, further progress to liberalize import restrictions did not occur until after the sample period. When compared with Chile (chapter 9), Colombia was characterized by a more stable macroeconomic environment and a more protectionist trade regime.

*Table 10.1 Average Annual Growth in Productivity and Real Output,
Colombia, 1977–85*
(percentages)

Industry	Productivity growth (ΔlnTFP)			Real output growth (ΔlnQ)		
	1977–80	1980–83	1983–85	1977–80	1980–83	1983–85
Food	−3.3	−1.3	7.3	7.3	2.4	11.8
Food—miscellaneous	−6.3	−4.2	5.1	3.6	2.0	14.1
Beverages	1.8	−5.5	4.0	11.7	1.6	6.4
Tobacco	−11.5	−5.4	0.1	2.7	3.7	9.6
Textiles	−3.8	−5.7	3.9	−0.1	−12.3	10.2
Apparel	7.2	−0.9	5.7	9.5	−3.1	8.4
Leather products	3.6	−0.5	−5.4	4.1	−5.1	5.7
Footwear	4.5	−4.1	−0.4	11.9	1.1	1.3
Wood products	−3.8	−3.2	−0.6	6.1	7.1	−3.7
Furniture	7.1	−7.5	7.1	9.3	−7.6	7.3
Paper	−1.7	−5.5	4.6	4.0	−1.9	13.8
Printing	−9.5	−5.5	−14.3	−1.0	2.7	−15.0
Industrial chemicals	4.3	−1.5	1.9	9.9	2.7	13.6
Other chemicals	−1.8	−0.4	−0.4	8.7	−1.9	10.3
Petroleum	−15.6	−6.8	−11.5	23.4	−2.4	11.3
Rubber products	−4.0	0.2	5.0	1.2	−5.2	10.3
Plastics	−2.5	−0.3	−10.3	15.8	2.6	2.8
Ceramics	7.6	−8.5	2.6	14.3	−7.9	11.4
Glass	3.1	0.1	3.2	11.0	0.8	−0.9
Nonmetallic minerals	9.2	−3.4	1.1	14.3	2.4	6.2
Iron and steel	−8.9	−1.2	−7.2	−4.2	11.3	−2.0
Nonferrous metals	−11.3	4.5	−7.1	−10.8	−0.7	−0.3
Metal products	−2.5	−2.4	1.6	5.6	−5.6	6.1
Nonelectrical machinery	8.0	3.4	−14.3	8.6	3.1	−16.7
Electrical machinery	0.2	−3.8	1.1	14.0	−5.6	5.3
Transport equipment	1.5	−3.2	−5.0	8.4	−12.8	3.5
Professional equipment	6.6	0.9	8.7	26.5	−0.5	15.9
Other manufacturing	2.0	−0.8	11.1	5.4	−6.6	21.2
Average	−0.7	−2.6	−0.1	7.7	−1.3	6.0

Note: Growth in total factor productivity was calculated using the Tornqvist index
defined in chapter 3.

Source: Author's calculations based on industrial survey data from DANE.

Characteristics of Manufacturing Plants

The data set analyzed in this study was constructed from the census of
Colombian manufacturing plants for 1977–85, which was collected by
the Departamento Administrativo Nacional de Estadística (DANE). The
census covers all plants in the manufacturing sector for 1977–82; after
1982, it covers only plants with ten or more employees. During the years

of complete coverage, the number of plants increased from 6,679 to 7,067. During the years of partial coverage, the number of plants varied from 6,249 to 6,406 (see table 10.2).

Plant heterogeneity can be summarized in several dimensions. According to the size of plants—measured as the number of employees—the distribution of plants was skewed toward a large group of small plants and was fairly stable over time. On average over the six years from 1977 to 1982, plants with fewer than fifty employees accounted for approximately 70 percent of all plants. The age distribution of plants indicates that the median age was approximately ten years, with between 20 and 25 percent of all plants being older than twenty years. The geographic distribution of plants was fairly concentrated, with approximately one-third of manufacturing plants in Bogotá, 20 percent in Medellín, and 10 percent in Cali. Three categories of ownership—proprietorship, limited partnership, and corporation—accounted for more than 90 percent of all plants in each year, with partnerships representing approximately two-thirds of that total. Over time, the share of limited partnerships and corporations increased, largely at the expense of proprietorships.[1]

Finally, the sectoral distribution of manufacturing plants was concentrated, with four industries—food processing, textiles, apparel, and metal products—accounting for approximately 44 percent of all manufacturing plants in each year. In general, there was little change over time in the distribution of plants across industries.

Patterns of Entry and Exit

The average annual entry rate for new plants for 1977–85 was 12.2 percent, with annual rates varying from a low of 8.7 percent in 1980–81 to a high of 14.9 percent in 1984–85 (see table 10.3; see the appendix for a discussion of how the longitudinal data set was constructed).[2] Entering plants tended to be smaller than incumbent plants, a fact reflected in their share of output, which averaged 4.9 percent for the period, with a high of 9.8 percent in 1978–79 and a low of 3.7 percent in 1983–84. With an average size only 39.2 percent of that of incumbent plants, entrants had a share in manufacturing output that was less than their share in the total number of plants.

Exit rates varied from 12.9 percent in 1979–80 to 8.3 percent in 1981–82, with an average of 11.1 percent for the period. Like entering plants, exiting plants tended to be small, averaging about 39 percent of the size of surviving plants. On average, exiting plants accounted for approximately 4.7 percent of the value of annual manufacturing output over 1977–85.

Few time-series patterns emerge in the entry and exit variables at the aggregate level that are contemporaneous with changes in trade policy.

Table 10.2 *Distribution of Plant Characteristics, Colombia, 1977–85*
(percentage share of each category in the total number of plants unless otherwise specified)

Characteristics	1977	1978	1979	1980	1981	1982	1983	1984	1985
Number of plants	6,679	6,625	6,765	6,850	6,792	7,067	6,249	6,258	6,406
Number of employees									
0–9	11.4	11.5	12.0	12.0	12.3	13.7	—	—	1.3
10–49	59.3	57.9	57.6	58.6	58.0	59.0	68.7	69.0	69.7
50–99	14.1	14.4	14.4	13.6	14.2	13.6	15.1	15.2	14.4
100–199	7.8	8.4	8.2	8.2	8.0	7.9	8.8	8.3	7.6
200 or more	7.4	7.8	7.9	7.5	7.4	6.8	7.4	7.5	7.1
Age (years)									
0–2	11.0	9.8	10.1	10.7	9.8	10.4	11.1	10.7	10.1
3–5	17.2	16.1	15.7	13.7	13.7	14.4	14.9	13.7	13.6
6–10	25.5	26.0	24.7	24.6	23.0	21.5	20.6	21.4	20.6
11–20	26.4	27.0	27.9	29.3	30.4	30.4	29.0	29.4	30.3
21 or more	19.9	21.0	21.4	21.6	22.9	23.3	24.4	24.8	25.4
Metropolitan area									
Barranquilla	6.9	7.0	7.2	7.6	7.2	7.1	7.0	6.7	6.5
Bogotá	33.8	34.2	33.5	32.8	32.5	31.8	32.5	32.9	33.1
Bucaramanaga	6.3	6.5	6.2	6.3	6.4	6.1	5.2	5.8	5.3
Cali	10.6	10.5	10.5	10.7	10.9	11.3	11.4	11.0	11.3
Cartagena	1.6	10.4	1.4	1.3	1.3	1.2	1.3	1.6	1.6
Manizales	1.8	1.7	10.1	1.7	1.7	1.7	1.5	1.5	1.5
Medellín	17.6	18.0	17.0	19.6	19.9	21.2	23.2	22.6	22.6
Pereira	3.4	3.3	3.1	3.0	2.9	2.8	2.5	2.4	2.6
Other	17.9	17.0	17.4	16.9	17.2	16.7	15.3	15.4	15.4

(Table continues on the following page.)

231

Table 10.2 (continued)

Characteristics	1977	1978	1979	1980	1981	1982	1983	1984	1985
Type of business									
Collective	1.4	1.4	1.0	1.0	1.0	0.8	0.7	0.6	0.5
Cooperative	0.6	0.6	0.3	0.2	0.3	0.3	0.4	0.4	0.4
Corporation	11.9	12.2	12.2	12.1	11.9	11.7	13.7	14.4	15.0
De facto corporation	3.2	3.2	2.8	2.4	2.3	2.3	1.5	1.5	1.3
Joint partnership	0.7	0.7	0.8	1.0	1.1	1.6	1.7	1.8	2.0
Joint stock company	1.0	1.0	0.9	0.9	1.0	1.0	1.0	0.9	0.8
Limited partnership	5.57	56.5	58.8	59.9	61.3	62.0	65.6	65.7	65.9
Official entity	1.0	0.9	0.6	0.6	0.6	0.6	0.6	0.6	0.6
Proprietorship	24.1	23.2	21.8	21.0	19.9	19.3	14.3	13.6	12.8
ISIC code and industry									
311 Food	15.7	15.1	15.1	14.8	14.8	14.7	14.4	14.6	14.4
312 Food—miscellaneous	2.9	2.9	2.9	3.0	3.0	2.9	2.8	2.8	2.7
313 Beverages	1.9	1.9	2.0	1.9	1.9	2.0	2.0	2.0	1.9
314 Tobacco	0.6	0.5	0.4	0.4	0.3	0.3	0.3	0.2	0.2
321 Textiles	7.5	7.5	7.5	7.3	7.2	6.8	7.0	6.8	6.9
322 Apparel	10.8	11.1	11.2	12.2	12.9	13.6	14.5	14.8	15.3
323 Leather products	1.6	1.6	1.5	1.6	1.5	1.5	1.4	1.5	1.4

Code	Industry									
324	Footwear	3.1	3.0	3.1	3.2	3.2	3.7	3.4	3.6	3.6
331	Wood products	3.1	2.9	2.8	2.8	2.7	2.9	2.8	2.7	2.6
332	Furniture	3.1	3.2	3.1	3.0	2.9	3.2	2.9	2.7	2.6
341	Paper	2.2	2.1	2.2	2.1	2.1	2.1	2.1	2.3	2.1
342	Printing	5.2	5.2	5.2	5.2	5.4	5.4	5.4	5.4	5.3
351	Industrial chemicals	1.6	1.6	1.6	1.4	1.5	1.6	1.7	1.8	1.8
352	Other chemicals	4.4	4.5	4.4	4.4	4.2	4.2	4.3	4.2	4.4
354	Petroleum derivatives	0.1	0.3	0.3	0.3	0.3	0.3	0.3	0.4	0.3
355	Rubber products	1.2	1.3	1.3	1.3	1.3	1.3	1.3	1.2	1.1
356	Plastics	2.9	3.1	3.1	3.5	3.5	3.8	4.1	4.3	4.5
361	Ceramics	0.6	0.7	0.7	0.6	0.6	0.5	0.4	0.4	0.4
362	Glass	0.8	0.8	0.8	0.7	0.8	0.8	0.7	0.7	0.8
369	Nonmetallic minerals	5.1	4.8	5.0	4.9	4.8	4.9	4.7	4.6	4.5
371	Iron and steel	1.0	0.8	0.9	0.8	0.8	0.8	0.8	0.8	0.9
372	Nonferrous metals	0.6	0.6	0.6	0.6	0.5	0.5	0.4	0.4	0.4
381	Metal products	9.0	9.4	9.7	9.2	9.0	8.9	8.8	8.1	7.9
382	Nonelectrical machinery	4.4	4.6	4.7	4.8	4.9	4.4	4.3	4.4	4.7
383	Electrical machinery	3.0	3.1	3.0	3.1	2.9	2.8	2.9	2.8	2.8
384	Transport equipment	3.5	3.4	3.4	3.5	3.3	3.4	3.2	3.2	3.2
385	Professional equipment	0.9	0.9	0.9	0.9	0.9	0.9	0.9	0.9	0.9
390	Other manufacturing	2.7	2.6	2.6	2.5	2.4	2.2	2.0	2.2	2.1

— Not available.

Source: Author's calculations based on industrial survey data from DANE.

Table 10.3 Aggregate Entry and Exit in the Manufacturing Sector, Colombia, 1977–85
(percentages)

Entry or exit statistic	1977–78	1978–79	1979–80	1980–81	1981–82	1982–83	1983–84	1984–85
Entry rate (ER)	10.8	12.6	14.1	8.7	12.4	11.9	12.2	14.9
Entering firms' share of output (ESH)	4.5	9.8	5.6	5.0	4.0	3.7	2.9	4.0
Entering firms' relative size (ERS)	38.5	77.8	36.5	54.2	31.3	29.4	21.5	24.5
Exit rate (XR)	11.6	10.5	12.9	9.6	8.3	a	12.0	12.6
Exiting firms' share of output (XSH)	3.6	5.9	8.9	6.3	3.6	a	2.6	3.7
Exiting firms' relative size (XRS)	28.8	53.6	66.4	64.0	41.0	a	20.0	27.1
Pearson correlations between entry and exit rates across industries	–0.106	0.507	0.666	0.404	0.436	a	0.455	0.585

a. Exit variables were not calculated for 1983 because of a reduction in survey coverage.
Source: Author's calculations based on survey data from DANE.

The only observable difference in these variables between the years of gradual trade liberalization (1977–81) and the years of increased trade restrictions (1981–85) is that entering firms were smaller in size and had smaller shares of output than incumbents in 1981–85 than in 1977–81. Entrants were about one-quarter the size of incumbents in 1981–85 and about half their size in 1977–81. With no significant difference in the average rate of entry between the two time periods, the difference in size was thus reflected in a lower average market share for entrants in the second period. One possible explanation is that trade restrictions allowed small, relatively inefficient producers to remain in operation. Another is that industrial composition within manufacturing had changed.

Entry cohorts reveal several patterns in their share of manufacturing output over time (see table 10.4). For virtually all observations, the market share of an entering cohort declined systematically in each year following entry, declining on average from 4.9 percent the first year to 3.3 percent the fourth year. The decline was more substantial for the 1978 and 1979 cohorts than for later entrants, perhaps reflecting the reduction of import competition in the 1980s, when quantitative restrictions were tighter and tariffs higher.[3]

The decline in the market share of each cohort over time was the result of two potentially conflicting forces: changes in the size of surviving members of the cohort and the exit of plants from the cohort. In general, the average size of each cohort's surviving plants relative to the average size of all plants increased as the cohort aged, indicating that a higher proportion of the older cohorts was concentrated in the upper tail of the distribution of plant size.[4]

Year-to-year survival rates increased as plants aged, rising from 79.4 percent after the first year to 85.8 percent after two years and to 86.8 percent after three years.[5] The survival rate stabilized at around 87 percent a year once plants were more than three years old. In each year, survival rates were higher for the oldest group of plants than for all later entrants, which is expected, because the oldest plants also tended to be the largest.[6] Overall, the high attrition rate for young cohorts contributed to the decline in their market share as they aged.

Several patterns emerge from an examination of average rates of entry and exit by manufacturing industry over three time periods: 1977–80, 1980–83, and 1983–85 (table 10.5). Average entry and exit rates fell between the first two periods, which coincided with periods of trade liberalization and increased import restrictions, and then rose in the third period. The decline in the average rate of entry between the first two periods affected twenty-two of the twenty-eight industries, with twenty-three industries experiencing a subsequent rise. Similarly, twenty industries experienced a decline in the rate of exit between 1977–80 and 1980–83, and the same number experienced an increase

Table 10.4 *Share of Manufacturing Output, Average Size of Firms, and Survival Rates of Entry Cohorts, Colombia, 1977–85*
(percentages)

Cohort	1977	1978	1979	1980	1981	1982	1983	1984	1985
Share of manufacturing output									
1977 plants	100.0	95.5	87.2	87.0	83.2	79.6	77.0	74.9	72.1
1978 entrants	n.a.	4.5	3.0	2.5	2.6	2.4	2.2	2.0	2.0
1979 entrants	n.a.	n.a.	9.8	4.8	4.2	4.1	3.6	3.4	3.3
1980 entrants	n.a.	n.a.	n.a.	5.6	4.9	4.8	4.5	4.3	4.2
1981 entrants	n.a.	n.a.	n.a.	n.a.	5.0	5.0	4.6	4.7	4.6
1982 entrants	n.a.	n.a.	n.a.	n.a.	n.a.	4.0	4.4	4.0	3.7
1983 entrants	n.a.	n.a.	n.a.	n.a.	n.a.	n.a.	3.7	3.7	3.4
1984 entrants	n.a.	n.a.	n.a.	n.a.	n.a.	n.a.	n.a.	2.9	2.6
1985 entrants	n.a.	n.a.	n.a.	n.a.	n.a.	n.a.	n.a.	n.a.	4.0
Size of surviving plants relative									
to that of all manufacturing plants									
1977 plants	100.0	107.2	109.7	124.1	127.6	136.4	145.2	154.9	166.1
1978 entrants	n.a.	41.3	36.2	37.9	42.9	45.8	49.2	53.8	60.2
1979 entrants	n.a.	n.a.	79.9	52.8	53.3	61.3	65.3	71.6	78.5

1980 entrants	n.a.	n.a.	n.a.	40.1	41.3	47.1	53.6	59.2	68.7
1981 entrants	n.a.	n.a.	n.a.	n.a.	56.5	66.4	70.1	86.3	98.1
1982 entrants	n.a.	n.a.	n.a.	n.a.	n.a.	34.1	42.8	45.4	50.5
1983 entrants	n.a.	n.a.	n.a.	n.a.	n.a.	n.a.	32.0	39.6	42.3
1984 entrants	n.a.	n.a.	n.a.	n.a.	n.a.	n.a.	n.a.	23.7	32.2
1985 entrants	n.a.	n.a.	n.a.	n.a.	n.a.	n.a.	n.a.	n.a.	27.5
Year-to-year cohort survival rates									
1977 plants	100.0	88.4	99.1	89.3	92.2	93.1	a	99.1	92.0
1978 entrants	n.a.	100.0	77.2	83.4	90.5	90.1	a	85.2	89.6
1979 entrants	n.a.	n.a.	100.0	75.6	85.6	87.8	a	87.1	91.4
1980 entrants	n.a.	n.a.	n.a.	100.0	84.3	89.2	a	86.7	86.8
1981 entrants	n.a.	n.a.	n.a.	n.a.	100.0	89.6	a	84.0	88.2
1982 entrants	n.a.	n.a.	n.a.	n.a.	n.a.	100.0	a	83.9	84.8
1983 entrants	n.a.	n.a.	n.a.	n.a.	n.a.	n.a.	100.0	80.7	87.1
1984 entrants	n.a.	n.a.	n.a.	n.a.	n.a.	n.a.	n.a.	100.0	68.8
1985 entrants	n.a.	n.a.	n.a.	n.a.	n.a.	n.a.	n.a.	n.a.	100.0

n.a. Not applicable.
a. Not reported because of a reduction in survey coverage.
Source: Author's calculations based on survey data from DANE.

Table 10.5 *Average Annual Entry, Exit, and Growth Rate of Plants, by Industry, Colombia, 1977–85* (percentages)

Industry	Entry rate 1977–80	Entry rate 1980–83	Entry rate 1983–85	Exit rate 1977–80	Exit rate 1980–83	Exit rate 1983–85	Growth rate of surviving plants 1977–80	Growth rate of surviving plants 1980–83	Growth rate of surviving plants 1983–85
Food	10.0	9.9	12.4	11.3	8.8	11.3	4.6	1.4	11.3
Food—miscellaneous	9.1	10.1	8.9	7.4	8.6	8.9	3.8	5.3	10.6
Beverages	6.7	4.9	4.4	5.4	6.0	5.6	6.9	0.7	-1.4
Tobacco	8.6	6.0	6.5	22.5	14.0	12.9	-17.0	2.0	10.8
Textiles	13.0	8.4	12.6	12.3	11.2	11.7	-3.8	-4.9	8.3
Apparel	20.2	18.5	18.3	15.0	10.4	14.8	6.0	-2.0	2.8
Leather products	17.8	9.9	20.2	18.7	10.3	12.9	0.8	1.6	3.1
Footwear	16.0	21.2	19.5	14.6	13.5	15.0	5.9	1.3	1.4
Wood products	11.0	15.1	16.5	13.5	11.5	18.6	3.5	2.8	-4.9
Furniture	15.0	15.1	17.4	16.9	10.6	19.6	1.8	-7.4	10.7
Paper	11.0	5.2	9.4	9.8	2.8	7.6	-0.6	-2.0	11.2
Printing	11.4	9.8	14.3	10.6	6.4	13.0	-0.7	-1.1	-6.3
Industrial chemicals	10.8	9.7	10.5	9.5	8.9	7.2	5.0	0.7	11.9
Other chemicals	8.0	5.5	9.0	7.4	5.5	7.3	7.5	-0.9	8.5
Petroleum	13.2	5.3	8.2	0.0	12.2	7.5	-1.4	0.9	8.9
Rubber products	10.6	11.4	6.9	7.5	8.0	12.5	-1.0	-2.6	7.7
Plastics	16.7	11.7	20.1	12.0	8.2	14.0	6.8	4.7	-0.5
Ceramics	13.4	8.3	12.8	13.4	14.1	10.9	13.1	-8.2	9.9
Glass	8.1	11.7	12.6	10.6	12.7	6.8	8.0	2.2	2.4
Nonmetallic minerals	11.2	9.5	11.6	11.8	8.4	12.6	12.4	0.1	10.6
Iron and steel	11.7	9.1	13.4	11.6	11.8	9.7	-7.0	11.5	-4.3
Nonferrous metals	8.1	3.9	9.3	7.9	8.7	12.8	-12.4	0.1	0.2
Metal products	12.7	8.8	11.1	11.3	8.3	14.3	-1.8	-3.9	6.2
Nonelectrical machinery	10.7	4.1	13.3	7.7	7.4	9.9	12.3	-1.5	-10.4
Electrical machinery	9.5	4.7	10.5	8.4	6.8	9.9	6.6	-4.0	4.0
Transport equipment	12.0	10.5	11.5	11.9	9.5	10.2	6.4	-14.0	0.5
Professional equipment	16.5	4.9	13.7	12.4	6.5	11.1	11.1	2.0	14.4
Other manufacturing	12.4	8.1	14.2	13.7	9.3	12.3	4.9	3.6	20.6
Average	12.0	9.3	12.5	11.3	9.3	11.4	2.9	-0.4	5.3

Source: Author's calculations based on industrial survey data from DANE.

238

in 1983–85. Overall, then, the time period effects in the data appear to be strong.

Aggregate rates of entry and exit in each time period are quite similar, with periods of high entry also being periods of high exit. This pattern also holds at the industry level. Except for 1978, the simple correlation between entry and exit rates across industries in the same year is generally large and positive. The large positive values indicate that industries with higher rates of entry tended to have high rates of exit, a finding common in other studies.[7] This suggests that industry-specific factors related to technology, such as sunk entry costs, rather than fluctuations in demand are primarily responsible for the observed patterns of entry and exit. It implies that industries can be categorized by their rate of turnover: high turnover is associated with high rates of entry and exit, while low turnover is associated with low rates.

The average growth rate of surviving plants in each industry tends to reflect the general trends in growth of the manufacturing sector. The average growth rate for surviving plants during 1980–83 was less than that during 1977–80 in twenty-five of the twenty-eight industries (table 10.5). This pattern reverses itself in 1983–85, when the rate was higher than in 1980–83 in twenty-three industries.

The results of the regression analysis of the entry variables are reported in table 10.6.[8] The model was estimated separately for each of two time periods, 1977–82 and 1983–85, because of the change in coverage of the manufacturing surveys.

For the 1977–82 period, output growth and the industry-level Herfindahl index are both positively and significantly correlated with plant-level entry rates. Import penetration has a negative but statistically insignificant effect on entry rates, and capital intensity has no effect. Over the 1983–85 period, none of the explanatory variables is significantly correlated with entry rate. Overall, the regression results indicate that, once industry and year are controlled for, there is no robust relationship between the structure or demand variables of the industry and the rate of plant entry.

The results on exit rates are similar. Growth of industry-level output, the structure variables, and import penetration are not significantly correlated with exit rates in a systematic way after industry and time effects are controlled for.

One robust result uncovered in exit studies of industrial countries is that the probability that a producer will fail declines systematically as its size and age increase.[9] Thus failure is concentrated among smaller, younger producers. To examine if this is true of Colombian manufacturing plants, we examined patterns of failure across size and age categories. The quartiles of each industry's distribution of plant size were identified, and the plants within each quartile were divided into three age

Table 10.6 Regression Coefficients with Entry Rate (ER) and Exit Rate (XR) as the Dependent Variable, Colombia, 1977–85

Variable	Entry rate		Exit rate	
	1977–82	*1983–85*	*1977–82*	*1983–85*
Independent variable				
Intercept	0.097 (0.034)*	0.091 (0.065)	0.096 (0.033)*	0.049 (0.043)
$\Delta \ln Q$	0.128 (0.023)*	−0.042 (0.086)	0.012 (0.022)	−0.020 (0.056)
H	0.406 (0.128)*	0.195 (0.431)	−0.146 (0.123)	−0.211 (0.281)
IMP	−0.039 (0.116)	−0.292 (0.350)	0.090 (0.111)	0.173 (0.228)
KQ	0.001 (0.039)	0.125 (0.077)	−0.007 (0.038)	0.117 (0.050)*
Year dummy variable				
1977–78	−0.022 (0.017)	n.a.	0.036 (0.016)*	n.a.
1978–79	−0.006 (0.014)	n.a.	0.012 (0.014)	n.a.
1979–80	0.024 (0.012)*	n.a.	0.044 (0.012)*	n.a.
1980–81	−0.036 (0.010)*	n.a.	0.020 (0.010)*	n.a.
1983–84		−0.004 (0.010)		−0.010 (0.007)
Mean dependent variable	0.109	0.125	0.105	0.115
$\hat{\sigma}^2$	0.001	0.001	0.001	0.001
$\bar{R}^2$	0.540	0.505	0.459	0.661
F-statistic	5.668	2.755	4.366	4.343

n.a. Not applicable.

* Significant at the $\alpha = 5$ percent level.

Note: H is the Herfindahl index of industry concentration, IMP is import penetration, and KQ is capital intensity. Industry dummy variables were not reported. Numbers in parentheses are standard errors.

Source: Author's calculations based on survey data from DANE.

categories; zero to four years old, five to ten years old, and more than ten years old. In effect, each plant in industry i in year t was assigned to one of twelve categories based on its size and age. The exit rate from each of these twelve size-age categories for industry i in year t was calculated as the number of plants that did not survive until year $t + 1$ as a proportion of the total number of plants in the category in year t.

The regression results reported in table 10.7 summarize the variation in exit rates using a set of eleven dummy variables to distinguish the twelve size-age classes. The excluded or base category is for the oldest plants in the largest quartile of the size distribution.

The dummy variable coefficients are all positive and virtually all statistically significant, indicating that, relative to the largest, oldest plants in an industry, smaller, younger plants have higher exit rates. More interesting, the coefficients indicate that, within each size quartile, the exit rate declines monotonically with age and that, within each age group, the exit rate declines with increases in size.[10]

Table 10.7 Regression Coefficients with Exit Rate (ER) as the Dependent Variable, Colombia, 1977–85

Variable	1977–82	1983–85
Independent variable		
Intercept	0.041 (0.039)	0.030 (0.082)
ΔlnQ	0.012 (0.032)	−0.037 (0.116)
H	0.207 (0.297)	0.689 (0.667)
IMP	0.130 (0.124)	−0.097 (0.466)
KQ	0.018 (0.039)	0.052 (0.095)
Size = 1, age = 1	0.142 (0.015)*	0.262 (0.026)*
Size = 2, age = 1	0.131 (0.015)*	0.145 (0.027)*
Size = 3, age = 1	0.114 (0.016)*	0.137 (0.029)*
Size = 4, age = 1	0.144 (0.018)*	0.172 (0.032)*
Size = 1, age = 2	0.105 (0.014)*	0.205 (0.025)*
Size = 2, age = 2	0.072 (0.015)*	0.120 (0.027)*
Size = 3, age = 2	0.072 (0.015)*	0.099 (0.028)*
Size = 4, age = 2	0.084 (0.017)*	0.077 (0.032)*
Size = 1, age = 3	0.095 (0.014)*	0.196 (0.025)*
Size = 2, age = 3	0.054 (0.144)*	0.058 (0.026)*
Size = 3, age = 3	0.042 (0.015)*	0.045 (0.027)
Year dummy variable		
1977–78	0.042 (0.017)*	n.a.
1978–79	0.024 (0.015)*	n.a.
1979–80	0.045 (0.012)*	n.a.
1980–81	0.018 (0.011)	n.a.
1983–84	−0.008 (0.013)	n.a.
Mean dependent variable	0.158	0.191
$\hat{\sigma}^2$	0.010	0.013
$\bar{R}^2$	0.363	0.435
F-statistic	14.304	8.409

n.a. Not applicable.
* Significant at the α = 5 percent level.
Note: H is the Herfindahl index of industry concentration, IMP is import penetration, and KQ is capital intensity. Industry dummy variables were not reported. Numbers in parentheses are standard errors.
Source: Author's calculations based on survey data from DANE.

To examine if this pattern of size-age differential is sensitive to the level of industry-level import penetration, the eleven size-age dummy variables were interacted with the level of import penetration. These results, which are not reported in the tables, indicate that an increase in import penetration raises the exit rate of the larger plants (third and fourth quartiles) in the younger age categories relative to that of the largest and oldest plants. There is no statistical evidence that an increase in import penetration affects the exit rate of smaller plants. This is consistent with the view that larger producers are the most likely to compete directly with imports.

Overall, the industry-level patterns suggest that time-series variations in structural or demand conditions are not highly correlated with entry or exit rates. Within industries, however, patterns of failure do reflect variations in plant size and age that are similar to those reported for industrial countries.

Performance, Market Structure, and Trade

This section looks at variations in industry-level performance and in the performance of plants within individual industries. In particular, the analysis considers the relationship between measures of performance and the extent of import penetration into the domestic market. Several patterns are evident in the key industry-level variables that were analyzed: concentration, import penetration rate, capital-output ratio, and price-cost margin for each industry (table 10.8).

The average price-cost margin for the manufacturing sector exhibits a distinct downward trend over time, with much of the decline occurring in 1982, the middle of the sample period, followed by a period of stabilization or reversal. The margins also differ across industries, with the differences becoming most pronounced in the middle of the sample period. The simple correlation of industry-level price-cost margins is 0.513 between 1977 and 1981 and 0.759 between 1981 and 1985, suggesting that the level of price-cost margins and the ranking of industries fluctuate more in the earlier than in the later period. The earlier period coincides with the end of the trade liberalization that began in 1967. The later period corresponds to a time of more restrictive import controls and declining manufacturing exports.

The Herfindahl index for industry-level concentration shows substantial variation across industries in each year and less variation within industries over time. The size distribution of plants within an industry tends to change very slowly over time, whereas at any given time, the mix of large and small plants can vary significantly across industries. High values of the Herfindahl index tend to indicate a larger dispersion in plant sizes within an industry.

The import penetration rate shows substantial differences across industries and over time. The rate is consistently high for some industries, most of which produce durable goods. Consistently high rates of import penetration are found in industrial chemicals, iron and steel, non-ferrous metals, electrical and nonelectrical machinery, and transport and professional equipment. Moderate rates are found for paper products, printing, other chemicals, and metal products. The lowest rates are in the

Table 10.8 Industrial Structure and Performance Variables for Selected Years, Colombia, 1977–85

Industry	Price-cost margin (PCM)			Herfindahl index (H)			Import penetration (IMP)			Capital-output ratio (KQ)		
	1977	1981	1985	1977	1981	1985	1977	1981	1985	1977	1981	1985
Food	0.155	0.172	0.210	0.007	0.008	0.008	0.066	0.087	0.039	0.396	0.556	0.525
Food—miscellaneous	0.192	0.200	0.170	0.026	0.027	0.025	0.036	0.025	0.031	0.193	0.400	0.455
Beverages	0.487	0.440	0.381	0.036	0.044	0.036	0.014	0.020	0.015	0.302	0.575	0.609
Tobacco	0.645	0.287	0.344	0.268	0.223	0.282	0.032	0.125	0.031	0.225	0.626	0.912
Textiles	0.316	0.235	0.243	0.043	0.046	0.048	0.022	0.038	0.023	0.459	1.143	1.423
Apparel	0.249	0.177	0.144	0.012	0.012	0.013	0.020	0.029	0.030	0.275	0.392	0.387
Leather products	0.205	0.154	0.080	0.067	0.071	0.094	0.011	0.024	0.016	0.292	0.535	0.615
Footwear	0.230	0.197	0.142	0.059	0.052	0.053	0.006	0.008	0.013	0.296	0.418	0.596
Wood products	0.364	0.301	0.244	0.144	0.115	0.131	0.062	0.089	0.035	0.514	1.058	1.828
Furniture	0.227	0.151	0.128	0.037	0.025	0.028	0.017	0.016	0.004	0.487	0.735	0.842
Paper	0.361	0.188	0.182	0.106	0.062	0.062	0.137	0.197	0.166	0.389	0.663	0.726
Printing	0.316	0.279	0.241	0.060	0.069	0.060	0.127	0.114	0.108	0.671	1.350	2.798
Industrial chemicals	0.242	0.205	0.189	0.052	0.060	0.046	0.408	0.405	0.420	0.721	1.073	0.897
Other chemicals	0.341	0.297	0.240	0.023	0.029	0.025	0.152	0.158	0.158	0.194	0.345	0.307
Petroleum	0.523	0.219	0.230	0.501	0.276	0.285	0.027	0.052	0.035	0.130	0.292	0.635
Rubber products	0.295	0.205	0.236	0.167	0.153	0.179	0.077	0.118	0.084	0.209	0.358	0.398
Plastics	0.274	0.153	0.145	0.031	0.032	0.026	0.024	0.027	0.022	0.620	1.242	1.380
Ceramics	0.231	0.216	0.259	0.142	0.157	0.150	0.040	0.043	0.022	0.612	1.044	1.588
Glass	0.266	0.232	0.307	0.100	0.096	0.205	0.096	0.135	0.060	0.318	0.650	0.737
Nonmetallic minerals	0.268	0.244	0.310	0.037	0.031	0.032	0.088	0.033	0.029	1.580	1.760	2.680
Iron and steel	0.235	0.188	0.173	0.138	0.113	0.108	0.318	0.421	0.486	0.609	1.063	3.804
Nonferrous metals	0.235	0.232	0.231	0.187	0.204	0.223	0.459	0.555	0.510	0.170	0.395	0.516
Metal products	0.348	0.196	0.175	0.026	0.014	0.017	0.087	0.215	0.143	0.355	0.746	0.830
Nonelectrical machinery	0.268	0.181	0.174	0.026	0.029	0.036	0.703	0.779	0.676	0.303	0.358	0.479
Electrical machinery	0.300	0.263	0.212	0.031	0.036	0.031	0.364	0.416	0.328	0.265	0.383	0.486
Transport equipment	0.220	0.142	0.073	0.135	0.117	0.108	0.338	0.445	0.356	0.550	0.604	0.795
Professional equipment	0.262	0.311	0.337	0.067	0.212	0.221	0.705	0.619	0.567	0.367	0.304	0.305
Other manufacturing	0.360	0.325	0.309	0.043	0.069	0.049	0.136	0.144	0.060	0.289	0.441	0.507
Average	0.301	0.228	0.218	0.092	0.085	0.092	0.163	0.191	0.160	0.421	0.697	1.000

Source: Author's calculations based on industrial survey data from DANE.

nondurable goods industries: beverages, textiles, apparel, leather goods, and footwear. Import penetration rates rose between 1977 and 1981 and then fell between 1981 and 1985, a pattern common among manufacturing industries. This reflects changes in the real exchange rate and the tightening of quantitative import restrictions in 1981. Twenty-five industries experienced an increase in import penetration between 1977 and 1981, and twenty-three experienced a decrease between 1981 and 1985. Cross-industry differences in import penetration rates indicate that Colombia did not have a major group of domestic producers in many industries. These differences are unlikely to reflect differences in trade policies across sectors alone but are more likely to reflect fundamental differences in resource endowments. The time-series variation in import penetration within each sector, however, does roughly parallel changes in Colombia's trade policy. This suggests that time-series, rather than cross-sectional, variations are most useful in identifying the effects of trade policy on market performance.

While capital-output ratios rose over time for virtually all industries, many industries with the lowest capital-output ratios in 1977 (other chemicals, apparel, and rubber) and several with the highest (iron and steel, other nonmetal products, ceramics and porcelain, and plastics) maintained their relative positions in 1985. Some industries commonly viewed as capital-intensive in industrial countries, such as industrial chemicals, transportation equipment, and petroleum derivatives, are not among the highly capital-intensive industries in Colombia, suggesting that producers in these industries use technologies different from those of their counterparts in industrial countries.

Price-Cost Margins at the Industry Level

Regression results show that price-cost margins rise with an increase in the industry-level Herfindahl index and fall with an increase in import penetration (table 10.9, model 1). In particular, a rise in the share of imports in total sales is associated with a statistically significant decline in the price-cost margin. This result is consistent with an increase in the competitiveness of the domestic industry as the rate of import penetration rises. Capital intensity has no significant effect on the margin.

The year effects—a measure of the difference in price-cost margin relative to 1977—are generally negative and increase over time, reflecting the downward trend in margins. The industry effects—a measure of the difference in price-cost margins relative to the miscellaneous manufacturing category—vary substantially across industries, reflecting differences in both capital intensity and profitability.

To see whether import penetration has a more pronounced effect on margins in highly concentrated, capital-intensive industries, a second

Table 10.9 Regression Coefficients with Price-Cost Margin (PCM) as the Dependent Variable, Colombia

Variable	Model 1	Model 2	Model 3	Model 4
Independent variable				
Intercept	0.342 (0.018)*	0.334 (0.020)*	0.277 (0.017)*	0.253 (0.018)*
H	0.921 (0.105)*	1.069 (0.127)*	0.352 (0.064)*	0.436 (0.080)*
IMP	−0.178 (0.087)*	−0.164 (0.105)	−0.058 (0.025)*	0.065 (0.048)
KQ	−0.000 (0.009)	−0.001 (0.016)	−0.001 (0.001)	0.028 (0.014)*
H·IMP	n.a.	−0.740 (0.356)*	n.a.	−0.452 (0.316)
KQ·IMP	n.a.	−0.021 (0.043)	n.a.	−0.136 (0.047)
Year dummy variable				
1978	−0.003 (0.010)	0.001 (0.010)	−0.006 (0.021)	−0.005 (0.021)
1979	0.007 (0.010)	0.001 (0.010)	−0.002 (0.021)	−0.003 (0.021)
1980	−0.040 (0.011)*	−0.034 (0.011)*	−0.050 (0.021)*	−0.051 (0.021)*
1981	−0.059 (0.011)*	−0.052 (0.011)*	−0.067 (0.021)*	−0.069 (0.021)*
1982	−0.062 (0.017)*	−0.056 (0.012)*	−0.075 (0.021)*	−0.076 (0.021)*
1983	−0.082 (0.012)*	−0.074 (0.013)*	−0.086 (0.022)*	−0.090 (0.021)*
1984	−0.079 (0.011)*	−0.072 (0.012)*	−0.082 (0.021)*	−0.086 (0.021)*
1985	−0.081 (0.011)*	−0.075 (0.012)*	−0.082 (0.021)*	−0.085 (0.021)*
Industry dummy variable				
Food	−0.120 (0.020)*	−0.116 (0.020)*	n.a.	n.a.
Food—miscellaneous	−0.131 (0.020)*	−0.129 (0.021)*	n.a.	n.a.
Beverages	0.111 (0.020)*	0.111 (0.021)*	n.a.	n.a.
Tobacco	−0.089 (0.026)*	−0.106 (0.021)*	n.a.	n.a.
Textiles	−0.066 (0.020)*	−0.061 (0.021)*	n.a.	n.a.
Apparel	−0.119 (0.020)*	−0.109 (0.021)*	n.a.	n.a.
Leather products	−0.206 (0.020)*	−0.211 (0.020)*	n.a.	n.a.
Footwear	−0.144 (0.020)*	−0.146 (0.020)*	n.a.	n.a.

(Table continues on the following page.)

Table 10.9 (continued)

Variable	Model 1	Model 2	Model 3	Model 4
Industry dummy variable (continued)				
Wood products	-0.094 (0.021)*	-0.098 (0.022)*	n.a.	n.a.
Furniture	-0.148 (0.021)*	-0.144 (0.021)*	n.a.	n.a.
Paper	-0.099 (0.018)*	-0.097 (0.019)*	n.a.	n.a.
Printing	-0.066 (0.020)*	-0.061 (0.021)*	n.a.	n.a.
Industrial chemicals	-0.052 (0.030)	-0.048 (0.031)	n.a.	n.a.
Other chemicals	0.008 (0.018)	0.009 (0.018)	n.a.	n.a.
Petroleum	-0.286 (0.029)*	-0.317 (0.032)*	n.a.	n.a.
Rubber products	-0.207 (0.021)*	-0.210 (0.021)*	n.a.	n.a.
Plastics	-0.125 (0.021)*	-0.118 (0.021)*	n.a.	n.a.
Ceramics	-0.181 (0.021)*	-0.189 (0.022)*	n.a.	n.a.
Glass	-0.137 (0.019)*	-0.144 (0.020)*	n.a.	n.a.
Nonmetallic minerals	-0.041 (0.024)	-0.029 (0.027)	n.a.	n.a.
Iron and steel	-0.150 (0.033)*	-0.136 (0.034)*	n.a.	n.a.
Nonferrous metals	-0.164 (0.045)*	-0.135 (0.050)*	n.a.	n.a.
Metal products	-0.065 (0.018)*	-0.119 (0.052)*	n.a.	n.a.
Nonelectrical machinery	0.019 (0.054)	0.022 (0.059)	n.a.	n.a.
Electrical machinery	-0.006 (0.029)	-0.005 (0.031)	n.a.	n.a.
Transport equipment	-0.206 (0.031)*	-0.198 (0.032)*	n.a.	n.a.
Professional equipment	-0.032 (0.051)	-0.006 (0.056)	n.a.	n.a.
Dependent mean	0.247	0.247	0.247	0.247
$\hat{\sigma}^2$	0.0014	0.0014	0.0061	0.0060
$\bar{R}^2$	0.820	0.822	0.227	0.253
F-statistic	31.056	29.949	7.705	7.541

n.a. Not applicable.

* Significant at the 5 percent level.

Note: H is the Herfindahl index of industry concentration, IMP is import penetration, and KQ is capital intensity. Numbers in parentheses are standard errors.

Source: Author's calculations based on 1977–85 survey data from DANE.

246

regression permits the effect of a change in import penetration to vary with the dispersion of plant size and capital intensity of the industry (model 2). Under these conditions, an increase in the share of imports reduces margins across all industries, but the largest and only statistically significant reduction occurs in highly concentrated industries. The coefficient on the interaction term between import penetration and industrial structure is negative and statistically significant, implying that the reduction in the price-cost margin that is associated with an increase in the share of imports occurs in the most highly concentrated industries. Again, this result is consistent with an increase in the degree of competition following an increase in import penetration.[11]

The results change markedly when the industry effects are not taken into account (models 3 and 4). Comparing the results with those for models that include the industry dummy variables (models 1 and 2) reveals that variables like capital intensity or import penetration, which differ more significantly across industries than over time, may act as proxies for industry effects in the cross-sectional regressions. Without the industry dummy variables, the results show no significant effect on price-cost margins for import penetration but show a significant, positive role for capital intensity, an effect that diminishes when import penetration rises. This differs substantially from the finding in model 2, which takes industry effects into account, that capital intensity has no effect on margins but that imports reduce margins in highly concentrated industries. The difference appears to arise because the industry dummy variables control for a host of industry-specific differences like capital intensity that are poorly controlled for without the dummies.

Overall, the results reveal significant differences in price-cost margins that persist across industries. The margins are systematically higher in highly concentrated industries, although increasing import penetration reduces the margins. Once industry fixed effects are controlled for, capital intensity appears to have no additional effect on margins. Finally, there is a systematic decline in the margins over time. These results are consistent with the view that imports introduce additional competitive pressure, whose strongest effects are felt in industries with the highest concentration of plant sizes.

Price-Cost Margin Correlations at the Plant Level

Price-cost margins are also found to be correlated with import penetration at the plant level (table 10.10). The results for the specification that includes all manufacturing plants show that a plant's price-cost margin falls as the rate of import penetration rises. The negative and significant coefficient on the interaction term between import penetration and market share indicates that an increase in import penetration has a larger

Table 10.10 Regression Coefficients for Type of Plant with Price-Cost Margin (PCM) as the Dependent Variable, Colombia

Variable	All plants	Proprietorships	Partnerships	Corporations
Independent variable				
Intercept	0.255 (0.014)*	0.256 (0.016)*	0.244 (0.009)*	0.303 (0.099)*
S	1.507 (0.182)*	2.784 (1.93)	2.839 (0.377)*	1.163 (0.511)*
S^2	-2.327 (0.549)*	-54.935 (64.854)	-15.428 (2.786)*	-1.341 (1.418)
IMP	-0.063 (0.063)	-0.127 (0.069)	-0.073 (0.041)	0.024 (0.349)
$IMP \cdot S$	-1.081 (0.402)*	16.486 (6.969)*	-1.539 (0.828)*	-1.070 (1.089)
KQ	-0.530 (0.035)*	-0.291 (0.054)*	-0.576 (0.025)*	-0.592 (0.151)*
KQ^2	0.048 (0.009)*	0.076 (0.018)*	0.045 (0.008)*	0.052 (0.031)
Year dummy variable				
1978	-0.005 (0.007)	-0.001 (0.007)	-0.002 (0.005)	-0.019 (0.037)
1979	-0.008 (0.007)	0.008 (0.007)	0.008 (0.005)	-0.083 (0.037)*
1980	-0.014 (0.007)	-0.010 (0.007)	-0.011 (0.005)*	-0.024 (0.038)
1981	-0.014 (0.007)	-0.010 (0.007)	-0.014 (0.005)*	-0.014 (0.038)
1982	-0.032 (0.007)*	-0.032 (0.007)*	-0.030 (0.005)*	-0.036 (0.038)
1983	-0.038 (0.007)*	-0.040 (0.007)*	-0.037 (0.005)*	-0.034 (0.038)
1984	-0.042 (0.007)*	-0.046 (0.007)*	-0.038 (0.005)*	-0.051 (0.037)
1985	-0.031 (0.007)*	-0.039 (0.008)*	-0.032 (0.005)*	-0.015 (0.036)
Industry dummy variable				
Food	-0.074 (0.013)*	-0.073 (0.014)*	-0.070 (0.008)*	-0.105 (0.091)
Food—miscellaneous	-0.064 (0.016)*	-0.099 (0.017)*	-0.054 (0.011)*	-0.088 (0.101)
Beverages	0.092 (0.018)*	-0.006 (0.037)	0.021 (0.015)	0.093 (0.099)
Tobacco	-0.009 (0.030)	-0.063 (0.023)*	-0.039 (0.041)	0.008 (0.123)
Textiles	-0.034 (0.014)*	-0.076 (0.017)*	-0.027 (0.009)*	-0.038 (0.098)
Apparel	-0.049 (0.014)*	-0.044 (0.015)*	-0.044 (0.009)*	-0.096 (0.104)
Leather products	-0.061 (0.019)*	-0.044 (0.020)*	-0.056 (0.012)*	-0.110 (0.119)
Footwear	-0.039 (0.016)*	-0.027 (0.016)	-0.049 (0.011)*	-0.084 (0.133)

Wood products	−0.055 (0.015)*	−0.049 (0.016)*	−0.054 (0.010)*	−0.088 (0.109)
Furniture	−0.064 (0.017)*	−0.023 (0.017)	−0.082 (0.011)*	−0.074 (0.133)
Paper	−0.034 (0.015)*	−0.064 (0.023)*	−0.031 (0.010)*	−0.058 (0.095)
Printing	0.016 (0.013)	−0.012 (0.014)	0.033 (0.008)*	−0.030 (0.097)
Industrial chemicals	0.078 (0.024)*	0.065 (0.035)	0.035 (0.017)*	0.463 (0.131)
Other chemicals	0.040 (0.013)*	−0.013 (0.017)	0.037 (0.009)*	0.030 (0.089)
Petroleum	−0.060 (0.032)	−0.239 (0.059)*	−0.043 (0.020)*	−0.167 (0.233)
Rubber products	−0.033 (0.018)	0.029 (0.022)	−0.018 (0.012)	−0.132 (0.107)
Plastics	−0.004 (0.016)	−0.037 (0.021)	0.003 (0.010)	−0.023 (0.105)
Ceramics	−0.067 (0.025)*	−0.079 (0.022)*	−0.054 (0.018)*	−0.096 (0.141)
Glass	−0.032 (0.021)	−0.041 (0.027)	−0.028 (0.014)*	−0.057 (0.117)
Nonmetallic minerals	0.003 (0.015)	−0.027 (0.016)	0.009 (0.010)	−0.009 (0.096)
Iron and steel	−0.024 (0.026)	0.019 (0.029)	−0.024 (0.018)	−0.073 (0.139)
Nonferrous metals	0.012 (0.035)	0.024 (0.044)	0.017 (0.022)	−0.052 (0.195)
Metal products	−0.031 (0.012)*	−0.044 (0.014)*	−0.027 (0.008)*	−0.027 (0.090)
Nonelectrical machinery	0.026 (0.039)	0.061 (0.042)	0.034 (0.025)	−0.041 (0.225)
Electrical machinery	−0.033 (0.021)	0.034 (0.025)	0.009 (0.014)	−0.213 (0.127)
Transport equipment	−0.010 (0.021)	0.001 (0.024)	0.004 (0.014)	−0.087 (0.130)
Professional equipment	0.041 (0.038)	0.063 (0.045)	0.046 (0.024)	−0.049 (0.221)
Dependent mean	0.193	0.185	0.184	0.235
$\hat{\sigma}^2$	0.137	0.026	0.040	0.636
$\bar{R}^2$	0.014	0.049	0.056	0.012
F-tests				
H_0: industry dummies are equal	16.57*	7.31*	42.62*	2.08*
H_0: all coefficients equal 0	25.77*	10.95*	49.32*	2.57*

* Significant at the 5 percent level.

Note: S is market share, *IMP* is import penetration, and KQ is capital intensity. Numbers in parentheses are standard errors. Data are for 51,340 plants, 8,843 proprietorships, 33,962 partnerships, and 8,533 corporations.

Source: Author's calculations based on 1977–85 survey data from DANE.

negative effect on the margins of relatively large plants. This may reflect the fact that larger domestic producers have products that compete most directly with imports, while smaller producers have specialized products for which imports substitute less easily. The results also indicate that the plant's market share varies significantly with the price-cost margin, while the coefficient on the squared market share is negative and significant. Together, these results indicate that price-cost margins rise with an increase in plant size, but at a diminishing rate. This finding is consistent with a diminution of the differences in efficiency across producers as plants increase in size. Overall, then, margins are higher for large plants in an industry, and imports are negatively correlated with margins, particularly for larger plants.[12]

Firms in an industry are often a diverse mix of individual proprietorships, small partnerships, and large corporations, including multinational corporations, and adjustments in trade policy are unlikely to affect all types of producers in the same way. Regression results for all three types of plant ownership show that an increase in the plant's market share increases the plant's price-cost margin, but at a decreasing rate (table 10.10). Both first- and second-order effects are significant for limited partnerships, the largest group of plants. Only the first-order effect is significant for corporations, and neither effect is significant for proprietorships.

An increase in import penetration affects the three types of plants quite differently. Increased import penetration reduces the margins of large plants owned by partnerships and corporations, but neither effect is statistically significant. In the case of proprietorships, import penetration has no significant effect on price-cost margins. Thus the finding from the regressions for all plants that import penetration reduces margins the most among larger plants seems to characterize only limited partnerships. For plants owned by corporations, price-cost margins are particularly insensitive to import penetration.

The model does the poorest job of explaining the variation in price-cost margins for the plants owned by corporations. For this group, few of the parameters are significant, and, contrary to the findings for the other groups, there is very little significant variation in margins across industries. These results suggest that import penetration does not affect all plants equally, raising the possibility that changes in the mix of producers may be an important outcome of trade adjustment.

Summary

Import penetration is correlated with price-cost margins at both the plant and industry level of analysis. In the industry-level analysis, imports reduce margins most substantially in highly concentrated industries. But there is significant heterogeneity in the size of plants and type of ownership, and the plant-level analysis shows that imports have a differential effect on the margins of large and small plants. They do not simply increase the level of market competition and lower the margins of all producers in the industry. Imports act to reduce margins, particularly for plants owned by limited partnerships. (These plants account for approximately 60 percent of the manufacturing plants in any year.) This suggests that plants differ in their efficiency and that import penetration may reduce the level of rents being earned by the larger producers within an ownership category. If differences in efficiency across plants are important, then estimates of the effects of the trade environment on market performance must recognize that trade policies may alter the mix of producers within an industry.

Conclusions

Patterns of producer turnover in Colombia do not differ markedly from those found for industrial countries. The relatively high rates of entry and exit, the small size of entering and exiting plants, lower failure rates as plants age and grow, and positive cross-sectional correlation between industry-level rates of entry and exit are all patterns that have been identified for industrial countries.

Another finding that matches the results found for industrial countries is that import penetration is strongly correlated with plant- and industry-level performance, with the strength of the relationship varying with industrial structure. Import penetration is negatively correlated with industry- and plant-level price-cost margins, the largest effect coming in more highly concentrated industries. These findings are consistent with the notion that import competition helps to reduce noncompetitive outcomes in domestic markets, although of course, the mechanism through which this occurs is not identified.

Above all, this analysis exposes the broad heterogeneity among producers within individual industries. Understanding that the response to changes in economic conditions may also vary across producers is an important step in analyzing aggregate and sectoral responses to a changing economic environment in developing countries.

Appendix: Data Preparation

Plant-level data for 1977–85 were obtained from an annual census of manufacturing plants conducted by Colombia's Departamento Administrativo Nacional de Estadística. The data were provided as separate annual cross sections, and plant observations were not linked over time.

The first task was to match individual plant observations across years so that longitudinal analysis could be conducted.

Constructing the Longitudinal Data Set

Constructing the longitudinal data set required locating the data for each manufacturing plant in each of the yearly cross-sectional data sets by identifying variables that are specific to individual plants and remain unchanged over time. Plant characteristics used in the matching process are the initial year of operation, the metropolitan area and section of the country (available only for 1981–85) in which the plant is located, and the four-digit industrial classification to which the plant is assigned. The first three variables do not change over time for a given plant and are very valuable in the matching process. The possibility that the industry may change over time was taken into account in the matching process.

By themselves, these plant characteristics, or discrete identifying variables, are insufficient to produce unique matches across adjoining years, particularly in regions with a large number of manufacturing plants. Two additional sets of continuous identifying variables were used to identify plants uniquely across adjacent years: end- and beginning-of-year inventories for a plant, a plant's flow of investment over the year, and the end-of-year book value of capital. In all cases, only nonzero values of the continuous variables were used in order to assure that matches are unique.

The matching process began with the 1984 and 1985 data sets and worked back to 1977 and 1978 in a four-step process. Thus, for example, a plant's end-of-year inventories in the 1984 data were matched with the beginning-of-year inventories in the 1985 data for four variables (finished goods, raw materials, goods in progress, and total inventory). For the six capital variables, the end-of-year book value of capital in 1984, say, was matched with a constructed beginning-of-year book value of capital in 1985 (reported end-of-year book value in 1985 minus the gross flow of investment in 1985 plus depreciation in 1985 plus the book value of assets sold in 1985). The measures of beginning- and end-of-year capital stocks were constructed for structures, equipment, land, transportation equipment, office equipment, and total stocks.

One limitation of this procedure is that matching is performed only across adjacent years. Any errors in the three discrete variables—initial year of plant operation, section of the country, or area of the country—will lead to a failure to identify a continuing plant. Matching across nonadjacent years might permit some additional continuing plants to be identified, but there are no continuous variables that can be used to match the plants across nonadjacent years.

The number of plant matches found at each stage of this process is summarized for each pair of years in table 10A.1. The first row reports

Table 10A.1 Number of Plant Matches in Colombia, 1977–85

Variable	1977–78	1978–79	1979–80	1980–81	1981–82	1982–83	1983–84	1984–85
Minimum number of possible matches $(N_t, N_t + 1)$	6,625	6,625	6,765	6,792	6,792	6,249	6,249	6,258
Number of matches on industry, initial year, section, area, and continuous variables								
Inventory variable								
Finished goods	3,186	3,915	1,782	3,781	3,853	3,552	3,595	3,474
Raw materials	1,775	1,743	1,744	1,521	1,555	1,314	1,290	1,330
Goods in progress	68	81	415	39	41	23	22	34
Total	49	45	35	30	20	17	17	33
Capital variable (book values)								
Structures	383	370	918	377	209	175	160	171
Equipment	37	25	227	12	197	147	144	150
Land	28	26	126	7	10	7	3	16
Transportation equipment	23	15	128	6	6	4	3	4
Office equipment	25	17	170	11	13	9	5	7
Total	5	6	21	2	2	1	0	4
Total number of matches	5,577	5,523	5,566	5,786	5,906	5,249	5,239	5,223
Total when all continuous variables equal 0	19	17	20	18	13	13	11	10

(Table continues on the following page.)

Table 10A.1 (continued)

Variable	1977–78	1978–79	1979–80	1980–81	1981–82	1982–83	1983–84	1984–85
Number of matches when industry switches are permitted								
Inventory variable								
Finished goods	171	228	88	259	208	178	166	158
Raw materials	100	120	93	86	70	54	62	55
Goods in progress	4	6	29	3	2	2	1	0
Total	2	5	3	7	1	1	1	0
Capital variable (book values)								
Structures	17	21	45	27	8	6	5	7
Equipment	2	1	6	2	13	6	4	8
Land	3	3	12	0	0	1	1	2
Transportation equipment	3	3	12	1	1	1	0	0
Office equipment	5	3	18	5	6	11	9	8
Total	1	2	2	1	0	1	0	1
Total	308	392	308	391	309	261	249	239
Total number of matches	5,904	5,932	5,892	6,195	6,228	5,523	5,499	5,472
Share of minimum number of possible matches (percentages)	89.1	89.5	87.1	91.2	91.7	88.4	88.0	87.4

Source: Author's calculations based on survey data from DANE.

254

the minimum number of plants in each of the two years in question. This is the maximum number of plant matches that are possible between the two years. This is followed by the number of matches on the four discrete matching variables plus each of the continuous variables. Two patterns are of interest. First, most matches occur on the first continuous variable used: finished goods inventories. This is not unexpected, since the set of nonmatched plants is largest at this point, and the number of plants with zero values for this variable is relatively small. The second pattern is an increase in the number of matches as the capital variables are applied in the matching. This result is expected if some plants do not report inventories consistently over time but do report book value of capital stocks consistently.

Next, table 10A.1 reports the additional matches when the industry matching requirement is dropped. When plants are not required to remain in the same four-digit industrial classification, approximately 300 additional matches are made, or about 5 percent of the plants operating each year.

Constructing Perpetual-Inventory Capital Stocks

The construction of perpetual-inventory capital stocks for each three-digit manufacturing industry began with capital stock and investment data for each of four classes of assets: buildings and structures, machinery and equipment, transportation equipment, and land. The capital stock of asset class k at the end of year t for industry j is denoted as K_{jt}^k and was constructed as

$$(10A.1) \qquad K_{jt}^k = I_{jt}^k + (1 - \delta^k)\, K_{jt-1}^k$$

where I_{jt}^k is the real flow of new investment of asset type k in industry j in year t, δ^k is a depreciation rate for asset type k, and K_{jt-1}^k is the previous year's capital stock of asset type k in industry j.

The real flow of new investment for each type of asset was constructed by deflating the flow of investment by a price index for new investments of type k. The flow of investment was constructed by summing the plant-level investment flows over all plants. Investment in asset type k is the sum of purchases of new and used assets and production of the asset for own use minus the sale of assets.

The price indexes for structures, machinery and equipment, and transportation equipment were constructed as the ratio of the current and constant unit (peso) flows of investment for the whole economy (Central Bank 1988, tables 7.1.5 and 7.1.6). The gross domestic product deflator was used as the price index for the fourth type of asset: land.

The rate of depreciation for each type of asset was assumed to be constant over time as follows: 5 percent for structures, 10 percent for machinery and equipment, 20 percent for transportation equipment, and 0 percent for land, which was assumed not to depreciate.

To construct a measure of the capital stock for each industry for 1977, the initial year of the data, the 1977 end-of-year book value of each type of asset was deflated by the value of the 1977 asset price index. Simply beginning the perpetual-inventory calculations in a year well before 1977—a better approach—was not possible because no data on the flow of investment are available prior to 1977. The procedure used to construct the 1977 figures for capital stock introduces two biases that work in opposite directions. First, the book value for 1977 does not include depreciation on the assets over their lifetime, so it tends to overvalue capital stock even if the price of investment goods does not change. Second, the price of new investment goods generally rises over time, so deflating the 1977 book value by the 1977 price of new investment goods is, in effect, based on a price that is too high, which tends to undervalue the capital stock. This bias would be present even if there was no depreciation of the assets over their lifetimes. Because there are both depreciation of the existing capital stock and inflation in the price of new investment goods, both of these biases are present in the constructed 1977 figures for capital stock.

Constructing Industry-Level Output Price Indexes

For 1981 through 1985, each manufacturing plant reported both its nominal and its real value of production. For all establishments in the same three-digit industry, the implicit output price index (ratio of nominal to real value of production) used to deflate the nominal value of production is identical. This indicates that the real value of a plant's production is constructed by deflating the nominal value of production by a three-digit industry-level output price index, so for 1981 through 1985, these implicit output price indexes are used as the industry-level output price indexes.

For 1977 through 1980, plants did not report the real value of establishment production, and so industry-level price indexes reported in *Colombia estadística 1986* (DANE 1986) are used instead. A problem, however, is that DANE reports price indexes for only twenty industries, grouping together some of the twenty-nine industries at the three-digit level of ISIC classification:

DANE *industry*	*ISIC code*
Food	311, 312
Beverages	313
Tobacco	314
Textiles	321
Clothing and shoes	322, 324
Leather goods except shoes	323

Wood and cork	331
Wood furniture	332
Paper and paper products	341
Printing and publishing	342
Chemicals	351, 352
Petroleum derivatives	354, 353
Rubber products	355, 356
Nonmetallic minerals	361, 362, 369
Metals	371, 372
Metal products	381
Nonelectrical machinery	382
Electrical machinery	383
Transport equipment	384
Other manufacturing	385, 390

For the industries with a one-to-one match, the 1981–85 output price indexes reported are identical to those constructed as described above, which verifies that these are the industry deflators used to construct real production data reported by firms in 1981–85. For the aggregate industries, price indexes for 1981–85 lie within the range of constructed prices for the constituent three-digit industries, indicating that DANE's aggregates are weighted averages. We have been unable to uncover the exact set of weights used.

To construct output prices for the twenty-eight three-digit industries for 1977–80, we used the year-to-year growth rates of the prices reported by DANE to extend the 1981 industry-level prices, constructed from plant-level data, back to 1977. The industry-level prices for all aggregate industries in the *Estadística* series were assumed to grow at the same rate. The growth rate of the price series for aggregate k between 1980 and 1981 was

(10A.2) $$g^k_{80,81} = \ln P^k_{81} - \ln P^k_{80}$$

(where P^k_t is the aggregate price index for year t). The 1980 output price index for three-digit industry j, included in aggregate k, was constructed as $P^k_{80} = \exp(\ln P^j_{81} - g^k_{80,81})$. The 1981 price index for industry j was constructed using the plant-level data reported above. The process was repeated for each year back to 1977.

Notes

The first section of the chapter, on Colombia's trade policy, is based on World Bank 1991 and García García 1991.

1. This trend appears to be exaggerated by the change in coverage of small plants beginning in 1983, although it is also evident in 1977–82 and 1983–85.

2. The entry rate for 1982–83 was calculated as the number of new plants present in 1983 divided by the number of plants with ten or more employees in 1982, in order to account for the change in survey coverage in the two years.

3. Although the share of any one cohort of entering plants in manufacturing output was fairly modest, the cumulative effect of multiple cohorts of entrants was more substantial. The market share of the plants in operation in 1977 declined consistently over time as entry occurred, so that by 1985, their share had declined to 72 percent.

4. This increase in average size could have occurred either because the surviving plants grew or because the failing plants were smaller than the surviving plants.

5. Survival rates are not reported for 1983 because of the reduction in survey coverage. Market shares after 1982 are also biased downward, but not seriously, because the plants omitted in 1983, 1984, and 1985 were very small. Similarly, the average sizes reported in the last three years are biased upward by the omission of the smallest plants, but the continued increase in the average size over time should not be affected significantly.

6. Several studies using U.S. data have found a similar pattern (Evans 1987a and 1987b; Dunne, Roberts, and Samuelson 1988 and 1989).

7. Geroski (1991) and Geroski and Schwalbach (1991) review entry studies in a number of countries; Dunne and Roberts (1991) document this pattern in U.S. data.

8. The regressions reported in table 10.6 all include industry dummy variables. In each case, between three and five of the twenty-seven industry dummy variable coefficients are significantly different from 0. The only systematic patterns in these coefficients are a significantly lower rate of entry and exit for industry 313 (beverages) and a significantly lower rate of exit for industry 341 (paper products). Both comparisons are relative to industry 390 (miscellaneous manufacturing).

9. The decline in exit rates as size increases, holding age fixed, and as age increases, holding size fixed, are reported for U.S. manufacturing plants in Dunne, Roberts, and Samuelson 1988.

10. The only exception to this pattern is that plants in the largest quartile have higher exit rates than plants in the third size quartile when they are in the youngest age category. This occurs in both time periods.

11. Domowitz, Hubbard, and Peterson (1986) report the same result using a set of panel data for U.S. manufacturing industries. Theirs is one of the few studies to control for fixed industry effects, as in models 1 and 2 reported here.

12. The explained variation in the plant-level margin regression is extremely low ($\bar{R}^2$ is 0.014) indicating substantial variation in the within-industry margin.

References

Central Bank. 1988. *Revista* (June). Bogotá.

DANE (Departamento Administrativo Nacional de Estadística). Various years. *Colombia estadística*. Bogotá.

Domowitz, Ian, R. Glenn Hubbard, and Bruce C. Peterson. 1986. "Business Cycles and the Relationship between Concentration and Price-Cost Margins." *Rand Journal of Economics* 17 (1): 1–17.

Dunne, Timothy, and Mark J. Roberts. 1991. "Variation in Producer Turnover across U.S. Manufacturing Industries." In Paul A. Geroski and Joachim Schwalbach, eds., *Entry and Market Contestability*. Oxford: Basil Blackwell.

Dunne, Timothy, Mark J. Roberts, and Larry Samuelson. 1988. "Patterns of Firm Entry and Exit in U.S. Manufacturing Industries." *Rand Journal of Economics* 19 (4): 495–515.

———. 1989. "The Growth and Failure of U.S. Manufacturing Plants." *Quarterly Journal of Economics* 104 (4): 671–98.

Evans, David S. 1987a. "The Relationship between Firm Growth, Size, and Age: Estimates for 100 Manufacturing Industries." *Journal of Industrial Economics* 35 (4): 567–82.

———. 1987b. "Tests of Alternative Theories of Firm Growth." *Journal of Political Economy* 95 (August): 657–74.

García García, Jorge. 1991. "Colombia." In Demetris Papageorgiou, Michael Michaely, and Armeane M. Choksi, eds., *Liberalizing Foreign Trade*, vol. 4, *The Experience of Brazil, Colombia, and Perú*. Cambridge, Mass.: Basil Blackwell.

Geroski, Paul A. 1991. *Market Dynamics and Entry*. Oxford: Basil Blackwell.

Geroski, Paul A., and Joachim Schwalbach, eds. 1991. *Entry and Market Contestability*. Oxford: Basil Blackwell.

World Bank. 1991. *Colombia: Industrial Competition and Performance*. Washington, D.C.

11

Mexico, 1985–90:
Trade Liberalization,
Market Structure, and
Manufacturing Performance

Jean-Marie Grether

Several elements make the Mexican case study especially interesting. One is the dramatic nature of the trade liberalization of the mid-1980s following decades of policies based on import substitution. Another is the timing of the reforms, which fall squarely in the middle of the sample period, neatly splitting the before- and after-reform periods in half. Also, detailed annual data are available on tariffs, nontariff barriers, and effective protection, permitting analysis of their association with various measures of performance in the manufacturing industries. The main issue considered here is whether the removal of protection, following decades of import-substitution policies, reduced the profitability and market power of domestic plants. Perhaps more strongly than any of the other case studies, the case of Mexico supports the hypothesis of import discipline, which posits that price-cost margins fall as protection is removed. (Because the data do not cover the smaller plants in each industry, patterns of entry and exit could not be examined.)

Recent Macroeconomic and Trade Policies

After two decades of sustained growth averaging more than 6 percent a year, the Mexican economy entered a period of stagflation in the mid-1980s, with the growth rate falling to 0.1 percent and inflation averaging 90 percent. Extreme fiscal laxity and excessive foreign borrowing led to the debt crisis of 1982, and the new government of Miguel De la Madrid (1983–88) was forced to adopt a hard-core program of fiscal retrenchment. Even that was inadequate, however, to prevent another crisis in 1986, as world oil prices collapsed and interest payments on the domestic debt soared with surging inflation. Together with the ensuing debt-reduction agreements and the wage and price freezes negotiated under two *pactos*, macroeconomic stabilization and austerity measures finally brought the public deficit and the inflation rate down to acceptable levels after 1988.[1]

Complementing the stabilization effort were major structural reforms, gradually introduced starting in 1985. Major initiatives included privatization of state-owned companies, deregulation of financial markets, liberalization of foreign investment regulations, and a complete reorientation of trade policy.

The change in trade policy was perhaps the most dramatic. Traditionally, trade policy had been Mexico's means of correcting balance of payments problems. Thus, the relative economic openness of the late 1970s gave way to dramatic restrictions in 1982 to cope with the shortage of foreign exchange. Along with a sharp devaluation and foreign exchange controls, all imports were subject to import licensing. Few changes occurred until 1985, when for the first time, trade liberalization measures were implemented despite a continuing external payments constraint. Import licensing was relaxed for most intermediate inputs and capital goods, which accounted for about half of all imports. To avoid an immediate boom in imports, the authorities also kept the peso undervalued, increased tariff rates slightly, and introduced new reference prices for customs valuation (see table 11.1).

Mexico initiated a first round of tariff reductions in April 1986, dropping the average rate from 29 to 24 percent and reducing dispersion as well. The procompetitive effects of this reform were softened by real devaluations. But an upsurge in inflation in 1987 generated concerns about this exchange rate policy. To contain inflationary pressure from imports, the government reversed its policy of keeping the peso undervalued and accelerated the tariff reduction. In December 1987, tariffs were cut by half, approaching the levels applied by most industrial countries, and the last reference prices were eliminated.

Mexican export policy had traditionally been less restrictive than its import policy. To encourage exports, regulations were relaxed even more during the 1980s. Taxes on exports were reduced in 1984 to 0.6 percent, and the coverage of export permits was cut back at the end of 1987 to 24.8 percent of exports, most of them agricultural goods with controlled prices or products subject to international agreements. The liberalization of imports and the undervaluation of the peso also helped to boost exports. Other incentives were also offered, including simplified

Table 11.1 Import Protection for Manufacturing Industries in Mexico, 1985–90
(percentages)

Indicator	1985		1986		1987		1988		1989		1990	
	June	December	June	December	June	December	June	December	June	December	June	December
Tariffs (ad valorem)												
Maximum	100.0	100.0	45.0	45.0	40.0	20.0	20.0	20.0	20.0	20.0	20.0	20.0
Average[a]	23.5	28.5	24.0	24.5	22.7	11.8	11.0	10.2	12.6	12.5	12.5	12.4
Dispersion	25.6	25.3	18.1	17.9	15.8	7.8	8.0	7.8	5.7	6.2	6.2	6.4
Coverage of import licenses[b]	92.2	47.1	46.9	39.8	35.8	25.4	23.2	22.1	22.1	20.3	19.9	17.9
Coverage of reference prices[b]	18.7	25.4	19.6	18.7	13.4	0.6	0.0	0.0	0.0	0.0	0.0	0.0
Index of real exchange rate (1970 = 100)[c]	95.9	128.2	151.5	170.6	173.7	171.2	138.2	131.6	124.9	127.4	121.7	122.7

a. Weighted by production; does not include the uniform 5 percent surcharge that was abolished in December 1987.
b. Average share of commodity categories subject to import licensing or reference prices, as a percentage of the value of the category's production.
c. Calculated by the Bank of Mexico on the basis of a world current price index estimated over 133 countries; an increase means a real depreciation of the Mexican peso.

Source: Ten Kate and de Mateo Venturini 1989; SECOFI data; Bank of Mexico 1991.

procedures, improved access to credit, and exemptions from tariffs and restrictions on imported inputs.[2]

Exports were also favored by reorienting industrial policy away from protection and fiscal incentives, policies that had been designed to promote local integration and the development of domestic manufacturing. These industrial programs were reduced drastically, and export promotion and price competitiveness received greater emphasis. Only a few priority industries were kept under special promotion programs, and domestic content requirements were gradually replaced by export targets (Ros 1992).

In short, Mexico liberalized its trade regime rapidly and dramatically. The liberalization process was more or less complete by the end of 1987, although the impact on the flow of imports remained softened somewhat by management of the exchange rate. All these changes helped to promote exports. In terms of both import penetration rates and export rates, the manufacturing sector was substantially more open as a consequence.

Price-Cost Margins and Trade

Prior to the Mexican liberalization, trade accounted for a small share of manufacturing production in most industries (the ratios of imports over domestic consumption and of exports over domestic production were both below 10 percent on average). Further, manufacturing firms numbered in the tens of thousands and must have imposed some degree of competitive pressure on one another. Ex ante, therefore, one might not have expected the new policies to have brought much pricing discipline to bear. This section investigates whether discernible changes in price-cost markups indeed accompanied the shift toward outward orientation, using equations 8.5 and 8.6 from chapter 8.

Both equations were adapted to the rich Mexican data base by replacing import penetration rates with two direct measures of commercial policy. One is the share of total industrial output that falls into commodity categories subject to import licenses ($QUOT$). The second is a production-weighted average official tariff rate ($MTAR$).[3] The measures are not available for 1984, but they are preferable to import penetration rates because they describe trade policy directly and are less likely to introduce simultaneity bias in the results.

Data on price-cost margins, capital stocks, output levels, and industry-level concentration are based on a panel of roughly 2,800 Mexican manufacturing plants (after excluding suspicious and incomplete observations). This sample was collected by Mexico's National Institute of Statistics, Geography, and Information (INEGI) and covers the period 1984–90. It is not representative; rather it covers the larger plants in each industry and exhibits very little entry and exit. Data on protection are industry-level tariff rates and license coverage ratios provided by the Secretary of International Commerce and Industrial Development (SECOFI). Both sources of data are summarized in the appendix to this chapter.

Industry-Level Analysis of Margins

We begin by analyzing the behavior of price-cost margins at the industry level, using variables constructed by aggregating across individual producers. (Table 11A.4 summarizes the data for the years 1985, 1988, and 1990.) Regression results are reported separately for each type of protective instrument to highlight differences between them (see tables 11.2 and 11.3). Models 1 and 2, which include dummy variables for industry, explain the temporal variation within each industry; models 3 and 4, without the industry variables, basically explain the variation between sectors.[4]

As Tybout finds for Chile (chapter 9) and Roberts for Colombia (chapter 10), an important part of the explanatory power comes from industry effects (the adjusted R^2 more than doubles from model 3 to model 1). This outcome may reflect sector-specific industrial policy, entry barriers, or technological differences not captured by the other explanatory variables. The time dummies for 1987 and 1988 are positive and significant when industry effects are controlled for, which is consistent with the increase in profitability preceding the anti-inflationary agreements (see Ize 1990). A fall in price-cost margins for 1989 and 1990 could reflect appreciation of the real exchange rate and the acceleration of structural reforms by the new administration.

The coefficient of the capital-output ratio has the expected positive sign when industry dummy variables are left out, but the sign turns negative when industry effects are controlled for (although the coefficient is significant only when the average tariff variable *MTAR* is used). Since only temporal variation is picked up in the model with the industry variables, this result may reflect underutilization of capacity during the recession, which prevailed for most of the sample period. Installed capital was not used to its full capacity, so variations in output (and profits) occurred without affecting the capital stock in the same proportion. The coefficient of the concentration index is positive, confirming a higher rate of profit in more concentrated industries, both across sectors and through time.[5]

The coefficient of import licenses is positive and significant in model 3 (table 11.2), confirming Roberts's finding for Colombia that less protected sectors seem to behave more competitively. In model 1, however, the impact is not significant, suggesting that differences in the level of protection across sectors are more important than variation over time. But adding interaction terms (in models 2 and 4) reveals a more complex picture. Even if the net impact of import licenses is not significant in explaining temporal variation, the interaction term for import licenses and industry-level concentration is positive and significant. Thus firms located in the most concentrated industries are more likely to experience a reduction in margins when protection is removed. In other words, a reduction in import license requirements does not affect profitability as much in an industry that is already quite competitive as in one characterized by a small number of firms.

The results are similar for the regressions using the average tariff rate variable, but the ability of the models to explain cross-industry variation is cut roughly in half (table 11.3). When both measures of protection are included in the regressions of model 2 (not reported), the global significance of the terms that include the tariff variable is weaker (F-statistic of 4.46) than that of the terms that include the import license variable (F-statistic of 8.26). These findings are consistent with the standard analytical result from trade theory that nontariff barriers have more to do with creating market power than do tariff rates.

Briefly, the main finding is that with lower protection comes lower profitability in Mexican manufacturing plants, corroborating the import-discipline hypothesis. This relationship is clearly established across sectors, particularly for quantitative restrictions, and somewhat less so across time, with trade liberalization seeming to affect only the most concentrated sectors. The probable explanation is that firms must have a certain amount of market power before they can be induced to behave more competitively—an explanation that is explored below.

Plant-Level Analysis of Margins

To examine intrasectoral variation in margins, we use plant-level models based on Schmalensee 1985 (see table 11.4). These explain only a small fraction of plant-level variation in price-cost margin when the entire sample is included in the regression (the adjusted R^2 is 0.07). This is not an uncommon outcome of regressions performed on large micro data sets. Besides, the model is globally significant, as the F-statistic indicates. Year dummy variables are all significantly positive until 1989, confirming the downward trend in profitability during the last two years of the sample period.

Both market share effects and industry dummy variables are significant at the plant level. A rise in market share increases the price-cost margin of the individual plant, but at a decreasing rate, and many of the industry dummies differ significantly from 0. The null hypothesis that the market share effects are not significant is always rejected at the 5 percent level (F-statistics are 109.28 using the import license variable $QUOT$ and 84.22 using the average tariff variable $MTAR$), and the same is true for industry effects (F-statistics of 39.91 and 40.17, respectively).

(Text continues on p. 272.)

Table 11.2 Regression Estimates at the Industry Level with Price-Cost Margin (PCM) as the Dependent Variable and Import License Coverage (QUOT) as the Indicator of Protection, Mexico

Variable	Model 1	Model 2	Model 3	Model 4
Independent variable				
Intercept	0.343 (0.012)*	0.345 (0.011)*	0.152 (0.028)*	0.234 (0.046)*
H	0.224 (0.075)*	0.185 (0.071)*	0.279 (0.106)*	-0.278 (0.105)*
$QUOT$	0.011 (0.009)	-0.010 (0.013)	0.261 (0.032)*	-0.059 (0.050)
KQ	-0.033 (0.020)	-0.033 (0.019)*	0.215 (0.029)*	0.148 (0.026)*
$H \cdot QUOT$	n.a.	0.284 (0.068)*	n.a.	1.664 (0.199)*
$KQ \cdot QUOT$	n.a.	0.008 (0.016)	n.a.	0.188 (0.068)*
Year dummy variable				
1985	0.003 (0.009)	0.003 (0.008)	-0.185 (0.038)*	-0.093 (0.033)*
1986	0.001 (0.005)	0.001 (0.005)	-0.049 (0.029)	-0.021 (0.023)
1987	0.016 (0.005)*	0.016 (0.005)*	-0.018 (0.029)	-0.001 (0.023)
1988	0.023 (0.005)*	0.023 (0.005)*	-0.007 (0.028)	-0.002 (0.022)
1989	0.005 (0.005)	0.005 (0.004)	-0.003 (0.028)	-0.001 (0.022)
Industry dummy variable				
Food	-0.125 (0.011)*	-0.121 (0.010)*	n.a.	n.a.
Beverages	0.127 (0.011)*	0.128 (0.010)*	n.a.	n.a.
Tobacco	0.359 (0.019)*	0.311 (0.021)*	n.a.	n.a.
Textiles	-0.075 (0.011)*	-0.075 (0.010)*	n.a.	n.a.
Apparel	-0.043 (0.010)*	-0.039 (0.009)*	n.a.	n.a.
Shoes	-0.073 (0.012)*	-0.083 (0.011)*	n.a.	n.a.

Wood products and furniture	−0.069 (0.010)*	−0.068 (0.009)*	n.a.	n.a.
Paper and publishing	−0.100 (0.010)*	−0.100 (0.010)*	n.a.	n.a.
Chemicals	0.047 (0.010)*	0.048 (0.010)*	n.a.	n.a.
Regenerated oils	0.002 (0.012)	−0.012 (0.012)	n.a.	n.a.
Plastics and rubber products	−0.032 (0.010)*	−0.032 (0.009)*	n.a.	n.a.
Glass	0.065 (0.014)*	0.064 (0.014)*	n.a.	n.a.
Cement products	0.168 (0.025)*	0.166 (0.024)*	n.a.	n.a.
Other nonmetal products	0.068 (0.013)*	0.068 (0.012)*	n.a.	n.a.
Iron and steel	−0.136 (0.010)*	−0.137 (0.010)*	n.a.	n.a.
Nonferrous metal	−0.215 (0.021)*	−0.210 (0.020)*	n.a.	n.a.
Metal products	−0.054 (0.010)*	−0.054 (0.009)*	n.a.	n.a.
Nonelectrical machinery	−0.053 (0.009)*	−0.052 (0.008)*	n.a.	n.a.
Electrical machinery	−0.045 (0.009)*	−0.043 (0.009)*	n.a.	n.a.
Transport equipment	−0.121 (0.010)*	−0.119 (0.010)*	n.a.	n.a.
Dependent mean	0.338	0.338	0.338	0.338
σ^2	0.0002	0.0002	0.0084	0.0051
Adjusted R^2	0.985	0.987	0.458	0.668
F-statistic	292.63	317.48	14.19	26.176

n.a. Not applicable.

* Significant at the 5 percent level.

Note: H is the Herfindahl index of industry concentration, $QUOT$ is the share of total industrial output that falls into categories subject to import licensing, and KQ is the capital-output ratio. Numbers in parentheses are standard errors.

Source: Author's calculations based on 1984–90 data from Bank of Mexico and INEGI.

Table 11.3 *Regression Estimates at the Industry Level with Price-Cost Margin as the Dependent Variable and Average Tariff Rate (MTAR) as the Indicator of Protection, Mexico*

Variable	Model 1	Model 2	Model 3	Model 4
Independent variable				
Intercept	0.343 (0.012)*	0.366 (0.015)*	0.139 (0.036)*	0.266 (0.052)*
H	0.224 (0.077)*	0.162 (0.088)*	0.526 (0.121)*	−0.346 (0.245)
MTAR	0.010 (0.026)	−0.088 (0.044)*	0.400 (0.104)*	−0.168 (0.216)
KQ	−0.038 (0.021)*	−0.066 (0.022)*	0.156 (0.033)*	0.064 (0.059)
H · MTAR	n.a.	0.277 (0.173)	n.a.	3.704 (0.925)*
KQ · MTAR	n.a.	0.131 (0.052)*	n.a.	0.437 (0.274)
Year dummy variable				
1985	0.009 (0.007)	0.011 (0.007)	−0.056 (0.039)	−0.043 (0.033)*
1986	0.002 (0.007)	0.003 (0.007)	−0.051 (0.038)	−0.042 (0.023)
1987	0.016 (0.006)*	0.017 (0.006)*	−0.033 (0.037)	−0.025 (0.023)
1988	0.024 (0.005)*	0.025 (0.005)*	0.007 (0.034)	0.009 (0.022)
1989	0.005 (0.005)	0.005 (0.005)	−0.001 (0.033)	−0.001 (0.022)
Industry dummy variable				
Food	−0.123 (0.011)*	−0.128 (0.010)*	n.a.	n.a.
Beverages	0.130 (0.010)*	0.127 (0.010)*	n.a.	n.a.
Tobacco	0.368 (0.018)*	0.361 (0.017)*	n.a.	n.a.
Textiles	−0.073 (0.011)*	−0.075 (0.010)*	n.a.	n.a.
Apparel	−0.041 (0.009)*	−0.038 (0.009)*	n.a.	n.a.
Shoes	−0.071 (0.012)*	−0.074 (0.012)*	n.a.	n.a.

	(1)	(2)	(3)	(4)
Wood products and furniture	−0.067 (0.010)*	−0.068 (0.010)*	n.a.	n.a.
Paper and publishing	−0.098 (0.011)*	−0.100 (0.011)*	n.a.	n.a.
Chemicals	0.050 (0.011)*	0.047 (0.011)*	n.a.	n.a.
Regenerated oils	0.011 (0.012)	0.005 (0.013)	n.a.	n.a.
Plastics and rubber products	−0.031 (0.009)*	−0.032 (0.009)*	n.a.	n.a.
Glass	0.067 (0.014)*	0.060 (0.015)*	n.a.	n.a.
Cement products	0.175 (0.027)*	0.183 (0.027)*	n.a.	n.a.
Other nonmetal products	0.031 (0.013)*	0.069 (0.013)*	n.a.	n.a.
Iron and steel	−0.134 (0.012)*	−0.136 (0.012)*	n.a.	n.a.
Nonferrous metal	−0.215 (0.022)*	−0.215 (0.022)*	n.a.	n.a.
Metal products	−0.053 (0.010)*	−0.055 (0.010)*	n.a.	n.a.
Nonelectrical machinery	−0.053 (0.009)*	−0.055 (0.009)*	n.a.	n.a.
Electrical machinery	−0.044 (0.009)*	−0.045 (0.009)*	n.a.	n.a.
Transport equipment	−0.117 (0.009)*	−0.118 (0.009)*	n.a.	n.a.
Dependent mean	0.338	0.338	0.338	0.338
σ^2	0.0002	0.0002	0.0117	0.0104
Adjusted R^2	0.985	0.986	0.244	0.328
F-statistic	288.81	286.21	6.03	7.09

n.a. Not applicable.

* Significant at the 5 percent level.

Note: H is the Herfindahl index of industry-level concentration, $MTAR$ is a production-weighted average official tariff rate, and KQ is the captial-output ratio. Numbers in parentheses are standard errors.

Source: Author's calculations based on 1984–90 data from Bank of Mexico and INEGI.

Table 11.4 Regression Estimates at the Plant Level with Price-Cost Margin (PCM) as the Dependent Variable and QUOT or MTAR as the Indicator of Protection, Mexico

Variable	All plants		Plant quintile with largest market share	
	QUOT	MTAR	QUOT	MTAR
Independent variable				
Intercept	0.235 (0.016)*	0.237 (0.018)*	0.271 (0.016)*	0.278 (0.019)*
Market share	2.991 (0.205)*	2.569 (0.251)*	1.108 (0.154)*	0.890 (0.183)*
Share · Share	−6.395 (0.509)*	6.376 (0.508)*	−2.667 (0.350)*	−2.700 (0.349)*
QUOT	−0.008 (0.017)	n.a.	−0.001 (0.020)	n.a.
Market share · QUOT	0.049 (0.242)	n.a.	0.334 (0.162)*	n.a.
MTAR	n.a.	−0.020 (0.044)	n.a.	−0.050 (0.052)
Market share · MTAR	n.a.	1.969 (0775)*	n.a.	1.538 (0.522)*
Year dummy variable				
1985	0.034 (0.016)*	0.028 (0.011)*	0.017 (0.019)	0.025 (0.014)*
1986	0.026 (0.009)*	0.024 (0.010)*	0.008 (0.011)	0.011 (0.013)
1987	0.032 (0.008)*	0.031 (0.010)*	0.018 (0.010)*	0.021 (0.012)*
1988	0.034 (0.007)*	0.034 (0.007)*	0.014 (0.009)	0.014 (0.009)
1989	0.011 (0.007)	0.011 (0.007)	−0.000 (0.009)	−0.000 (0.009)
Industry dummy variable				
Food	−0.089 (0.016)*	−0.090 (0.017)	−0.050 (0.018)*	−0.049 (0.019)*
Beverages	0.087 (0.018)*	0.087 (0.018)*	0.127 (0.018)*	0.133 (0.018)*
Tobacco	0.222 (0.052)*	0.194 (0.047)*	0.307 (0.038)*	0.324 (0.031)*
Textiles	−0.061 (0.017)*	−0.059 (0.017)*	−0.037 (0.017)*	−0.034 (0.017)*
Apparel	−0.052 (0.018)*	−0.052 (0.017)*	−0.014 (0.018)	−0.009 (0.018)

	(1)	(2)	(3)	(4)
Shoes	−0.123 (0.021)*	−0.124 (0.021)*	−0.040 (0.020)*	−0.037 (0.020)*
Wood products and furniture	−0.070 (0.019)*	−0.070 (0.019)*	−0.065 (0.017)*	−0.062 (0.017)*
Paper and publishing	−0.028 (0.017)	−0.027 (0.018)	−0.059 (0.018)*	−0.058 (0.019)*
Chemicals	0.071 (0.016)*	0.072 (0.017)*	0.078 (0.018)*	0.080 (0.018)*
Regenerated oils	−0.048 (0.034)	−0.032 (0.034)	−0.003 (0.028)	0.032 (0.028)
Plastics and rubber products	−0.018 (0.017)	−0.017 (0.017)	0.014 (0.018)	0.016 (0.019)
Glass	−0.006 (0.028)	−0.009 (0.028)	0.044 (0.019)*	0.043 (0.019)
Cement products	0.049 (0.027)*	0.055 (0.028)*	0.113 (0.019)*	0.114 (0.021)*
Other nonmetal products	−0.017 (0.018)	−0.016 (0.018)	0.080 (0.018)*	0.082 (0.018)
Iron and steel	−0.109 (0.020)*	−0.106 (0.020)*	−0.084 (0.020)*	−0.083 (0.021)*
Nonferrous metal	−0.046 (0.027)*	−0.042 (0.028)	−0.039 (0.022)*	−0.039 (0.022)*
Metal products	−0.043 (0.017)*	−0.041 (0.018)*	0.026 (0.018)	0.027 (0.018)
Nonelectric machinery	−0.028 (0.017)	−0.027 (0.018)	0.014 (0.018)	0.015 (0.019)
Electrical machinery	−0.055 (0.017)*	−0.053 (0.017)*	0.008 (0.017)	0.010 (0.017)
Transport equipment	−0.109 (0.019)*	−0.111 (0.018)*	−0.115 (0.021)*	−0.110 (0.019)*
Dependent mean	0.242	0.242	0.314	0.314
σ^2	0.072	0.072	0.024	0.024
Adjusted R^2	0.070	0.070	0.207	0.208
F-statistic	43.72	43.95	30.98	31.17
Sample size	16,473	16,473	3,334	3,334

n.a. Not applicable.
* Significant at the 5 percent level.
Note: QUOT is the share of total industrial output that falls into categories subject to import licensing; MTAR is a production-weighted average official tariff rate. Numbers in parentheses are standard errors.
Source: Author's calculation based on 1984–90 data from Bank of Mexico and INEGI.

Unlike Schmalensee's findings for U.S. manufacturing, market share effects for Mexican industries are not only significant but also have strong explanatory power. Starting from the naive model with only time dummies, the increase in the adjusted R^2 following inclusion of market share or industry effects is fairly comparable (+0.024 and +0.055, respectively). This result suggests that in the Mexican case, although the variation in price-cost margin at the plant level does depend on industry-level differences in the degree of competition, it is also correlated with plant-level differences in efficiency. These results are similar to those for Colombia (chapter 10) but differ from those for Chile (chapter 9), which find markets to be basically competitive.

For protective instruments, the only significant impact is from the interaction term between average tariff rate and a plant's market share. This is not surprising, given that the import-discipline effect at the sector level has already been shown to be strongest in the most concentrated industries (tables 11.2 and 11.3). A similar outcome would be expected at the plant level since the Herfindahl index is constructed by aggregating market shares.[6]

To pursue further the relation between market power and protection, plants are sorted by ascending market share into five groups of equal size, and regressions are performed separately for each group. As expected, the impact of protective instruments is stronger in the groups with the higher market shares. The best explanatory power is obtained for the fifth quintile (last two columns of table 11.4).[7] Price-cost margins now appear to increase with both measures of protection, and as before, only the interaction terms are significant, even for the biggest plants.

Finally, of the protective instruments, average tariff seems to have a stronger impact on price-cost margins than do licensing requirements at the plant level (when both protective instruments are included in the same regression, only the average tariff $MTAR$ is significant). The opposite is true at the sector level, a troublesome finding that suggests the need for careful consideration of the type of theoretical model that may best explain the collusive behavior of domestic plants.[8]

Conclusions

Mexico has a relatively large number of producers, and presumably they impose some degree of competitive pressure on one another. Further, most of its industries were not very involved in trade prior to the scaling back of tariffs and license requirements. Nonetheless, empirical evidence suggests that exposure to foreign competition significantly reduced the profit rate of Mexican manufacturers. The greater the market power of an industry, the stronger was the impact of trade liberalization on price-cost margins.

Appendix: Data Preparation and Summary Statistics

Data on 3,218 manufacturing plants for the period 1984–90 were collected by Mexico's National Institute of Statistics, Geography, and Information (INEGI); these data provide the basis for all inferences regarding industrial production, profitability, and use of inputs. Within manufacturing, INEGI's objective was to cover enough plants to account for 80 percent of cumulative value added—the smaller plants were excluded.[9]

The original sample provided annual observations on roughly 100 variables. The following variables were used in subsequent calculations. (All monetary variables were converted to millions of 1980 Mexican pesos using deflators indicated by superscripts.)

1. Labor force
TWRK	Total workers (blue-collar, white-collar, and nonremunerated workers)
NBHR	Work hours logged by blue-collar workers (thousands of hours)
$BSAL^a$	Blue-collar salary
$WSAL^a$	White-collar salary
$TLPM^a$	Total labor remunerations (including BSAL and WSAL)

2. Inputs and other expenditures
$PMAT^b$	Primary materials and auxiliary inputs consumed (including the use of related inventories)
$TMAT^b$	Total inputs consumed (including PMAT)
$CONT^a$	Expenditures on maquila services
$TSRV^a$	Total expenditures on industrial services (including CONT)
$RENT^a$	Rent
$TNIS^a$	Total expenditures on nonindustrial services (including RENT)
$VELC^c$	Value of electricity consumed

3. Income from sales and other services
$GVAL^d$	Gross value of products (including net increase of inventories)
$OINM^a$	Income from maquila services

4. Replacement cost of capital (end of year)
$MERC^e$	Machinery and equipment
$CIRC^f$	Construction and installation
$LNRC^{ae}$	Land
$TERC^g$	Transport equipment
$OARC^h$	Other fixed assets

5. Capital produced for own use
MEOU^e Machinery and equipment
CIOU^f Construction and installation
TEOU^g Transport equipment
OAOU^h Other fixed assets

6. Industry-level price deflators (superscripts)
a   General wholesale price index, annual average
b   Primary materials price index, annual average (at a two-digit
         national accounts classification level)
c   Electricity price index, annual average
d   Industrial output price index, annual average (at a four-digit
         census classification level)
e, f, g, h   Corresponding capital price indexes[10]
ae   General wholesale price index, end of year

Several variables were created from the original data base. First, efficiency units of labor were calculated as an index of total labor services used at each plant: $LEU = NBHR \cdot [1 + (WSAL / BSAL)]$. This variable, used especially in productivity analysis, is based on the assumption that the wage differential between white- and blue-collar workers is equal to the productivity differential.

Second, total capital stock at each plant was calculated as the sum of the replacement cost of its components and the capitalized value of the rent at an annual discount rate of 10 percent: $TKS = (MERC + CIRC + LNRC + TERC + OARC) + (RENT / 0.10)$.

Next value added, output, and intermediate inputs for subcontracting (*maquila*) work were corrected.[11] The census recorded all primary materials and output associated with this type of work at the plant that ordered the job, not the one that actually did the work. Consequently, the value of production reported by the plant that did the subcontracted work is below its true value—$GVO = GVAL + (MEOU + CIOU + TEOU + OAOU)$—as is the cost of its primary inputs. Further, because total labor and capital were reported fully, plants heavily engaged in subcontracted work often show negative value added—$VA = GVO - (TMAT + VELC)$. The reverse observations hold for those plants that ordered subcontracted work.

A corrected value added ($CORVA$) was therefore obtained for *maquila* work by adding the net value of income from *maquila* services: $CORVA = VA + (OINM - CONT)$. Of course, the value of output is biased by the same problem but is more difficult to correct for. One alternative was to drop from the sample all plants that ordered or supplied subcontracted work. But this would have eliminated half of the selected plants and substantially reduced the range of the analysis. Instead, two additional assumptions were made in order to impute figures for gross output: the ratio between value added and output and the ratio between primary materials and total inputs are constant through time and among plants. Then $CORGVO = GVO + b*(OINM - CONT)$. The mean value of b was calculated at a two-digit national accounts classification level (forty-eight industry groups) using the plants that did not conduct *maquila* activity and then was used to calculate the estimated value of $CORGVO$. This variable was used in all subsequent calculations except for estimation of the Herfindahl index and the individual plant's share, which are intended to reflect the effective share of the market controlled by each plant.

Finally, given the above variables, corrected intermediate inputs ($CORINT$) were constructed as $CORINT = CORGVO - CORVA$.

Of course, these assumptions are fairly restrictive and, ideally, should be supported by empirical tests. In this study, they mainly serve to correct the bias that would otherwise eliminate a significant number of plants. Over the whole sample finally retained (see the next section), 45 percent of the observations are affected by the *maquila* bias. However, among those, the share of subcontracted work was usually low, under 10 percent in two-thirds of the cases. Only a small group of 784 observations (less than 10 percent of the total) relied on subcontracted jobs for more than 90 percent of their total production.

Finally, three cost measures were constructed: variable costs ($VCOST$), fixed costs ($FCOST$), and total costs ($TCOST$):

$VCOST = (TMAT + VELC) + TLPM$
$FCOST = TSRV + TNIS + 0.10*(MERC + CIRC + LNRC + TERC +$
$\qquad OARC)$
$TCOST = VCOST + FCOST$

These helped to identify outliers, as discussed below.

Selection of Observations

A rough 15 percent of the 22,442 observations involved were eliminated by applying the following selection criteria:

- *Elimination of missing and zero variables.* All observations with missing or zero values for each of the following variables were immediately excluded: $TWRK$, $NBHR$, $BSAL$, VA (at current prices), TKS, $VCOST$, $FCOST$, $TCOST$, GVO, and INT. This eliminated 587 observations.
- *Elimination of odd observations.* If a key variable (either $TWRK$, $NBHR$, $TLPM$, $GVAL$, $PMAT$, $TMAT$, or $RENT$) grew or shrank at an inordinately rapid pace, the associated observation was excluded. Such anomalies were considered to reflect errors in entering or recording the data. An additional nineteen observations were eliminated by this criterion.

Table 11A.1 Trade and Production Characteristics of Manufacturing Industries in Mexico, 1984–90

Characteristic	1984	1985	1986	1987	1988	1989	1990
Growth rate (percentages)	5.32	7.03	-3.42	3.93	2.95	6.54	5.04
Deviation from predicted rate (percentages)[a]	-4.17	0.68	-4.56	-2.63	-1.61	2.89	6.09
Import penetration rate (percentages)	9	10	9	8	11	14	18
Export share (percentages)	7	6	7	8	8	9	10
Trade share (percentages)	16	17	16	15	19	23	29
Number of plants	2,801	2,816	2,799	2,764	2,738	2,713	2,643
Value added per plant (millions of 1980 pesos)	164.22	182.63	178.12	187.67	197.76	243.23	273.42
Gross output per plant (millions of 1980 pesos)	351.52	392.20	373.07	390.10	400.39	474.28	530.03
Capital stock per plant (millions of 1980 pesos)	216.60	191.38	168.41	186.53	236.10	239.20	247.90
Labor per plant[b]	944.75	986.75	975.35	984.21	1,035.80	1,151.10	1,212.81
Labor productivity[c]	0.36	0.36	0.34	0.35	0.35	0.39	0.40
Capital productivity[d]	5.69	5.83	6.32	5.79	4.32	4.59	4.60

a. Percentage of deviation from the predicted value of a trend fitted over the 1980–90 period.
b. Thousands of blue-collar equivalent working hours (see the appendix text).
c. Unweighted average of plant-level values of gross output / labor efficiency units.
d. Unweighted average of plant-level values of gross output / capital stock.
Source: Author's calculations based on Bank of Mexico, various years, INEGI data, and National Bank of Foreign Trade, various years.

- *Elimination of incomplete series.* Plants that were discarded in at least one year for the reasons mentioned above were discarded for all the other years as well. This eliminated 1,116 observations.
- *Entry and exit.* The remaining subset of observations was then sorted by plant identification code and year. Although the sample is essentially closed, seventeen plants were identified as entrants—all in 1986. Also 175 exiting plants were identified. Finally, 142 plants were discarded because they entered and exited the sample more than once, or because they were dormant in more than one year. Dormant plants were defined as having *TWRK, NBHR, BSAL, CORVA, VCOST, GVO,* and *INT* all missing or equal to 0 but as having *TKS, FCOST,* and *TCOST* strictly positive.

The final sample contained 19,726 observations (about 2,800 per year) that were used in the rest of the analysis and represented roughly 95 percent of the initial total workers and of the initial corrected value added.

Trade Statistics

Trade data at the overall manufacturing level (table 11A.1) were taken from National Bank of Foreign Trade (various years). At the sector level (table 11A.2), data on imports and exports were taken from the Commodity Trade data base of the United Nations Statistical Office, which provides information at a four-digit level of the ISIC. Several standard problems arose in merging these data with INEGI's industrial survey. First, ISIC codes distinguish products by end use, but INEGI's industrial classifications distinguish products by production technology. Thus, for example, processed and fresh foods are similar in the trade data, but one is an industrial product and one is an agricultural product in the Mexican system. Nonetheless, because detailed product codes are available in INEGI's data base, it was possible to achieve a reasonable match. Second, the trade statistics are in dollars, and the (clean) INEGI data base is in 1980 pesos. To avoid large swings in the share of output exported or the share of consumption imported, the trade data were first put in 1980 dollars and then converted to pesos at the 1980 exchange rate. Thus fluctuations in the exchange rate were essentially removed from the series.

Data on commercial policy were provided by Adrian Ten Kate of SECOFI and were already aggregated according to a classification scheme compatible with that of the industrial census. These data are summarized by industry and time period in table 11A.3, which clearly demonstrates that most of the changes in commercial policy took place between 1985 and 1988.

Table 11A.2 Share of Trade and Production by Industrial Sector in Mexico, 1984
(percentages)

ISIC code	Industry	Number of plants	Share of total output	Share of imports	Share of exports
311,312	Food	378	14.5	6.2	10.2
313	Beverages	134	7.4	0.1	1.3
314	Tobacco	7	1.3	0.0	0.0
321	Textiles	190	3.5	1.1	3.4
321,322	Apparel	181	1.4	1.0	2.0
324	Shoes	54	0.8	0.2	0.6
331,332	Wood products and furniture	82	0.8	0.5	1.2
341,342	Paper and publishing	188	5.1	3.3	1.3
351,352	Chemicals	355	16.0	19.0	12.7
354	Regenerated oils	16	0.4	0.4	2.7
355,356	Plastics and rubber products	222	3.9	2.5	2.0
362	Glass	23	2.2	0.5	1.9
369	Cement products	26	2.3	0.1	1.2
369	Other nonmetal products	129	1.4	0.6	1.1
371	Iron and steel	85	9.0	6.5	4.7
372	Nonferrous metal	23	5.2	2.7	8.5
381	Metal products	160	2.8	5.0	3.5
382	Nonelectrical machinery	167	2.5	16.5	6.6
383	Electrical machinery	179	6.2	23.2	24.9
384	Transport equipment	146	12.9	10.1	9.3
390,352	Other manufacturing	56	0.5	0.5	1.0

Note: The trade figures relate only to the industrial categories included in the sample and therefore do not cover the entire range of Mexican imports and exports. Also, the classifications of the Commodity Trade data do not correspond exactly to the industrial classifications of the sample firms.
Source: Author's calculations.

Table 11A.1 combines INEGI data on production and inputs with data on trade flows to impute import penetration rates, export shares, and trade shares. Once again, a clear trend toward increased openness emerges.

Sample Characteristics

Table 11A.1 summarizes the INEGI data by presenting the number of plants and various indicators of plant size. Except for 1986, average plant growth was positive, whether measured by output, value added, or labor. Further analysis reveals that exiting plants were markedly smaller than incumbents, so increases in the average size of firms partly reflect plants exiting the panel.[12]

Average capital stock per plant decreased from 1984 to 1986, probably as a consequence of physical destruction caused by the earthquake of

Table 11A.3 Average Annual Change in Import Protection in Mexico,
1985–90
(percentages)

Industry	Change in import license coverage		Change in average tariff	
	1985–88	*1988–90*	*1985–88*	*1988–90*
Food	−24.5	−0.9	−3.0	0.3
Beverages	−32.0	−0.4	−21.8	0.0
Tobacco	0.0	0.0	−10.0	0.0
Textiles	−29.5	−0.7	−6.6	0.2
Apparel	−33.3	0.0	−9.9	0.0
Shoes	−32.6	0.0	−8.6	−0.3
Wood products and furniture	−33.3	0.0	−7.2	0.0
Paper and publishing	−28.5	−0.3	−7.1	1.8
Chemicals	−26.5	−0.5	−5.5	0.7
Regenerated oils	−2.4	−0.4	−0.4	1.7
Plastics and rubber products	−32.7	0.0	−6.5	−0.6
Glass	−32.2	−0.2	−13.0	1.4
Cement products	−33.3	0.0	0.0	0.0
Other nonmetal products	−30.0	−1.8	−6.9	0.2
Iron and steel	−30.2	0.0	−2.1	1.5
Nonferrous metal	−24.0	0.0	−3.8	0.8
Metal products	−24.0	0.0	−7.1	−0.2
Nonelectrical machinery	−25.4	−0.3	−2.0	0.3
Electrical machinery	−32.4	0.0	−5.2	0.0
Transport equipment	−13.9	−7.0	−7.9	0.6
Other manufacturing industries	−30.6	0.0	−11.1	0.2

Source: Author's calculations based on data from SECOFI.

1985 and the low level of net investment during the recession of 1986. Its upward trend after 1987 is consistent with both the recovery of the economy and the elimination of the smallest firms—more than 50 percent of the increase in the average capital stock per plant in 1989 and 1990 was due to the exit of small firms.

The only years in which output was clearly above the 1980–90 trend were 1989 and 1990, while 1984, 1985, and 1987 should be viewed as recovery years. The import penetration rate (corrected for changes in the real exchange rate) remained constant over the period until 1988, when it began to increase markedly, reflecting the delayed effects of liberalization. The increase in the export rate was less dramatic, despite favorable conditions, suggesting that some producers were still relying on the domestic market rather than on export opportunities.[13]

Both labor and capital productivity rose in 1989 and 1990, reflecting the increase in production.[14] But while labor productivity remained roughly constant from 1984 through 1988, capital productivity underwent important changes, increasing until 1986 and then falling sharply.

These variations may be due to underutilization of capacity and delays in replacing obsolescent equipment.[15]

Growth of total factor productivity was negative in most industries for the first part of the sample period, 1985–88, as was growth of output (see table 11A.4). Regressions (not reported here) confirm that annual growth of productivity was strongly correlated with annual growth of output, controlling for characteristics of the industry. This suggests that the fall in productivity during the initial phase of trade liberalization was due at least partly to the recession.

Productivity rebounded during the second period at the same time that real appreciation of the exchange rate heightened competitive pressures. The rate of productivity expansion in the second period was greater than the rate of contraction in the first period. So heightened foreign competition was associated with more than a reduction in price-cost margins; it coincided with more efficient production.[16]

Finally, price-cost margins and other variables that support regressions reported in the text are summarized in table 11A.5.

Table 11A.4 Average Annual Growth of Productivity and Real Output in Mexico, 1985–90
(percentages)

Industry	Productivity		Real output	
	1985–88	1988–89	1985–88	1988–90
Food	1.8	6.0	3.7	9.6
Beverages	−0.2	2.2	4.1	10.7
Tobacco	0.3	2.8	0.5	14.8
Textiles	−6.7	9.4	−6.4	10.0
Apparel	−4.6	0.5	−7.4	7.2
Shoes	−4.9	1.8	−16.8	9.4
Wood products and furniture	−9.9	7.2	−12.9	13.0
Paper and publishing	−3.7	4.3	−3.5	6.9
Chemicals	−4.0	6.0	−1.1	9.7
Regenerated oils	−1.6	−1.7	10.5	5.0
Plastics and rubber products	−6.2	2.6	−5.3	6.9
Glass	1.2	9.5	1.9	18.5
Cement products	−5.3	2.7	−4.5	6.8
Other nonmetal products	−10.4	9.5	−9.8	16.9
Iron and steel	−0.1	6.5	−6.5	11.6
Nonferrous metal	4.2	−2.9	0.6	−7.4
Metal products	−4.1	6.2	−1.5	14.1
Nonelectrical machinery	2.0	5.9	1.7	11.7
Electrical machinery	−2.0	11.4	−3.6	19.5
Transport equipment	−1.8	3.5	2.3	21.9
Other manufacturing industries	−3.0	6.1	−2.1	13.9

Source: Author's calculations based on data from INEGI and Bank of Mexico.

Table 11A.5 Industrial Structure and Performance Variables for Mexico, 1985, 1988, and 1990

Industry	Price-cost margin (PCM)			Average tariff rate (MTAR)			Average coverage of import licenses (QUOT)			Herfindahl index (H)			Capital-output ratio (KQ)		
	1985	1988	1990	1985	1988	1990	1985	1988	1990	1985	1988	1990	1985	1988	1990
Food	0.212	0.225	0.226	0.203	0.112	0.117	0.945	0.210	0.192	0.007	0.008	0.009	0.258	0.280	0.243
Beverages	0.454	0.477	0.478	0.849	0.196	0.196	0.995	0.034	0.025	0.030	0.036	0.036	0.740	0.708	0.640
Tobacco	0.747	0.767	0.760	0.500	0.200	0.200	1.000	1.000	1.000	0.234	0.253	0.238	0.506	0.499	0.473
Textiles	0.256	0.254	0.253	0.345	0.148	0.151	0.909	0.024	0.010	0.014	0.013	0.014	0.625	0.905	0.701
Apparel	0.309	0.321	0.298	0.498	0.200	0.200	1.000	0.000	0.000	0.022	0.030	0.033	0.305	0.411	0.380
Shoes	0.368	0.332	0.246	0.426	0.168	0.162	0.978	0.000	0.000	0.238	0.153	0.156	0.304	0.491	0.497
Wood products and furniture	0.273	0.267	0.264	0.387	0.170	0.170	0.999	0.000	0.000	0.028	0.035	0.038	0.502	0.870	0.622
Paper and publishing	0.239	0.248	0.219	0.264	0.051	0.086	0.859	0.005	0.000	0.025	0.025	0.024	0.592	0.818	0.705
Chemicals	0.384	0.379	0.375	0.291	0.126	0.140	0.820	0.025	0.016	0.010	0.012	0.013	0.583	0.772	0.602
Regenerated oils	0.378	0.385	0.366	0.022	0.011	0.044	0.943	0.872	0.864	0.129	0.131	0.125	0.332	0.377	0.404
Plastics and rubber products	0.307	0.318	0.313	0.364	0.169	0.158	0.982	0.000	0.000	0.039	0.046	0.042	0.405	0.609	0.565
Glass	0.425	0.408	0.358	0.527	0.138	0.165	0.969	0.003	0.000	0.065	0.079	0.074	0.988	1.013	0.769
Cement products	0.491	0.483	0.463	0.100	0.100	0.100	1.000	0.000	0.000	0.054	0.054	0.055	1.191	1.858	1.688
Other nonmetal products	0.403	0.417	0.391	0.369	0.161	0.165	0.934	0.035	0.000	0.028	0.028	0.027	0.666	1.090	0.831
Iron and steel	0.233	0.234	0.236	0.134	0.072	0.101	0.907	0.000	0.000	0.091	0.077	0.075	0.638	0.759	0.560
Nonferrous metal	0.188	0.206	0.199	0.222	0.109	0.124	0.719	0.000	0.000	0.185	0.336	0.342	0.419	0.451	0.483
Metal products	0.269	0.302	0.281	0.362	0.149	0.145	0.733	0.012	0.011	0.026	0.039	0.035	0.582	0.697	0.534
Nonelectrical machinery	0.300	0.319	0.298	0.210	0.150	0.156	0.798	0.036	0.031	0.032	0.089	0.137	0.439	0.453	0.371
Electrical machinery	0.291	0.325	0.302	0.327	0.172	0.172	0.971	0.000	0.000	0.018	0.032	0.057	0.304	0.391	0.287
Transport equipment	0.233	0.251	0.230	0.390	0.152	0.164	0.992	0.573	0.433	0.047	0.050	0.052	0.256	0.325	0.226
Other manufacturing industries	0.354	0.374	0.341	0.508	0.176	0.180	0.918	0.000	0.000	0.063	0.059	0.070	0.371	0.492	0.383

Source: Author's calculations based on data from Bank of Mexico and INEGI.

Notes

The author wishes to thank François Bourguignon, Fernando Clavijo, Jaime de Melo, James Tybout, and Milad Zarin-Nejadan for their support and helpful comments.

1. The Pacto de Solidaridad Económica (December 1987–December 1988) and the Pacto para la Estabilidad y el Crecimiento Económico (since January 1989), negotiated among government, labor, and business organizations, consist mainly of agreements for price and wage freezes and smooth depreciation of the peso. For a detailed analysis of the external debt agreement of July 1989, see van Wijnbergen 1991.

2. This last measure was already part of the favorable treatment that had been granted to the *maquiladora* producers after 1965. The *maquilas* (mainly in the apparel and automobile industries) import duty-free components, which are then processed in Mexico and exported again. Although there is as yet no general agreement about their impact on the domestic economy, their growing importance in Mexican manufacturing exports in the 1980s is clear. The production of *maquilas* accounted for approximately 44 percent of Mexican exports to the United States in 1987. For a recent survey of the *maquiladoras*, see Fatemi 1990.

3. The measures of tariff and import license coverage are as calculated by the Mexican Secretary of International Commerce and Industrial Development (SECOFI). Adriaan Ten Kate provided recent data on these measures.

4. Between regressions were also run, using the temporal average of each variable. They confirmed the results of models 3 and 4.

5. Regression results involving the concentration proxy must be approached with caution. Diagnostic tests (studentized residuals, changes in predicted value) reveal that outliers and influential observations are located mainly in the tobacco and nonferrous metals industries, which happen to be the most concentrated ones. However, excluding them from the sample does not affect the main results of our study, and since there is no obvious economic reason to treat them separately, these two industrial groups are kept in the following regressions.

6. There is a strong similarity between the specifications at the sector and plant levels. In a simple model of Cournot-type oligopoly, Jacquemin (1982) has shown that the sectoral relationship can be obtained by multiplying the plant-level equation by the plant's market share and summing over all plants in the industry.

7. The number of observations for the fifth quintile is slightly greater than one-fifth of sample firms, because the number of exiting plants was relatively smaller in this quintile than in others over the sample period.

8. In the simple model in which a domestic monopoly faces competitively supplied imports, quantitative restrictions create more market power than tariffs. But the result can be different in the case of a collusive domestic oligopoly. For a recent survey, see Helpman and Krugman 1989.

9. Further comparisons with national accounts data reveal that the coverage of the original sample varies industry by industry and may be smaller than 80 percent overall.

10. Purchased capital is recorded in end-of-year prices, while capital produced for own use is expressed in roughly mid-year prices. As the original sample does not include end-of-year price indexes, interpolation was necessary using geometric means of mid-year price series.

11. Contrary to popular usage of this term, in the industrial survey it includes subcontracting between two domestic firms as well as transactions across the border.

12. Application of the method of decomposing the growth of size proposed by Tybout (1992) results in a global exit effect for certain years that explains more than 30 percent of the increase in size.

13. Ros (1992) shows that during the 1980s the fastest growing exports originated mainly from sectors under specific industrial programs and from the *maquiladoras*. The export performance of the remaining sectors was particularly vulnerable to economic recovery.

14. The measure of productivity presented in table 11.1 was calculated at the plant level, a factor that gives more importance to small plants, whose level of capital productivity is greater than that of larger plants (this relationship has been checked throughout the sample period). This explains why capital productivity is markedly larger than the ratio between average output and average capital stock. Both measures follow approximately the same time pattern.

15. Capital measurement errors may also explain some of the variation, particularly during the years of high inflation. In valuing end-of-year replacement costs of capital, surveyed firms can choose between market prices and government accounting rules. Furthermore, end-of-year price indexes are not available and have to be estimated using the mean of the annual average price indexes. This procedure overstates the value of the end-of-year price index when inflation is accelerating.

16. Plant-level analysis based on estimated cost functions and production functions confirms that the efficiency of most sectors improved overall during the sample period (Tybout and Westbrook 1995).

References

Bank of Mexico. Various years. *Indicadores económicos.* Mexico City.

Fatemi, Khosrow. 1990. *The Maquiladora Industry: Economic Solution or Problem?* New York: Praeger Publishers.

Helpman, Elhanan, and Paul Krugman. 1989. *Trade Policy and Market Structure.* Cambridge, Mass.: MIT Press.

Ize, Alain. 1990. "Trade Liberalization, Stabilization, and Growth: Some Notes on the Mexican Experience." IMF Working Paper 90/15. International Monetary Fund, Washington, D.C.

Jacquemin, Alexis. 1982. "Imperfect Market Structure and International Trade: Some Recent Research." *Kyklos* 35 (1): 75–93.

National Bank of Foreign Trade. Various years. *Comercio exterior.* Mexico City.

Ros, Jaime. 1992. "Mexico's Trade and Industrialization Experience since 1960: A Reconsideration of Past Policies and Assessment of Current Reforms." University of Notre Dame, Notre Dame, Ind.

Schmalensee, Richard. 1985. "Do Markets Differ Much?" *American Economic Review* 75 (3): 341–51.

Ten Kate, Adriaan, and Fernando de Mateo Venturini. 1989. "Apertura comercial y estructura de la protección en México." *Comercio Exterior* 39: 313–29.

Tybout, James R. 1992. "Researching the Trade/Productivity Link: New Directions." *World Bank Economic Review* 6 (2, May): 189–211.

Tybout, James R., Jaime de Melo, and Vittorio Corbo. 1991. "The Effects of Trade Reforms on Scale and Technical Efficiency: New Evidence from Chile." *Journal of International Economics* 31: 231–50.

Tybout, James R., and M. Daniel Westbrook. 1995. "Trade Liberalization and the Dimensions of Efficiency Change in Mexican Manufacturing Industries." *Journal of International Economics* 39: 53–78.

van Wijnbergen, Sweder. 1991. "Mexico and the Brady Plan." *Economic Policy* 12 (April): 14–56.

12

Morocco, 1984–89:
Trade Liberalization, Exports,
and Industrial Performance

Mona Haddad, Jaime de Melo, and Brendan Horton

Until 1983 the Moroccan foreign trade regime was riddled with import controls, cumbersome administrative procedures for exports, and a wide range of tariff duties (up to 400 percent) that heavily protected domestic industry. In 1983 Morocco began a progressive dismantling of quantitative restrictions, reduction of tariffs, and simplification of administrative procedures, all designed to improve industrial performance by forcing greater competition, exploiting economies of scale, and improving technical efficiency. This chapter looks for signs of positive results in the industrial sector, drawing on data from a panel of Moroccan industrial firms surveyed during 1984–89.

Although the data do not permit a before-and-after analysis of the effects of trade liberalization on the industrial sector's performance, the Moroccan case is interesting for at least two reasons. First, the liberalization was gradual rather than sudden, so that it provides an opportunity to study how industrial performance evolves during gradual liberalization. Second, the data set includes exports at the firm level and information on the number of products produced by firms in 1987, permitting examination of the mix of exports and products, two aspects on which little evidence has been available.

Changes in the Moroccan Trade Regime

As internal and external disequilibria worsened in the early 1980s, the government began a program of reforms built around stabilization and structural adjustment measures. The program included a flexible

Table 12.1 Chronology of Trade Liberalization in Morocco, 1983–89

Year	Nontariff barrier	Tariff barrier
1983	Transfer from list B to list A of raw materials and spare parts not produced in Morocco; share of manufacturing output protected by restrictions: 60 percent	Maximum customs tariff: 400 percent; unweighted average tariff rate: 36 percent
1984	Continued liberalization, with particular emphasis on products not produced in Morocco; import value coverage: list A, 82.2 percent; list B, 17.5 percent; list C, 0.3 percent	Reduction of special import tax from 15 to 10 percent; reduction of maximum customs duty to 100 percent
1985	Continued liberalization, with particular emphasis on products not produced in Morocco	Reduction of the special import tax to 7.5 percent; reduction of maximum customs duty to 60 percent
1986	Continued liberalization; abolition of list C	Reduction of maximum customs duty to 45 percent; substitution of the sales tax, accompanied by a rate increase from 17 to 19 percent; introduction of an interest-free 25 percent prior import deposit; selective use of reference prices; unweighted average tariff rate: 26 percent
1987	Liberalization of an additional 332 tariff items	Reduction of special import tax to 5 percent; increase of all customs duties of 42.5 percent and below by 2.5 percentage points
1988	Liberalization of additional tariff items; import value coverage: list A, 87.3 percent; list B, 12.7 percent	Replacement of special import tax and customs stamp tax by a fiscal import duty of 12.5 percent
1989	Liberalization of additional tariff items; share of domestic manufacturing output protected by restrictions: 20 percent	Distribution of port values by tariff: 8.6 at 0.0 percent, 32.2 at 2.5 percent, 16.9 at 12.5 percent, 13.3 at 17.5 percent, 5.5 at 22.5 percent, 7.6 at 45.0 percent

Note: List A, goods freely imported; list B, goods requiring a license; list C, goods for which imports are prohibited.
Source: World Bank 1988, 1990; World Bank and UNDP 1990.

exchange rate policy to improve Morocco's external competitiveness and a set of liberalization measures to improve the efficiency of resource allocation in manufacturing (see table 12.1). Before 1983 all imported goods except those on a free import list required a license. After 1983 the annual import programs became progressively less restrictive as goods—classified by tariff line—were transferred to list A, for which no prior authorization was required, and list B, for which prior permission was usually granted automatically. By 1986 the list of prohibited imports (list C) was abolished. However, despite the transfer of goods to the free import list between 1984 and 1988, there was little change in the share of imports that fell under lists A and B.

Customs duties were also gradually reduced, with the maximum duty falling from 400 percent in 1983 to 45 percent by 1988, although twenty-six categories of tariffs remained. Also in 1988 the special import tax and customs stamp tax were replaced by a fiscal levy on imports that was larger than the two taxes it replaced. Numerous exemptions were granted on the fiscal levy (more than 25 percent of imports were exempt in 1988).[1]

The evolution of the average nominal tariff and the share of imports under lists A and B for the period 1982–90 shows that most of the liberalization had taken place by 1984, the first year covered in the analysis of industrial sector performance. It is also clear that the protective regime favored industry over agriculture.[2] The average level of nominal protection remained quite high, especially in manufacturing. For example, in 1987 average nominal protection in manufacturing was 37 percent—higher than the 34 percent average for all developing countries.

The reform program also reduced the bias against exports. Barriers to exports were eliminated, and administrative procedures were simplified. Several export incentives were also introduced, including insurance, fiscal and financial incentives, and, in 1987, a temporary admission scheme that allowed exporters to obtain imported inputs duty-free. Finally, Morocco's accession to the General Agreement on Tariffs and Trade (GATT) in 1987 must also have boosted the confidence of exporters, since membership offered a bulwark against political pressures for protection.

Changing Patterns of Industry-Level Structure and Performance

All in all, the Moroccan reform program resulted in a relatively modest liberalization of a tightly controlled foreign trade regime. No dramatic shifts in resources or productivity in manufacturing would be expected from such a gradual trade liberalization, although some rationalization of the allocation of resources within manufacturing toward exporting activities might be expected if the reforms were significant enough.

Table 12.2 *Characteristics of the Manufacturing Sector in Morocco, 1987*

Sector and percentage share of manufacturing value added	Number of firms	Thousands of workers	Concentration ratio[a]	Value added as a percentage of output	Labor cost as a percentage of value added	Capital-output ratio	Price-cost margin	Export sales (thousands of dirhams)	Import penetration[b]	Foreign ownership (percent)	Public ownership (percent)	Tariff (percent)	Export-oriented sector[c]
Food products, 7.8	899	25.1	26	17	39	33	118	2	4	5	38	31	No
Other food products, 10.8	422	51.2	27	21	37	19	47	24	12	12	24	31	Yes
Beverages and tobacco, 16.9	33	9.8	78	72	10	21	12	1	8	15	15	39	No
Textiles, 10.8	464	55.7	16	31	45	35	59	32	38	12	12	35	Yes
Clothing, 4.4	473	43.7	18	30	55	14	11	84	3	20	4	44	Yes
Leather and shoes, 2.1	248	13.3	23	29	55	39	10	42	21	17	2	22	Yes
Wood products, 2.2	194	10.1	38	31	47	19	20	21	42	14	0	29	Yes
Paper and printing, 4.5	336	11.9	47	30	38	36	69	11	17	22	17	37	No
Mineral products, 9.0	305	25.5	31	45	30	70	85	1	9	22	23	28	No
Basic metals, 3.5	26	2.8	81	34	13	54	4	15	53	3	84	9	Yes
Metallic products, 4.3	328	16.1	25	27	47	18	49	1	18	20	7	31	No
Machinery and equipment, 2.0	202	6.5	50	41	46	21	28	0	66	21	5	17	No
Transport materials, 3.5	99	7.6	60	33	38	17	15	9	52	26	18	24	Yes
Electronics, 3.6	110	9.9	35	37	47	24	20	11	43	28	10	26	Yes
Precision equipment, 0.2	22	0.8	45	44	43	31	6	4	83	18	0	29	No
Chemical products, 11.1	241	22.2	52	19	39	49	64	36	30	10	71	21	Yes
Rubber and plastics, 2.8	195	8.1	45	32	41	26	23	5	22	12	2	29	No
Other industrial products, 0.1	26	0.4	52	43	62	14	−8	10	87	23	0	38	No

a. Of the four largest firms in the industry.
b. Defined as imports / (output + imports − exports).
c. Based on authors' judgment.
Source: Authors' calculations based on survey data.

Characteristics of the Manufacturing Sector

Average yearly growth in the manufacturing sector was 2.9 percent between 1977 and 1981 and 4.5 percent during 1985–89, compared with growth in gross domestic product (GDP) of 2.3 percent in real terms and 5.2 percent, respectively.[3] Employment in manufacturing grew 5.6 percent a year during 1976–80 and 10.3 percent (including temporary workers) during 1984–90. Not surprisingly, little significant difference can be detected in manufacturing performance from these aggregate statistics before and after the reform. However, changing patterns of resource allocation and productivity may be detected at the sector and firm level. This study looks for those changes using data from annual surveys from 1984 to 1989 of all firms with more than ten employees or sales revenue of more than DH100,000 (Morocco's currency is the dirham). The results suggest that the reforms did alter incentives in a sustained and credible manner.

The manufacturing sector in Morocco in 1987 had a well-developed set of light manufacturing activities and relatively high levels of employment in sectors that use natural resources intensively (see table 12.2). Data on export sales at the firm level show that the sectors exporting the largest proportion of their production were clothing, leather and shoes, chemical products, textiles, and other food products. Except for chemicals (which are natural resource-intensive), all these activities exhibited relatively high ratios of labor to gross output. The import-competing sectors (those with high rates of import penetration and high tariffs) were concentrated in the capital goods and heavy industry sectors, although the textile sector also had relatively high rates of nominal protection and import penetration.

The data on sector-level share of exports were also used to construct a classification of export-competing sectors, supplemented by assessments of which sectors have the potential for a supply response to a change in incentives (last column of table 12.2). Export subsectors were identified in other food products, textiles, clothing, leather and shoes, wood products, basic metals, electronics, and chemical products. Among these sectors, the chemicals sector had a steadily declining share of exports during 1984–89, and other food products, leather and shoes, and electronics had a steadily rising share of exports (at the four-digit level, 50 of 228 sectors were classified as exporting).

Concentration rates in manufacturing were relatively high. In six sectors, half of sectoral sales was accounted for by four or fewer firms. High concentration rates are often observed in developing economies, especially when the domestic market is small in size. There is a statistically significant positive correlation between share of public ownership and industrial concentration (0.15) and between share of foreign ownership and both share of exports (0.11) and share of import penetration (0.11).

Patterns of Entry and Exit

On average during 1984–89, 13 percent of the firms operating in each sector were new firms, though the entry rate fell by a third between 1985 and 1989; 3 percent of the firms switched sectors (see table 12.3). New entrants accounted for 3 percent of each sector's output. Comparison of entry rates and entrants' share of the market reveals that entrants tended to be smaller than existing producers. New entrants produced at 24 percent of the level of output of incumbent firms in the industry, while switching entrants produced at 58 percent. About 6 percent of firms

Table 12.3 Entry and Exit Rates of Manufacturing and Export Sectors in Morocco, 1984–89
(percentages)

Entry or exit statistic	1984	1985	1986	1987	1988	1989	Period average
Entry rates							
New entry	—	15.4	15.4	12.3	10.6	11.3	13.0
Switch entry	—	3.7	2.3	3.8	1.4	2.9	2.8
Entry to export sectors[a]	—	14.9	16.9	14.4	15.9	17.9	16.0
Entering plants' share of output							
New entry	—	4.4	4.7	2.7	2.0	2.3	3.2
Switch entry	—	2.6	1.2	1.8	0.7	1.6	1.6
Entry to export sectors	—	3.3	4.7	2.7	2.1	3.5	3.3
Entering plants' relative size							
New entry	—	28.1	29.9	21.1	18.3	20.4	23.6
Switch entry	—	76.0	57.0	49.9	51.8	56.3	58.2
Entry to export sectors	—	21.2	27.2	18.1	13.1	19.5	`19.8
Exit rates							
Exit and disappear	7.1	6.8	6.1	5.2	4.6	—	6.0
Exit and switch	3.7	2.3	3.8	1.4	2.9	—	4.8
Exit from export sectors	8.4	6.9	5.7	5.9	4.5	—	6.3
Exiting plants' share of output							
Exit and disappear	1.0	2.4	1.2	1.1	0.7	—	1.3
Exit and switch	2.0	1.1	2.6	0.7	1.5	—	1.6
Exit from export sectors	1.1	0.8	1.1	0.6	0.7	—	0.9
Exiting plants' relative size							
Exit and disappear	13.7	34.2	18.5	21.0	13.9	—	20.3
Exit and switch	52.5	46.9	67.3	47.6	51.7	—	53.2
Exit from export sectors	12.6	10.7	18.8	10.3	14.2	—	13.3

— Not available.

a. Export sectors are defined at the four-digit level. For a definition of export sectors at the two-digit level, see table 12.2 and text.

Source: Authors' calculations based on survey data.

exited each year, though the average exit rate (for disappearing firms) fell from 7 percent in 1985 to 5 percent in 1989. Exiting firms had a tiny market share (1 percent on average), and their average size was some 13 to 34 percent of that of other firms.[4] Entry rates exceeded exit rates in all years, indicating net expansion of firms in manufacturing. The share of output was also larger for entering than for exiting firms.

The same decomposition analysis was conducted for the export-oriented sectors. Comparisons with the patterns for other manufacturing sectors clearly show a higher than average rate of entry starting in 1986. Firms entering export-oriented activities were smaller than average for new entrants, suggesting that Morocco had a comparative advantage in small-scale activities, although new firms generally were smaller than existing firms and small firms were subsidized. Exit rates were similar across export and nonexport activities during the period of trade liberalization, possibly suggesting that competition in international markets was as tough for export firms as competition from imports was for firms producing for the domestic market.

Does market structure or trade regime affect entry and exit? Regression results for models that exclude dummy variables for industry reveal a strong statistically significant correlation between share of exports and rate of entry, suggesting that firms were attracted to industries with export potential—the reforms sought to reduce the bias against exports and to promote small exporting firms (model 1 in table 12.4). As expected, there is a negative correlation between rates of entry and industry-level concentration, a proxy for barriers to entry. There is also a negative correlation between rates of exit and industry-level concentration (model 3), a relationship observed in Chile as well. Although the reasons for this relationship are not clear, concentration may have been highest in sectors characterized by technologies with large fixed costs.

As in the other country studies, there is not a significant correlation between growth of real output and rate of entry or exit. One possible explanation is that these models do not take into account the fact that demand conditions might affect entry and exit with a lag. The macroeconomic environment is more powerful in explaining entry rates, as the significant coefficients on the time dummies indicate, but is not helpful in explaining contemporaneous exit rates. The capital-output ratio (a proxy for scale and capital intensity) is also not correlated (negatively) with entry and exit. Finally, import penetration is only weakly associated with rates of entry (positively) and exit (negatively), suggesting that most variation in the data is generated by domestic demand shocks.

When industry dummy variables are included (models 2 and 4), all variables become insignificant in explaining entry and exit rates. Now all the explanatory power lies with the industry effects, meaning that entry and exit rates are highly influenced by factors that are not included in the

Table 12.4 Regression Coefficients at the Industry Level with Entry Rate and Exit Rate as the Dependent Variable

	Entry rate		Exit rate	
Variable	Model 1	Model 2	Model 3	Model 4
Independent variable				
Intercept	0.031 (0.022)*	n.a.	0.079 (0.012)*	n.a.
EXS	0.126 (0.026)*	−0.260 (0.242)	−0.014 (0.015)	−0.001 (0.190)
GRQ	0.023 (0.039)	−0.001 (0.054)	−0.004 (0.024)	−0.016 (0.038)
IMP	0.024 (0.032)	0.162 (0.286)	−0.034 (0.019)	−0.359 (0.193)
H	−0.229 (0.078)*	0.598 (0.405)	−0.127 (0.044)*	0.269 (0.237)
H · IMP	0.268 (0.193)	−0.508 (0.687)	0.314 (0.124)*	−0.111 (0.580)
KQ	−0.003 (0.039)	0.024 (0.151)	−0.020 (0.022)	0.016 (0.119)
Year dummy variable				
1987	−0.032 (0.014)*	−0.029 (0.014)*	n.a.	n.a.
1988	−0.052 (0.015)*	−0.047 (0.015)*	−0.007 (0.007)	−0.011 (0.008)
1989	−0.049 (0.015)*	−0.038 (0.017)*	−0.014 (0.007)	−0.015 (0.009)
Industry dummy variable	No	Yes	No	Yes
Dependent mean	0.115	0.115	0.050	0.050
ô²	0.042	0.038	0.020	0.020
$\overline{R}^2$	0.461	0.912	0.109	0.864
F-statistic	7.365	27.964	1.762	14.000

n.a. Not applicable.

* Significant at the 5 percent level.

Note: EXS is the share of exports in total outputs, GRQ is the growth in real output, IMP is the rate of import penetration, H is the Herfindahl index of concentration, and KQ is the capital-output ratio. The sample consists of sixty-eight Moroccan industries with entry and fifty-one with exit. Numbers in parentheses are standard errors.

Source: Authors' calculations based on 1984–89 survey data.

regressions, such as technology and tradability. Entry and exit rates are expected to be lower in sectors with technologies that have high fixed costs. But other factors, including institutional arrangements (regulatory policy, public sector ownership, government intervention), are also likely to affect the rates of entry and exit.

Price-Cost Margins

Industry-level results for price-cost margins show a good overall fit compared with similar regressions for other countries (as seen from the F-statistic), suggesting that the models have good explanatory power (table 12.5). When industry variables are not included, industry-level concentration has a strong positive effect on margins. Import penetration is negatively correlated with the gross margin in model 1, supporting the import-discipline hypothesis. Alternatively, the result can be interpreted as consistent with a specific-factors trade model that predicts a lower return for the fixed factor employed in the import-competing sector or with a standard Hecksher-Ohlin model in which the import-competing sector is capital-intensive. More convincing support for the import-discipline hypothesis comes from the significantly negative sign (and relatively large magnitude) of the coefficient of the interaction term between the concentration index and import penetration (model 3). Thus the disciplining effect of import competition is felt most strongly in the highly concentrated sectors.

In contrast, export-oriented sectors have lower profit margins. This result could reflect either more competitive pressures in export markets than in domestic markets or lower productivity in exporting activities. (The link between productivity and exports is explored later.)

With industry dummy variables included (models 2 and 4), the regressions test for the influence of changes in market structure through time. Most other variables become insignificant in the models that control for time-invariant industry-level characteristics. Clearly, industry and time effects play an important role, casting some doubt on the usefulness of models that only analyze structure and performance in a cross-sectional framework, a finding corroborated by other studies in this volume. The results for import penetration are not robust to the inclusion of industry dummy variables, suggesting that domestic demand shocks—which increase both import penetration and capacity utilization—are the dominant source of variation in profitability.

In examining the determinants of margins at the firm level, the issue of concern is whether firm-level variation in performance (measured by price-cost margins) is due more to industry-specific effects or to firm-specific effects. Schmalensee (1985) shows that if variation is due mostly to industry-specific effects, barriers to entry or the effects of other industrial policies are probably playing an important role. The results show

Table 12.5 Regression Coefficients with Price-Cost Margin as the Dependent Variable

Variable	Model 1	Model 2	Model 3	Model 4
Industry level				
Independent variable				
Intercept	0.250 (0.033)*	n.a.	0.106 (0.029)*	n.a.
H	0.715 (0.089)*	-0.175 (0.124)	1.547 (0.118)*	-0.314 (0.226)
IMP	-0.200 (0.041)*	0.174 (0.034)*	0.099 (0.046)*	0.157 (0.041)*
KQ	-0.098 (0.066)	-0.062 (0.070)	0.006 (0.050)	-0.067 (0.071)
EXS	-0.183 (0.049)*	-0.072 (0.143)	-0.083 (0.038)*	-0.084 (0.144)
H · IMP	n.a.	n.a.	-2.431 (0.284)*	0.312 (0.422)
Year and industry dummy variables	No	Yes	No	Yes
Dependent mean	0.187	0.182	0.187	0.187
$\hat{\sigma}^2$	0.090	0.031	0.066	0.031
$\bar{R}^2$	0.506	0.982	0.733	0.982
F-statistic	23.781	194.112	49.868	185.364

Firm level

Independent variable				
Intercept	0.195 (0.009)*	n.a.	0.191 (0.009)*	n.a.
SHARE	0.568 (0.189)*	0.682 (0.193)*	0.731 (0.202)*	0.798 (0.021)*
SHARESQ	−0.532 (0.278)	−0.715 (0.282)*	−0.421 (0.282)	−0.640 (0.290)
IMP	−0.064 (0.031)	−0.007 (0.049)	0.091 (0.033)	0.157 (0.286)
EXS	−0.056 (0.020)*	0.033 (0.024)	−0.055 (0.020)*	−0.033 (0.052)
KQ	−7.332 (0.132)*	−7.314 (0.024)*	−7.333 (0.132)*	−7.315 (0.245)*
SHAREIMP	n.a.	n.a.	−0.651 (0.024)*	−0.450 (0.290)
Year and industry dummy variables	No	Yes	No	Yes
Dependent mean	0.140	0.140	0.140	0.140
$\hat{\sigma}^2$	0.648	0.648	0.649	0.646
$\bar{R}^2$	0.162	0.165	0.162	0.165
F-statistic	620.77	122.96	518.35	118.50

n.a. Not applicable.

* Significant at the 5 percent level.

Note: EXS is the share of exports in total outputs, *IMP* is the rate of import penetration, *H* is the Herfindahl index of concentration, *KQ* is the capital-output ratio, *SHARE* is the firm's market share, *SHARESQ* is its square, and *SHAREIMP* is its interaction with the import penetration rate. Numbers in parentheses are standard errors. The sample consists of 90 Moroccan industries and 16,104 firms.

Source: Authors' calculations based on 1984–89 survey data.

that for the Moroccan data as a group, industry dummy variables explain very little, suggesting a fairly competitive environment among Moroccan manufacturers.[5] Of the other variables, only market share and capital-output ratios remain significant at the plant level when industry dummy variables are included. Capital-output ratios bear a strong negative relationship to margins, probably because most of the variation is due to output shocks. The lack of significant correlations between trade variables and firm-level margins when industry variables are included thus fails to support the import-discipline hypothesis.

To sum up, concentration seems to be the most important factor correlated with profitability. Beyond that, little significance can be attached to the other determinants of profitability. In particular, import penetration is not consistently found to affect price-cost margins. Therefore, there is only weak support for the import-discipline hypothesis. This result is not surprising, considering that most trade liberalization took place around 1983 and that import penetration rates are likely to be a poor proxy for sectoral rates of protection.[6]

Productivity Growth and Its Correlates

Next we looked for any evidence of correlation between measures of industry- and firm-level productivity and industrial growth, market structure, and trade orientation. Productivity was measured by total factor productivity growth (*TFPG*), using the Solow residual (described in chapter 3). Because of data limitations, value added was used as the measure of output, and materials were excluded from the set of factor inputs.[7] The usual caveats concerning Solow residuals apply—biases can arise from underutilization of capacity, noncompetitive behavior, nonconstant returns to scale, and measurement errors.

We began with the following model of industry-level total factor productivity growth:

$$(12.1) \quad TFPG_{jt} = f\left(GEXP_{jt}, GRQ_{jt}, GIMP_{jt}, H_{jt}, HGIMP_{jt}, DT_t, DS_j\right)$$

where *GEXP* is growth in exports, *GRQ* is growth in output, *GIMP* is growth in import penetration, and *HGIMP* is the interaction term between the Herfindahl index and growth in import penetration. Industry *(DS)* and year *(DT)* dummy variables were also included to capture industry and time effects. The same model was fit at the firm level, with all variables except *H* and *GIMP* measured at the firm level.

Three results stand out. First, the growth in real output is by far the most significant variable in accounting for variations in productivity growth, suggesting that measured growth in factor productivity is affected by changes in capacity utilization and scale, both being controlled by growth in output (table 12.6). Second, the index of concentration, the measure of import penetration, and the interaction between the two are insignificant in all models.[8] There is thus no evidence that greater competition from imports enhances productivity, at least as captured by the import penetration proxy. Third, the results for firm- and industry-level coefficients for export growth are contradictory: the coefficient is statistically significant and negative at the industry level and statistically positive at the firm level. Literally taken, these results suggest

Table 12.6 Regression Coefficients with Total Factor Productivity Growth as the Dependent Variable

Variable	Model 1	Model 2
Industry level		
Independent variable		
Intercept	0.008 (0.031)	n.a.
GEXP	−0.069 (0.033)*	−0.056 (0.032)**
GIMP	−0.218 (0.226)	0.174 (0.269)
H	0.039 (0.186)	−0.082 (0.851)
GRQ	0.731 (0.163)*	0.950 (0.189)*
HGIMP	1.540 (1.283)	1.192 (1.316)
Industry dummy variable (two-digit)	No	Yes
Dependent mean	0.021	0.021
ô²	0.187	0.172
R̄²	0.206	0.321
F-statistic	4.483	2.288
Firm level		
Independent variable		
Intercept	−0.062 (0.020)*	n.a.
GEXP	0.062 (0.167)*	0.063 (0.017)*
GIMP	0.000 (0.024)	−0.002 (0.025)
H	0.127 (0.131)	0.017 (0.169)
GRQ	0.220 (0.030)*	0.230 (0.030)*
HGIMP	−0.030 (0.319)	−0.064 (0.334)
Industry dummy variable (two-digit)	No	Yes
Dependent mean	−0.021	−0.021
ô2	0.606	0.604
R̄²	0.078	0.084
F-statistic	25.236	6.759

n.a. Not applicable.
* Significant at the 5 percent level.
** Significant at the 10 percent level.
Note: GEXP is growth in exports, GRQ is growth in real output, GIMP is the growth in the import penetration rate, H is the Herfindahl index of industry concentration, and HGIMP is the interaction between H and GIMP. Numbers in parentheses are standard errors. The sample consists of 68 Moroccan industries and 1,440 firms.
Source: Authors' calculations based on 1984–89 survey data.

that export growth enhances productivity growth at the firm level but has a negative spillover effect at the industry level. However, since the data set includes exports at the firm level and unknown measurement errors may occur as a result of constructing import penetration rates from trade data at the industry level, greater weight is attached to the firm-level results, and the negative correlation at the industry level is attributed to the effects of omitted variables or aggregation. The contrast may also be due to the fact that firm-level results give all firms equal weight, whereas the industry-level results give more weight to big firms.

Using the same data base, Haddad (1993) also finds a positive relation between productivity and exports at the firm level. She constructs measures of productivity *levels* relative to the most efficient firm in each industry and regresses these measures on the same proxies for trade liberalization used here.[9] She finds that firms closest to the maximum level of efficiency tend to have a high share of exports. She also finds that high import penetration rates reduce (at a decreasing rate) the gap between the firm's productivity index and the efficiency frontier.

Association does not, of course, imply causation. It is natural to ask whether growth of exports brings high growth of productivity (say, from learning through exporting) or whether high growth of productivity is a precondition for high growth of exports (say, good management techniques not associated with exporting). Consider the view that export growth tends to increase productivity growth. Contacts with foreign competitors that arise in exporting may lead to more rapid technical change and the development of local entrepreneurship. Or competitive pressures from international markets may reduce X-inefficiency and improve the quality of products. It could also be the case that because of capacity utilization effects, measured productivity growth is strongly procyclical, and, therefore, to the extent that output growth and export growth are correlated, exports may appear to cause productivity.

An equally plausible hypothesis is that productivity growth causes export growth. Consider a growing economy in which learning and technical change are proceeding rapidly in a few industries or a few firms, unrelated to any conscious government policy to promote exports. Perhaps the change is related to the transfer of technology from abroad through licensing or direct investment. Or import protection may serve as export promotion, as in Krugman 1984. Under these circumstances, producers are likely to turn to foreign markets to sell their goods. Here, the causal relationship proceeds from productivity growth to export growth.

Answering the question satisfactorily requires more information, including a much longer time series with a higher frequency. The data allow us to use two future lags and one past lag, which is clearly not enough, so the results of the Sims (1972) causality tests shown below should be interpreted even more cautiously than usual (*t*-statistics are in parentheses).[10]

(12.2) $TFPG(87) = -0.12 + 0.07\ EXPG(86) + 0.17\ EXPG(87)$
             $(-4.0)\quad (2.4)\qquad\qquad\qquad (5.2)$

$$+\ 0.01\ EXPG(88) - (0.03)\ EXPG(89)$$
$$(0.4)\qquad\qquad\quad (-0.8)$$

$$R^2 = 0.08;\ F\text{-statistic} = 7.87;\ N = 335$$

(12.3) $TFPG(87) = -0.12 + 0.16\ EXPG(87) + 0.06\ EXPG(86)$
             $(-4.0)\quad (5.4)\qquad\qquad\qquad (2.3)$

$$R^2 = 0.08;\ F\text{-statistic} = 15.14;\ N = 335$$

(12.4) $EXPG(87) = 0.22 - 0.11\ TFPG(86) + 0.46\ TFPG(87)$
             $(4.0)\ (-1.5)\qquad\qquad\qquad (3.3)$

$$-\ 0.29\ TFPG(88) + 0.02\ TFPG(89)$$
$$(-2.1)\qquad\qquad\quad (0.4)$$

$$R^2 = 0.07;\ F\text{-statistic} = 8.19;\ N = 375$$

(12.5) $EXPG(87) = 0.24 - 0.09\ TFPG(86) + 0.6\ TFPG(87)$
             $(4.3)\ (-1.3)\qquad\qquad\qquad (4.9)$

$$R^2 = 0.06;\ F\text{-statistic} = 13.2;\ N = 375$$

Based on computed F-ratios of 0.65 for equations 12.2 and 12.3, and 3.30 for equations 12.4 and 12.5, 3.0 is the critical value of F.[11] We accept the hypothesis that export growth causes productivity growth, and we reject the hypothesis of causality in the opposite direction.[12]

Characteristics of Exporters and Determinants of Product Diversity

These tentative results on the likely causality pattern of the correlation of high rates of export growth and high rates of measured total factor productivity growth tell us little about the characteristics of exporting firms. Are they young? Do they have a significant share of the domestic market, suggesting that scale matters for exporting? Do they export one or many products? Who owns them? Answers to these questions can provide some clues about the characteristics of exporting firms. When combined with similar information for a large number of countries, these answers can be used to piece together a description of what it takes to be an export manufacturing firm.

As a first step, the sample was divided into exporting and nonexporting firms, using a 25 percent share of exports in total sales as the arbitrary cutoff point. This classification gave 1,126 exporting firms and

5,045 nonexporting firms over the sample period. The characteristics of the two sets of firms were then compared over the entire 1985–89 sample period to see whether the two groups exhibited significantly different characteristics at the two-digit classification level.[13] The mean export share was 84 percent for the exporting group and 6 percent for the nonexporting group, many of which did not export at all or at least not directly.

Several clear patterns emerge from this comparison of group characteristics (see table 12.7). If sales are a good proxy for size, exporting firms are 1.7 times larger than nonexporters. Although this does not tell us that a firm must be large to start exporting, it certainly suggests the importance of characteristics usually associated with size but not captured here, such as scale or access to credit. This difference is statistically significant in eight of eighteen sectors. Age also matters, but not uniformly. In seven sectors there is a statistically significant difference in mean age between the two groups, but in three of these sectors the younger firms belong to the exporting group, while in four of them, the older firms export.[14]

Next, we constructed five two-way classifications and tested for differences in mean export share across each of them (see table 12.8). New entrants had a higher share of exports than surviving firms, and exiting firms had a lower share, confirming the results presented earlier that the

Table 12.7 Characteristics of Exporting Firms in Morocco, 1984–89
(mean value of exporting firms: mean value of nonexporting firms)

Sector	Sales (millions of dirhams)	Age (years)	Real wage (thousands of dirhams)	Real gross margin (thousands of dirhams)	Level of total factor productivity
Other food products	25:31*	20:17*	18:15	10:6	4.5:4.2*
Textiles	22:13*	15:15	12:19	11:7	3.6:3.5
Clothing	9:1*	8:13*	10:9	8:12	3.5:3.2*
Leather and shoes	10:4*	10:14*	13:10*	0:9*	3.4:3.3
Wood products	24:8*	25:16*	17:13*	7:4	3.9:3.6
Basic metals	182:89	25:21	20:30	8:28	—
Transport materials	37:32	16:19	25:23	16:12	4.4:3.6*
Electronics	46:22*	13:14	25:26	10:16	3.8:3.9
Chemical products	457:32*	19:19	25:27	16:16	4.6:3.8*
All sectors[a]	26:15*	13:16*	14:18	9:12*	3.7:3.3*

— Not available.
* Difference is significantly different from 0 at the 5 percent level.
Note: Exporting firms are firms with export share in total sales exceeding 25 percent.
a. Includes all eighteen two-digit sectors listed in table 12.2.
Source: Authors' calculations based on survey data; total factor productivity from Haddad 1993.

Table 12.8 Share of Exports for Various Groups of Firms in Morocco

Group of two-way classifications	Mean share of exports (percent)	Number of firms
Entering firms	18.2	2,753
Surviving firms	13.1	20,286
Exiting firms	10.1	1,001
Surviving firms	13.1	16,839
Direct foreign investments[a]	23.6	3,938
Nondirect foreign investment firms	11.7	19,101
Large firms[b]	32.0	6,414
Small firms	6.6	16,625
High public share[c]	13.4	310
Low public share	13.7	22,729

Note: The difference in the true means is significantly different from 0 at the 5 percent confidence level for all groups except the last.

a. Foreign ownership over 5 percent.
b. Firms that employ fifty or more workers.
c. Firms with public ownership over 50 percent.

Source: Survey data for 1984–89.

sales of exiting firms during the sample period were concentrated in the domestic market. Also, as expected, firms with larger foreign ownership and a larger number of employees had higher shares of exports. The share of public ownership, however, seems to have made no difference in share of exports.

These threads were pulled together in a regression relating the firm's share of exports to the characteristics described above (coefficients for industry and time dummies are not reported; *t*-statistics are in parentheses):[15]

$$(12.6) \quad EXS_{ijt} = 0.15 + 0.15 \cdot FORSH_{ijt} - 0.0002 \cdot AGE_{ijt}$$
$$\phantom{(12.6) \quad EXS_{ijt} = } (42.0) \; (18.19) (-13.98)$$

$$+ \; 0.56 \cdot SHARE_{ijt} - 0.49 \cdot SHARESQ_{ijt} - 0.002 \cdot KQ_{ijt}$$
$$(8.80) (-5.43) (-4.62)$$

$$+ \; (4.44) \cdot LQ_{ijt}$$
$$(0.019)$$

$$R^2 = 0.44; \; F\text{-statistic} = 465; \; N = 16,107$$

where *EXS* is the export share in sales, *FORSH* is foreign share in ownership, *AGE* is age of the firm, *SHARE* is share of the firm's sales in total sales of three-digit industries, *KQ* is the capital-output ratio, and *LQ* is the labor-output ratio.

The positive significant correlation between share of exports and share of foreign ownership is consistent with the hypothesis that knowledge gained from foreign markets is an important determinant of export performance. This result makes sense in the Moroccan context, where subcontracting by foreign firms is common. There is also evidence of an inverted U-pattern between export share and domestic market share, because firms tend to specialize. The export share is negatively correlated with the capital-output ratio and positively correlated with the labor-output ratio, suggesting that Morocco has a comparative advantage in labor-intensive production. Also, export share is negatively correlated with age, perhaps because older firms become less efficient and so less competitive in the international market.

Because the data also contain information on the number of products at the firm level for 1987, the relationship between product diversity and trade flows was also explored. Specifically, it has been argued that the international exchange of varieties allows each firm to specialize and to reap efficiency gains from longer production runs (Cox and Harris 1985). If this phenomenon is important in Morocco, we should find that firms in tradable sectors had relatively few product lines.

Overwhelmingly, Moroccan firms were single-product firms: 50 to 92 percent of respondent firms in each sector manufactured only one product (see table 12.9). In only four sectors did 10 percent or more of firms produce three products or more, and three of these sectors were classified as exporting (textiles, clothing, and chemical products). Compared with Canada, the only other country for which comparable data on product diversity are available (Baldwin and Gorecki 1986, chap. 2), Moroccan industrial firms were preponderantly single-product firms. Thus, in contrast with the results for the Canadian manufacturing sector, there is no prima facie evidence of scale inefficiency in Moroccan manufacturing caused by too much product diversity or short production runs, as can occur in multiproduct firms.

The following firm-level product homogeneity index (PH) was constructed to relate product diversity and trade:

$$(12.7) \qquad PH_i = \sum_k \left(\frac{N_{ki}}{\sum_k N_{ki}} \right)^2$$

where i refers to a firm at the four-digit industrial classification, and N_{ki} is the output of the kth product of the ith firm. A value of 1 for the index indicates a single-product firm. Regressions with this index yield several interesting results (table 12.10). First, as is expected from the analytical literature, there is a statistically significant positive correlation between product concentration and import penetration. Second, counter to

Table 12.9 Product Diversification across Industries in Morocco, 1987
(percentage of firms at the six-digit level)

Sector	Number of products						Number of firms
	1	2	3	4	5	6	
Food products	51	36	9	3	1	1	899
Other food products	70	15	8	4	2	1	421
Beverages and tobacco	79	12	9	0	0	0	33
Textiles	63	17	12	3	2	3	463
Clothing	51	20	12	7	4	5	472
Leather and shoes	77	12	9	2	0	0	248
Wood products	68	19	8	3	2	1	194
Paper and printing	77	14	5	2	1	0	336
Mineral products	77	14	6	2	1	0	305
Basic metals	50	27	4	12	8	0	26
Metallic products	64	18	10	4	2	2	329
Machinery and equipment	70	15	7	5	1	2	202
Transport materials	69	12	9	4	3	3	99
Electronics	56	20	8	6	5	5	109
Precision equipment	64	23	9	5	0	0	22
Chemical products	61	14	12	6	2	5	241
Rubber and plastics	65	19	8	2	4	2	195
Other industrial products	92	0	0	8	0	0	26

Source: Authors' calculations based on survey data.

expectations, firms with high shares of exports are *more* diversified, a challenge to the notion that trade allows firms to increase productivity by specializing. Haddad (1993, table 3), in correlations of product concentration and a firm-level productivity index, finds that more diversified firms are also *more* productive, conditioning on trade flows and other variables.

Other results also merit note. The industry dummy variables have considerable explanatory power (model 2, table 12.10). This is not surprising, since product diversification is expected to vary from sector to sector. A significantly negative correlation between product concentration and age of the firm suggests that younger firms are less diversified. More concentrated sectors are less diversified as well, which makes sense in that concentration is a proxy for scale economies and more product specialization is expected in sectors with scale economies.

Conclusions

Several useful insights emerge from this investigation of the behavior of Moroccan manufacturing firms during 1984–89, a period of slow but progressive opening to foreign competition and the establishment of some incentives to export. First, the results suggest that the reforms did

Table 12.10 Regression Coefficients at the Firm Level with the Product Homogeneity Index, 1987, as the Dependent Variable

Variable	Model 1	Model 2
Independent variable		
Intercept	0.862 (0.007)*	n.a.
SHARE	−0.552 (0.131)*	−0.594 (0.131)*
SHARESQ	0.444 (0.186)*	0.490 (0.186)*
IMP	0.081 (0.021)*	0.106 (0.030)*
FORSH	−0.020 (0.016)	−0.005 (0.16)
PUBSH	0.047 (0.039)	0.027 (0.039)
EXS	−0.074 (0.012)*	−0.051 (0.015)*
SUBHERF[a]	0.023 (0.040)	0.025 (0.045)
AGE	−0.001 (0.000)*	−0.002 (0.000)*
Industry dummy variable (two-digit)	No	Yes
Dependent mean	0.839	0.839
ô	0.261	0.258
$\bar{R}^2$	0.023	0.914
F-statistic	14.2	1958.7

n.a. Not applicable.
* Significant at the 5 percent level.
Note: For the definition of the dependent variable, see equation 12.7. Standard errors are in parentheses. The sample consists of 4,597 Moroccan firms for both models.
a. Computed at the three-digit level.
Source: Authors' calculations.

alter incentives in a sustained and credible manner and so led to noticeable changes. Supporting this claim is the finding that entering firms consistently located in exporting sectors throughout the five-year period examined.

Second, a positive correlation is found between growth of total factor productivity and growth of exports at the firm level. Further tests suggest that in the Moroccan case, it is more likely that exports were driving higher productivity growth than the other way around.

Finally, no clear pattern of correlation emerges between trade flows and price-cost margins. Sectors with high rates of import penetration had relatively low profit margins. In itself, this result might be interpreted to mean that foreign competition disciplines domestic pricing. However, this result is not robust to the inclusion of industry dummy variables, so *changes* in protection cannot be said to induce changes in the degree of market power among domestic producers.

Appendix: Data Description and Preparation

This appendix presents an overview of the Moroccan industrial data, along with the calculation of the major variables used in this study.

Description of the Data

The empirical analysis of the Moroccan industrial performance is based on firm-level industrial survey data covering 1984–89 collected by the Ministry of Commerce and Industry. The surveys include all enterprises with ten or more employees and those with fewer than ten employees if sales revenues were greater than DH100,000 (approximately US$11,000 at the average 1984–89 official exchange rate).

A firm's activity is described by a four-digit Moroccan nomenclature of economic activities, often referred to as the nomenclature of national accounting. There are eighteen industrial sectors at the two-digit level of aggregation (table 12.9). The annual surveys contain standard statistics at the firm level, including sales revenue, value of production, total exports, cost of labor, and number of employees. Other detailed features are specific to each year—capacity utilization (1984, 1987, and 1989), exports by product and destination (1985), and employment breakdown by skill group (1986 and 1988).

Definition of Major Economic Variables

A major problem arose in using the survey data: the lack of data on value added and on capital stock. We attempted to calculate them using available information. Most variables were computed at both the industry or sector level (two-digit level) and the firm level. However, some variables, such as the Herfindahl index or the rate of import penetration, could not be computed at a level of aggregation lower than a three-digit level.

VALUE ADDED. Because a price index for intermediate inputs is not available, measurement of growth in total factor productivity was based on growth in real value added, labor, and capital. It was necessary to estimate each plant's value added, because beginning in 1983, the industrial survey questionnaire asked for only the principal components of value added, namely labor remuneration, indirect taxes, operating subsidies, depreciation of fixed capital, and operating balance. These components of value added are available for all years under consideration except 1984 (which explains this year's exclusion). However, they are more detailed and disaggregated for the last years (1987, 1988, and 1989). Table 12A.1 shows the components of value added available in each year. A brief definition of each is given below.

Labor remuneration comprises all payments or benefits provided by employers as remuneration for work done by salaried employees during the accounting period, before deductions are made for social security and taxes. It includes direct payments (salaries, commissions, cost-of-living

Table 12A.1 Components of Value Added for Morocco, 1984–89

Year	Components of value added in addition to labor cost and depreciation available in the survey
1984	Not available
1985	Taxes Subsidies Balance of exploitation (includes amortization, profit, fees, and gifts)
1986	Taxes Subsidies Insurance premiums Balance of exploitation (includes amortization, profit, fees and gifts, directors' fee)
1987	Taxes Insurance premiums Financial costs Balance of exploitation Allocation to amortization and provisions Subscription fees and gifts Directors' fee Transportation and moving expenses Water, electricity, and heating
1988	Taxes Subsidies Insurance premiums Financial costs Balance of exploitation Allocation to amortization and provisions Subscription fees and gifts Directors' fee
1989	Taxes Subsidies Insurance premiums Financial costs Balance of exploitation Allocation to amortization and provisions Subscription fees and gifts Directors' fee

Source: Ministry of Commerce and Industry, *Situation des industries de transformation,* various years.

compensation, and housing allowance) and indirect payments (medical examinations, recreational installation expenses, and indemnities).

Depreciation of fixed capital is, in a general sense, the part of output used to replace the fixed capital used to produce this output during a specified period of time. Depreciation of fixed capital is linked to the life span of material and equipment, since it serves to compensate for the loss in equipment due to deterioration, obsolescence, and normal wear and tear. It does not include the wear and tear of natural resources. It is applied to all equipment except, for practical reasons, public capital goods such as roads, dams, and all construction other than buildings.

Indirect taxes are taxes that are imposed on a producer's production or sales, or its purchase or use of goods and services, and that are paid by the producer. These taxes include import and export taxes, domestic consumption taxes, taxes on goods and services, patents, and vehicle taxes.

Operating subsidies constitute the payments from the state to private or public enterprises for the purpose of influencing prices of goods and services, maintaining the profitability of certain activities, and encouraging others. These subsidies were added to the revenue of producers. Government transfers to compensate for destruction of the capital stock were not included.

Net operating balance is the profit obtained from production, defined as the excess of value added by producers over the costs incurred, during an accounting period. More specifically, net operating balance equals value added minus labor remuneration minus depreciation of fixed capital minus indirect taxes plus subsidies. Despite the availability of information on some of the components of value added, it is difficult to reproduce the way in which value added is calculated at the sector level by the Ministry of Commerce and Industry (and published in *Situation des industries de transformation,* various years). Therefore, firm-level data were aggregated at the sector (two-digit) level, and the Moroccan calculation of value added was approximated. The closest fit that we could reach for each year suggests that value added (*VA*) was obtained as follows:

- *VA* (1985) = wage bill plus tax plus gross operating balance, where gross operating balance incorporates profit, depreciation, and gifts
- *VA* (1986) = wage bill plus tax plus gross operating balance plus financial costs minus insurance premiums, where gross operating balance incorporates profit, depreciation, gifts, and directors' fee
- *VA* (1987, 1988, and 1989) = wage bill plus tax plus profit plus depreciation plus gifts plus directors' fee plus financial costs minus insurance premiums.

Table 12A.2 shows the difference between value added at the two-digit sectoral level as available in *Situation des industries de transformation* (Ministry of Commerce and Industry, various years) and the value added as reproduced by us. The approximation appears to be accurate in all years except 1987.

Table 12A.2 Value Added and Reproduced Value Added for Morocco, 1985–88
(thousands of dirhams)

	1985			1986		
Sector	Moroccan value added	Reproduced value added	Percentage difference	Moroccan value added	Reproduced value added	Percentage difference
Food products	1,108,478	1,108,478	0	1,493,000	1,507,052	−1
Other food products	1,469,305	1,439,253	2	2,124,000	2,040,682	4
Beverages and tobacco	2,440,187	2,389,099	2	2,920,000	2,902,913	1
Textiles	1,733,693	1,694,626	2	2,055,000	2,070,911	−1
Clothing	457,274	448,258	2	681,000	680,603	0
Leather and shoes	308,371	302,361	2	402,000	399,924	1
Wood products	413,016	404,000	2	406,000	396,521	2
Paper and printing	643,716	628,690	2	800,000	795,073	1
Mineral products	1,359,820	1,329,768	2	1,506,000	1,531,757	−2
Basic metals	463,288	454,272	2	436,000	436,941	0
Metallic products	964,871	943,835	2	914,000	918,475	0
Machinery and equipment	351,378	342,362	3	350,000	348,483	0
Transport materials	492,951	480,930	2	648,000	656,119	−1
Electronics	563,878	551,857	2	655,000	658,976	−1
Precision equipment	20,140	20,146	0	260,00	253,38	3
Chemical products	1,670,540	1,634,478	2	1,869,000	1,884,080	−1
Rubber and plastics	547,124	535,103	2	556,000	548,501	1
Other industrial products	10,495	10,495	0	15,000	14,622	3

Note: Moroccan value added is not available for 1989.
Source: Ministry of Commerce and Industry, *Situation des industries de transformation*, various years.

CAPITAL STOCK. Data on the components of capital stock are not available in the surveys. A measure of capital stock is included only in 1988 as the total equipment—goods and assets—owned by the firm. This figure was converted to constant 1985 prices (using the wholesale price deflator; see table 12A.3) and then used as the benchmark to construct capital stock for the remaining years from the perpetual-inventory method forward and backward:

$$(12A.1) \qquad K_{i,t} = K_{i,t-1} (1 - d) + I_{i,t}$$

where K is the capital stock in constant 1985 prices, subscripts i and t refer to the firm and time, d is the depreciation rate (set at 4 percent), and I is the level of investment in constant 1985 prices.

The perpetual-inventory method can be used only for firms included in the 1988 survey. All firms that are not included that year had to be omitted from analysis involving capital stocks.

1987			1988			
Moroccan value added	Reproduced value added	Percentage difference	Moroccan value added	Reproduced value added	Percentage difference	Sector
1,635,763	1,168,042	40	1,692,771	1,692,616	0	Food products
2,287,310	1,303,568	75	3,572,185	3,572,052	0	Other food products
3,571,176	3,101,649	15	3,937,583	3,923,932	0	Beverages and tobacco
2,275,559	1,440,088	58	2,348,383	2,347,037	0	Textiles
944,470	739,669	28	1,115,973	1,115,405	0	Clothing
449,805	402,914	12	470,149	469,504	0	Leather and shoes
480,565	406,959	18	572,540	563,246	2	Wood products
958,152	703,302	36	1,081,285	1,079,516	0	Paper and printing
1,873,591	1,193,928	57	2,096,295	2,118,107	−1	Mineral products
711,680	189,219	76	814,825	837,731	−3	Basic metals
948,551	717,389	32	1,172,185	1,170,541	0	Metallic products
432,333	346,805	25	385,523	409,070	−6	Machinery and equipment
734,322	505,551	45	777,847	771,814	1	Transport materials
713,782	555,269	29	745,505	754,872	−1	Electronics
51,694	39,401	31	59,593	51,769	15	Precision equipment
2,244,754	1,387,345	62	3,991,248	4,098,304	−3	Chemical products
599,838	459,446	31	625,090	614,749	2	Rubber and plastics
14,713	21,875	−33	23,065	24,175	−5	Other industrial products

LABOR. The surveys provide data on the total number of permanent employees for each firm and the total number of hours worked by temporary employees. These hours were converted into the equivalent number of employees (250 days of work a year are considered to be comparable to one full-time employee) and were included in the total number of employees for each firm.

Labor is also expressed as efficiency units, calculated as the total labor cost (of both temporary and permanent employees) divided by the wage of the least productive workers. We approximated this wage with the legally mandated minimum wage. The minimum wage was changed in September 1985, in January 1988, and in May 1989. Therefore, the labor efficiency units (LEF) were calculated for each year using relevant weights for minimum wage as follows:

- LEF (1985) = labor cost / $[(0.67 \times 8.935) + (0.33 \times 9.809)]$
- LEF (1986 and 1987) = labor cost / 9.809
- LEF (1988) = labor cost / 10.782
- LEF (1989) = labor cost / $[(0.33 \times 10.782) + (0.67 \times 11.856)]$.

Table 12A.3 Deflators Used for Morocco, 1986–89
(1985 = 100)

Sector	1986	1987	1988	1989
Industry-specific price index[a]				
Food products	109.78	109.52	111.64	124.35
Other food products	113.57	115.82	111.71	116.28
Beverages and tobacco	116.53	130.82	150.46	179.28
Textiles	107.23	112.67	118.67	117.92
Clothing	107.23	112.67	118.67	117.92
Leather and shoes	107.68	108.70	128.85	128.00
Wood products	112.94	127.37	145.68	147.64
Paper and printing	110.87	116.11	145.67	154.51
Mineral products	105.86	110.39	110.50	107.68
Basic metals	102.26	100.56	112.24	124.64
Metallic products	115.82	119.65	126.22	136.48
Machinery and equipment	131.73	133.37	134.08	135.94
Transport materials	119.96	128.56	141.67	147.31
Electronics	104.19	99.55	113.72	124.19
Precision equipment	100.29	100.57	100.57	100.58
Chemical products	116.85	121.81	128.48	146.46
Rubber and plastics	120.52	121.29	132.19	150.29
Other industrial products	100.00	108.61	107.62	112.29
Wholesale price index[b]	104.0	106.6	113.1	114.9

a. Used as a deflator for value added and production.
b. Used as a deflator for investment and capital stock.
Source: For the industry-specific index, Ministry of Commerce and Industry, *Annuaire statistique du Maroc*, various years; for the wholesale price index, IMF 1990.

ENTRY AND EXIT RATES. Entering and exiting firms are identified by numbers collected as part of the survey. If a firm's identification number is missing in any year, the firm was considered to have exited. Since the surveys include only firms with more than ten employees or with more than DH100,000 in sales revenue, entry rates might incorporate firms that already existed but did not previously qualify to enter the survey. Similarly, exit rates might include firms still in operation but that no longer qualified to enter the survey.

IMPORT PENETRATION. Import penetration at the three-digit level was calculated as the ratio of imports to domestic sales, with domestic sales defined as output of domestic industries minus exports plus imports. All firms with the same three-digit activity had the same rate of import penetration.

There is one problem with data on imports. Data are available for 1985 to 1987 in one code (the nomenclature of national accounting classification) at the three-digit level and for 1988 in another code (nomen-

clature groupe produit) at the six-digit level. The 1988 data were converted to the nomenclature of national accounting. Moreover, some
aggregation was made for the three-digit 1985–87 data (table 12A.4).
Therefore, the 1988 data had to be changed accordingly. Disaggregate
data are not available on imports.

For the industry-level data, the two-digit nomenclature of national
accounting classification is available for all years.

OTHER VARIABLES. Variables requiring no new calculations include sales
revenue, value of production, exports, and investment. Sales revenue
(sales of goods and services) includes all taxes. The value of production
is the sales revenue corrected for variation in stocks of finished and semi-
finished goods. Exports are given as part of the sales revenue and are
expressed at their f.o.b. (free on board) value. Investments realized each
year refer to the expenses allocated to the acquisition or creation of physical production goods.

Other variables were constructed using simple calculations:

• Export share was calculated as the ratio of exports to total sales at the
  industry as well as the firm level.
• The firm's share of the market was calculated as the ratio of the sales
  of the firm to total sales at the three-digit level.
• The age of the firm was computed as the difference between the year
  of the survey plus one and the starting year of the firm.
• Gross profit margin was computed as the ratio of profit to production,
  where profit is defined as value added minus labor cost.
• The capital output ratio was computed as capital stock in 1985 prices
  divided by output in 1985 prices.
• Foreign share in total ownership was computed as foreign equity
  divided by total equity.

*Table 12A.4 Aggregation of Imports at the Three-Digit Level
for Morocco*

Subsectors aggregated	Definition of the subsectors
11.2 + 11.3	Slaughtering + canned meat processing
14.2 + 14.3	Underwear + clothes and linens made to measure
15.1 + 15.2 + 15.3	Tannery + leather-substitute products + leather products except shoes
18.4 + 18.8	Cement + lime and plaster
23.4 + 23.5	Electronic components + electronic equipment and material

Note: There were no imports for subsector 13.5 (textile finishing), so imports were
assumed to be 0. There were no firms in subsector 12.3 (alcoholic beverages) in 1987 and
1988; therefore the imports for this subsector were deleted.

Notes

1. Reference prices were used to calculate customs duties for 367 tariff headings. These are intended as a safeguard against dumping, but there is suspicion that the reference prices used for calculating tariffs may act as binding quantitative restrictions.

2. The pattern of tariff rates is dominated by manufacturing because only 600 of the 20,000 tariff lines cover agricultural products. However, a similar pattern arises from a weighted calculation using either production or imports as weights.

3. The comparisons are only indicative, since they do not control for weather conditions, an important determinant of agricultural performance (droughts occurred in 1983, 1985, and 1987). Also, Morocco's terms of trade were affected both by hikes in the price of oil on the import side and by changes in the price of phosphates on the export side (phosphates have traditionally accounted for about 55 percent of Morocco's export earnings).

4. The calculations were carried out at the four-digit level and then aggregated.

5. Nonetheless, given the extremely large number of observations, time and industry dummies are jointly significant, with an $F(21, 16102)$ ratio of 3.76.

6. The superiority of tariffs over import penetration rates emerges clearly in the case study of Mexico (chapter 11).

7. Our firm-level measure of capital stock was constructed using a base year figure based on book value and not including rented capital.

8. Similar results were obtained from regressions that omit the interaction term. All signs and significant levels were unchanged, so these results are not reported.

9. In the estimations, the dependent variable is the deviation of a firm's total factor productivity from the efficiency frontier, and the set of regressors also includes age of the firm, pattern of ownership, and product and geographic dispersion indexes.

10. According to Sims (1972), one can regress Y on past and future values of X, and if causality runs from X to Y only, future values of X in the regression should have coefficients insignificantly different from 0, as a group.

11. To test the hypothesis that coefficients for future values of independent variables are jointly equal to 0, F-statistics were calculated as follows: $F = [(RSS_2 - RSS_1) / (df_1 - df_2)] / (RSS_1 / df_1)$, where RSS_1, RSS_2 are the residual sum of squares of the unconstrained and constrained equations, and df_1, df_2 are the degrees of freedom in the unconstrained and constrained equations.

12. In closely related causality testing, Jung and Marshall (1985) find bidirectional causality between output growth and export growth. Our results differ in that they pertain to productivity rather than output, to a single country, and to a relatively short time period.

13. The proportion of firms that derived 75 percent (or more) of their revenues from exports was stable over the sample period, justifying the aggregation over the entire time period. For a detailed description of the characteristics of exporting firms over time, see Sullivan 1993.

14. The statistical results are for the eighteen sectors listed in table 12.2. A similar pattern holds for the nine exporting sectors reported in table 12.7.

15. We do not report the results when time and industry dummies are omitted, since all signs and significance levels are unchanged.

References

Baldwin, John, and Paul Gorecki. 1986. *The Role of Scale in Canada–U.S. Productivity Differences in the Manufacturing Sector: 1970–1979.* Toronto: University of Toronto Press.

Cox, David, and Richard Harris. 1985. "Trade Liberalization and Industrial Organization: Some Estimates for Canada." *Journal of Political Economy* 93 (1): 115–45.

Haddad, Mona. 1993. "How Trade Liberalization Affected Productivity in Morocco." PRE Working Paper 1096. Policy Research Department, World Bank, Washington, D.C.

IMF (International Monetary Fund). 1990. *International Financial Statistics.* Washington, D.C.

Jung, Woo S., and Peyton J. Marshall. 1985. "Exports, Growth, and Causality in Developing Countries." *Journal of Development Economics* 18 (1): 1–12.

Krugman, Paul. 1984. "Import Protection as Export Promotion." In Henryk Kierzkowski, ed., *Monopolistic Competition and International Trade.* Oxford: Oxford University Press.

Ministry of Commerce and Industry. Various years. *Annuaire statistique du Maroc.* Rabat, Morocco.

———. Various years. *Situation des industries de transformation.* Rabat, Morocco.

Schmalensee, Richard. 1985. "Do Markets Differ Much?" *American Economic Review* 75 (3): 341–51.

Sims, Christopher. 1972. "Money, Income, and Causality." *American Economic Review* 62 (4): 540–52.

Sullivan, Theresa. 1993. "Morocco Industrial Survey: Data Preparation." Department of Economics, Georgetown University, Washington, D.C.

World Bank. 1988. *Morocco: The Impact of Liberalization on Trade and Industrial Adjustment.* Washington, D.C.

———. 1990. *Morocco: Sustained Investment and Growth in the Nineties.* Washington, D.C.

World Bank and UNDP (United Nations Development Programme). 1990. *Morocco 2000: An Open and Competitive Economy.* Washington, D.C.: World Bank

13

Turkey, 1976–85: Foreign Trade, Industrial Productivity, and Competition

Faezeh Foroutan

D uring the early 1980s, Turkey launched an ambitious trade liberalization program that dramatically increased the openness of the manufacturing sector. This chapter examines the resulting changes in performance. Unlike some of the other country studies presented in this volume, this chapter does not examine entry and exit patterns or cohort behavior, because comprehensive plant-level data are not available. Industry-level data do distinguish public and private enterprises, however, and that distinction is a primary focus of this chapter, along with sectoral price-cost margins and growth of productivity. Also, cross-sectoral comparisons are made of industries sorted into producers of importables, exportables, and nontradables. The study finds that trade reform has a positive, though modest, impact on manufacturers by reducing market power where it exists and accelerating the growth of productivity. However, these positive effects are limited mainly to privately owned firms. Public enterprises remain largely unaffected.[1]

Reforms in Turkey during the 1980s

A foreign debt crisis in 1977 ushered in two years of economic recession in Turkey.[2] Beginning in 1980, Turkey responded by adopting a stabilization program that represented a radical break with its traditional inward-looking strategy. Liberalization of foreign trade and payments policies was a key feature of the program.

The aim was to shift the economy toward export-led growth by dismantling the set of complex and restrictive regulations that had governed Turkey's transactions with the outside world. Import liberalization and export promotion were key features of the reform. Import liberalization encompassed a gradual shift from nontariff barriers to tariffs and a reduction in the rate and variability of import taxes. Export promotion was achieved directly through a generous package of incentives for exporters and indirectly through devaluation of the real exchange rate.

Import Liberalization

In the first of two series of import reforms, the import licensing system was liberalized in 1981. Quotas were abolished, and goods from the quota list were moved to the two liberalized lists—one requiring import licenses, the other not. Approximately 200 tariff positions, equivalent to 4 percent of the value of imports in 1980, were transferred from the license list to the fully liberalized list. Other administrative reforms and a reduction of other taxes on imports completed the reforms of 1981.

In late 1983 and early 1984 the government adopted an even more far-reaching program of import reform that represented a major break with the past. The most significant feature of the new import regime was the switch from a positive list of permitted imports to a negative list of prohibited imports. The prohibited list initially included some 219 tariff positions consisting mostly of consumer goods. By May 1985 the banned list was for all practical purposes abolished, and the goods on the list either were transferred to the license list or became freely importable. The list of licenses was similarly reduced, shrinking from 369 items (28 percent of imports) in 1984 to 33 items in 1988.

The import reforms of 1983–84 introduced a new list called the levy or fund list. Goods on this list—primarily luxury goods—paid a specific, dollar-denominated surcharge in addition to customs duties and other import taxes. The levies were intended to finance social projects, such as mass housing, and to provide *temporary* protection to domestic industries that lost quota protection. The reach of the levies expanded over the years, however, from an initial 200 goods and an implicit average tariff equivalent of 2 percent in 1984 to more than 570 items and a tariff equivalent of 6.1 percent by 1987.

The tariff schedule was also rationalized. The overall import-weighted average tariff rate for goods whose rates were modified fell from 38.8 percent before December 1983 to 22.7 percent in 1984. Rates continued to fall in subsequent years, and in 1987 the overall import-weighted average tariff rate stood at 9.5 percent. The realized rate (tariff revenues as a proportion of total imports) was even lower because of widespread exemptions.

Export Promotion

Export promotion measures involved maintaining a competitive real exchange rate, providing direct subsidies, and simplifying administrative and bureaucratic procedures.

In 1980 the government devalued the Turkish lira by more than 50 percent in nominal terms and abolished the system of multiple exchange rates except for a few agricultural inputs. The government also adopted a flexible exchange rate based on daily adjustments to prevent appreciation.

A generous package of direct incentives for exporters was also put together:

- An export tax rebate was designed initially to compensate exporters for indirect taxes on their inputs. The rebate included a substantial subsidy element. Indeed, after January 1985, with the introduction of a value added tax that rated exports at 0, the entire rebate constituted a subsidy. The subsidy has declined steadily, however, in line with the government's declared objective of gradually phasing it out.
- Duty drawbacks on imported inputs used to produce exports are an important incentive to produce for export rather than for the domestic market. On average during the 1980s, duty drawbacks constituted 5 percent of the value of exports for the manufacturing industry.
- Access to credit at preferential interest rates constituted an important incentive during the early 1980s, when the rates applied to export credits were substantially lower than the general short-term rates. This scheme gradually dwindled in importance and was abolished in 1985. A new export credit regime was instituted in January 1987, and its subsidy content appears to be slight.
- Cash grants, financed through various extrabudgetary funds, were also intended to support exports. In January 1985 the government established the Resource Utilization and Support Fund to encourage exports by granting a flat 4 percent cash subsidy to all exporters. The program was phased out by November of the same year. In January 1987 the government reintroduced the subsidy program, but this time subsidies were granted only to select products.

The immediate and most dramatic outcome of these trade policy reforms was a substantial increase in the degree of openness of the manufacturing sector, reflecting an increase in both imports and, more substantially, exports (see table 13.1). Manufacturing imports increased from 10 percent of domestic consumption in 1979 to 18 percent in 1985. Manufacturing exports soared over the same period from 2 to 19 percent of total output.[3]

Table 13.1 Average Share of Exports and Imports by Type of Industry in Turkey, 1976–85
(percentages)

Year	Exportable industries		Importable industries		Nontradable industries	
	Exports	Imports	Exports	Imports	Exports	Imports
1976	3.9	19.8	1.9	35.6	1.0	5.5
1977	3.7	19.8	1.6	32.5	0.7	5.5
1978	3.8	14.5	1.2	24.1	0.8	4.0
1979	3.8	12.0	1.4	21.1	1.0	4.9
1980	6.4	17.1	2.4	25.3	1.6	4.8
1981	15.2	18.6	4.4	29.8	4.0	3.5
1982	23.5	19.5	7.1	32.5	4.8	3.2
1983	20.7	18.9	7.5	31.2	4.4	3.8
1984	29.7	22.2	9.5	38.2	7.5	6.3
1985	42.2	25.4	14.0	40.9	9.8	6.7

Note: Exports as a share of total production; imports as a share of domestic absorption.
Source: Author's calculations based on industry-level data from Turkey's State Institute of Statistics.

The following sections explore the extent to which the greater openness of the economy and the increased exposure to foreign competition affected the performance of the Turkish manufacturing industry.

Trade Liberalization and Price-Cost Margins

The impact of trade liberalization on price-cost margins in manufacturing was examined separately for public and private sector firms for 1976–85. The analysis considered twenty-two industries for the public sector and twenty-four industries for the private sector at the three-digit level of industrial classification.[4]

Calculations of capital-output ratios and price-cost margins confirm what has long been known about Turkey's industrial structure. State enterprises have historically been engaged in the most capital-intensive industries, and the pursuit of profitability has not been a strong concern. Average capital-output ratios are much higher in the public than in the private sector, while the public sector's price-cost margin is generally below that of the private sector (see table 13.2). During the years of slow economic growth in 1978–80, the average capital-output ratio increased in both private and public sectors and the price-cost margin decreased, with the exception of nontradable producers in the public sector. In the subsequent years, this trend was reversed. This pattern reflects cyclical variations in rates of capacity utilization, since capital stocks rather than flows of capital services were used to compute capital-output ratios. The

Table 13.2 Average Capital-Output Ratio and Price-Cost Margin in Turkey, 1976–85

Year	Private sector		Public sector	
	Capital-output ratio	Price-cost margin	Capital-output ratio	Price-cost margin
1976	0.446	0.178	1.393	0.213
1977	0.487	0.212	1.643	0.111
1978	0.487	0.236	2.403	0.123
1979	0.594	0.186	1.394	0.077
1980	0.742	0.204	1.757	0.011
1981	0.570	0.208	1.622	0.128
1982	0.506	0.228	1.772	0.185
1983	0.541	0.201	1.540	0.192
1984	0.542	0.207	1.464	0.124
1985	0.519	0.190	0.897	0.156

Source: Author's calculations based on data from Turkey's State Institute of Statistics.

data also show a narrowing of the difference in capital-output ratios between private and public firms due to a gradual but steady decline in the public sector's capital intensity.

Breaking out the data for importables, exportables, and nontradables shows that the capital-output ratio was greater for public than for private firms for all three categories, with the difference more pronounced for industries engaged in the production of nontradables (see table 13.3). Moreover, for both private and public sector firms, the average capital-output ratio was higher for nontradables than for tradables and for exportables than for importables. However, importables were relatively more capital-intensive than exportables for both public and private sector firms, as shown by the average capital-labor ratio. (That ratio, not the capital-output ratio, is the correct measure of relative factor intensity.)[5]

The price-cost margin was higher in the industries producing nontradables than in those producing tradables, a pattern that is compatible with the capital-output ratios for the private and public sectors. However, for private firms, there was no appreciable difference in price-cost margins between importables and exportables. For public firms, the price-cost margin was systematically higher in industries producing exportables than in those producing importables.

These results, which run contrary to the pattern of capital-output ratios for the two groups of industries, suggest that private firms are more or less equally profitable in the two sectors but that public firms are less efficient and less profitable in import-competing industries than in exporting sectors. The smallest difference between private and public firms for both capital-output ratios and price-cost margins is in the industries producing for export. Public firms also seem to perform better in nontradables than in importables. Even after the liberalization of the 1980s, public firms in import-competing industries received a high degree of protection, which allowed them to continue operating at very low levels of efficiency and profitability. The higher margins for private firms in nontradables than in tradables sectors seem to be due mostly to differences in their capital-output ratios.

For the regression analysis of price-cost margins, data were pooled for all industries, but the distinction between private and public sectors was maintained. For the private sector, all variables in model 1 have the expected sign (see table 13.4). However, the capital-output variable is insignificant, and the import penetration variable, although significant, has a very small coefficient. For the public sector, import penetration has the expected sign but is not significant. The capital-output ratio has a negative sign but is also insignificant. In model 2, which allows the effect of import penetration to vary with the capital-output ratio and concentration (the Herfindahl index) for each industry, the interaction term for import penetration and concentration is negative and significant, with a higher coefficient than that for import penetration alone in model 1.[6] This result is expected (by construction, $0 < H < 1$).[7] Given that this interaction variable in model 2 is not more significant than import penetration in model 1 and that the adjusted R^2 is the same in both models, it can be concluded that import penetration has no differential impact on industries with a higher degree of concentration. Nor does the capital-output ratio of industries appear to affect the impact of import penetration on price-cost margins. For the public sector, the results are reversed, with import penetration affecting price-cost margins only in sectors with high capital-output ratios.

The results for models 3 and 4, which drop the industry effects, reveal that most of the explanatory power of the basic model derives from the industry dummy variables (see table 13.4). Without them, the adjusted R^2 for both the private and the public sectors is greatly reduced, while the level of significance of the remaining variables generally increases. For the private sector, import penetration becomes insignificant (model 3) and the interaction term for capital-output ratios and import penetration becomes significant and negative (model 4). For the public sector, both import penetration and the interaction variable become significant. The capital-output ratio continues to have a negative association with price-cost margins for the public sector but turns positive and strongly significant for the private sector.

In Turkey greater exposure to international trade apparently exerts a modest effect on the market power of firms in both the private and the public sectors. For the private sector, when industry-specific effects are

Table 13.3 Average Capital-Output Ratio, Price-Cost Margin, and Capital-Labor Ratio in the Private and Public Sectors in Turkey, 1976–85

Type of good and year	Private sector			Public sector		
	Capital-output ratio	Price-cost margin	Capital-labor ratio	Capital-output ratio	Price-cost margin	Capital-labor ratio
Exportable						
1976	0.580	0.155	1,274.5	0.684	0.138	1,126.3
1977	0.669	0.198	1,415.7	0.639	0.121	1,047.7
1978	0.586	0.240	1,256.8	0.867	0.232	1,191.5
1979	0.694	0.176	1,375.0	0.933	0.140	1,209.8
1980	0.952	0.191	1,457.2	0.963	−0.203	1,378.6
1981	0.649	0.192	1,408.7	0.746	0.012	1,438.8
1982	0.539	0.201	1,394.1	0.957	0.316	1,754.6
1983	0.535	0.173	1,403.0	0.713	0.199	1,485.1
1984	0.498	0.197	1,395.5	0.755	0.108	1,688.3
1985	0.470	0.178	1,347.6	0.578	0.213	1,730.2
Importable						
1976	0.310	0.166	1,559.1	1.243	0.114	2,080.7
1977	0.322	0.172	1,693.1	0.725	0.095	2,149.9
1978	0.343	0.243	1,860.0	1.182	−0.049	2,148.6

Year					
1979	0.434	0.160	1,872.6	1.262	−0.015	2,229.7
1980	0.521	0.202	1,962.5	1.283	−0.080	2,203.5
1981	0.433	0.179	2,124.0	1.011	−0.051	2,232.1
1982	0.407	0.236	2,137.4	0.978	0.136	2,267.0
1983	0.389	0.165	2,302.1	0.948	0.112	2,102.0
1984	0.369	0.182	2,388.3	0.833	0.093	2,135.3
1985	0.406	0.172	2,695.9	0.821	0.060	2,143.6
Nontradable						
1976	0.421	0.192	—	1.347	0.300	—
1977	0.463	0.220	—	2.163	0.142	—
1978	0.478	0.217	—	3.333	0.126	—
1979	0.575	0.198	—	1.485	0.038	—
1980	0.674	0.190	—	2.027	−0.021	—
1981	0.538	0.234	—	2.017	0.202	—
1982	0.481	0.247	—	2.209	0.238	—
1983	0.550	0.235	—	1.940	0.243	—
1984	0.585	0.226	—	1.798	0.181	—
1985	0.537	0.203	—	0.965	0.213	—

— Not available.

Source: Author's calculations based on industry-level data from Turkey's State Institute of Statistics.

Table 13.4 Regression Estimates with Price-Cost Margin as the Dependent Variable

Variable	Model 1	Model 2	Model 3	Model 4
Private sector				
Independent variable				
Intercept	0.335 (3.7)	0.347 (3.7)	0.109 (6.0)	0.104 (5.8)
KQ	0.000 (0.0)	−0.005 (0.2)	0.160 (9.0)	0.172 (9.2)
IMP	−0.002 (1.8)	n.a.	−0.000 (0.8)	n.a.
KQ · IMP	n.a.	0.000 (0.2)	n.a.	−0.001 (1.6)
H · IMP	n.a.	−0.022 (1.9)	n.a.	0.007 (0.9)
Year dummy variable				
1977	0.031 (1.9)	0.033 (2.0)	0.027 (1.2)	0.027 (1.2)
1978	0.048 (2.8)	0.050 (3.0)	0.050 (2.2)	0.049 (2.2)
1979	−0.004 (0.2)	−0.001 (0.0)	−0.017 (0.7)	−0.017 (0.7)
1980	0.018 (1.0)	0.019 (1.1)	−0.022 (1.0)	−0.019 (0.9)
1981	0.025 (1.5)	0.026 (1.6)	−0.010 (0.4)	0.011 (0.5)
1982	0.046 (2.8)	0.046 (2.8)	0.090 (1.8)	0.039 (1.8)
1983	0.018 (1.1)	0.019 (1.2)	0.007 (0.3)	0.006 (0.3)
1984	0.032 (1.9)	0.032 (1.9)	0.014 (0.6)	0.012 (0.6)
1985	0.017 (1.0)	0.015 (0.9)	0.001 (0.0)	−0.000 (0.0)
Industry dummy variable	Yes	Yes	No	No
R^2	0.6047	0.6035	0.2593	0.2664
F-test	11.755	11.393	8.606	8.231
Public sector				
Independent variable				
Intercept	0.178 (1.9)	0.224 (3.5)	0.257 (5.6)	0.263 (5.3)
KQ	−0.008 (1.1)	−0.003 (0.4)	−0.020 (2.5)	−0.005 (1.0)
IMP	−0.002 (0.6)	n.a.	−0.030 (3.2)	n.a.
KQ · IMP	n.a.	−0.005 (2.7)	n.a.	−0.003 (2.4)
H · IMP	n.a.	−0.006 (0.4)	n.a.	0.004 (0.3)
Year dummy variables				
1977	−0.101 (2.2)	−0.129 (2.8)	−0.102 (1.6)	−0.118 (1.8)
1978	−0.098 (2.0)	−0.135 (2.8)	−0.101 (1.6)	−0.117 (1.7)
1979	−0.143 (2.9)	−0.173 (3.6)	−0.151 (2.3)	−0.159 (2.4)
1980	−0.203 (4.3)	−0.220 (4.7)	−0.207 (3.2)	−0.212 (3.2)
1981	−0.086 (1.7)	−0.111 (2.4)	−0.089 (1.4)	−0.099 (1.5)
1982	−0.027 (0.6)	−0.046 (1.0)	−0.028 (0.4)	−0.036 (0.5)
1983	−0.022 (0.5)	−0.042 (0.9)	−0.024 (0.4)	−0.032 (0.5)
1984	−0.069 (1.4)	−0.078 (1.7)	−0.079 (1.2)	−0.091 (1.4)
1985	−0.055 (1.2)	−0.074 (1.6)	−0.051 (0.8)	−0.069 (1.0)
Industry dummy variable	Yes	Yes	No	No
R^2	0.5207	0.5397	0.0822	0.0601
F-test	8.253	8.585	2.686	2.103

n.a. Not applicable.

Note: KQ is capital-output ratio, *IMP* is import penetration, and *H* is the Herfindahl index of industry concentration. Numbers in parentheses are *t*-statistics.

Source: Author's calculations based on 1976–85 industry-level data from Turkey's State Institute of Statistics.

allowed for, greater import penetration appears to affect all industries alike; when industry-specific effects are excluded, greater import penetration appears to affect price-cost margins only in industries with high capital-output ratios. However, in both cases, the impact of trade penetration is small, most likely indicating that private manufacturing industries had little market power even before the reforms of the 1980s. For the public sector, import discipline appears to affect only the capital-intensive industries with higher capital-output ratios. The negative sign for the capital-output ratio in the public sector conforms to the earlier finding that public enterprises are more concentrated in capital-intensive, nonprofitable industries.

Trade Liberalization and Productivity

For both private and public enterprises, average growth of total factor productivity was negative during 1976–80, a period of recession, high inflation, and an inward-looking trade regime (see table 13.5). The decline was more severe in the public sector (–7.5 percent a year) than in the private sector (–4.1 percent). During that time, only four of twenty-six industries registered positive growth in productivity among private sector firms and three among public sector firms. During 1981–85, a period of radical reform marked by a significant liberalization of foreign trade, both these trends were reversed. The greatest gains were in the public sector, where growth of productivity (5.7 percent a year) surpassed that in private firms (3.4 percent). Productivity growth was negative during this period in only five industries each in both the private and the public sectors.

To isolate the effect of the debt crisis of 1979–80, which led to a substantial fall in output, a three-digit rate of inflation, and a contraction in foreign trade, the data were analyzed again for three rather than two time periods, 1976–78, 1979–80, and 1981–85 (see table 13.6). During 1976–78, growth of productivity was modestly positive in the private sector and modestly negative in the public sector. Growth of both productivity and output was strongly negative in the crisis years of 1979–80, but employment and the stock of capital continued to rise in both private and public sectors, indicating the difficulty of adjusting the growth of inputs to outputs over the short to medium run. In the next period, 1981–85, growth of productivity was positive and higher in the public sector than in the private sector. The reform of state enterprises, including greater autonomy in the hiring and firing of labor, may explain some of the improvement in the public sector. But some of it probably comes from overestimating the growth of productivity for the public sector. Because the price of outputs paid by public enterprises rises more rapidly

Table 13.5 Average Growth of Total Factor Productivity in the Private and Public Sectors in Turkey, 1976–85
(percentages)

		Private sector		Public sector	
ISIC code and industry		1976–80	1981–85	1976–80	1981–85
311	Food	2.3	−1.0	−2.5	6.9
313	Beverages	−2.1	−7.8	−12.3	20.8
314	Tobacco	4.3	7.0	1.7	15.2
321	Textiles	0.4	1.7	−3.3	1.1
322	Apparel	2.8	2.8	−22.7	20.9
323	Leather products	−10.8	2.3	—	—
324	Footwear	−8.6	6.3	−10.1	−7.0
331	Wood products	−8.4	0.1	−9.2	0.1
332	Furniture	−6.7	8.3	4.4	−7.7
341	Paper	−1.6	−2.9	−10.4	7.1
342	Printing	−4.8	−1.4	−9.5	−0.3
351	Industrial chemicals	−3.1	2.1	−1.2	−2.2
352	Other chemicals	−3.3	7.8	−5.0	2.9
353	Petroleum refining	—	—	−18.2	8.6
354	Petroleum derivatives	−3.9	−0.1	−17.0	14.1
355	Rubber products	−7.0	3.0	—	—
356	Plastics	−9.3	3.1	−13.4	−3.6
361	Ceramics	−7.8	6.8	−12.6	12.5
362	Glass	−5.1	3.9	—	—
369	Nonmetal minerals	−2.8	2.3	−5.3	1.0
371	Iron and steel	−2.9	9.8	−4.8	7.2
372	Nonferrous metals	0.0	4.5	4.2	6.7
381	Metal products	−6.3	5.0	−3.3	8.8
382	Nonelectrical machinery	−4.9	6.3	−6.7	5.5
383	Electrical machinery	−5.2	5.6	−12.8	11.3
384	Transport equipment	−5.9	5.4	−2.8	2.1
385	Professional equipment	−6.7	8.7	—	—

— Not available.
Source: Author's calculations based on data from Turkey's State Institute of Statistics.

than that paid by private firms (internal World Bank reports), using the same price deflator for public firms as for private ones when computing real output overestimates the growth of productivity.

For the private sector, the rate of growth of total factor productivity during the 1980s was much higher for industries producing exportables and importables (5 percent each) than for nontradables (2 percent), perhaps because of heightened exposure to international competition. Productivity growth contributed to 26 percent of output growth for exportables, 30 percent for importables, and 17 percent for nontradables.

*Table 13.6 Average Annual Rates of Growth of Output and Total
Factor Productivity in Turkey, 1976–85*
(percentages)

Sector and type of good produced	Growth of output			Growth of total factor productivity		
	1976–78	1979–80	1981–85	1976–78	1979–80	1981–85
Private sector						
Exportable	7.3	−17.1	19.2	1.0	−10.9	5.0
Importable	10.9	−20.0	15.5	7.4	−20.7	4.8
Nontradable	5.2	−12.5	10.7	0.2	−11.0	1.9
Public sector						
Exportable	−14.2	−1.7	2.7	−1.7	−15.2	4.3
Importable	11.5	−23.5	15.4	8.2	−21.9	4.7
Nontradable	−2.1	−6.2	7.0	−5.2	−16.3	6.5

Source: Author's calculations based on data from Turkey's State Institute of Statistics.

The same pattern is not true for the public sector. Average growth of productivity during the 1980s was higher in nontradables sectors (6.5 percent) than in tradables sectors (4.3 and 4.7 percent in industries producing exportables and importables, respectively). Growth of productivity contributed 92 percent of output growth in nontradables industries and, in the tradables industries, it contributed 30 percent in industries producing importables and 159 percent in industries producing exportables. These results indirectly support the hypothesis that growth of public sector output is overestimated. In tradables industries, where international competition prevents public firms from raising prices above international levels, there is no difference in growth of productivity in the private and public sectors. But in nontradables industries, where public enterprises have greater liberty to raise the price of output, growth of productivity appears to have been substantially higher in the public sector than in the private sector, because real output in the public sector is clearly overestimated.

It is also interesting to note that trade liberalization does not appear to have had a negative impact on employment in Turkey. During 1981–85, employment increased 5.1 percent in the private sector and decreased 0.7 percent in the public sector. Because public enterprises accounted for about 25 percent of industrial output, employment in industry rose overall. Employment in the private sector increased not only in exportables-producing industries, but in import-competing and nontradables industries as well. For the public sector, employment increased only in importables industries. Thus as Michaely, Papageorgiou, and Choksi (1991) find for developing countries generally, trade liberalization does not appear to have hurt employment in Turkey.

Productivity and Market Power

So far, the analysis has tested whether greater exposure to foreign trade reduces the market power of Turkish manufacturing firms but has made no attempt to measure the degree of market power. The marginal significance of the openness variable (import penetration) is interpreted as an indirect sign that Turkish manufacturing firms had little market power even before the reforms. Yet the strongly procyclical pattern in the growth of total factor productivity may reflect market power as well as changes in capacity utilization or scale economies (Hall 1986 and 1988). If it does, the measures of productivity growth reported in the previous section are biased. This section attempts to determine the extent of market power in the Turkish manufacturing industry before reform and how the reforms of the 1980s affected that market power.

Growth of total factor productivity was previously defined residually as the excess growth of output over growth of inputs, a definition that accurately measures productivity only under the restrictive assumptions of perfect competition, constant returns to scale, and freely adjustable factors. When any one of these assumptions is violated, the Solow residual is no longer a true measure of productivity. To demonstrate this, Hall (1986 and 1988) derives the following relationship between inputs, outputs, and productivity among imperfectly competitive firms:

$$(13.1) \qquad \hat{q} = \mu(a_L \hat{l} + a_M \hat{m}) + (\beta - 1)\hat{K} + \frac{dA}{A} .$$

Here $\hat{q}$ is $d\ln(Q / K)$, $\hat{l}$ is $d\ln(L / K)$, $\hat{m}$ is $d\ln(M / K)$, Q is output, L is labor, K is capital, M is intermediate inputs, and A is the level of total factor productivity. μ is price over marginal cost, β measures the returns to scale, a_L and a_M indicate the share of labor and raw materials in the total value of output, and dA / A is productivity growth. The equation shows clearly that unless both μ and β are set equal to 1—that is, unless there is marginal cost pricing and firms exhibit constant returns—the Solow residual is a biased measure of productivity growth. With positive markups and increasing returns to scale, the bias is generally procyclical. Similarly, adjustment costs associated with changes in the stock of capital bias measure productivity and introduce the appearance of a procyclical burst of productivity growth.

To test for the existence of market power and nonconstant returns to scale, Hall estimates the equation and tests whether μ and β are significantly different from 1. Following Harrison (1994) a slightly modified version of equation 13.1 was estimated here to allow for shifts in the level of productivity and market power in Turkish industry in the period following reform:

$$(13.2) \quad \hat{q} = \beta_0 + \beta_1(a_L\hat{l} + a_M\hat{m}) + \beta_2[D(a_L\hat{l} + a_M\hat{m})] + \beta_3\hat{K} + \beta_4 D + u$$

where the coefficient β_1 equals μ; β_2 measures the shift in markup; β_3 equals $\beta - 1$; and D is a dummy variable distinguishing the observations in the 1980s. The productivity term dA / A is given by an industry-specific constant β_0 and a residual u.

If the trade reform of the 1980s caused a positive shift in the overall level of productivity, the coefficient of the intercept dummy variable, β_4, should be positive. Similarly, if the reforms led to more competitive behavior by Turkish firms, the coefficient of the markup shift variable, β_2, should be negative.

Equation 13.2 was estimated for the private sector for individual industries at the two-digit level for 1976–85.[8] The public sector was excluded, because its behavior, especially during the 1970s, was heavily influenced by considerations other than market forces. Industry dummies were included in equation 13.2 for each of the three-digit industries in the pooled data.

Regression results using ordinary least squares show that except for one case in which the coefficient that measures the price-cost margin (β_1) is negative, its value is never significantly different from unity, indicating that private industry did not have a significant degree of market power even before the trade reforms of the 1980s (table 13.7). For the manufacturing industry as a whole, the coefficient is nearly 1 and is highly significant. In six of ten cases, the estimated value of the coefficient of the shift in markup (β_2) is positive although significant in only one case. Moreover, the coefficient is positive not only for industries with a small coefficient for the price-cost margin but also for those in which that coefficient is substantially greater than 1. Cyclical variations in capacity utilization rather than increased market power probably account for the positive relationship, since stock rather than measures of capital flow are used in the equation.

The coefficient that measures the returns to scale (β_3) is generally not significant except for food and beverage industries (ISIC groups 311–313), where it is nearly −1. This means that capital is unproductive in the short run—changing the stock of capital has little effect on output in the short run. The usual explanation for this phenomenon is error in measuring the capital variable (see Abbott, Griliches, and Hausman 1989). For the manufacturing industry as a whole, the coefficient is nearly 0, meaning that the assumption of constant returns to scale cannot be rejected.

The coefficient of the intercept dummy (β_3) is always positive except for the food and beverage industry, indicating that there is a positive shift in the overall level of productivity in Turkey in the period following reform. The coefficient is positive and highly significant for the

Table 13.7 Regression Estimates of the Productivity Equations for the Private Sector: Ordinary Least Squares Estimates

ISIC code[a]	Equation 1						Equation 2				Equation 3		
	β_1	β_2	β_3	β_4	R^2	F-test for $\beta_1 = 1$	β_1	β_2	β_3	R^2	β_1	β_4	R^2
311–313	0.46 (1.2)	0.35 (0.7)	−1.04 (1.9)	−0.02 (0.4)	0.569	1.97	0.83 (2.3)	0.60 (1.1)	0.04 (0.7)	0.488	1.10 (4.1)	−0.05 (0.9)	0.479
311–314	1.18 (6.8)	0.51 (1.5)	−0.15 (0.3)	−0.06 (1.0)	0.761	1.16	1.19 (7.0)	0.54 (1.7)	−0.06 (1.3)	0.770	1.34 (9.2)	−0.06 (1.0)	0.754
321–324	0.94 (3.8)	0.30 (0.9)	0.11 (0.3)	0.05 (0.7)	0.636	0.06	0.92 (3.8)	0.27 (0.9)	0.05 (0.7)	0.646	1.09 (7.3)	0.06 (0.8)	0.648
331–332	1.26 (3.6)	−0.57 (1.2)	−1.06 (1.1)	0.03 (0.3)	0.651	0.57	1.41 (4.3)	−0.70 (1.4)	0.11 (1.6)	0.644	1.11 (4.4)	1.0 (1.4)	0.677
341–342	−0.36 (0.7)	2.0 (3.1)	0.57 (1.3)	0.01 (0.2)	0.701	8.18*	−0.16 (0.3)	1.51 (3.0)	0.03 (0.5)	0.689	1.09 (4.8)	0.00 (0.0)	0.534
351–356	1.07 (5.4)	−0.12 (0.5)	0.60 (1.3)	1.00 (2.8)	0.633	0.12	0.92 (5.9)	0.00 (0.0)	0.08 (2.5)	0.627	0.92 (8.2)	0.08 (2.5)	0.628

Industry / Eq.	β_1	β_2	β_3	β_4	R^2	
361–369						
(1)	1.35 (3.4)	0.13 (0.2)	0.47 (1.1)	0.08 (1.2)	0.473	0.75
(2)	1.25 (3.2)	0.09 (0.1)		0.07 (1.0)	0.466	
(3)	1.30 (9.9)			0.07 (1.1)	0.485	
371–372						
(1)	0.85 (4.8)	−0.18 (0.5)	−0.02 (0.0)	0.09 (1.8)	0.650	0.68
(2)	0.85 (5.0)	−0.18 (0.6)		0.09 (2.0)	0.675	
(3)	0.79 (6.0)			0.09 (2.0)	0.687	
381–385						
(1)	1.15 (4.1)	−0.02 (0.06)	0.43 (0.5)	0.11 (1.5)	0.499	0.30
(2)	1.15 (4.1)	−0.03 (0.1)		0.09 (1.4)	0.508	
(3)	1.13 (5.2)			0.09 (1.4)	0.519	
All industries						
(1)	1.03 (11.6)	0.12 (1.0)	0.04 (0.3)	0.06 (3.0)	0.603	0.12
(2)	1.03 (11.7)	0.12 (1.0)		0.06 (3.1)	0.605	
(3)	1.09 (17.7)			0.07 (3.1)	0.605	

* Significant at the 5 percent level.

Note: Numbers in parentheses are standard errors. The equations are as follows:

(1) $\hat{q} = \beta_0 + \beta_1 (\alpha_L \hat{l} + \alpha_M \hat{m}) + \beta_2 \{D \cdot (\alpha_L \hat{l} + \alpha_M \hat{m})\} + \beta_3 \hat{K} + \beta_4 D + \Sigma \Theta_i I_i$

(2) $\hat{q} = \beta_0 + \beta_1 (\alpha_L \hat{l} + \alpha_M \hat{m}) + \beta_2 \{D \cdot (\alpha_L \hat{l} + \alpha_M \hat{m})\} + \beta_4 D + \Sigma \Theta_i I_i$

(3) $\hat{q} = \beta_0 + \beta_1 (\alpha_L \hat{l} + \alpha_M \hat{m}) + \beta_4 D + \Sigma \Theta_i I_i$

a. See table 13.4 for industry identities.

Source: Author's calculations based on 1976–85 industry-level data from Turkey's State Institute of Statistics.

manufacturing industry as a whole in all the estimated versions of equation 13.2.

Because of the simultaneous determination of inputs and outputs, regressions using ordinary least squares produce biased estimates. In particular, the estimate of the coefficient that measures the price-cost margin (β_1) exaggerates the degree of market power (Abbott, Griliches, and Hausman 1989). The obvious solution is to use instrumental variables, but choosing good instruments is difficult in this context.[9] One test for assessing the validity of the instruments chosen is to compare estimates of the markup coefficient (μ) using ordinary least squares and instrumental variables. If the estimate is higher using instrumental variables, the instruments are invalid because the upward bias implicit in the ordinary least squares estimates is clearly not taken care of.

The instruments chosen for the estimates here are the second lag of the levels of labor, materials, and capital stock. The second rather than the first lag of inputs was chosen, because the explanatory variable—the rate of growth of inputs—includes current and lagged values.

In general the results for the instrumental variable estimates (table 13.8) are not satisfactory, but using gross national product or the lagged rate of growth of inputs as an instrument does not improve the results either. In the full model, the estimated markup coefficients have a higher standard error than the ordinary least squares estimates and are significant for industry 38 and for the manufacturing industry as a whole. The pattern of results also differs. The two set of estimates are equivalent for industries 31, 32, and 34 and for industries 35, 36, 37, and 38 using instrumental variables but are substantially higher than they are using ordinary least squares. And instrumental variables estimates of the price-cost markup after the trade reform (the sum of $\beta_1 + \beta_2$) are higher than ordinary least squares estimates in all but one case. When constant returns to scale are imposed and the dummy for shift in markup is dropped, the instrumental variables estimates are still higher in 60 percent of cases. By the criterion of Abbott, Griliches, and Hausman (1989), therefore, it can be concluded that the instruments used are not satisfactory, even though they are the best available.

The findings here confirm that a positive shift in productivity occurred in Turkish industry in the period following reform but provide no clear evidence of market power either before or after the trade reforms of the 1980s. This finding is very sensitive to the estimation procedure used, however, and the methodology applied is more appropriate for firm-level than industry-level data.

Comparison with Findings of Other Studies

How do the results of this study on foreign trade, productivity, and competition in Turkey compare with those of other studies? Four studies are

Table 13.8 Regression Estimates of the Productivity Equations for the Private Sector: Instrumental Variables Estimates

ISIC code[a]	Equation 1				Equation 2			Equation 3	
	β_1	β_2	β_3	β_4	β_1	β_2	β_4	β_1	β_4
311–313	0.46	1.22	–0.69	–0.02	0.72	1.23	–0.02	0.92	–0.09
	(0.5)	(1.2)	(0.3)	(0.3)	(1.3)	(1.2)	(0.5)	(1.8)	(0.6)
311–314	0.47	1.50	0.00	0.00	0.47	1.50	0.00	1.55	–0.08
	(0.6)	(0.9)	(0.00)	(0.0)	(0.6)	(1.0)	(0.0)	(1.9)	(0.7)
321–324	0.73	0.49	–0.75	0.00	0.83	0.79	0.00	1.31	0.01
	(0.7)	(0.3)	(0.4)	(0.0)	(0.8)	(0.6)	(0.0)	(1.9)	(0.1)
331–332	0.30	0.22	–2.00	0.00	0.32	0.15	0.19	0.66	0.16
	(0.2)	(0.1)	(1.0)	(0.0)	(0.2)	(0.1)	(1.1)	(0.6)	(1.0)
341–347	–0.33	2.77	1.43	–0.02	0.77	0.24	0.01	1.13	0.00
	(0.1)	(0.9)	(1.0)	(0.2)	(0.5)	(0.1)	(0.1)	(2.6)	(0.0)
351–358	1.85	–0.85	2.3	0.12	0.50	0.11	0.10	–1.19	0.17
	(1.3)	(0.8)	(1.0)	(2.6)	(1.0)	(0.2)	(2.5)	(0.3)	(1.0)
361–369	1.51	–0.16	0.82	0.10	1.42	–0.28	0.08	1.18	0.08
	(2.2)	(0.1)	(1.08)	(1.0)	(2.0)	(0.1)	(0.8)	(1.6)	(1.0)
371–372	1.62	–0.62	–0.92	0.13	1.38	0.25	0.08	1.21	0.08
	(1.3)	(0.2)	(0.2)	(0.6)	(2.1)	(0.2)	(1.0)	(2.5)	(1.5)
381–385	2.40	–0.79	2.10	0.01	2.21	–0.12	–0.08	2.0	–0.06
	(2.4)	(0.4)	(0.6)	(1.0)	(2.3)	(0.1)	(0.4)	(2.2)	(0.3)
All industries	1.67	0.11	1.5	0.04	1.08	0.49	0.03	2.07	–0.04
	(2.0)	(0.1)	(1.5)	(1.0)	(1.8)	(0.5)	(0.9)	(3.4)	(0.5)

Note: Numbers in parentheses are standard errors. The equations are as follows:

(1) $\hat{q} = \beta_0 + \beta_1 (\alpha_L \hat{l} + \alpha_M \hat{m}) + \beta_2 \{D \cdot (\alpha_L \hat{l} + \alpha_M \hat{m})\} + \beta_3 \hat{K} + \beta_4 D + \Sigma \Theta_i I_i$

(2) $\hat{q} = \beta_0 + \beta_1 (\alpha_L \hat{l} + \alpha_M \hat{m}) + \beta_2 \{D \cdot (\alpha_L \hat{l} + \alpha_M \hat{m})\} + \beta_4 D + \Sigma \Theta_i I_i$

(3) $\hat{q} = \beta_0 + \beta_1 (\alpha_L \hat{l} + \alpha_M \hat{m}) + \beta_4 D + \Sigma \Theta_i I_i$

a. See table 13.5 for industry identities.
Source: Author's calculations based on 1976–85 industry-level data from Turkey's State Institute of Statistics.

considered, one on the effect of trade liberalization on market power and three on the relation between trade and productivity.

In a study examining the impact of trade liberalization on the market power of manufacturing firms in Turkey, Levinsohn (1993) applies a methodology similar to that applied in the previous section. Levinsohn's unit of observation is the firm, rather than the industry, and his period of observation (1983–86) is shorter than that used in this study, but to the extent that comparison is possible, his results do not conflict with those presented here. For example, Levinsohn finds evidence of market power in only three of eleven import-competing industries examined for the year just before the import liberalization and in four industries during the two years after liberalization. He also finds that, except in one case, whenever protection decreases in an industry, the market power of the firms in that industry also decreases, a finding congruent with that of the margin regressions in this study: greater openness generally has a negative, if modest, effect on price-cost margins.

Several other studies evaluate the effects of trade policy on productivity in Turkish industry. Krueger and Tuncer (1980 and 1982) find that "Productivity growth might uniformly be more rapid during periods of liberalization of the foreign trade regime than during periods of severe foreign exchange shortage" (1980, p. 4). They compute the rate of growth of total factor productivity in Turkish manufacturing industries during 1963–76 for the private and the public sectors. They find that not only did productivity grow modestly in Turkey over the entire period (2 percent), but that it slowed considerably during periods of stringent import restriction. The implication that trade liberalization has a positive effect on the growth of productivity in industry matches the findings reported here.

Krueger and Tuncer also find, as does this study, a relatively more rapid rate of productivity growth in the public sector. Despite several attempts, they are not able to provide a satisfying explanation for this seemingly paradoxical result. They are, however, able to infer something about the absolute level of efficiency in the two sectors. Public enterprises generally have higher levels of labor and capital input per unit of output. They also are able to purchase material inputs at subsidized prices. If these enterprises had to pay market prices for their intermediate inputs, their level of efficiency, Krueger and Tuncer argue, would be lower than that of private enterprises.

In another study, Nishimizu and Robinson (1984) analyze the relation between growth of total factor productivity and trade orientation in four countries. The analysis for Turkey covers 1963–76 for thirteen broadly defined industries. Nishimizu and Robinson do not distinguish public from private enterprises. They find that for nine industries growth of productivity is significantly and positively correlated with expansion of exports, and for four industries it is negatively and significantly correlated with import substitution. During this period, Turkey was a relatively closed economy with exports accounting for less than 4 percent of total manufacturing output and imports contributing to only 11 percent of the domestic supply of manufactured goods. Total factor productivity growth was therefore modest during this period, increasing some 1 percent a year and contributing to 12 percent of growth in output.

An internal World Bank report on structural adjustment loans to Turkey also considers productivity in the public sector during the 1980s.

After examining the evolution of labor productivity during 1982–86, the report concludes that improvements in the profitability of state enterprises were due to price increases, rather than to efficiency gains. That conclusion supports the finding here that the productivity gain in public enterprises may be more apparent than real, deriving mainly from mismeasurement of the growth in real output in publicly owned firms.

Conclusions

Turkey's radical import liberalization and export promotion program of the early 1980s generated a spectacular surge in trade, especially in exports. Although external factors also played a role, there is no doubt that the reforms transformed Turkey from a closed, inward-looking economy into an open, outward-oriented one.

Increased import penetration led to a small but significant decrease in price-cost margins and a small but significant increase in total factor productivity growth in Turkey. These beneficial effects of a more liberal trade regime occurred primarily in the private sector. There was no appreciable impact on public enterprises. The higher rate of growth in factor productivity in the public sector in the first half of the 1980s was attributed principally to an overestimation of the public sector's growth in real output, stemming from the use of the same price deflator for public as for private enterprises.

No correlation was found between export shares and price-cost margins. One reason could be that export-oriented industries, which had to compete in international markets, were the most competitive and efficient of Turkish manufacturing industries to begin with.

The small impact of the reforms of the 1980s on private industry's price-cost margins suggests that Turkish private enterprises did not enjoy a great deal of market power before the reform. This interpretation is supported by additional empirical analysis that quantifies the degree of market power in each industry by testing for a significant departure of prices from marginal costs.

Appendix: Data Preparation

Industry-level data were obtained from Turkey's State Institute of Statistics. The data for 1973 to 1982 cover all manufacturing firms with ten or more employees. From 1983 onward the data cover only firms with twenty-five or more employees. The change in coverage is not important for industries with a few large firms, but it is important for industries with a large number of small, family concerns. Data are available at the level of the three-digit ISIC code, distinguished by private or public ownership. The data covered include

- Labor input, defined as total number of production workers
- Total labor cost, which comprises wages and other payments such as overtime payment, bonuses, and employers' contributions to retirement funds
- Total value of intermediate inputs at current prices
- Total value of output at current prices
- Beginning- and end-of-year value of inventories of final output and intermediate inputs. Inventory data were corrected for inflation bias using the methodology described in Tybout 1988
- Sectoral output price deflators.

Capital stock series were constructed using the perpetual-inventory method. Industry-specific input price deflators were computed using input-output coefficients and output price deflators.

Data on the total value of imports and exports by industry were obtained from the United Nations data base. Foreign trade data were converted from U.S. dollars to Turkish lira using mid-year average exchange rates. Trade figures in local currency were then used to derive import penetration and export share series.

Most of the data series cover the period 1973–85, although in the process of transforming the data, several years were lost. As a result, the regression analyses normally cover the years 1976–85.

The Herfindahl concentration indexes were computed from plant-level data covering all plants in the greater Istanbul area from 1983 to 1985. Because of the heavy concentration of industry in the Istanbul area, the data are fairly representative of the national picture.

The industries were grouped into exportables, importables, and non-tradables. Industries that produce exportables were defined as those that showed an increase in exports during the sample period and whose average exports in 1984–85 constituted at least 25 percent of their output (see table 13A.1). Among the remaining industries, industries that produced importables were defined as those for which the share of imports in total domestic sales (output minus exports plus imports) in 1984–85 exceeded 25 percent. All remaining industries were classified as non-tradables. The years 1984–85 were chosen because they were most favorable in the sample period for both export promotion and import liberalization. Because the data refer only to three-digit industry disaggregation, industries such as iron and steel and professional equipment showed a high degree of both import penetration and export share. Industries were classified in only one category, however, and the exportable industries were chosen first, so both of these industries were included among exportables.

Table 13.A1 International Standard Industrial Classification for Turkey

ISIC code	Industry	Category[a]
311, 312	Food	Nontradable
313	Beverages	Nontradable
314	Tobacco	Nontradable
321	Textiles	Exportable
322	Apparel	Exportable
323	Leather products	Nontradable
324	Footwear	Nontradable
331	Wood products	Exportable
332	Furniture	Exportable
341	Paper	Nontradable
342	Printing	Nontradable
351	Industrial chemicals	Importable
352	Other chemicals	Nontradable
353	Petroleum refining	Nontradable
354	Petroleum derivatives	Nontradable
355	Rubber products	Nontradable
356	Plastics	Nontradable
361	Ceramics	Nontradable
362	Glass	Exportable
369	Nonmetallic minerals	Nontradable
371	Iron and steel	Exportable
372	Nonferrous metals	Importable
381	Metal products	Nontradable
382	Nonelectrical machinery	Importable
383	Electrical machinery	Nontradable
384	Transport equipment	Importable
385	Professional equipment	Exportable

a. See the appendix for classification criteria.
Source: Author's calculations based on 1976–85 industry-level data from Turkey's State Institute of Statistics.

Notes

The author gratefully acknowledges the assistance of Kaniz Siddique in preparing the data and refers interested readers to chapter 4 of her doctoral dissertation for more details (Siddique 1992).

1. Public sector enterprises were most prominent in nontraded sectors, where they accounted for 31 percent of output. Among tradables, they accounted for 23 percent of output in import-competing sectors and 15 percent of output in export sectors.

2. This section is based on Baysan and Blitzer 1991, Milanovic 1986, Aricanli and Rodrik 1990, Foroutan 1991, and Nas and Odekon 1992.

3. In this computation and in all analysis in the chapter, the apparel industry was omitted because of inconsistent trade figures. The value of exports exceeded the value of total output by as much as 100 percent toward the end of the sample period. Because trade data include all firms, whereas output data exclude

small firms (those with fewer than ten employees up to 1982 and fewer than twenty-five thereafter), output figures underestimate the true value of output in the apparel industry, where small firms are common. Also, the policy of subsidizing exports is known to have induced a certain degree of overinvoicing of exports. Thus the share of exports and, to some extent, of imports may be slightly exaggerated for all industries. However, the trend is reliable.

4. In addition to the apparel industry, the tobacco processing industry was also excluded from the regression analysis, because complete data are lacking for the sample period.

5. Where there are intermediate inputs, the correct measure of factor intensity is the direct capital-labor ratio for gross output and the total (direct plus indirect) capital-labor ratio for net output (see Derr 1979).

6. The Herfindahl index for each industry could be constructed only for 1983, 1984, and 1985, so it could not be entered as an independent variable in the regression analysis. Instead, the average of the index over the three years was calculated for each industry and entered in the regression as an interaction variable with import penetration. This method assumes implicitly that the Herfindahl index for each industry remains unchanged over time. If the technical characteristics of the production technology determine the degree of concentration in an industry, this assumption is not too unrealistic. (See, for example, the analysis for Colombia in chapter 10, which finds that the Herfindahl index for any particular industry changes very little over time.)

7. In fact, if industry concentration (H) is constant over all industries as well as over time, the coefficient of the import penetration variable in model 1 is exactly equal to the coefficient of the interaction term for concentration and import penetration in model 2 multiplied by H^{-1}.

8. Because of the limited number of observations in the data set, the twenty-six three-digit industries were pulled together to form nine two-digit industries. The pooled data set contains between twenty and fifty observations.

9. See, for example, Hall 1986 and 1988, Shapiro 1987, and Harrison 1994 on the type of instruments.

References

Abbott, Thomas A., Zvi Griliches, and Jerry A. Hausman. 1989. "Short Run Movement in Productivity: Market Power Versus Capacity Utilization." Department of Economics, Harvard University, Cambridge, Mass.

Aricanli, Tosun, and Dani Rodrik. 1990. "An Overview of Turkey's Experience with Economic Liberalization and Structural Adjustment." *World Development* 18 (10): 1343–50.

Baysan, Tercan, and Charles Blitzer. 1991. "Turkey." In Demetris Papageorgiou, Michael Michaely, and Armeane M. Choksi, eds., *Liberalizing Foreign Trade*, vol. 6, *The Experience of New Zealand, Spain, and Turkey*. Cambridge, Mass.: Basil Blackwell.

Derr, William. 1979. "Multi-Intermediate Goods Trade: The Gains and the Heckscher-Ohlin Analysis." *American Economic Review* 69 (4): 575–86.

Foroutan, Faezeh. 1991. "Turkey: Structural Transformation and the Threat to Sustainability." In Vinod Thomas, Ajay Chhibber, Mansoor Dailami, and

Jaime de Melo, eds., *Restructuring Economies in Distress: Policy Reform and the World Bank*. New York: Oxford University Press for the World Bank.

Hall, Robert E. 1986. "Market Structure and Macroeconomic Fluctuations." *Brookings Papers on Economic Activity* 2: 285–322.

————. 1988. "The Relation between Price and Marginal Cost in U.S. Industry." *Journal of Political Economy* 96 (5): 921–47.

Harrison, Ann E. 1994. "Productivity, Imperfect Competition, and Trade Reform: Theory and Evidence." *Journal of International Economics* 36 (1): 53–73.

Krueger, Anne, and Baran Tuncer. 1980. *Estimating Total Factor Productivity Growth in a Developing Country*. Staff Working Paper 422. Washington, D.C.: World Bank.

————. 1982. "Growth of Factor Productivity in Turkish Manufacturing Industry." *Journal of Development Economics* 11 (3): 307–25.

Levinsohn, James. 1993. "Testing the Imports-as-Market-Discipline Hypothesis." *Journal of International Economics* 35 (1): 1–22.

Michaely, Michael, Demetris Papageorgiou, and Armeane M. Choksi. 1991. *Lessons of Experience in the Developing World*. Vol. 7 of Demetris Papageorgiou, Michael Michaely, and Armeane M. Choksi, eds., *Liberalizing Foreign Trade*. Cambridge, Mass.: Basil Blackwell.

Milanovic, Branko. 1986. *Export Incentives and Turkish Manufacturing Exports 1980–84*. Staff Working Paper 768. Washington, D.C.: World Bank.

Nas, Tevfik F., and Mehmet Odekon, eds. 1992. *Economics and Politics of Turkish Liberalization*. Toronto: Associated University Presses.

Nishimizu, Mieko, and Sherman Robinson. 1984. "Trade Policies and Productivity Change in Semi-Industrialized Countries." *Journal of Development Economics* 16 (1–2): 177–206.

Shapiro, Matthew D. 1987. "Measuring Market Power." NBER Working Paper 2212. National Bureau of Economic Research, Cambridge, Mass.

Siddique, Kaniz N. 1992. "Sources of Efficiency Gain Due to Trade Liberalization: A Dynamic Domestic Resource Cost Analysis of the Turkish Manufacturing Sector, 1976–85." Ph.D. diss., George Washington University, Washington, D.C.

Tybout, James R. 1988. "The Algebra of Inflation Accounting." *International Economic Journal* 2 (2): 83–100.

Index

Abbott, Thomas A., 330
Age of firms: Chilean survival patterns
  and output share and, 210–11;
  employment flows and, 26–27; entry
  and exit patterns and, 7–9, 192; productivity differences and, 54, 89–91
Aitken, Brian, 172, 175, 177
Allocative efficiency index (proposed),
  100n5
Arrow, Kenneth, 46
Asymmetrical oligopoly model of output
  adjustment, 143–48

Baily, Martin Neil, 49, 50, 51, 55, 93,
  136n16
Baldwin, John, 26, 51, 52, 128
Bartelsman, Eric, 55
Berry, Albert, 111, 113
"Between" regression equations: foreign
  direct investment and, 166–67; production functions, exit functions, and,
  117
"Big push" development models, 44
Business cycle effects: employment flows
  in semi-industrialized countries and, 5,
  25–27; plant entry and exit patterns
  and, 6–7; productivity growth and,
  59–60

Caballero, Ricardo J., 37–38, 55
Cameroon, 132
Campbell, David, 49, 50, 51, 55, 93,
  136n16
Canada: computable general equilibrium
  (CGE) models for, 128, 131; cost function estimates for, 121; employment
  flows in, 20, 23–27, 40nn19, 20; heterogeneity-based productivity growth
  in, 51; product diversity and export
  patterns in, 302

Capital-output ratios: in Chile, 215–17;
  in Colombia, 244; in Mexico, 264,
  281; in Morocco, 296; in Turkey,
  317–19
Capital stock data: for Chile, 99,
  221–24; for Colombia, 255–56; for
  Mexico, 274, 278–80; for Morocco,
  308; for Turkey, 334
Caves, Douglas W., 135n4
Chile: capital-output ratios in, 215–17;
  capital stock data for, 99, 222–24;
  cohort analysis in, 89–91; constant
  price data for, 221; data preparation
  for country study of, 218–24; employment flows in, 3–5, 23–36, 201–2;
  entry and exit patterns in, 6–9, 19,
  28–30, 32–34, 60, 84–87, 189,
  191–92, 202–11; heterogeneity-based
  productivity growth in, 52–54, 84, 87;
  incentive structure in, 188; labor and
  capital costs in, 100n7; macroeconomic and political conditions in, 3,
  78–79; plant characteristics in, 203–4;
  plant size and import competition in,
  159n3; price-cost margins in, 195,
  215–17; producer heterogeneity in,
  1–2; productivity in, 81–87; productivity growth in, 73–74, 91–97;
  returns to scale studies for, 119–123;
  simultaneity bias in productivity measurements in, 101n22; size distribution
  of manufacturing plants in, 26;
  survival patterns in, 210; total factor
  technical efficiency vs. Divisia indexes
  for, 81–82; trade liberalization in,
  200–201, 211–15, 217–18
Choksi, Armeane M., 325
Christensen, Laurits R., 135n4
"Cleansing effect of recessions" hypothesis, 26, 93–94, 96

338